Commentary
on the
Book of Mormon

Volume VII

Commentary

on the

Book of Mormon

VOLUME VII – THE BOOKS OF III and IV NEPHI –
MORMON and MORONI

The Ministry of Jesus Christ among the Nephites — The Reign
of Peace and Good Will Thereafter — The Destruction
of the Nephites and the Close of Their Record.

From the notes of:

GEORGE REYNOLDS

and

JANNE M. SJODAHL

Amplified and Arranged by
PHILIP C. REYNOLDS

DISTRIBUTED BY
DESERET BOOK COMPANY
SALT LAKE CITY, UTAH
1976

Lithographed by

DESERET PRESS

in the United States of America

GEORGE REYNOLDS

In a note near the close of his great contribution to L.D.S. Church literature, *New Witnesses for God*, President B. H. Roberts penned this remarkable tribute to the labors of Elder George Reynolds:

"It is a pleasure to note the work of this my brother, and fellow President in the First Council of the Seventies, in this field of Book of Mormon labor. I feel myself much indebted to him because of his great achievements in this field of research.

"First, for his excellent *Book of Mormon Chronological Table*, published now for many years in connection with the late Elder F. D. Richards' *Compendium.*

"Second, for his *Myth of the Manuscript Found.*

"Third, for his *Story of the Book of Mormon.*

"Fourth, for his *Dictionary of the Book of Mormon.*

"Fifth, for a series of articles appearing in the *Contributor*, Vol. 5, on the *History of the Book of Mormon.*

"Sixth, for a second series of articles in the *Contributor*, Vol. 17, under the title, *Evidences of the Book of Mormon; Some External Proofs of Its Divinity.*

"Seventh, and last, and greatest achievement of all, I thank him for his *Complete Concordance of the Book of Mormon.* The amount of patient, painstaking labor required for the production of this magnificent work will never be known to the general reader. Only the close student of the Nephite Scriptures will ever appreciate it. What Cruden and Young have done for Bible students, Elder Reynolds has more abundantly done for Book of Mormon students. The Elders of the Church through all generations to come will, I am sure, feel deeply grateful to Elder Reynolds for his great work which will stand as a monument to his painstaking habits of thorough application to a task; but what is better still, the work will stand as a monument of his love for the Book of Mormon."

JANNE M. SJODAHL

An editorial published in the *Deseret News*, June 25, 1939, will serve to acquaint those who know little of the life and labors of the co-author of this *Commentary.*

"Physically frail but mentally energetic; of serious manner, studious volition and sendentary habit; Janne Mattson Sjodahl lived simply and labored faithfully beyond the eighty-fifth anniversary of his birth. A native of Sweden, he was educated in Stockholm and London, becoming identified in early manhood with the Scandinavian Baptist Union having headquarters in Trondhjem, Norway.

"At the age of 33 he came to the United States and was converted to Mormonism after his arrival in Utah over a half century ago. His ability as a writer, his faculty for research, his skill as a translator brought him instant recognition and a lifetime of labor.

"As a writer and as an editor he had been connected with the *Deseret News,* the *Improvement Era,* the *Millennial Star* and various foreign language publications once circulated by his Church. He served on various missions to Palestine, Switzerland, England, and Sweden. In the latter country he presented a special edition of the Book of Mormon to the king, who received the Utah delegation at the Royal Palace.

"Mr. Sjodahl was the author of many ecclesiastical works and a prolific writer of pamphlets and special articles relating to the organization of which he was a distinguished member. He devoted his whole time, energy, ability, and thought to religious issues and inquiries. Absorbed in meditation almost to a point of asceticism, subjecting his vigor and vitality to constant exertion, he lived many years longer than his acquaintances believed possible for a tireless soul that occupied a frame so fragile."

With the late Elder Hyrum M. Smith, of the Council of Twelve Apostles, Elder Sjodahl was the author of, and the compiler of the *Doctrine and Covenants Commentary.*

The Bible and the Book of Mormon

The Finger of God

The story of the Book of Mormon is a true one. Its origin, its teachings, and its message, together, proclaim, "Jesus is the Son of God."

It opens the way for this generation to learn of the millions of God's children who lived upon the Western Continents hundreds of years ago; it is their history. It contains many biographies and autobiographies combined into one which is interwoven with the proofs of Providential care.

It is America's contribution to Holy Writ!

It is the Bible of the New World. Not that it supersedes the Bible, or in any way interferes with it, any more than the history of Peru interferes with or supersedes the history of Greece; but, on the other hand, in many places it confirms Bible history, demonstrates Bible truths, sustains Bible doctrines, and fulfills Bible prophecy.

In the hearts of many, the Book of Mormon has established itself among the finest books of literature, and has taken its place at the side of the Bible as the inspired and revealed *Word of God*.

When the magicians of Pharaoh's Court could not do what they saw Moses and Aaron do, they said, "This is the finger of God." That expression is used throughout the Scriptures, and means the *presence*, or *the power*, or *the purpose of God*.

In contemplating the Book of Mormon, all the evidence that is presented and all the witnesses bound, join with us in repeating the words the magicians said to Pharaoh in Ancient Egypt: *"This is the finger of God."*

The authors of the Book of Mormon lived in the Land of America hundreds of years ago. Their writings have been preserved by the *finger of God* to come forth in these Last Days.

To a doubting world they proclaim that *God lives*. To the honest in heart, throughout the world, they reaffirm the glad tidings that *His Son, Jesus Christ, is the Savior and the Redeemer of the world*. They also testify as trustworthy deponents that the records kept by the Jews — that is the Bible — are true. Again and again, their words establish them to be the "other sheep," of which the *Good Shepherd* spoke to His flock gathered in Old Jerusalem: "Other sheep I have which are not of this fold, them also must I bring, and they shall hear My voice; and there shall be one fold and one Shepherd." (Matthew 19:29; III Nephi 15:17)

The Book of Mormon has a message for all, for Jew and for Gentile. Every nation under heaven; every kindred, tongue, and people who dwell upon the face of the Earth, shall see in it the Salvation of the Lord and shall hear its voice; and they shall know "that I am He that doth speak." (*Ibid.*, 20:39) This glorious information is given with the added assurance that: "For because of My Spirit he shall know that these things are true." (Ether 4:11)

To the Jew, it says:

"And as surely as the Lord liveth, will he gather in from the four quarters of the earth all the remnant of the seed of Jacob, who are scattered abroad upon all the face of the earth.

"And as he hath covenanted with all the house of Jacob, even so shall the covenant wherewith he hath covenanted with the house of Jacob be fulfilled in his own due time, unto the restoring all the house of Jacob unto the knowledge of the covenant wherewith he hath covenanted with them.

"And then shall they know their Redeemer, who is Jesus Christ, the Son of God; and then shall they be gathered in from the four quarters of the earth unto their own lands, from whence they have been dispersed; yea, as the Lord liveth so shall it be. Amen. (*Mormon*, III Nephi 5:24-26)

The promises of the Book of Mormon are great unto the Gentiles. To them it says that they shall be blessed upon this Land, that is Zion; the Land of the Lord, our King; America:

"This land shall be a Land of Liberty unto the Gentiles, and there shall be no kings upon this land . . . for I the Lord, the King of Heaven, will be their King, and I will be a light unto them forever, that hear My words." (II Nephi 11:14)

To you and to me, who, when the storms of life descend, begin to say, "The Lord hath forsaken me, and my Lord hath forgotten me," it says in the words of Isaiah, God's holy Prophet, "But He will show that He hath not." (I Nephi 21:14)

To all men, everywhere, it says: "The Lamb of God is the Son of the Eternal Father, and the Savior of the world; and that *all men* must come unto Him, or they cannot be saved." (I Nephi 13:40)

The Book of Mormon answers, formally, the questions we have so often heard debated: "Who are the American Indians? and Whence did they come?" It is a history of their ancestors. In his own beautiful, but simple words, William W. Phelps, the inspired writer of many of the songs of Zion, both asks and answers these questions:

O, stop and tell me, Redman,
  Who are you? Why you roam?
And how you get your living;
  Have you no God, no home?

With stature straight and portly,
  And decked in native pride,
With feathers, paints, and brooches,
  He willingly replied.

I once was pleasant Ephraim,
  When Jacob for me prayed,
But O, how blessings vanish,
  When man from God has strayed.

Some people are under the impression that the Latter-day Saints do not believe in the Bible, and that they have discarded that sacred volume for the Book of Mormon. That is not true. They have not! To the Latter-day Saints, the Bible is God's Book. It contains the Word of God, and they believe it all the more because they have been almost untouched by the destructive criticism, which under the name "Higher," aims at the abrogation of all channels of divine revelation. The Bible is a book of God. It has been called, "The god of books." It was written by inspired men — men whom the Apostle Peter says, "Were moved upon to speak by the Holy Ghost." (II Peter 1:21)

The Book of Mormon is a translation of the originals. The Bible is a translation of other translations. Each, however, is subjected to the same bitter criticism of faultfinding skeptics who love to point to the errors they have found in both volumes of sacred literature. They point frequently, and sometimes carelessly "to the lack of grammatical correctness, to the wrongful use of language, and to the absence, in places, of the propriety of speech."

They let this be a reason to reject the Bible, to deride the Book of Mormon, and to deny that both are the *Word of God.*

When the ages that have passed since the books of the Bible were written, the many translations that have been made of them, the vicissitudes through which they have passed in their transmission to the present generation, the wonder is, not that there are errors and parts left out, but that there is a Bible at all.

The diluting influences that accompany each translation, has surrounded the Bible with a mist, which like an imperfect glass, distorts and confuses the vision of those who desire to know the mind and will of God.

In turning the pages of the Bible — that dear and precious Book — many fail to see the Plan of Life and Salvation unfold before them. They refuse to listen to the greatest story ever told,

The Resurrection of Jesus Christ. They sit in darkness although the Sun shines brightly. From their position they cannot see the mountain because of the molehills. In rejecting the Bible "they cast away the cup and lose the precious wine that is in that cup." The wine is God's holy word.

We admit that there are errors in the Bible, but we deny they are errors of belief or doctrine. The text of the Bible may be faulty, but it is full of Life and Salvation.

This is also true of the Book of Mormon. In places its grammar may be incorrect, its story appear to be weak, its narrative unended, but Moroni writes of his difficulty in placing his words, his lack of adequate means of expression, and that, because of weakness in writing he is unable to give his thoughts their full meaning.

Moroni was the last to write in the Book of Mormon; Nephi was the first. About a thousand years separated their times. Moroni was commanded by the Lord to include in the record he was making that the Gospel would come unto his brethren, the Lamanites, through the Gentiles.

Moroni did as he was commanded, but, nevertheless, he felt incapable of fully fulfilling the Lord's requirements. He sought the help of the Lord, and of his prayer to the Almighty, he said:

"And I said unto him: Lord, the Gentiles will mock at these things, because of our weakness in writing; for Lord thou hast made us mighty in word by faith, but thou hast not made us mighty in writing; for thou hast made all this people that they could speak much, because of the Holy Ghost which thou hast given them.

"And thou hast made us that we could write but little, because of the awkwardness of our hands. Behold, thou hast not made us mighty in writing like unto the brother of Jared, for thou madest him that the things which he wrote were mighty even as thou art, unto the overpowering of man to read them.

"Thou hast also made our words powerful and great, even that we cannot write them; wherefore, when we write we behold our weakness, and stumble because of the placing of our words; and I fear lest the Gentiles shall mock at our words." (Ether 12:23-25)

The thoughtful reader of the Book of Mormon will remember the conversation in which Moroni apologized to the Lord for not being great in writing. He said:

"Lord, the Gentiles will mock at these things, because of our weakness in writing; for Lord Thou hast made us mighty in word by faith, but Thou hast not made us mighty in writing."

In finishing the abridgment of the Larger Plates of Nephi which his father, Mormon, had made, Moroni also said: "Behold, I speak unto you as though I spake from the dead; for I know that ye shall hear my words. Condemn me not because of mine imperfection, neither my father, because of his imperfection, neither them who have written before him; but rather give thanks unto God that He hath made manifest unto you our imperfections, that ye may learn to be more wise than we have been." (Mormon 9:30-31) "And whoso receiveth this record, and shall not condemn it because of the imperfections which are in it, the same shall know of greater things than these." (*Ibid.*, 8:12)

Skeptics and students of sacred literature may point to the errors they allege to have found in the Book of Mormon, to the wrongful use of words, to improper forms of speech, but in doing this they fail to point out, "If there are faults they are the mistakes of men," (Inspired Preface) and not the inspirations of God. They do not say, "This is the finger of man, and not the Finger of God."

"Wherefore, condemn not the things of God, that ye may be found spotless at the Judgment-Seat of Christ." (*Ibid*)

* * * *

Thanks be to God, the Book of Mormon is written. It is, however, not a romance. It is not a tale of fiction written for our entertainment. It is not a mixture of folklore and tradition, nor is it, as some allege, "a pious fraud." But holy men of God, great prophets and teachers, recorded their prophecies and their wisdom upon metal plates from which the Book of Mormon was translated. Also, Heaven-inspired historians and leaders engraved thereon the important events of their times. Thus, together, they preserved for over a thousand years, the annals of the Nephite people in spirit and in truth.

The Nephites were a branch of the House of Israel. They believed in God Who was the Father of all men. They believed that His Son, Jesus Christ, was the Savior and the Redeemer of mankind. Also, they believed that He was the Messiah of Whose coming all the prophets had spoken. In their possession was a copy of the Law of Moses, and of it their practice was complete. They had revelations from Heaven to guide them; angels ministered unto them; they prospered in material things, and those who were zealous in keeping the commandments of the Lord were benefited and blessed.

Again, thanks be to God, these beliefs and the incidents surrounding their observance are written. They were not left to treacherous memory; they were not left to the diluting influence of oral transmission; they were not bequeathed to hearts, diseased and depraved, who might corrupt them, but they are written, and written at the very command of Him Who said: "Other sheep I have which are not of this fold; them also must I bring, and they shall hear My voice; and there shall be one fold and one Shepherd." (John 10:16)

In meditating upon the scenes presented by the Sacred Records, the Bible and the Book of Mormon, and the doctrines therein proclaimed, we are constantly reminded of King David's 23rd Psalm: "Yea, though I walk through the valley in[1] the shadow of death, I will fear no evil: for Thou art with me; *Thy rod and Thy staff* they comfort me." Thy rod and Thy staff means the *Word of God.* The Book of Mormon and the Bible are His rod and His staff. They bring comfort to every heart. They raise up the heart that is bowed down. They regenerate a bad heart and sanctify a sinful one. They quicken one that is dead in trespass and in sin. They help the helpless, and those who have no Helper but the Lord. They give succor according to the power and the hour of one's need. And, when at last the shadows of night gather about us, and we know that our day's pilgrimage upon earth is near an end, the Word of the Lord spreads over us a canopy of peace and fills our hearts with a joyous hope of Life Everlasting.

Heeding the words of God's Nephite servants, and following the path to which they point, we marvel at the beauties along the way. Our guide, the Book of Mormon, which we have identified as the *Word of the Lord,* leads us neither to the right nor to the left, but along that *Way* which is straight and narrow unto the *Eternal City of God.*

Our backs may be bent with the weight of years and our feet unsteady, but our souls are gladdened and our steps made firm as a voice — a pleasant voice, "as if it were a whisper" — reaches our ears and pierces to our inmost parts, causing our hearts to burn. (*See* Helaman 5:46; III Nephi 11:3) Yea, the voice of *One from On High.* Whose voice is unto the ends of the Earth, to all mankind, even the voice of Jesus Christ: "Come unto Me." (*See Ether* 4:13-14)

Enraptured, we proclaim God's holy Name, and in ecstasy shout to those about us who also journey to the Holy City: "O magnify the Lord with me, and let us exalt His Name together." (Psalm 34:3)

In wonderment we pause in our footsteps and listen. Not a sound disturbs the solemn air. But hearken! Again we hear the

---

[1]We have changed the preposition OF to IN (King James Translation). We think it is the better understanding of the thought, and just what the Psalmist meant. The Hebrews of old did not include the vowels in their writing, and but a few prepositions. The expression, "Valley of the Shadow of Death," is a beautiful name, but otherwise it signifies but little. The use of the word OF by the translators of the text shows that they had little understanding of the Psalmist's meaning, and was by them an arbitrary selection of the word. (*See,* Isaiah 9:2; Matthew 4:16; II Nephi 19:2)

In this Psalm, David sings of man's journey through life which he calls *a valley.* He pictures man therein as always being overshadowed by death. Death has a shadow. But there can be no shadow unless there is sunshine. And that sunshine is the *Word of God.*

"I will fear no evil," says King David, "for Thou art with me." Amid much that is painful to the heart and perplexing to the mind, surrounded by storms that at times would overwhelm us, the Word of the Lord, whether it comes to us through Judah or Joseph, the Bible or the Book of Mormon, the prophets of old, or the seers of our own times, we will remember that "Thou hidest not Thy face from any generation of Thy children who seek after Thee."

voice of the Savior. Not a voice like rushing mighty waters, nor like thunder upon the distant mountain tops; but a voice like the calm of eventide with healing in its wings; a still voice of perfect mildness. Not in these exact terms but with a meaning all may understand, it says: The words you heed are the words of My servants "whom I have sent unto you to declare good tidings," (Helaman 5:29) Their words are My words, "For I am He Who speaketh." (Ether 4:8-14)

As we walk farther and farther along that path which the Nephites themselves trod, and in our imagination partake with them the sweet fruits of righteousness of which they had a joyous harvest, we feel more and more constrained to join with them, not to say, but to "Shout praises unto the Holy One of Israel." (II Nephi 31:13)

The Book of Mormon contains the Gospel of Jesus Christ in its fulness (the Angel Moroni said to the Prophet Joseph Smith). It publishes anew the Glad Tidings of man's Redemption, and makes plain the precious truths of his Salvation. Like the Bible, the Book of Mormon is the Word of God. It reveals His holy mind and will.

And now, let us urge all to study prayerfully and carefully the pages of these Sacred Records, and receive through them the priceless truths of Life and Salvation. "Now, behold, I say unto you that if ye will do this ye shall always rejoice, and be filled with the love of God, and always retain a remission of your sins; and ye shall grow in the knowledge of the glory of Him that created you, or in the knowledge of that which is just and true." (King Benjamin, Mosiah 4:12)

Moroni, who was the last to write in the Book of Mormon, makes this glorious promise to all men who have a desire to know the mind and will of God: "And when ye shall receive these things, I would exhort you that ye would ask God, the Eternal Father, in the Name of Christ, if these things are not true; and if ye shall ask with a sincere heart, with real intent, having faith in Christ, He will manifest the truth of it unto you, by the power of the Holy Ghost." (Moroni 10:4)

In conclusion, may we suggest the admonition of Solomon, the wise old Hebrew King: it is the sum and substance of all the lessons carried to us by both the Sacred Records, the Book of Mormon and its companion in holiness, the Bible: "Fear God, and keep His commandments: for this is the whole duty of man." (Ecclesiastes 12:13)

"Fear God, and keep His commandments." To what end?

To the end "That ye may remember, and do all My commandments, and be holy unto your God. I am the Lord your God." (See, Numbers 15:40-41)   PHILIP C. REYNOLDS

REFERENCE TO VOLUME V

It was now the Eighteenth Year of the Reign of the Judges over the people of Nephi, or about 73 years before the birth of the Savior in the Land of Jerusalem, that Alma, weighted down by the many years he carried, realized that age was weakening his efforts to advance the Church of God and notwithstanding his labors and his prayers, the Nephites were again backsliding into iniquity. But nevertheless and in spite of his many afflictions, to every Nephite city and to every land he went or sent to revive the Gospel fires in the souls of the inhabitants. However, many became offended on account of the strictness of the Gospel's laws, which forbade not only sin, itself, but the very appearance of sin. As this feeling grew in the hearts of many Church members, Alma's own heart became exceedingly sorrowful and he mourned the depravity into which his people had fallen.

Like many of the ancient patriarchs, when he felt that his day's pilgrimage on earth was rapidly coming to an end, he called his sons to him and gave each one of them his last charge and blessing, speaking to every one as the spirit of prophecy inspired. To Helaman, the eldest, he transferred the custody of the Sacred Plates with many words of warning and caution regarding them. With hearts strengthened and their courage renewed by the inspiration of his fervent admonitions, his sons went forth among the people; nor could Alma, himself, rest while there was a soul to save or a wrong to make right. He also went forth once again in the spirit of his holy calling, and raised his voice in advocacy of the principles of the Everlasting Gospel.

In the Nineteenth Year of the Judges, Alma took his beloved son, Helaman, and after having discovered, through divers questions, the strength and integrity of his faith, prophesied to him of many important events in the future, especially with regard to the destruction of the Nephites. This prophecy he commanded Helaman to record on the Plates, but not reveal it to anyone. Alma then blessed Helaman, and also his other sons; indeed he blessed all who should stand firm in the truth of Christ from that time forth. Shortly after this Alma departed out of the Land of Zarahemla as if to go to the Land of Melek, and was never heard of more. Of his death and burial no men were witnesses. Then the saying went abroad throughout the Church that the Lord had taken him as He beforetime had taken Moses. This event occurred exactly one hundred years from the time of the elder Alma's birth.

After the departure of Alma we learn nothing more of the life of his associate, Zeezrom, though his name and teachings are more than once referred to by later servants of God. We read of a City of Zeezrom, and, as it was the custom of the Nephites to name their cities, towns, and villages after whoever founded them, it is highly probable that, in the colonization of the country so vigorously carried on in the age that these men dwelt, he very likely commenced the building of this place, and it would not be unreasonable to suppose that he lived in the midst of its citizens as their High Priest or Chief Judge.

Alma's son, Helaman, appears to have succeeded his father as the Presiding High Priest of God's Church. After Alma's departure from this earth, Helaman and others went through the cities and regulated the affairs of the Church. Owing to the pride of many of its members who would not give heed to the instructions given them, nor walk uprightly, dissensions arose, which in after years led to numerous evils, among the greatest of which was a long continued war, or series of wars, between the faithful Nephites on one side, and certain apostates on the other, who were later joined by the Lamanites. Still for four years, Helaman and his associates in the Priesthood were enabled to maintain order in the Church. Many died in full faith of the Gospel and in joyous hope of its never-ending rewards; indeed, during that period there was much peace and great prosperity enjoyed by those who remained faithful.

Peace, however, was but short lived. Internal dissension created by the intrigues of apostates and royalists convulsed the Nephite community. The rebels were led by a descendant of Zoram, the servant of Laban, named Amalickiah, one of the most ambitious, cunning, and unscrupulous characters that ever disgraced the history of ancient America. It was a perilous day for the Nephite Nation when this subtle creature bent all his brilliant energies to the fulfillment of his dreams. True, he had been a member of Christ's holy Church, but now the love of God had given place to the hatred of His servants; he was a citizen of the Republic, but he aspired to overthrow its liberties, and for himself to reign as king over his fellow-Nephites. Indeed, he had cherished thoughts of still greater power, even to be monarch of the entire continent; both Nephite and Lamanite should bow to his undisputed sway. Such were his nightly dreams, and the continual thoughts of his waking hours, and to this end he bent all the energies of his mind, all the craft of his soul, all the cunning of his tongue, all the weight of his influence. With promises rich beyond all hope of keeping, and numerous as the snowflakes in a winter's hurricane, he beguiled his weaker fellows; men, who, like him, loved power, hated truth, delighted in iniquity, but who had not the secret ambition, the unhallowed valor, and the deep, designing cunning, that distinguished their leader. To his call the dissatisfied, the corrupt, and the apostate, rallied.

Opposed to him stood Moroni, the dauntless leader of the Nephite armies. Inspired by an unquenchable love for truth and liberty, he sensed with every one of his heart's pulsations that no man could fight for a holier, more precious cause than virtue and liberty. Thus inspired, he tore a portion of his cloak from its surrounding parts, and inscribing thereon his battle-cry, he lifted it high upon a pole. Then girding on his body-armor, incasing his head with a fit covering, shielding his body with its breastplates, placing the proper pieces round his thighs and loins, he kneeled in humble, heartfelt prayer before Jehovah, presented his *Title of Liberty* before Him and asked His blessing, protection, guidance, and victorious aid in the coming struggle. Then he gathered the Nephite hosts; from place to place he sped, waving the ensign on which all could read the burning words he had inscribed: In memory of our God, our religion and freedom, and our peace, our wives and our children.

Nor did he cry in vain; the patriot Nephites, the members of the Church of Christ, hastened with ready feet to the response. The streets of Zarahemla were alive with the gathering hosts. Each warrior, to show his devotion to the liberties with which God had endowed them, and his fealty to the Great Giver, rent his robe, as the young general had done, and thereby made a covenant with God and his brethren to be faithful and true, in life and in death, in the council chamber and on the battlefield, while an enemy remained to menace their liberties, national or religious.

Nor was Zarahemla alone in the manifestation of her patriotic love. Moroni's stirring appeal was spread far and wide throughout the lands of the Nephites. Swift-footed, banner-bearing messengers hastened down the Sidon's banks to the dwellers in the north, arousing the patriots of each peaceful city to the peril of the hour. Onward they hurried until Desolation echoed back to Bountiful the battle cry of liberty. Others gave no rest to the soles of their feet until Mulek, and her sister cities that lined the Caribbean Sea had flung from their tower tops the hallowed banner. Through the narrow defiles and rocky canyons that lay between the Andes' lofty peaks, other couriers pushed their unwearied way into the western wilderness and hence to the Pacific's strand, until every city held by the Nephites had gathered her sons to the defense of their rights and freedom, their altars and their firesides. Nor were Manti and the other cities of the south forgotten; the faithful and the brave who lined the borders of the great southern wilderness heard the rallying call. From every city, every vale, the converging hosts poured forth with sword and spear, with bow and arrow, with slings and stones; while from the top of every tower and citadel throughout the Nephite Commonwealth the sacred standard of liberty fluttered to the breeze. Men of strong arms and stout hearts were they, of faith unfaltering, and courage undiminished.

No wonder, then, that when Amalickiah's emissaries brought the evil-boding news of this great awakening to his unwilling ears, that he faltered in his purpose, that his followers lost heart, that retreat was deemed the fittest show of wisdom, and discretion the better part of valor. No wonder that when, by Moroni's vigilance, that retreat was cut off, that the rebels succumbed and surrendered, that Amalickiah fled for safety to the Lamanites, and that the *Title of Liberty* continued to float uninterruptedly from the Atlantic to the Pacific Coast as far as Nephite children ruled or Nephite homes were found, and that Moroni and his people rejoiced with intensified joy in their liberties, now more than ever dear to them through the valorous efforts they had put forth for their preservation.

When Amalickiah fled to the court of the Lamanite king he evolved a scheme or plot worthy only of a demon, which only ceased with life. On the first favorable opportunity after reaching the Lamanite court, he commenced to rekindle the fires of hatred toward his former friends. At first he was unsuccessful; the recollection of their past defeats was too fresh in the memory of the multitude. The king issued a proclamation, but it was disregarded. Much as his subjects feared the imperial power, they dreaded a renewal of war more. Many gathered to resist the royal mandate. The king, unused to such objections, raised an army to quell the advocates of peace, and placed it under the command of the now zealous Amalickiah.

The peace-men had chosen an officer named Lehonti for their leader, and he had assembled his followers on a mountain nearby called Antipas. Thither Amalickiah marched, but with no intention of provoking a conflict; he was working for the good feelings of the entire Lamanite people. On his arrival he entered a secret correspondence with Lehonti, in which he agreed to surrender his forces on condition that he should be appointed second in command of the united armies. The plan succeeded. Amalickiah surrendered to Lehonti and assumed the second position in command. It was but a little thing then to remove Lehonti. He died of a slow poison administered by Amalickiah's connivance.

Amalickiah now assumed supreme command, and at the head of his forces he marched towards the Lamanite Capital. The king, supposing that the approaching hosts had been raised to carry the war into Zarahemla, came out of the royal city to greet and congratu-:

late him. As the monarch drew near he was traitorously slain by some of the creatures of the subtle general, who at the same time raised the hue and cry that the king's own servants were the authors of the vile deed. Amalickiah assumed all the airs of grief, affection, and righteous indignation that he thought would best suit his purpose. He next made apparently desperate, but futile and purposely ineffectual, efforts to capture those who were charged with the crime, and so adroitly did he carry out his plans that before long he wheedled himself into the affections of the queen, whom he married, and was then recognized by the Lamanites as their king. Thus far his ambition was realized, but it was far from satisfied; ambition seldom is.

Amalickiah now cherished the stupendous design of subjugating the Nephites and ruling singly and alone from ocean to ocean (B.C. 73). To accomplish this iniquitous purpose he dispatched emissaries in all directions, whose mission was to stir up the angry passions of the Lamanites against the Nephites. When the vile object was accomplished to a sufficient degree, and the deluded people had become clamorous for war, Amalickiah raised an immense army, equipped them with an excellence never before known among the Lamanites. This force he placed under the command of Zoramite officers and ordered its advance into the western possessions of the Nephites, where, amongst others, stood the cities of Ammonihah, now rebuilt, and Noah.

The Nephites, during this time, had been watching Amalickiah's movements and were energetically preparing for war. When the Lamanites reached Ammonihah they found it to be too strongly fortified to be taken by assault; they therefore retired to Noah, originally a very weak place, but now, through Moroni's foresight and energy, made stronger than Ammonihah. The Zoramite officers well knew that to return home without having attempted something would be most disastrous to them, and therefore, though with little hope, made an assault upon Noah. This step resulted in throwing away a thousand lives outside its walls, while its well-protected defenders had but fifty men wounded. After this disastrous attempt the Lamanites marched home. Great was the anger of Amalickiah at the miscarriage of his schemes; he cursed God and swore that he yet would drink the blood of the Nephite Commander, Moroni.

During the next year the Lamanites were driven out of the eastern wilderness, which was occupied by numerous Nephite colonists who had laid the foundations of several new cities along the Atlantic Coast. Moroni also established a line of fortifications along the Nephites' southern border, which stretched from one side of the continent to the other.

A few years of peace and prosperity now followed. The Nephites multiplied exceedingly and grew very rich. They also were greatly blessed of the Lord; and the sacred historian informs us that there never was a happier time among the people of Nephi than at this time. Sad it is to say, this blessed era lasted but a few years. A local quarrel between two cities on the Atlantic Seaboard regarding their respective boundaries was the cause of the first outbreak of internecine strife. At this point we are introduced to another great Nephite general, named Teancum.

Teancum appears to have had command of the Nephite army of the north (under the direction of Moroni, the Commander-in-Chief of all the forces of the Republic), and to have had committed to him the defense of the Land Bountiful and the Isthmus of Panama. His first exploit to which our attention is drawn is the defeat of the dissatisfied people of Morianton, who, having unjustly quarreled with their neighbors, the people of the City of Lehi, and being apparently aware of the unrighteousness of their cause, determined to migrate to the land northward, and there establish an independent government.

Such a movement being dangerous to peace and to the stability of the Republic, Moroni determined to prevent the accomplishment of their resolve. He dispatched Teancum with a body of troops to head them off. This the gallant officer succeeded in doing, but not until they had reached the Isthmus, where a stubbornly-fought battle ensued, in which Teancum slew Morianton with his own hands, and compelled the surrender of his followers (B.C. 68). The prisoners were brought back, the grievances of the two people were investigated, a union between them brought about, and both were restored to their own lands.

In the following year, Amalickiah commenced his devastating invasion of the Atlantic provinces of the Nephites. Commencing at Moroni, on the extreme southeast, he gradually advanced northward, capturing and garrisoning all the Nephite cities along the coast, until toward the close of the year he reached the borders of the Land Bountiful, driving the forces of the Republic before him. At this point he was met by Teancum and a corps of veterans renowned for their courage, skill, and discipline. The Lamanite leader endeavored to force his way to the Isthmus, with the intention of occupying the North Continent. In this he was foiled, for the trained valor of Teancum's men was too much for that of Amalickiah's half-savage warriors. All day the fight lasted, and at night the worn-out soldiers of the two armies camped close together, the Lamanites on the sea-beach, and the Nephites on the borders of Bountiful.

It was the last night of the old year, according to Nephite

reckoning. The great heat and the terrible efforts of the past day had overcome both officers and men. The murmur of the Atlantic's waves sounded a soft lullaby in the ears of Amalickiah and his hosts, who, for the first time during the campaign had suffered a check in their triumphal march. Even Amalickiah slept; but not so Teancum. He was brooding over the wrongs and perils of his beloved country, as well as his own sufferings, both the deadly fruit of one man's ambition. As he pondered, he grew more angry, and at last he determined by one desperate stroke to put an end to the war; or if not that, at least to slay the cause of it. Taking one servant with him, he stole out of his own camp into that of the enemy. A death-like silence reigned in both. Cautiously and unobserved, he searched out the royal tent. There lay the foe; there lay his guards, all overcome with resistless fatigue. To draw his javelin, thrust it into the king's heart and then flee was but the work of a minute, and so adroitly did he fulfill his purpose that Amalickiah died without a struggle or a cry, and it was not until the morning that his guards discovered that the Lamanite hosts were without a leader.

When Teancum returned to his own warriors he awoke them from their slumbers and rehearsed to them all that had happened. It is not difficult to imagine their enthusiasm, which, for fear they would arouse the enemy, they were compelled to restrain. They, however, kept a strong guard on the alert, lest when the Lamanites awoke and discovered that their king was dead, they should, in their anger make a sudden onslaught on the Nephite lines. This thought, however, was not realized. When the Lamanites found that Amalickiah was slain, they hastily retreated to the fortified City of Mulek.

Amalickiah was succeeded on the Lamanitish throne by his brother, Ammoron, who continued the war with unrelenting vindictiveness.

JACOB THE ZORAMITE

The general who commanded the Lamanite forces at Mulek was named Jacob. He was a Nephite apostate, who had accepted the errors of the Zoramites. His appointment was one characteristic of the prevailing policy of Amalickiah and of his successor, Ammoron. It was to give the command of the Lamanite armies to men who, like themselves, were traitors to their own government; for, in such cases, to military knowledge was almost invariably added intense religious hate, which neither asked nor gave quarter on the battlefield, but fought to the last extremity with unconquerable fury.

Such a one was Jacob. He had entrenched himself in the strongly fortified city of Mulek, the most northern of the Nephite cities that had fallen into the enemy's hands. It was a key to the surrounding country. While it remained in Lamanite possession it was very little use for Moroni to attempt to recover the cities that lay yet farther south along the shores of the east sea. The Nephite generals did not consider themselves justified in making an attempt to carry the place by assault. Such an effort would have cost too many noble lives, and probably have proven unsuccessful. Moroni had with him at this time two of his most trusted lieutenants, Lehi and Teancum, both of whom were little inferior to the chief captain in wisdom and valor. At a council of war it was determined to attempt the capture of Mulek by strategy. They had already sent embassies to Jacob desiring him to bring his armies into the open plain to meet the Nephites in battle, but the Lamanite commanders were too well acquainted with the discipline and courage of the Nephite forces to take such a risk. There was, therefore, but one plan left, other than to patiently sit down before the city and reduce it by a regular siege, and that was to decoy a portion of its defenders beyond the protection of its walls, and when it was thus weakened to carry it by storm. Moroni determined on this course.

By command of Moroni, the gallant Teancum, with a small force, marched along the seashore to the neighborhood of Mulek, while Moroni, with the main body of the army, unperceived by the enemy, made a forced march by night into the wilderness which lay on the west of the city. There he rested. Lehi, with a third corps, remained in the City of Bountiful.

On the morrow Teancum's detachment was discovered by the Lamanite outposts, and from the smallness of its numbers they judged it would fall an easy prey. Jacob at once sallied forth at the head of his warriors to attack the presumptuous Nephites. On their approach Teancum cautiously retreated along the seashore towards the City of Bountiful. Jacob followed in vigorous pursuit. Moroni, in the meanwhile, divided his army into two corps, one of which he dispatched to capture the city, and with the other he closed in between Jacob's army and Mulek. The first corps accomplished its work without difficulty, for Jacob had left but a small force behind him, and all who would not surrender were slain.

The Lamanites crowded after Teancum in hot pursuit until they came nigh unto Bountiful, when they were met by Lehi and the small force under his command. At his appearance the Lamanite captains fled in confusion, lest they should be out-generaled and cut off from their fortifications. Jacob's warriors were weary by reason of their long and hasty advance, while Lehi's soldiers were fresh and unfatigued. But Lehi refrained from pressing too vigorously on his retreating foes, as his object was not to exhaust his men before the hour of battle came, and he was anxious to avoid a conflict till he and Moroni could at the same moment attack the Lamanites in front and rear.

When Jacob drew near the city he found himself confronted by the soldiers of Moroni, who closed in around his warriors and barred their further progress southward; while Lehi, putting forth his pent-up energies, fell with fury on their rear. Weary and worn though his troops were, Jacob would not surrender. Whatever his faults may have been, and they were doubtless numerous, he had a resolute, unconquerable spirit that would fight to the last. He determined, if possible, to cut his way through to Mulek. With this intent he made a desperate, though ineffectual, charge on Moroni's lines. The Nephites being fresh and unwearied, never wavered, but received the shock firm as a rock upon which the waves of the ocean break in vain. The battle here raged with indescribable fierceness, and with heavy losses to both sides. The wild Lamanites, in the frenzy of desperation, dashed with all their strength and prowess against the well-ordered ranks of the Nephites in the one absorbing endeavor to force their way through; while the Nephites, in the heroic courage which religion and patriotism inspire, stood cool and undismayed, breaking the force of the shock of each charge.

In this desperate encounter Moroni was wounded and Jacob slain.

While Jacob was thus impetuously charging on Moroni's corps, Lehi with his "strong men" was furiously driving in the Lamanite rear. At last the soldiers of Jacob in that part of the field surrendered. Their leader being slain, the remainder of the troops hesitated between throwing down their arms and continuing the hopeless strife. Moroni, with his intense hatred of unnecessary bloodshed, when he noticed that they wavered, cried out that if they would lay down their weapons and deliver themselves up he would spare their lives. His offer was accepted. The chief captains, who remained, came forward and placed their weapons at his feet and commanded their men to do the same. Most of the warriors obeyed, yet numbers would not. They preferred death to surrender, and force had to be used to wrest their weapons from them. The Lamanite prisoners were then sent under an escort to the City of Bountiful, and when counted were found to exceed in numbers the slain on both sides in the late battle. Thus fell Mulek, and thus died its defender, Jacob the Zoramite.

HELAMAN AND HIS TWO THOUSAND YOUNG MEN

The war had been raging about a couple of years, and was working disastrously to the Nephites, when the people of Ammon, feeling that they were a burden rather than a help to their benefactors, though indeed they were not, desired to be released from their oath and covenant never again to take up deadly weapons against their fellows. They desired in this hour of extreme peril to take up arms in defense of the liberties of their adopted country. From this rash step Helaman and his brethren dissuaded them, lest by so doing they should imperil their eternal salvation. But they had sons who had grown far towards manhood who had not entered into this covenant, and consequently were not shut off from participating in the dangers and glories of the war. So with their fathers' and mothers' consent, faith, prayers and words of encouragement, two thousand of these youths were mustered into the Nephite army (B.C. 66). These striplings were all men of truth, faith, soberness and integrity, and were conspicuous for their courage, strength and activity. Being organized they desired that Helaman, for whom they had great love and respect, should be their leader. He consented, and at their head marched to the relief of the forces of the republic that were struggling against considerable odds on the southern borders of the Nephite dominions, from the shores of the Pacific Ocean eastward.

Helaman found the Nephite forces, numbering about six thousand warriors, in a somewhat deplorable condition. The Lamanites, in the strength of greatly superior numbers, had captured the cities of Manti, Cumeni, Zeezrom and Antiparah, and held possession of the country round about. These cities had not been taken without much bloodshed on both sides. The Nephites especially had lost large numbers in prisoners, who were generally put to death by their captors, except the superior officers, who were sent to the land of Nephi. Antipus, the Nephite commander, was locked up in the city of Judea, where, dispirited and weakened by excessive toil and fighting, his troops were making a desperate and painful effort to fortify the city. The arrival of Helaman and his corps brought hope and joy again to their hearts, and renewed vigor to their endeavors.

King Ammoron, learning that reinforcements had reached the defenders of Judea, ordered all active operations to be suspended for a season. This suspension was most providential for the soldiers of Antipus, as it gave them time to finish the work of fortifying the beleagured city, and also to recruit their health and energies. By the commencement of the following year the works of defense were completed, and the Nephites became anxious for the onslaught they had so greatly dreaded a few months previous. But they were disappointed. The Lamanites did not feel sufficiently strong to renew aggressive movements. They contented themselves with occupying the Nephite cities they had already captured. In the second month of this year (B.C. 65) a convoy of provisions and two thousand additional warriors arrived from the Land of Zarahemla. The Nephites in the city of Judea were now ten thousand strong, with abundant provisions, and they were anxious for a forward movement in order, if possible, to retake some of their cities in the hands of the enemy.

Antipus and Helaman resolved on a ruse to entice the Lamanites from behind their fortifications. It was decided that Helaman and his command should march out of Judea with the apparent intention of carrying supplies to one of the cities in the hands of the Nephites, that was built near the seashore. In executing this maneuver, they purposely passed at no great distance from the City of Antiparah, in which was stationed the most numerous of the Lamanite armies, in the hope that the Lamanites would notice that their numbers were few, and thus be led to attack them. The stratagem proved successful. The garrison of Antiparah issued forth in pursuit of Helaman, who, with all haste, retreated into the wilderness northward, his intent being to draw his pursuers as far as possible from Antiparah. When the Lamanites had started in pursuit of Helaman, Antipus, with a considerable portion of his army, marched out of the city of Judea and fell in the Lamanites' rear. The retreat soon became a race. The Lamanites crowded forward with all possible expedition in the endeavor to reach Helaman before Antipus caught them. Helaman, on the other hand, used his utmost energy to keep out of their clutches. Neither of the three bodies turned to the right nor to the left, but kept straight on in the effort to out-march their foes. Night came and went, and on the morrow the double pursuit was still kept up. Another night fell, but neither dared turn from its course.

On the third morning the race for life and victory was again renewed, but before long the Lamanites, concluding they could not overtake Helaman, suddenly stopped, and awaited the coming of Antipus and his weary soldiers, whom they unexpectedly attacked with great fury, slew Antipus and several of his captains, threw the Nephites troops into great confusion and forced them to commence a retreat.

In the meantime, Helaman discovered that he was no longer pursued, and not knowing the reason, was in doubt what course to take. He called a hasty council of war, at which it was determined to return at once, and risk the chances of being caught in a trap by the crafty Lamanites.

The statement which Helaman makes regarding the conduct of his young soldiers at this council is very interesting. After he had explained the situation to them, he inquired, What say ye, my sons, will ye go against them in battle? Without hesitancy they answered in the affirmative, saying: Father, behold our God is with us, and he will not suffer that we shall fall; then let us go forth; we would not slay our brethren if they would let us alone; therefore let us go lest they should overpower the army of Antipus. Here Helaman remarks: Now they never had fought, yet they did not fear death; and they did think more of the liberty of their fathers than they did upon their lives; yea, they had been taught by their mothers that if they did not doubt God would deliver them. And they rehearsed unto me the words of their mothers, saying, We do not doubt our mothers knew it.

Helaman and his sons arrived none too soon on the field of battle. The soldiers of Antipus were already fleeing before their more numerous foes, but the valor and impetuosity of the youthful Ammonites was irresistible. They fell on the Lamanite rear with a daring and miraculous strength possessed only by men who put their whole trust in God. Thus attacked in the rear, the Lamanites immediately halted, changed front, and threw their whole force against the Ammonites. The surviving officers of Antipus' army, finding that Helaman had come to their rescue, stopped the retreat, reorganized their scattered bands, and renewed the attack. The Lamanites were compelled to succumb; they could not resist the desperate courage of the Nephites that was driving them in at both front and rear. Their legions all surrendered, and, by Helaman's orders, were sent as prisoners of war to Zarahemla.

And what about the young warriors of Ammon? So great was their faith, so potent its workings, that when, after the battle, Helaman called the roll of his youthful heroes, not one was missing. The faith sown by their mothers' words had borne fruit — they were all preserved. To their undaunted prowess, for they fought as if with the strength of God, the Nephites unhesitatingly accorded the glory of the day.

Still the hotly contested war continued. Six thousand men, with provisions, reached Helaman from Zarahemla and the regions round about (B.C. 63), besides sixty more young Ammonites who had grown sufficiently vigorous to assume the hardships of military life. The City of Cumeni shortly afterwards surrendered through the want of provisions, their supplies having been continuously cut off by Helaman's troops. This surrender threw so many prisoners on the hands of the Nephites that they were unable to guard or feed them. An officer named Gid, with a sufficient force, was detailed to convey them to Zarahemla, but on their way, passing near to an invading body of Lamanites, the prisoners made a desperate attempt to escape. A few succeeded in getting away, but the greater number were slain by their guard. Gid and his command returned to headquarters, as it proved, just in time, for the Lamanites had made a sudden and unexpected attack at Cumeni, and but for Gid's timely arrival the

Nephite forces would probably have received a severe defeat. As it was, defeat was turned to victory by their coming.

In this desperate battle every one of the young Ammonites was wounded, but not one was slain. According to the promise made to them they were preserved by the marvelous power of God.

THE OVERTHROW OF THE KINGMEN

After the battle at Cumeni, the Lamanites retreated eastward to Manti, which was situated on the upper waters of the Sidon. Nor was it for several months that this city could be taken, as owing to internal dissensions at the Nephite capital, and the attempts on the part of some of the people to overthrow the republic and establish a monarchy, Pahoran, the chief judge, was unable to supply the necessary provisions and reinforcements.

In this strait Helaman and his fellow officers called on the Lord in fervent prayer, which was not unanswered. They received assurances of deliverance and victory. These blessed assurances inspired fresh faith and infused renewed courage in the war-weary hearts of those not given to the love of carnage. Fired with the determination, by God's grace, to conquer, they entered on a campaign against the city of Manti, which, by strategy, they captured before the end of the year (B.C. 63). The moral effect of this victory was so great that the Lamanites retreated into the wilderness, evacuating the whole of the territory on the west, but unfortunately taking with them, as prisoners, many women and children.

For more than a year Moroni could not send the needed help to Helaman. The rebels in Zarahemla had driven the chief judge out of the city, and he had taken refuge in Gideon. From there he wrote to Moroni to come to his assistance, which that officer did at the earliest possible moment, leaving the armies in the northeast under the command of Lehi and Teancum. As he advanced he rallied the people on his line of march to the defense of the liberties of the republic, and was so successful that, after having joined the chief judge, Pahoran, he succeeded in overthrowing the "king men," killing their leader, Pachus, and completely crushing the rebellion. This being accomplished, he sent 6,000 men with the necessary provisions to reinforce Helaman (B.C. 61).

The campaign during this year, along the Atlantic coast, was a decisive one. At last the soldiers of Ammoron were driven out of Omner, Morianton, Gid, Lehi, Nephihah, and every other Nephite city on that seaboard, except the outlying one, called Moroni, where the whole of the invading host was massed for a final desperate stand, and around which Moroni, by hurried and lengthened marches, had concentrated his warriors.

It was the night before an expected decisive battle, and the Nephite officers and soldiers were too fatigued to either devise stratagems or execute them. Teancum alone did not seek rest. He remembered with intense bitterness all the bloodshed, woes, hardships, famine, etc., that had been brought about in this great and lasting war between the two races, which he rightly attributed to the infamous ambition of Amalickiah and Ammoron. He reflected how he had slain the former, and determined that as he had slain Amalickiah, so should Ammoron fall. In his anger he stole forth into the enemy's camp, let himself over the walls of the city, sought out the king's tent, and when he had found the object of his search, he cast a javelin at him, which pierced him near the heart. But, unlike Amalickiah, Ammoron's death was not instantaneous. He had time to awaken his servant before he passed away. The alarm was given, the guards started in pursuit; Teancum was overtaken, caught and slain. On the morrow, Moroni attacked the Lamanites, defeated them with great slaughter, captured the city, and drove them entirely out of Nephite territory. (B.C. 61)

The writer of the Book of Alma records: When Lehi and Moroni knew that Teancum was dead, they were exceedingly sorrowful; for behold, he had been a man who had fought valiantly for his country; yea, a true friend to liberty, and he had suffered very many exceeding sore afflictions. But behold, he was dead, and had gone the way of all the earth.

In that glorious galaxy of patriot-priests, or warrior-prophets, call them which we may, to whose stern integrity, inspired valor, and unflinching virtue the Nephite republic, in the days of which we write, owed so much of its stability and was so greatly indebted for its perpetuity, Teancum shines among the brightest. View him from whatever point we please, there is no mistaking the man. His ardent disposition, his fiery impetuosity, his zealous patriotism, his undaunted courage, his love of liberty, his entire disinterestedness, shine forth in every action. Indeed, we might almost call him rash, so little did he consider his personal safety when he thought the good of his country required the sacrifice.

In picturing the heroes of those days, Teancum looms up before us almost as a Hotspur or Murat. In our mind's eye we can see him charging the solid phalanxes of the Lamanites, rushing at full speed towards the enemy several lengths ahead of his line of battle; his commanding presence inspiring confidence, his unwavering voice ringing out the word of command, his bright armor shining in the sun, and his hair streaming from beneath his helmet, as, regardless of all save the liberties of his country, he falls upon the thickest of the foe, seeking out their chief captains, that by their death an end may possibly be put to the horrors of war. Thus we find him slaying with his own hand, at different times, Morianton, Amalickiah and Ammoron. In fact, it is quite noticeable that in nearly all the great battles of this age, the Nephites appear to have made it a conspicuous part of their policy to slay the commander of the opposing hosts. So fell Amlici, Morianton, Jacob, Coriantumr and others.

HAGOTH, THE SHIPBUILDER

In the next year after the capture of the city of Moroni peace was established in all the land; not a Lamanite warrior remained on Nephite soil. Then Pahoran returned to his judgment seat, and Helaman recommenced his labors in the ministry.

The long-continued and savage war just closed had brought various evils to the church. In many parts of the land it may be said to have been disorganized. The occupancy of so many of the Nephite cities by the unbelieving Lamanites had produced numerous demoralizing effects. Murders, contentions, dissensions and all manner of iniquity had become rife, and the hearts of the people had grown hardened. Yet not altogether so, for there were some who acknowledged the hand of the Lord in all their afflictions. These humbled themselves in the depths of humility; and because of the prayers of the righteous the people were spared.

Such was the state of affairs when Helaman went forth to call the people to repentance and set the church in order. In this blessed work he had much success, and with the help of his brethren he again established the Church of God throughout all the land. These labors he continued until the time of his death, and his joy therein was greatly increased by the continued faithfulness of the people. They, notwithstanding their abundant prosperity, which, as ever, followed their repentance, remained humble, fervent in prayer and diligent in well-doing. Such was the happy condition of the people of Nephi when Helaman died (B.C. 57), he having survived his illustrious father sixteen years. Shiblon, at the death of his brother, took possession of the sacred things that had been delivered unto Helaman by Alma, and held them for four years.

The next year (B.C. 56), the valiant Moroni, one of the greatest and most virtuous of God's sons, passed away from this state of mortality to the glories of eternity, at the early age of forty-three years. Some time before his death he had given the chief command of the armies of the Nephites to his son, Moronihah, who, from the history of later years, we judge to have been a worthy son of so illustrious a sire.

The four years that Shiblon held the plates are principally note-worthy for the commencement of Nephite emigration to the northern continent. It was during this period that Hagoth established his shipbuilding yards on the Pacific, near the Land Bountiful. It is probable that ships were built by the Nephites before Hagoth's time, but he being an exceedingly expert mechanic, constructed much larger ones than had hitherto been built, and thus inaugurated a new feature in Nephite colonization.[1]

When Shiblon died he committed the records to the care of Helaman, the son of his brother Helaman. The history of the Nephites and Lamanites still continued a history of wars. In the same year that Shiblon died, the Lamanites again raised a numerous army and went down against their traditional foes. The campaign was a short one. Moronihah, the son of Moroni, inflicted a signal blow upon their advancing legions, and drove them back to their own lands. Their loss in this deservedly ill-fated expedition was great.

Still this bloodthirsty race never seemed to gain experience by the things it suffered. This, no doubt, arose to a great extent from the continued irritation kept up by the wily apostates, who had much private spleen to gratify in the sufferings of the Nephites, and who held no particular love or respect for their credulous dupes and cat's-paws, the Lamanites.

It was in the year B.C. 53 that Helaman took charge of the sacred plates, etc. In the next year Pahoran, the chief judge, died, which event gave rise to serious contention amongst the Nephite people. Three of his sons, named Pahoran, Pacumeni and Paanchi, were ambitious to fill the exalted position left vacant by their father's death. Each had his adherents and following, but, according to the national law, the matter was decided by the voice of the people, and Pahoran was chosen.

Pacumeni assented to the decision of the citizens, but Paanchi attempted to raise a rebellion, for which crime he was arrested, tried by law, and condemned to death. Still the more wicked part of the community supported his unlawful claims. These determined to slay Pahoran, which resolve they carried into effect, and the chief judge was slain by an assassin named Kishkumen.[2] This foul murder was committed while the chief magistrate was sitting in the judgment seat administering the law, but through the connivance of the murderer's associates in iniquity he escaped.

---

[1]These ships of Hagoth carried many colonies to the land northward; as it was their custom to take one load of emigrants and when they had disembarked, to return for another. Some of these vessels were eventually lost; that is, the ships and their passengers never reached their destination. It is supposed by many that a part of them were carried out to mid-ocean by storms and probably wrecked; and that the survivors found safety and shelter on some of the islands of the Pacific Ocean. In this way, it is suggested, the Hawaiian, Samoan and other islands were first peopled.

[2]Pacumeni was chosen to succeed Pahoran as Chief Judge.

These lawless men bound themselves together by a secret oath and covenant, that they would never divulge who was the murderer of Pahoran, and they swore, by the most horrible oaths, one to another, to conceal each other's crimes, to aid and sustain each other in their villainies, and to carry out the designs and directions of their leaders. Over this band of conspirators, assassins and robbers, Gadianton stood as the head.

The next year after Pahoran's assassination, the Lamanites invaded the lands of the Nephites. The Lamanite armies were commanded by a Nephite dissenter named Coriantumr. He was a descendant of Zarahemla, therefore, presumedly, of the tribe of Judah. He determined on new and venturesome tactics, and caused his forces to make an unexpected dash through the Nephite territory. The Nephites everywhere gave way before them. They marched through the center of the country, ravaging its most populous and richest districts. Before the astonished Nephites could collect their armies the enemy had assaulted and captured their beautiful and strongly fortified capital, and for the first time the savage soldiery of Laman held possession of the towers, temples and palaces of Zarahemla. On this occasion the chief judge, Pacumeni, was slain. Intoxicated with his uninterrupted success, the Lamanite general crowded yet further north, neglecting to keep up his line of communication in the rear.

Coriantumr's hope was to obtain possession of the narrow isthmus which was the key to both continents. In this he failed. The Nephite commander first checked his progress northward, and then cut off his retreat. In a fierce battle that followed he was killed, his armies surrendered, and the remnants hastened ingloriously home, Moronihah, the Nephite commander, magnanimously permitting them to return unmolested. (B.C. 51)

HELAMAN CHOSEN CHIEF JUDGE

As Pacumeni, the chief judge, had been slain at the capture of Zarahemla, no sooner was the war over than an election took place to fill his vacant seat. The choice fell upon Helaman, the more righteous of the people providentially being still in the majority.

Helaman being a God-fearing, just man, his election was very distasteful to the Gadianton band and its sympathizers. They resolved to slay him as they had before slain the younger Pahoran, and place Gadianton on the judgment seat in his stead. To accomplish this the same vile instrument was chosen—Kishkumen. But the protecting hand of the great Jehovah was over and around Helaman, and he preserved him from the assassin's knife. A servant of Helaman, possibly a detective commissioned in such time of peril to watch the movements of the dangerous classes, by disguise became acquainted with the doings of the robber band, and of their intentions toward his master.

As Kishkumen was on his way to fulfill his bloody work, this servant, whose name is not recorded, met him, and gave him one of their secret signs. This admitted him into the confidence of the assassin, who explained his errand, and asked to be conducted privately into the judgment hall, where Helaman was then sitting in the performance of his duties. This was agreed upon; the two proceeded to where the murderer expected to find his victim. The strategy of the servant disarmed his suspicions; he was off his guard. At the opportune moment the servant stabbed Kishkumen, and so adroitly did he perform his work, that the robber fell dead without a groan. The servant immediately ran to the judgment hall, and informed Helaman of all that he had heard, seen and done. Without delay, orders were issued for the arrest of the band, but its members, finding that Kishkumen did not return, and hearing he had miscarried in his unholy work, under the guidance of their leader, fled precipitately into the wilderness by a secret way, and, in the depths of its luxuriant vegetation, hid in a place where they could not be found. (B.C. 50)

The succeeding years were of peculiar prosperity, though not of great righteousness, amongst the Nephite people. They spread out and colonized in every direction. Many thousands emigrated to the northern continent, among them great numbers of Ammonites. Numerous new cities were built, and old ones repaired; shipbuilding was largely carried on and the arts and manufactures encouraged. Temples, tabernacles and sanctuaries were erected in great numbers; in fact, the people spread out and covered both continents north and south, east and west. The sacred historian states that he has not recorded one hundredth part of the doings of the people — their wickedness and righteousness, their wars and contentions, their peace and prosperity; but many records were kept, upon which the history of the things were engraved, and all that is necessary for the world's good will be brought to light in heaven's own time.

The annals of the remainder of Helaman's rule are very short. In the years B.C. 45 and 44 there were many contentions in the land, but in the latter portion of the succeeding years they measurably ceased, and tens of thousands were baptized unto repentance. So great was the prosperity of the church at this time that even the priesthood were surprised thereat, and at the multiplicity of blessings that were poured out upon the people. This happy state of affairs continued until the death of Helaman, though somewhat marred by the increasing pride and vanity that long-continued prosperity had begotten in the hearts of many of the Christians.

Helaman himself was a righteous judge: He did observe to keep the judgments, and the statutes, and the commandments of God; and he did do that which was right in the sight of God continually, and he did walk after the ways of his father, insomuch that he did prosper in the land. So writes the historian of Helaman; what more can be said of any man?

Helaman had two sons to whom he gave the names of Nephi and Lehi, to remind them, when they heard their own names called, of the faith and goodness of their great ancestors, who, by God's direction, led their fathers to the promised land. When Helaman died he was succeeded by his son Nephi.

NEPHI AND LEHI, SONS OF HELAMAN

In Nephi we have one of the greatest prophets that ever trod the earth, or to whom the God of our salvation revealed his glorious will. He lived during the greater portion of the first century before Christ, and disappeared from the knowledge of mankind but a short time before the advent of the Messiah as a babe in Bethlehem. He is first referred to in the Book of Mormon (B.C. 44) as the elder of Helaman's two sons, Lehi being the younger. These two brothers appear to have been inseparable during their lives. They are nearly always mentioned as associated in the great and ofttimes perilous labors of the ministry undertaken for the salvation of either Nephites or Lamanites. We have no information with regard to the time of Nephi's birth, but when his father died, in the year B.C. 39, he succeeded him as chief judge, the duties of which office he filled with wisdom and justice for about nine years, when owing to the wickedness of the people, he resigned that office, and Cezoram was chosen by the people in his stead (B.C. 30).

The years that Nephi judged his people are some of the darkest in Nephite history. Owing to their great pride and iniquity, the Lord left them to themselves, and they became weak like unto the Lamanites, man for man. When war was declared, the latter, being much the more numerous, carried everything before them. In vain the Nephites struggled for their homes and their liberties. They were forced back by the hordes of the Lamanites from city to city, from land to land. Manti, Gideon, Cumeni, Moroni, and even Zarahemla fell. Nor did the war end when the bloodthirsty Lamanites held high carnival in the midst of its towers and palaces. Onward swept the invading host; backward fled the defenders of the commonwealth, and backward they continued until every town and city, every tower and fort, from Melek to Moroni, from Manti to Bountiful, were filled with the savage, half-disciplined, dark-skinned warriors of Laman. Not a place could be found in the whole southern continent where the soldiers of the Nephites successfully held their ground. Zarahemla, with its hallowed associations, its glorious temples, where the daily sacrifice was unceasingly offered, its proud palaces, its luxurious homes, its courts of justice, where the chief judge sat in the magnificence of almost kingly authority to administer the law — this, their queen city, the seat of government, the center of their civilization, the home of their highest priesthood, was in the hands of their merciless, vandal-like foes. Nor had the danger stopped; with hurried hands the Nephites built a line of defense across the Isthmus of Panama from sea to sea, for the unnumbered hosts of their conquerors were still pushing forward. This line of fortification was effectual; it stopped the roll of the barbaric tide northward, and the Lamanite commanders rested with the possession of a continent.

In this war the Nephite dissenters took active part against their white brethren, and to this fact, in part, may be attributed the sudden success that shone on the Lamanite arms. But little by little in succeeding years the half repentant Nephites regained their lost ground, until (B.C. 31), the most northerly half of their possessions had again fallen into their hands; but because of their only partial repentance, their leaders had not strength to lead them further, and Zarahemla still remained in the hands of the warriors of Laman.

When Nephi retired from the judgment seat, it was with the intention of devoting his entire time to the preaching of the gospel. He associated his brother Lehi with him, and commencing at Bountiful, he journeyed and preached throughout all the land southward in the possession of the Nephites. From thence the two brothers passed onwards to Zarahemla, where they found many Nephite dissenters, to whom they proclaimed the word of God in great power. Numbers of these confessed their sins, were baptized unto repentance, and immediately returned to their brethren to repair, if possible, the wrongs they had done, and make such restitution as lay in their power.

Numbers of the Lamanites also received the truth gladly, insomuch that eight thousand of that race were baptized in Zarahemla and the regions round about.

From Zarahemla the prophets proceeded to the Lamanite capital in the Land of Nephi, where yet mightier power attended them. The voice of God from heaven sustained their testimony; angels ministered to the people who assembled to see them; neither prisons, nor chains, nor bonds could restrain or hold them, and they accomplished an ever blessed and marvelous work amongst the benighted children of Laman (B.C. 30). God's power was manifested at these times in mercy to the darkened condition of the minds of the Lamanites, when only extraordinary manifestations of His divine goodness could reach their hearts. They had no records to which they could appeal, and all their traditions were opposed to the Holy Being whose message of eternal joy the Nephite prophets bore. Thus in their weakness they were strengthened by signs and wonders which a people better educated in the things of God could with but ill grace claim.

The story of the ministration of Nephi and Lehi in the Land of Nephi is of the deepest interest. When they reached its chief city they were thrust into that same prison into which Ammon and his companions were cast by the guards of King Limhi. Here they were kept with little or no food for a number of days. At the end of this time the officers of the Lamanites went to the prison with the intention of slaying the two brothers. But to their intense surprise the Lamanites found them encircled about as if by fire. At this strange spectacle fear fell upon the officers. They dared not touch the two prisoners lest they should be burned. Yet when they saw that Nephi and Lehi were not consumed their hearts took courage, though they still stood as if struck dumb with amazement.

At this point the two brethren stood forward and began to explain that what was seen was manifested that the spectators might learn that no one could harm them, and that they were the servants of the Most High, and his all-powerful arm shielded them. Nor was this all: a sudden earthquake shook the ground, the prison walls tottered to their foundations, a pall of thick darkness covered all whom curiosity or other motives had gathered to the prison. The unburning flame, the tottering walls, the quivering earth, the impenetrable cloud of blackness, all conspired to fill the hearts of the Lamanites with solemn fear and awful dread. They realized the almighty power of God; they were filled with the sense of their own insignificance. A voice, the voice of One whom they knew not, sounded in their affrighted ears. Once again, yea, a third time, and each time that the voice came it was followed by the trembling of the earth and the shaking of the prison walls. All nature quivered at the presence of the Majesty on High, whilst the heavy, palpable, impenetrable darkness still enshrouded them.

From above the voice descended; it was outside the cloud; its tones came not to their quaking hearts with the roar of the pealing thunder; nor was it like the tumultuous flow of angry waters; but a still voice of perfect mildness, almost a whisper, that pierced to their inmost souls. That voice was the voice of the mighty God of Jacob, and he called upon all those who heard him to repent, and to do his servants no hurt. With the third repetition of this command were added marvelous words of salvation that cannot be uttered by men. And because of the darkness that enveloped them, and the fearful dread that filled their hearts, none dared to move. Fear, astonishment, apprehension of what was to come, had riveted each to the spot on which he stood.

Among the crowd was a Nephite dissenter, an apostate from the true church, named Aminadab. This man, happening to turn his face in the direction in which the two disciples stood, beheld that their faces shone with a glorious light, and that they were conversing with someone who appeared to be above them, for their eyes were turned heavenward. Aminadab drew the attention of those who surrounded him to this glorious appearance, and the spell that bound them was sufficiently removed to enable them to turn towards the prisoners and to become witnesses of the fact also. What do all these things mean? they anxiously inquired. They do converse with the angels of God, answered Aminadab. What shall we do that this cloud of darkness may be removed? was their next question. You must repent and cry unto the Voice, even until ye shall have faith in Christ, he replied. They did cry unto God with all the energy that their terrifying surroundings inspired, and so continued to supplicate until the cloud was dispersed. Then, to their great surprise, they discovered that they also were entombed in a pillar of living fire. Yet this fire did not hurt them; it did not singe their garments; it did not consume the prison walls, but their terror was swept away, and they were filled with a joy that was unspeakable, for the Holy Spirit of God filled their souls, and they broke forth in marvelous words of praise and rejoicing. Again a pleasant, searching whisper reached their gladdened ears. It said unto them, Peace, peace be unto you because of your faith in my Well-beloved, who was from the foundation of the world. Now there were about 300 souls who heard and saw these things, and they cast up their eyes unto heaven, which was opened to their vision, and holy angels came down and ministered unto them.

The tidings of this glorious appearing were quickly spread near and far in the lands where the Lamanites dwelt. So powerful was the testimony, and so great were the evidences, that the major portion of the people believed, repented and obeyed the gospel. Then, like all true saints, they manifested the sincerity of their repentance by works of restitution; they laid down their weapons of war, they cast aside their false traditions, their hatred gave place to love, and they restored to the Nephites Zarahemla and the other lands which they had taken from them (B.C. 30).

So great was the reformation in their character that the Lamanites soon exceeded the Nephites in their faith and good works. Extraordinary as it may appear, instead of Nephite missionaries visiting the Lamanites, Lamanite missionaries were soon ministering the precious truths of the gospel among the Nephites. Then a universal peace, such as had never before been known since the division of the two races, extended over the whole land. Indeed. from this time the history of the two nations, to a great extent, becomes one. Together they worshiped the Lord; together they rose and sank; together they battled with the assassin hosts of Gadianton; together they triumphed over those desperadoes, and together they sought refuge in one vast body when there was no safety but in massing the people in one land; together the more unrighteous portions of both races were destroyed at the crucifixion of the Savior, and together the more righteous ones witnessed his appearing, listened to his words, received his law, and became members of his holy church. Henceforth, for generations, they were no more of Nephi, no more of Laman, no more of Jacob, no more of Ishmael — all were of Christ.

GROWTH OF EVIL AMONG THE NEPHITES

This goodly reign of universal peace, brought stability, stability developed wealth, wealth engendered pride, pride gave birth to numerous sins, to be followed by contentions, dissensions, and then wars. These evils begat sorrow, sorrow softened the hearts of the people to repentance, repentance was followed by the blessing of God, which again brought peace, prosperity and, by-and-by, riches. At this era of Nephite national life, this is the one eternal round which their inspired historians are compelled to chronicle. Within four short years of the happy time of universal peace we have just referred to, the riches of the world had induced stubbornness and rebellion towards God, combined with the insane desire to rob, plunder and murder their fellow men. If there ever were a people swift to do evil, it was the Nephites of this generation. In the year B.C. 26, Cezoram, the chief judge, was murdered by an unknown hand as he sat on the judgment seat, and his son, who succeeded him, suffered in like manner within the year. The Gadianton robbers grew in strength, both in numbers and influence, and were actually fostered amongst the Nephites, while the more righteous Lamanites utterly destroyed all that they found within their borders. The one people dwindled in unbelief; the other grew in grace and in the power of God's divine Spirit.

Nephi, who had gone to the northern continent, tarried there until the year B.C. 23, when, his teachings and prophecies having been rejected by its inhabitants, he returned in sorrow to Zarahemla; but he found no comfort there. The Gadianton robbers filled the judgment seats, and perverted the law to their own avarice and lust. The life, the property, the liberty, the virtue of righteous men and women were counted but things of naught, the playthings or their spoil.

Nephi's house in Zarahemla was situated on one of the principal thoroughfares. It led to the chief marketplace. In his garden, near the highway, he built a tower whither it was his wont to repair for prayer. On one occasion, shortly after his return from the north, he became so deeply concerned because of the iniquities of the people, that in earnest supplication to the Lord he raised his voice so high that he was heard by the passers-by in the street below. A listening crowd soon gathered, and when the prophet had ended his devotions and became aware of their presence, he commenced to teach them. His words were not sugar-coated to adapt them to the tastes of his congregation. To the contrary, he boldly rebuked their sins, their murders, and their secret wickedness; at the same time, in the love of the gospel, he entreated and pled with them to amend their lives and do better. He also warned them of the terrible judgments that would fall upon them if they did not turn from their sinful ways.

Towards the conclusion of his address, Nephi surprised his hearers by stating that the chief judge, Seezoram, had been murdered by his brother, Seantum, who was anxious to obtain the chief judgeship himself. Both these men were members of the vile band who owned Gadianton as their chief.

The people did not believe Nephi's statement, so five incredulous men ran to the judgment hall to find out the truth of the matter. When they reached there they discovered Seezoram lying dead in a pool of blood near the judgment seat. The five messengers were so overcome with fear at this awful sight that they fell to the earth.

Soon after, other citizens who had not heard Nephi, came in. Finding the dead judge and the five men all there, they concluded that the latter must be the murderers, who, by some manifestation of the power of heaven, had been prevented from leaving the scene of their shameful deed. The officers therefore took the five and cast them into prison.

When the wicked learned that Nephi's words had proven true, they charged him with being an accomplice. They did not believe in revelation from God, so argued that Nephi must have had a hand in the murder or he could not have known anything about it. He was therefore taken and bound and brought before the multitude. Then they cross-examined him, abused him, and finally offered him money to confess that he had employed someone to commit the dreadful crime. They were anxious to bring reproach and trouble upon him that they might have an excuse for not believing his words nor heeding his teachings.

Nephi, to establish his innocence, sent his accusers to the house of Seantum, and instructed them what to say. He further told them how the fratricide would act; how he would acquit him (Nephi) of all complicity in the murder, assert his own innocence, until shown stains of blood on his cloak, and then, overwhelmed with terror, he would confess.

The people went and followed Nephi's instructions, and all that he had told them came to pass; for according to his words Seantum did at first deny, and according to the words he did afterwards confess; acknowledging also that Nephi knew nothing of the matter, without it had been revealed to him of God.

Some of the citizens now acknowledged that Nephi was a prophet, others declared that he was a god, whilst many remained hardened in their sins. So violent became the contention that the people gathered in excited crowds upon the streets, wrangling and disputing about the events of the past two days, and in their excitement they entirely forgot Nephi, and left him standing alone in the street.

With a sorrowful heart he wended his way homeward; but before he reached there, the voice of the Lord came to him with many words of comfort and commendation. As with others of his servants, the Lord made a covenant with him, that he would bless him forever; that whatsoever he bound on earth should be bound in heaven, and whatsoever he loosed on earth should be loosed in heaven; that he should have power over the elements to bless and to curse; to smite the earth with famine, and pestilence, and destruction.

Notwithstanding the many proofs the ungodly Nephites had that Nephi was a true prophet, they continued to reject his teachings. They persecuted him, and even went so far as to seek his life. But he was conveyed out of their midst by the power of God, and ministered among other peoples.

The general character of the Nephites continued to grow worse and worse. The Gadianton robbers grew stronger and stronger. For a few years there was increasing commotion, disunion and bloodshed. At last, wearied at beholding so much misery and contention, Nephi prayed that the Lord would not suffer these people to be destroyed by the sword, but rather let a famine desolate the land, and, peradventure, bring the people to an understanding of their awful condition, and cause them to humble themselves and repent. The Holy One heard and answered his petition, the heavens became as brass over the land, the rains ceased, the earth dried up, the crops failed, the people perished for want of food.

Two years passed (B.C. 19 and 18) and the third came, and still the refreshing rain was withheld (B.C. 17). During this year the people, humbled by their sufferings, turned towards the Lord. They endeavored to root out iniquity from their midst. They destroyed the Gadianton robber bands, and established the government on a more righteous foundation. Nephi, observing the change in their conduct and feelings, interceded with the Lord in their behalf.

His prayers were answered, the welcome rain descended on the parched soil, and a bounteous harvest once more crowned the labors of the husbandmen (B.C. 16).

The repentant people now regarded Nephi in his true light; they revered him as a great prophet, and for a few short years they listened to his teachings. While they did so they prospered. But the leaven of unrighteousness had too thoroughly permeated the national life for their faithfulness to God to be of long duration. Two, three, or perhaps half a dozen years they would maintain their integrity, and then corruption would seethe, the vile would snatch the reins of government, the good would be oppressed, and contention and war, with all their horrors, would again reign supreme. Thus it was after three years of famine. For two years there was peace, in the third there began to be much strife (B.C. 13), in the next, the Gadianton bands reappeared, and carried havoc amongst their more peaceable fellow countrymen. Going on, year by year they grew in iniquity and ripened for destruction. For many years Nephi strove to stem the tide of vice. At times partial success rewarded his unceasing efforts, and he had joy in the baptism of some honest souls. But the great bulk of the people had rejected the gospel, they had no love for its holy principles, and were unfit for its blessings.

SAMUEL THE LAMANITE

We come now to the days of Samuel the Lamanite (B.C. 6). Without any previous reference to him, he appears suddenly in the foreground of ancient American history, bearing a weighty and solemn message; a messenger of God's displeasure, he stands a Jonah to the Nephites. That message is faithfully delivered; then he disappears forever from our sight.

The condition of society in the days of Samuel was somewhat peculiar. The Nephites and Lamanites had, so far as righteousness is concerned, to a great extent changed places. The former were puffed up with worldly pride, were full of vain boastings, envyings, strifes, malice, persecutions, murders and all manner of iniquities. They cast out, they stoned, they slew the servants of God, while they encouraged, exalted and rewarded the false teachers who flattered them in their vileness and sung in their ears the siren's song of "all is well." They reveled in all the luxury that the fatness of the land brought forth; they were ostentatious in the use of gold and silver and precious things; but their hearts never turned in thankfulness to the great Giver of all these bounties. The majority of the Lamanites, on the contrary, walked circumspectly before God; they were full of faith and integrity, were zealous in the work of converting their fellows, and kept the commandments, statutes and judgments of the Lord according to the law of Moses.

Such was the condition of affairs when the Lamanite prophet Samuel appeared among the sin-stained citizens of Zarahemla, and for many days preached repentance in their midst. Their eyes were blind and their ears were deaf, sin filled their souls, and in their anger they cast him out. But the work of his mission was not yet accomplished. As he was preparing to return to his own country, a holy angel visited him and proclaimed the voice of the Lord. That voice commanded that he should turn back and prophesy to the people of Zarahemla the things that should come into his heart.

He returned to the city, but was refused admission at its gates. The iniquitous dwellers therein had no desire to have their peace disturbed by the voice of divine threatenings. But the prophet had the word of the Lord burning within him, and could not be restrained. He mounted the walls of the city, and from this conspicuous vantage ground, with outstretched hands and loud voice, he proclaimed to the wicked unwelcome tidings of their coming destruction. Many listened to his proclamation, some few were pricked in their hearts, repented of their evil deeds, and sought the prophet Nephi, that they might be baptized. Others were angry; they gathered up the stones in the roadway and hurled them at Samuel; they drew forth their bows and shot arrows at him. But to no effect; the protecting power of the Holy Spirit was around him, and he could not be harmed.

When some beheld how wonderfully the prophet was preserved, it was a testimony to them that God was with him, and they also sought Nephi, confessing their sins. But the great body of the populace grew more enraged at the want of success that attended their murderous efforts. They called upon their captains to seize and bind him. They cried out, He hath a devil, and it is by this power he is preserved; take the fellow, bind him, and away with him! Following the wild satanic cry of the multitude, the officers of the law endeavored to arrest Samuel. But he cast himself down from the wall of the city and fled out of the lands of the Nephites into his own country. There he preached and prophesied among his own people; but among the people of Nephi he was never heard of more.

The prophecies of Samuel are among the most wonderful recorded in holy writ. He especially foretold many things regarding the life and death of our Savior, and concerning the future destiny of his people, and of the Nephites.

With regard to the birth of the Redeemer he said:

Behold, I give unto you a sign; for five years more cometh, and behold, then cometh the Son of God, to redeem all those who shall believe on his name.

And behold, this will I give unto you for a sign at the time of his coming; for behold, there shall be great lights in heaven, insomuch that in the night before he cometh there shall be no darkness, insomuch that it shall appear unto man as if it was day.

Therefore there shall be one day and a night and a day, as if it were one day and there were no night; and this shall be unto you for a sign; for ye shall know of the rising of the sun, and also of its setting; therefore they shall know of a surety that there shall be two days and a night; nevertheless the night shall not be darkened; and it shall be the night before he is born.

And behold there shall a new star arise, such an one as ye never have beheld; and this also shall be a sign unto you.

And behold this is not all, there shall be many signs and wonders in heaven.

And it shall come to pass that ye shall all be amazed and wonder, insomuch that ye shall fall to the earth.

Regarding the death of the Lord Jesus he declared:

But behold, as I said unto you concerning another sign, a sign of his death, behold, in that day that he shall suffer death, the sun shall be darkened and refuse to give its light unto you; and also the moon, and the stars; and there shall be no light upon the face of this land, even from the time that he shall suffer death, for the space of three days, to the time that he shall rise again from the dead.

Yea, at the time that he shall yield up the ghost, there shall be thunderings and lightnings for the space of many hours, and the earth shall shake and tremble, and the rocks which are upon the face of this earth, which are both above the earth and beneath, which ye know at this time are solid, or the more part of it is one solid mass, shall be broken up;

Yea, they shall be rent in twain, and shall ever after be found in seams and in cracks, and in broken fragments upon the face of the whole earth; yea, above the earth and beneath.

And behold there shall be great tempests, and there shall be many mountains laid low, like unto a valley, and there shall be many places, which are now called valleys, which shall become mountains, whose height thereof is great.

And many highways shall be broken up, and many cities shall become desolate.

And many graves shall be opened, and shall yield up many of their dead; and many saints shall appear unto many.

And behold thus hath the angel spoken unto me; for he said unto me, that there should be thunderings and lightnings for the space of many hours:

And he said unto me that while the thunder and the lightning lasted, and the tempest, that these things should be, and that darkness should cover the face of the whole earth for the space of three days.

And the angel said unto me, that many shall see greater things than these, to the intent that they might believe that these signs and these wonders should come to pass, upon all the face of this land; to the intent that there should be no cause of unbelief among the children of men.

We shall see as we proceed how wonderfully all these sayings of Samuel the Lamanite were fulfilled. He closed his prophecy with these emphatic words. First regarding the Lamanites:

Therefore, saith the Lord, I will not utterly destroy them; but I will cause that in the day of my wisdom they shall return again unto me, saith the Lord.

And now behold, saith the Lord, concerning the people of the Nephites, if they will not repent and observe to do my will, I will utterly destroy them, saith the Lord, because of their unbelief, notwithstanding the many mighty works which I have done among them; and as surely as the Lord liveth shall these things be, saith the Lord.

Chronology -- Volume VII

	B.C.	N.A.
The Third Book of Nephi opens. Nephi departs out of the land, and is never again seen. Lachoneus, chief judge and governor.	1	600

	A.D.	N.A.
The promised signs of the Redeemer's birth appear, to the joy of believers. The two days and one night of constant light; a new star appears. The majority of the people join the church. The Nephites reckon their time from the Messiah's advent.	1	601
The Gadianton robbers commit many murders; the people not strong enough to overpower them.	2	602
Dissensions increase, owing to many joining the robber bands, especially among the young.	3	603
Wickedness and unbelief greatly increase.	4	604
Evil continues to gain strength to this time. Gadianton bands grow so numerous that both Nephites and Lamanites take up arms against them.	13	613
The robbers driven into their secret fastnesses in the mountains and the wilderness.	14	614
Owing to dissensions, the robbers gain many advantages.	15	615
Giddianhi, the robber chief, writes an epistle to Lachoneus, calling upon the Nephites to surrender. Gidgiddoni chosen commander of the Nephite forces. Lachoneus decides to gather all the Nephites from both continents into the lands of Zarahemla and Bountiful, and fortify against the attacks of the robbers.	16	616
The people, with all their movable substance and seven years' provisions, gather at the appointed place.	17	617
In the latter part of the year the robbers leave their hiding places and occupy the lands deserted by the people.	18	618
The robbers, under Giddianhi, attack the Nephites. The slaughter more terrible than in any previous battle among the children of Lehi; Giddianhi is slain, the robbers are defeated and pursued to the wilderness.	19	619
The robbers do not venture to again attack the Nephites. Zemnarihah made chief of the robber bands.	20	620
The robbers surround and ineffectually besiege the Nephites, who make many sorties and slay tens of thousands of them; the robbers attempt to concentrate in the north but are cut off, their armies destroyed, and thousands taken prisoners; among whom is Zemnarihah, who is afterwards hanged. The Nephites greatly rejoice in their marvelous deliverance.	21	621
All the Nephites believe the words of the prophets; righteousness prevails. They preach to their prisoners; all who make a covenant to murder no more are released, those who refuse are punished according to the law.	22	622
The Nephites all return to their own lands on both continents.	26	626

	A.D.	N.A.
The law revised according to justice and equity; great order throughout the land.	27	627
Many new cities built and old ones repaired; numerous other improvements made.	28	628
Disputings and contentions recommence; pride and other evils increase.	29	629
Lachoneus, the younger, governor. The church broken up, except among a few Lamanites. Many prophets testify and are persecuted; some are executed contrary to law. The officers committing these crimes, on being called to account, rebel and seek to establish a monarchy, with Jacob as king. The chief judge is slain, and the ancient iniquitous combination reintroduced. The Nephite Republic is broken up, and the people divided into numerous tribes. Jacob leads his band into the northernmost part of the land.	30	630
The various tribes more fully regulated. Nephi performs many miracles; among others, raises his brother Timothy from the dead. But few are converted.	31	631
Nephi continues his preaching and ministry; a few accept his message.	32	632
Many join the church.	33	633
On the fourth day of the new year the signs of Christ's crucifixion commence. An unparalleled storm rages for three hours, convulsing the land and destroying many cities. It is followed by three days' darkness. The voice of the Lord is heard proclaiming the destruction that had happened. Jesus appears to the people in the Land Bountiful. He preaches his gospel, performs many mighty works, and chooses twelve disciples. Nephi, the son of Nephi, takes the records.	34	634
All the people are converted, and the church becomes universal. The believers have all things in common.	36	636
The disciples of Jesus work many wonderful miracles.	37	637
The people again becoming numerous. Zarahemla and other cities rebuilt.	59	659
All the original twelve disciples, except the three who were to tarry, have died by this date.	100	700
The first generation in Christ have passed away. Nephi dies, and his son Amos takes charge of the records.	110	710
Amos dies. In his days a few apostatize and become Lamanites. His son Amos takes charge of the records.	194	794
All the second generation have passed away, except a few.	200	800
Pride appears in the church; its members have their goods no more in common, and sects arise.	201	801
Many churches established opposed to the true church.	210	810
The wicked increase; the disciples and saints persecuted. The Three Nephites perform many miracles, from the last date to	230	830
The people divided into Nephites and Lamanites.	231	831
The more wicked portion of the people have grown much the stronger.	244	844
The wicked build up many expensive churches to their false faiths.	250	850
The members of the true church, or Nephites, begin to grow proud and sinful. The Gadianton iniquities are again developed.	260	860

	A.D.	N.A.
Both Nephites and Lamanites have grown very wicked; none are righteous except the three disciples. The Gadianton robbers have spread over all the land.	300	900
Amos transfers the records to his brother Ammaron, and dies.	306	906
Mormon born.	311	911
Ammaron hides up the records in the hill Shim.	321	921
Mormon, the father of Mormon, takes his son to Zarahemla. War commences between the Nephites and Lamanites; a number of battles fought in which the Nephites prevail. Mormon's record opens.	322	922
The Three Nephites cease to minister among the people, because of their iniquities. Things hidden in the earth become slippery. Mormon endeavors to preach, but his mouth is shut. War recommences, and Mormon is chosen general of the Nephites.	326	926
The Nephites retreat before the Lamanites to the north countries. The Lamanites capture Angola.	327	927
The Lamanites drive the Nephites out of the land of David into the land of Joshua.	328	928
Revolution and carnage throughout all the land. The Nephite warriors gather for battle into one place.	329	929
The Lamanite king, Aaron, defeated by Mormon.	330	930
Great sorrow among the Nephites, because of their pitiable condition.	331	931
Mormon obtains the plates, as Ammaron directed.	335	935
Wars, with much slaughter, until	344	944
The Lamanites drive the Nephites to the land of Jashon, thence northward to the land of Shem. The Nephites fortify the city of Shem.	345	945
Mormon, with 30,000 Nephites, defeats 50,000 Lamanites in the land of Shem; he pursues and again defeats the enemy.	346	946
The Nephites regain the lands of their inheritance by the end of the year.	349	949
The Nephites as one party, and the Lamanites and Gadiantons as the other, make a treaty, by which the Nephites possess the country north of the Isthmus, and the Lamanites that south of it. Ten years' peace follows.	350	950
By the command of the Lord, Mormon preaches repentance, but the Nephites harden their hearts, during the ten years ending	360	960
The Lamanite king declares war; the Nephites gather at the Land Desolation.	360	960
The Lamanites march to Desolation, are defeated and return home.	361	961
The Lamanites make another invasion and are defeated. Mormon refuses to lead the Nephites any longer.	362	962
The Nephites invade South America, and are driven back. The Lamanites capture the City of Desolation.	363	963
The Lamanites besiege Teancum, are repulsed, and the Nephites recapture Desolation.	364	964
The Lamanites recommence war; they capture the cities of Desolation and Teancum, but are afterwards driven entirely out of the lands of the Nephites.	367	967

The Lamanites again commence war. A fierce battle is fought in the

THIRD NEPHI

THE BOOK OF NEPHI

THE SON OF NEPHI, WHO WAS THE SON OF HELAMAN

And Helaman was the Son of Helaman, Who was the Son of Alma, Who was the Son of Alma, being a Descendant of Nephi Who was the Son of Lehi, Who Came Out of Jerusalem in the First Year of the Reign of Zedekiah, the King of Judah.

CHAPTER 1

1. *Nephi, Son of Helaman, Departs*—2. *Signs Given of the Savior's Birth*—3. *Opposite Effects Manifest*—4. *Again the Gadianton Band.*

1. Nephi, son of Helaman, departs.

1. Now it came to pass that the ninety and first year had passed away and it was six hundred years from the time that Lehi left Jerusalem; and it was in the year that Lachoneus was the chief judge and the governor over the land.

2. And Nephi, the son of Helaman, had departed out of the land of Zarahemla, giving charge unto his son Nephi, who was his eldest son, concerning the plates of brass, and all the records which had been kept, and all those things which had been kept sacred from the departure of Lehi out of Jerusalem.

3. Then he departed out of the land, and whither he went, no

VERSES 1-3. *Nephi, the son of Helaman, departed out of the land.* The story of Lehi's descendants as it is recorded by Nephi, the grandson of Helaman who in turn was the grandson of Alma, who organized the Church of God in the Land of Nephi, and who led the faithful from there down to Zarahemla, begins at the end of the Ninety-first year of the Reign of the Judges over the People of Nephi. Sometime in this year, he transferred the Plates of Brass and other records to his own son, Nephi, gave him charge concerning them, and departed from the Land of Zarahemla. Whither he went, or what became of him, is hidden from the knowledge of mankind. That he did not return to his usual place of abode, or to any of the known places of humanity is testified to by his son some ten years afterwards.

Lachoneus, the elder, was then Chief Judge and the Governor of the Land. His reign was long and troublesome. It was one of continued warfare with the Gadianton Robbers, who, year by year, grew in numbers and audacity.

Six hundred years had now passed since Lehi and his companions left Jerusalem. The time had arrived of which Samuel, the Lamanite, and other prophets had borne testimony as to when the phenomena should appear bearing witness of the birth of the Son of God: "Yea, even six hundred years from the time that my father left Jerusalem, a prophet would the Lord God raise up among the Jews—

man knoweth; and his son Nephi did keep the records in his stead, yea, the record of this people.

2. Signs given of the Savior's birth.

4. And it came to pass that in the commencement of the ninety and second year, behold, the prophecies of the prophets began to be fulfilled more fully; for there began to be greater signs and greater miracles wrought among the people.

5. But there were some who began to say that the time was past for the words to be fulfilled, which were spoken by Samuel, the Lamanite.

6. And they began to rejoice over their brethren, saying: Behold the time is past, and the words of Samuel are not fulfilled; therefore, your joy and your faith concerning this thing hath been vain.

7. And it came to pass that they did make a great uproar throughout the land; and the people who believed began to be very sorrowful, lest by any means those things which had been spoken might not come to pass.

8. But behold, they did watch steadfastly for that day and that night and that day which should be as one day as if there were no night, that they might know that their faith had not been vain.

9. Now it came to pass that there was a day set apart by the unbelievers, that all those who believed in those traditions should be put to death except the sign should come to pass, which had been given by Samuel the prophet.

10. Now it came to pass that when Nephi, the son of Nephi, saw this wickedness of his people, his heart was exceedingly sorrowful.

11. And it came to pass that

even a Messiah, or, in other words, a Savior of the world." (I Nephi 10:4) "And behold He cometh according to the words of the angel, in six hundred years from the time my father left Jerusalem." (I Nephi 19:8) "For according to the words of the prophets, the Messiah cometh in six hundred years from the time that my father left Jerusalem; and according to the words of the prophets, and also the word of the angel of God, His Name shall be Jesus Christ, the Son of God." (II Nephi 25:19) Listen again to the words of Samuel, "And behold, he said unto them: Behold, I give unto you a sign; for five years cometh, and behold, then cometh the Son of God to redeem all those who shall believe on His Name." (Helaman 14:2. About B.C. 6)

VERSES 4-9. *The prophecies began to be fulfilled more fully.* As the day by prophets long foretold drew near, signs and miracles increased among the people. But the hardened in heart, who were ever on the watch to entrap those who believed in the prophet's words, began to circulate the idea that the time had passed and the prophecies had failed. Not content with mocking and reviling those who were anxiously looking for the promised two days and a night when there should be no darkness, they went as far as to appoint a day when all who believed in the coming of the Savior should be slain, except the sign be first given.

VERSES 10-16. *When Nephi saw this great wickedness, his heart was exceedingly*

he went out and bowed himself down upon the earth, and cried mightily to his God in behalf of his people, yea, those who were about to be destroyed because of their faith in the tradition of their fathers.

12. And it came to pass that he cried mightily unto the Lord, all the day; and behold, the voice of the Lord came unto him, saying:

13. Lift up your head and be of good cheer; for behold, the time is at hand, and on this night shall the sign be given, and on the morrow come I into the world, to show unto the world that I will fulfil all that which I have caused to be spoken by the mouth of my holy prophets.

14. Behold, I come unto my own, to fulfil all things which I have made known unto the children of men from the foundation of the world, and to do the will, both of the Father and of the Son —of the Father because of me,

and of the Son because of my flesh. And behold, the time is at hand, and this night shall the sign be given.

15. And it came to pass that the words which came unto Nephi were fulfilled, according as they had been spoken; for behold, at the going down of the sun there was no darkness; and the people began to be astonished because there was no darkness when the night came.

16. And there were many, who had not believed the words of the prophets, who fell to the earth and became as if they were dead, for they knew that the great plan of destruction which they had laid for those who believed in the words of the prophets had been frustrated; for the signal which had been given was already at hand.

17. And they began to know that the Son of God must shortly appear; yea, in fine, all the people upon the face of the whole earth

---

sorrowful. This great wickedness caused Nephi great sorrow; his only recourse was to Heaven. Before God, in mighty prayer, he bowed in behalf of his imperiled people. All the day long he continued his earnest supplications. At last the word of the Anointed One came unto him, saying: "Lift up your head and be of good cheer, for behold the time is at hand, and on this night shall the sign be given, and on the morrow come I into the world, to show unto the world that I will fulfill all that which I have caused to be spoken by the mouth of My holy prophets." As was thus declared, so was it fulfilled, for at the going down of the Sun, it was light as day and so continued until the morning when the Sun arose again in its usual course. A new star also appeared in the skies. Then the faithful rejoiced, their hearts were filled to overflowing, they knew that their Redeemer was born, and that the great Plan of Salvation had entered its most glorious phase; *God, the great Jehovah, was tabernacled in the flesh.* But the wicked quaked with awful dread: they realized the extent of their iniquity, they sensed that they were murderers at heart, for they had plotted to take the lives of the righteous, and in the terror that this overwhelming sense of their piteous condition wrought, they sank to the earth as though they were dead.

VERSES 17-26. *They began to know that the Son of God must shortly appear.*

from the west to the east, both in the land north and in the land south, were so exceedingly astonished that they fell to the earth.

18. For they knew that the prophets had testified of these things for many years, and that the sign which had been given was already at hand; and they began to fear because of their iniquity and their unbelief.

19. And it came to pass that there was no darkness in all that night, but it was as light as though it was mid-day. And it came to pass that the sun did rise in the morning again, according to its proper order; and they knew that it was the day that the Lord should be born, because of the sign which had been given.

20. And it had come to pass, yea, all things, every whit, according to the words of the prophets.

21. And it came to pass also that a new star did appear, according to the word.

22. And it came to pass that from this time forth there began to be lyings sent forth among the people, by Satan, to harden their hearts, to the intent that they might not believe in those signs and wonders which they had seen; but notwithstanding these lyings and deceivings the more part of the people did believe, and were converted unto the Lord.

23. And it came to pass that Nephi went forth among the people, and also many others, baptizing unto repentance, in the which there was a great remission of sins. And thus the people began again to have peace in the land.

24. And there were no contentions, save it were a few that began to preach, endeavoring to prove by the scriptures that it was no more expedient to observe the law of Moses. Now in this thing they did err, having not understood the scriptures.

25. But it came to pass that they soon became converted, and were convinced of the error which they were in, for it was made known unto them that the law was not yet fulfilled, and that it must be fulfilled in every whit; yea, the word came unto them that it must be fulfilled; yea, that one jot or tittle should not pass away till it should all be fulfilled; therefore in this same year were they brought to a knowledge of their error and did confess their faults.

26. And thus the ninety and second year did pass away, bringing glad tidings unto the people because of the signs which did come to pass, according to the words of the prophecy of all the holy prophets.

Many now believed who previously had scorned the divine messages that the prophets bore; but others inspired of Satan, as soon as they recovered from the fright which the appearance of the promised signs had produced, began to explain them away, and, by various lying rumors, endeavored to nullify the good that had been done in the hearts of many. Others began to teach that it was no longer expedient to

3. *Opposite Effects Manifest.*

4. *Again the Gadianton Band.*

27. And it came to pass that the ninety and third year did also pass away in peace, save it were for the Gadianton robbers, who dwelt upon the mountains, who did infest the land; for so strong were their holds and their secret places that the people could not overpower them; therefore they did commit many murders, and did do much slaughter among the people.

28. And it came to pass that in the ninety and fourth year they began to increase in great degree, because there were many dissenters of the Nephites who did flee unto them, which did cause much sorrow unto those Nephites who did remain in the land.

29. And there was also a cause of much sorrow among the Lamanites; for behold, they had many children who did grow up and began to wax strong in years, that they became for themselves, and were led away by some who were Zoramites, by their lyings and their flattering words, to join those Gadianton robbers.

30. And thus were the Lamanites afflicted also, and began to decrease as to their faith and righteousness, because of the wickedness of the rising generation.

---

observe the Law of Moses, drawing their conclusions from a false interpretation of the Scriptures. Notwithstanding these efforts of the evil one, Nephi and others went forth among the people preaching, baptizing many, and bringing a short period of peace to the land. Thus did the Ninety-second year pass away.

VERSES 27-30. *The Ninety and third year also passed away in peace save for the Gadianton Robbers.* Those of the Nephites who believed that the wonderful signs and miracles which they had seen heralded the coming of the promised Messiah, experienced during the Ninety-third year of the Judges a peace that was founded upon their righteous lives. However those who were righteous were not strong enough to overcome the vast hosts of Gadianton Robbers, who, time and time again, swarmed from their mountain retreats and carried carnage, rapine, and desolation to the homes of both Nephites and Lamanites.

In the Ninety-fourth year many Nephites dissented from the regularly constituted authority of the Commonwealth, and took refuge among the robber group, which defection caused "much sorrow unto those Nephites who did remain in the land," while at the same time it increased greatly the number of Gadiantons with whom the loyal citizens of the Republic were compelled to contend.

The rising generation of Lamanites brought sore affliction upon their fathers and mothers by their listening to some apostate Zoramites, who, "by their lyings and their flattering words," caused them to join the Robber Bands. In this manner the Lamanites, who had become even more righteous than were the Nephites, were themselves deprived of much spiritual strength "because of the wickedness of the rising generation."

NEPHI, THE DISCIPLE

Nephi, like his illustrious father, was the leading spirit of the age. Previous to the visit of the risen Redeemer to the Nephites he was their High Priest and prophet. When the Messiah came to them and chose twelve Disciples to be special ministers of His Name and glory, Nephi was the first that He called. To him, on various occasions, the Savior immediately directed His conversation and instructions.

Shortly before the birth of our Savior, Nephi received the Sacred Plates with their appendages from his father with strict instructions as to their care. From that time the elder Nephi was no more seen by mortals and his son took his place as the representative of Jehovah to the inhabitants of the western world.

When 600 years had passed since Lehi left Jerusalem, the wicked and perverse raised a great outcry that the prophecies had failed and the believers were deluded, that the delusion was a danger to the State and those who adhered to it should be slain. They even appointed a day on which to carry out their sanguinary threats should the promised signs not be first given. These were days of anxiety and dread to Nephi. For consolation he sought the Lord in long and fervent prayers. And his prayers received a full and joyous answer. The word of the Lord came to him that night the looked-for sign should be given and on the morrow Jesus would come into the world. And so it came to pass. The new star appeared in the heavens, there were two days and a night of undiminished light and all the people, both the righteous and the evildoers, recognized the sign and accepted its signification, the Lord of Life and Glory was clothed with humanity.

For about thirty years we have no direct statement of the work done by Nephi as a minister of God's word. Those thirty years were a period marked with many vicissitudes in the national and spiritual history of the Nephites. For seventeen years from the time of the birth of our Savior they gradually increased in wickedness; war and desolation afflicted them until, in their extremity, they were brought to repentance. But their repentance did not bring immediate deliverance from earthly troubles — the Gadianton Robbers held the upper hand and it was not until 21 A.D. that, by a signal victory, they freed themselves from their oppressors and invaders. Then followed a short period of peace and prosperity with its usual train of consequences — riches, pride, inequality, oppression and varied iniquities and year by year they grew worse until 29 A.D. But even then they had not descended to their lowest; the next year we read of them unjustly and unlawfully condemning to death the prophets who were sent to them. They overrode the laws, filled the country with sedition and sought to establish a monarchy in the place of the Republic. The royalists, however, did not effect their purpose but they succeeded in breaking up the government. The people then split up and divided into numerous factions, each governed by its peculiar laws and regulations and having its own chief. (31 A.D.)

At this time Nephi is again brought to our notice. He comes forth as a servant of the Most High God, administering the words of Eternal Life with such power and great authority that none could disbelieve his testimony, for angels ministered to him daily. His cry was faith in the Lord Jesus Christ, repentance and baptism for the remission of sins. Many were the mighty works he performed; he cast out devils and unclean spirits; he healed the sick and even raised the dead. But the wicked were actually angered at these manifestations of God's goodness and but few were converted. Still, Nephi continued his labors and at the end of three years he rejoiced in the re-establishment of the Church among the righteous, the organization of the Priesthood and the development of the purposes of God. For all this, the greater portion of the people continued to delight in sin; the day of their destruction had come.

Thus passed away thirty and three years. The time had now come for the fulfillment of the prophecy of Samuel, the Lamanite, when there should be darkness over the face of the land for the space of three days. On the fourth day of the first month of the thirty-fourth year a great and terrible tempest arose, the horrors of which exceeded all others since the deluge. Huge tidal waves swept the coasts, swift cyclones and irresistible hurricanes mowed down forest, wilderness, city and tower, leaving blank desolation in their train; the earth trembled to its foundations, belched forth fire, uprose in giant peaks or sank in deep abysses. The whole face of the land was changed by these indescribable commotions. Some cities were burned, some sank in the depths of the sea, some were entombed in the earth, while mountains covered the place where others had before stood. It is not our intention here to detail the horrors of the three days of mental and physical darkness that followed the hurricane and the earthquake nor to dilate upon the great and terrible mourning of the people for their kindred slain, their cities destroyed and their treasures lost. The mental horror of these black days was intensified by the fear that they had sinned away their day of grace, as they realized the tens of thousands of the dead had done. Then was heard a voice from Heaven, crying, "Wo, wo, unto this people, except they shall repent." That voice was the voice of the Redeemer and He recounted to them the destructions, the tribulations, the sorrow that had come upon them because of their abominations but added the pleasing news that they who survived had been spared because they were more righteous than those who had fallen victims to the fury of the storm. He had given His life as a ransom for the sins of the world — and many words of counsel and instruction He added to His testimony for their future guidance. When the voice ceased there was silence throughout the land for the space of many hours. Afterwards the voice of the Savior was again heard, repeating to the humbled Nephites how often he would have gathered and spared His people Israel, but they would not. Thus did the three days of terror pass away. At its close the darkness dispersed and wailing of the people stopped for their mourning was turned into praise and thankfulness unto the Lord Jesus, their Redeemer.

The horrors of the desolation past was succeeded by the most glorious age in Nephite history. The extreme of misery was followed by a fullness of joy. The crucified Redeemer Himself appeared and ministered among the people; with His own voice He explained the beauties and harmonies of Salvation's wondrous plan. The simple, heart-reaching truths of the Everlasting Gospel He repeated in the same plain and gentle terms in which He had taught His disciples at Jerusalem and even greater truths did He announce and greater works perform because of the more abundant faith of the Nephites. He also organized His Church in their midst and called twelve Disciples, who became His special representatives and the presiding authorities of His Church. These are to sit in the great Day of Judgment as the judges of the seed of Nephi and be themselves judged by the Twelve Apostles whom He had called from among the Jews.

First of these Nephite Twelve stood Nephi, who, by virtue of his seniority, his previous position, or his goodness, or, perhaps, all combined, was recognized by the Savior on various occasions as the foremost of his race. Nephi, at this time, was most probably advanced beyond the middle age of man, as he had held the records more than thirty-three years after his father's departure from this earth and as that event occurred when the elder Nephi was quite aged and Nephi was his eldest son, it is presumable that, if he were one of those who died when he was seventy-two years old, his day on the earth was not a long one after the departure of his Divine Master.

Though Nephi had himself been baptized, and had in times past baptized many yet a new dispensation being now opened Jesus commanded the Twelve whom He had chosen to baptize all the people. He afterwards gave them power and authority to confer the Holy Ghost. Nephi was the first who was baptized among all the people, he then baptized the remaining eleven of his quorum, which, having been done, they were filled with the Holy Ghost and with fire; indeed they were encircled around with fire which came down from Heaven, while holy angels ministered to them the unspeakable things of the Kingdom.

After the final departure of the Savior we are told but little of Nephi's personal life. His son, Nephi, appears to have taken charge of the records almost immediately after these events, while another son, Jonas, was a member of the quorum of the Twelve.

CHAPTER 2

1. Nephite Degeneracy—2. Both Peoples Unite for Defense Against Robbers and Murderers—3. White Lamanites.

1. Nephite Degeneracy.

1. And it came to pass that thus passed away the ninety and fifth year also, and the people began to forget those signs and wonders which they had heard, and began to be less and less astonished at a sign or a wonder from heaven, insomuch that they began to be hard in their hearts, and blind in their minds, and began to disbelieve all which they had heard and seen—

2. Imagining up some vain thing in their hearts, that it was wrought by men and by the power of the devil, to lead away and deceive the hearts of the people; and thus did Satan get possession of the hearts of the people again, insomuch that he did blind their eyes and lead them away to believe that the doctrine of Christ was a foolish and a vain thing.

3. And it came to pass that the people began to wax strong in wickedness and abominations; and they did not believe that there should be any more signs or wonders given; and Satan did go about, leading away the hearts of

---

VERSES 1-3. *The people began to forget those signs and wonders which they had heard.* Human nature was then as it is now, the slave of passion, the victim of corruption. In a few words that describes the Nephites of Samuel's time. They hated truth, and each walked in his own way. As a nation of much-favored people, they, however, were quick to forget, and slow to remember God's goodness. Heaven's greatest gift to mankind, the Savior of the world, was declared by them to be folly, and the idea of Christ was foolishness. Even when their eyes and ears, and even their hearts, told them of His reality, they sought ways to explain by a purely materialistic concept that they were deceived, and that Samuel and others of the prophets were peddlers of mischief. They imagined vain things to excuse their iniquity; and as a pretext for choosing evil asserted that the wonders they had seen both in the heavens and on the earth were "wrought by men and by the power of the devil, to lead away and deceive the hearts of the people," forgetting all the while that *Beelzebub does not scourge Beelzebub.* Of such a course there could be only one result; they become *servants of evil, and of their wickedness they were victims.* Their choice between good and evil was prescribed by iniquity, which like a growth of rank grass smothered the fair and fragrant flowers of God's promise of a Redeemer, to beautify, and purify, and sanctify the hearts of His children. It is well to remember in reading this verse, the words of King David: "O ye that love the Lord, hate evil," and also, "Light is sown for the righteous, and gladness for the upright in heart." (Psalm 97:10-11)

It is true, it ever was and ever will be, that when a people choose darkness rather than light; when they prefer error instead of truth; when they persecute the righteous because of their righteousness and applaud the wicked in their sins, that people is ripe for destruction. So it was with the Nephites of that period. We shall shortly learn how the more wicked part of them were destroyed. However,

the people, tempting them and causing them that they should do great wickedness in the land.

4. And thus did pass away the ninety and sixth year; and also the ninety and seventh year; and also the ninety and eighth year; and also the ninety and ninth year;

5. And also an hundred years had passed away since the days of Mosiah, who was king over the people of the Nephites.

6. And six hundred and nine years had passed away since Lehi left Jerusalem.

7. And nine years had passed away from the time when the sign was given, which was spoken of by the prophets, that Christ should come into the world.

8. Now the Nephites began to reckon their time from this period when the sign was given, or from the coming of Christ; therefore, nine years had passed away.

9. And Nephi, who was the father of Nephi, who had the charge of the records, did not return to the land of Zarahemla, and could nowhere be found in all the land.

10. And it came to pass that the people did still remain in wickedness, notwithstanding the much preaching and prophesying which was sent among them; and thus passed away the tenth year also; and the eleventh year also passed away in iniquity.

---

the Lord is long-suffering and slow to anger, but nevertheless the cup of their iniquity was rapidly filling, "Satan did go about, leading away the hearts of the people, tempting them and causing them that they should do great wickedness in the land."

VERSES 4-10. *The people did still remain in wickedness.* The sacred historian in these verses makes it certain that the time in which all these things happened is thoroughly understood by the reader; so that, also, he may understand the exact time of future events that will influence and give shape and form to Nephite history.

These are dates which to him were important:

One hundred years had passed away since the days of Mosiah, or the same number of years that the Nephite Republic had existed. It was also one hundred years of the Reign of the Judges over the people of Nephi.

"And six hundred and nine years had passed away since Lehi left Jerusalem."

Nine years had passed away from the time that Samuel and other prophets had foretold certain signs that would herald the birth of the Savior, or that Christ should come into the world. "Now the Nephites began to reckon their time from this period when the sign was given, or from the coming of Christ; therefore, nine years had passed away."

It was twelve years since Nephi, the son of Helaman, departed out of the Land of Zarahemla, and had not been seen since, or his whereabouts noted. (See III Nephi 1:2)

For upwards of a dozen years, the Nephites waxed stronger and stronger in wickedness, and notwithstanding that many inspired men appeared among them, *preaching and prophesying and warning the people of things to come,* each year more adroitly than in the preceding one, the Nephites sought for that which would please their fancy and satisfy their whims. Unashamed, they looked for the baser things of life; everything human ingenuity could suggest, or evil power achieve.

11. And it came to pass in the thirteenth year there began to be wars and contentions throughout all the land; for the Gadianton robbers had become so numerous, and did slay so many of the people, and did lay waste so many cities, and did spread so much death and carnage throughout the land, that it became expedient that all the people, both the Nephites and the Lamanites, should take up arms against them.

12. Therefore, all the Lamanites who had become converted unto the Lord did unite with their brethren, the Nephites, and were compelled, for the safety of their lives and their women and their children, to take up arms against those Gadianton robbers, yea, and also to maintain their rights, and the privileges of their church and of their worship, and their freedom and their liberty.

13. And it came to pass that before this thirteenth year had passed away the Nephites were threatened with utter destruction because of this war, which had become exceedingly sore.

2. *Both peoples unite for defense against robbers.*
3. *White Lamanites.*

VERSES 11-13. *The Gadianton Robbers had become so numerous.* We cannot understand this period in Nephite history. It is a mystery. It may be likened to a night of horror. Its whole nature is but a composite of crime and cruelty. In the darkness thereof we are not surprised to find the plans of the evil one enmeshed with those of his servants. In addition to its blackness, this lightless season was a prolific progenitress. Its evil offspring were those of which we may imagine the devil and his servants were the legitimate parents. He was their sire; they were his children, his issue, his fruit. Robbery, rapine, and murder, were the midwives who assisted in their birth.

The greatest evil which this night brought forth was a resurgence of the Gadianton band of robbers; a conspiring group of murderers and plunderers who were first bought together by Kishkumen and one, Gadianton, over sixty years before. (Helaman Chapters 2 and 6) The degrading influences of this organic structure appealed to many Nephites who saw in it a sure way to gain wealth without effort. Its leaders taught its carnally-minded adherents to steal, plunder, commit whoredoms and murder, at will; not stopping at any manner of wickedness.

Only thirteen years had passed since the signs of the Savior's birth had been given, yet in this year the robbers had become so numerous that armed conflict with them almost overwhelmed the whole nation. In their vile endeavors to get riches that were not theirs, they "did slay so many of the people, and did lay waste so many cities, and did spread so much death and carnage throughout the land" that it was necessary that both Nephites and Lamanites should unite in mutual defense even to "take up arms against them."

For that purpose, and for that alone, the Christian believers of both peoples threw their lots together, but in spite of each other's help, reciprocally given and received, "the Nephites were threatened with utter destruction because of this war, which had become exceedingly sore."

VERSES 14-16. *The skin of the Lamanites became white like unto the Nephites.* Previously, we have mentioned that the Nephites and the Lamanites, Christians of both peoples, united for their common welfare, to protect their families, their free-

14. And it came to pass that those Lamanites who had united with the Nephites were numbered among the Nephites;

15. And their curse was taken from them, and their skin became white like unto the Nephites;

16. And their young men and their daughters became exceedingly fair, and they were numbered among the Nephites, and were called Nephites. And thus ended the thirteenth year.

17. And it came to pass in the commencement of the fourteenth year, the war between the robbers and the people of Nephi did continue and did become exceedingly sore; nevertheless, the people of Nephi did gain some advantage of the robbers, insomuch that they did drive them back out of their lands into the mountains and into their secret places.

18. And thus ended the fourteenth year. And in the fifteenth year they did come forth against the people of Nephi; and because ' of the wickedness of the people of Nephi, and their many contentions and dissensions, the Gadianton robbers did gain many advantages over them.

19. And thus ended the fifteenth year, and thus were the people in a state of many afflictions; and the sword of destruction did hang over them, insomuch that they were about to be smitten down by it, and this because of their iniquity.

dom, and their Church, which was the Church of God. Unity in evil is conspiracy, the environment in which the Gadiantons were born; unity without permanency of purpose is merely coalition, but unity that is lasting and real must be upheld by righteousness; the inspiration of the heart, not the discipline that bound together the soul-destroying robbers. (Helaman 6:22-30) We shall presently see that this display of Christian unity heralded the beginning of that grand era of peace and prosperity that bound together all the people of the land as one who loved the Lord, who loved truth, and who loved one another.

This unity of the righteous brought them many blessings; the converted Lamanites were numbered among the Nephites, and the curse with which the Lamanites had been visited (II Nephi 5:21) was no more; it had been removed from their bodies; their dark skins "became white like unto the Nephites." The prophecy of Nephi, made over five hundred years previously, had been, as far as they were concerned, fulfilled. (II Nephi 30:6) "Their young men and their daughters became exceedingly fair, and they were numbered among the Nephites, and were called Nephites."

They became *a white and delightsome people.*

VERSES 17-19. *The sword of destruction did hang over them.* The combined strength of the righteous was not enough to overcome the vast hosts of Gadianton Robbers, who, time and time again, swarmed from their mountain retreats, and carried carnage, rapine, and desolation, to the homes of the Saints.

Year by year these marauding bands repeated their incursions. Sometimes one party conquered, sometimes the other. This condition of affairs kept the people in such a state of terror and anxiety that life, itself, became a burden to them. Still they did not repent in sincerity of heart, and their many afflictions were permitted by the Lord because of their continued iniquity. The abridger of Nephi's record here makes the comment that thus ended the fifteenth year after the birth of Christ.

CHAPTER 3

1. and 2. *Lachoneus receives demand to surrender from chief of the robbers.*

1. And now it came to pass that in the sixteenth year from the coming of Christ, Lachoneus, the governor of the land, received an epistle from the leader and the governor of this band of robbers; and these were the words which were written, saying:

2. Lachoneus, most noble and chief governor of the land, behold, I write this epistle unto you, and do give unto you exceeding great praise because of your firmness, and also the firmness of your people, in maintaining that which ye suppose to be your right and liberty; yea, ye do stand well, as if ye were supported by the hand of a god, in the defence of your liberty, and your property, and your country, or that which ye do call so.

3. And it seemeth a pity unto me, most noble Lachoneus, that ye should be so foolish and vain as to suppose that ye can stand against so many brave men who are at my command, who do now at this time stand in their arms, and do await with great anxiety for the word—Go down upon the Nephites and destroy them.

4. And I, knowing of their unconquerable spirit, having proved them in the field of battle, and knowing of their everlasting hatred towards you because of the many wrongs which ye have done unto them, therefore if they should come down against you they would visit you with utter destruction.

5. Therefore I have written this epistle, sealing it with mine own

---

VERSES 1-10. *Giddianhi's demand for Nephite surrender.* With words tending toward hostile action, yet couched in fulsome praise which he hoped would seduce the Chief Judge and subject that Nephite official to his will, Giddianhi, the leader of the Gadianton Robbers, wrote an epistle to Lachoneus, who, besides being Chief Judge was also the supreme Governor of all Nephite lands, demanding the surrender of his people.

With threatenings of destruction and other baleful penalties if surrender was not concluded, the robber chieftain hoped to force the relinquishment of Nephite power into his own hands at an early date. The *morrow month* Giddianhi put as the limit of any delay in yielding to his demand. He wanted to frighten Lachoneus in giving up to evil without a struggle. "It is so foolish and vain," he argued, "as to stand against so many brave men who are at my command, who do now at this time stand in their arms, and do wait with great anxiety for the word — Go down upon the Nephites and destroy them." Many other afflictions he promised to impose upon the peace-loving Nephites, but none of them were sore enough to estrange

hand, feeling for your welfare, because of your firmness in that which ye believe to be right, and your noble spirit in the field of battle.

6. Therefore I write unto you, desiring that ye would yield up unto this my people, your cities, your lands, and your possessions, rather than that they should visit you with the sword and that destruction should come upon you.

7. Or in other words, yield yourselves up unto us, and unite with us and become acquainted with our secret works, and become our brethren that ye may be like unto us—not our slaves, but our brethren and partners of all our substance.

8. And behold, I swear unto you, if ye will do this, with an oath, ye shall not be destroyed; but if ye will not do this, I swear unto you with an oath, that on the morrow month I will command that my armies shall come down against you, and they shall not stay their hand and shall spare not, but shall slay you, and shall let fall the sword upon you even until ye shall become extinct.

9. And behold, I am Giddianhi; and I am the governor of this the secret society of Gadianton; which society and the works thereof I know to be good; and they are of ancient date and they have been handed down unto us.

10. And I write this epistle unto you, Lachoneus, and I hope that ye will deliver up your lands and your possessions, without the shedding of blood, that this my people may recover their rights and government, who have dissented away from you because of your wickedness in retaining from them their rights of government, and except ye do this, I will avenge their wrongs. I am Giddianhi.

3. *Lachoneus ignores demand and prepares for defence.*

11. And now it came to pass when Lachoneus received this epistle he was exceedingly astonished, because of the boldness of

the Nephites from the God in Whom they trusted. It is well to remember that throughout the ages, "None that put their trust in God were overcome." Lachoneus had learned that lesson; he thought of the words of the Psalmist which were engraved upon the Brass Plates of Laban: "Ye that love the Lord, trust in the Lord." "Trust in Him at all times, ye people, pour out your heart before Him." And he knew that the freedom offered his people by Giddianhi was not true liberty; that the reward of iniquity is serfdom. His feelings then were closely like those expressed in a prayer offered by the Jews of our day: "May our lives prove the strength of our own belief in the truths we proclaim. May our bearing toward our neighbors, our faithfulness in every sphere of duty, our compassion for the suffering, and our patience under trial, show that He Whose law we obey, is indeed the God of all men, that to serve Him is *perfect freedom and to worship Him the soul's purest happiness.*" And as a final showing of devotion, he resolved to follow the Psalmist's advice: "Commit thy way unto the Lord," "He will not forsake you, nor leave you in your grief."

Giddianhi demanding the posses- sion of the land of the Nephites, and also of threatening the people and avenging the wrongs of those that had received no wrong, save it were they had wronged them- selves by dissenting away unto those wicked and abominable robbers.

12. Now behold, this Lacho- neus, the governor, was a just man, and could not be frightened by the demands and the threaten- ings of a robber; therefore he did not hearken to the epistle of Gid- dianhi, the governor of the rob- bers, but he did cause that his people should cry unto the Lord for strength against the time that the robbers should come down against them.

13. Yea, he sent a proclama- tion among all the people, that they should gather together their women, and their children, their flocks and their herds, and all their substance, save it were their land, unto one place.

14. And he caused that fortifi- cations should be built round about them, and the strength thereof should be exceeding great. And he caused that armies, both of the Nephites and of the La- manites, or of all them who were numbered among the Nephites, should be placed as guards round about to watch them, and to guard them from the robbers day and night.

15. Yea, he said unto them: As the Lord liveth, except ye repent of all your iniquities, and cry unto the Lord, ye will in nowise be delivered out of the hands of those Gadianton robbers.

16. And so great and marvelous were the words and prophecies of

VERSES 11-26. *Lachoneus was a just man, and was unafraid.* So great was the misery entailed by the repeated incursions of the robbers, that the Chief Judge, Lachoneus, at last determined to gather all the people into one place, and by a policy of masterly inactivity wear out or starve out the invaders. We can scarcely understand how terrible must have been the misery endured by the Nephites at this time, to have caused the conception and execution of such a measure. Can we picture to ourselves the scenes that must have occurred as the people, near and far, converged to the gathering places? Zarahemla and Bountiful, were the gathering places. They came with their flocks and herds, their grain and provisions, leaving nothing behind that would help to sustain the robber bands while they continued their unhallowed war.

Now when the people had all gathered as Lachoneus had directed them, he caused that they should fortify the land, making it impregnable to their enemies, and at the same time he called upon them to "repent of all your iniquities and cry unto the Lord." Unless you do this in full measure, he commented, "ye will in nowise be delivered out of the hands of those Gadianton Robbers." The people believed his warnings insomuch that they did cast aside their evil ways, "and they did exert themselves in their might to do according to the words of Lachoneus."

As a further defense, and as a greater means to protect their women and children and their store of grain and other commodities, including their horses, cattle and flocks of domestic animals, Lachoneus appointed captains with full military authority to command the new army he had formed of all the able-bodied men, both Nephite and Lamanite, to guard them from the robbers both day and night.

Lachoneus that they did cause
fear to come upon all the people;
and they did exert themselves in
their might to do according to the
words of Lachoneus.

17. And it came to pass that
Lachoneus did appoint chief captains over all the armies of the
Nephites, to command them at
the time that the robbers should
come down out of the wilderness
against them.

18. Now the chiefest among all
the captains and the great commander of the armies of the Nephites was appointed, and his
name was Gidgiddoni.

19. Now it was the custom
among all the Nephites to appoint for their chief captains,
(save it were in their times of

wickedness) some one that had
the spirit of revelation and also
prophecy; therefore, this Gidgiddoni was a great prophet among
them, as also was the chief judge.

20. Now the people said unto
Gidgiddoni: Pray unto the Lord,
and let us go up upon the mountains and into the wilderness, that
we may fall upon the robbers and
destroy them in their own lands.

21. But Gidgiddoni saith unto
them: The Lord forbid; for if we
should go up against them the
Lord would deliver us into their
hands; therefore we will prepare
ourselves in the center of our
lands, and we will gather all our
armies together, and we will not
go against them, but we will wait
'till they shall come against us;

Among them was one Gidgiddoni, who was a stalwart in not only obeying the
word of God, but by example he taught righteousness. It was the custom, Mormon
the abridger of Nephi's record of these events, informs us, for, except in times of
wickedness, the Nephites to appoint such a man as Commander-in-Chief of their
armies.

The people were quick to see in Gidgiddoni a proper man to command, and
knowing this, implored him to pray unto the Lord for success in the event they
should go up in the mountains and into the wilderness, "that we may fall upon
the robbers and destroy them in their own lands."

"But Gidgiddoni saith unto them: The Lord forbid; for if we should go up
against them the Lord would deliver us into their hands; therefore we will prepare
ourselves in the center of our lands, and we will gather all our armies together, and
we will not go against them, but we will wait till they shall come against us;
therefore as the Lord liveth, if we do this He will deliver them into our hands."

At the end of almost one more year, Lachoneus' proclamation had reached the
most distant parts of the Nephite domain. The people obeyed his word, and with
their entire substance migrated to the place previously chosen for gathering. The
Nephites came by the thousands and tens of thousands. In their wake they left
nothing the robbers might subsist upon.

As we have already noted, the land appointed as a gathering place was the
Land of Zarahemla and the Land Bountiful which lay south of the Land Desolation.
Into this inviting land, Lachoneus caused the people to congregate because a curse
had been placed upon the land northward, which was the Land Desolation. A
great many thousands of Nephites gathered there.

The Sacred Record says that "they did fortify themselves against their enemies;
and they did dwell in one land, and in one body, and they did fear the words of

therefore as the Lord liveth, if we do this he will deliver them into our hands.

22. And it came to pass in the seventeenth year, in the latter end of the year, the proclamation of Lachoneus had gone forth throughout all the face of the land, and they had taken their horses, and their chariots, and their cattle, and all their flocks, and their herds, and their grain, and all their substance, and did march forth by thousands and by tens of thousands, until they had all gone forth to the place which had been appointed that they should gather themselves together, to defend themselves against their enemies.

Lachoneus, insomuch that they did repent of all their sins; and they did put up their prayers unto the Lord their God, that He would deliver them in the time that their enemies should come down against them to battle."

Under Gidgiddoni's instructions his soldiers made themselves strong armor and shields to protect their bodies, as well as all kinds of weapons, so that they might be fully prepared for the day of battle. Lachoneus, in the meantime, continued to preach to them in great power, so much so, that they feared his denunciations of their wickedness. They therefore forsook all their sins and turned to the Lord in great humility and devotion.

GIDDIANHI

A Gadianton Robber chief and general, who lived contemporaneously with the Savior. He was a leader of great boldness and ability and in his days the robbers gained many advantages over the Nephites, so much so, that the existence of the Nephite race was imperiled. In 16 A.D., Giddianhi had the effrontery to write to Lachoneus, the Chief Governor of the Nephites, threatening to utterly destroy the people if they did not surrender to the robbers, accept their secret oaths and become like them in all things. This epistle, which gives an interesting insight into the condition of the times, is found in III Nephi, chapter 3. Lachoneus did not hearken to the epistle of Giddianhi but perceiving the desperate straits in which his people were placed, issued a proclamation directing them to leave their various homes throughout the two continents and all gather in one vast host in a place selected in the lands of Zarahemla and Bountiful, bringing with them everything that would help to sustain the besieging forces of the robbers. The people obeyed and in the trust of the Lord awaited the coming of the foe. In the latter end of 18 A.D. the armies of the robbers were prepared for the war and they began to sally forth from the wilderness and the mountains and from their other strongholds and to occupy and revel in the deserted homes and lands of the Nephites. But difficulties soon stared them in the face, the greatest of which was the want of food. As the Nephites had removed everything edible the robbers' only source of supply was the game in the wilderness, which soon proved insufficient. Thus pressed, in the year 19 A.D., Giddianhi gave command to his armies to attack the Nephites. It was in the sixth month of the year (September, we presume) that this command was carried out. Terrible, we are told, was the appearance of the robber hosts. They wore a lamb skin, dyed in blood, about their loins; their heads were shaven but covered with armor — head-plates, as they are called. When the Nephites perceived them coming they bowed before the Lord in prayer. The robbers, seeing their action counted it as a sign of fear and set up a horrible shout and rushed upon them. The slaughter was terrible; never had there been so much blood shed in a single fight since the day that Lehi's children first inhabited the land. At last the Nephites

23. And the land which was appointed was the land of Zarahemla and the land Bountiful, yea, to the line which was between the land Bountiful and the land Desolation.

24. And there were a great many thousand people who were called Nephites, who did gather themselves together in this land. Now Lachoneus did cause that they should gather themselves

were victorious and pursued their foes to the borders of the wilderness, giving no quarter. Giddianhi himself fought with great courage but being weary through his exertions, was overtaken in the retreat and slain. Zemnarihah succeeded him as commander of the robbers.

LACHONEUS, THE ELDER

One of the greatest prophets and Judges of the Nephites. We are not informed when he was elected to the Judgment Seat but we are told that he occupied it at the time of the Redeemer's birth in Bethlehem. His reign was a long and troublesome one; it was one of continued warfare with the Gadianton bands, who, year by year, grew in numbers and increased in audacity. The forces of both Nephites and Lamanites were unable to cope with them and their leader, Giddianhi, had the effrontery to write an epistle to Lachoneus (16 A.D.) asserting the powers of the robbers, their undoubted ability to conquer all opposed to them and suggesting that the people whom Lachoneus judged should surrender and affiliate with them and become like them. This arrogant proposition was indignantly rejected.

So great was the misery entailed by the invasions of the robbers that Lachoneus at last determined to gather all the people into one place and by a policy of masterly inactivity wear out or starve out the invaders. We can scarcely understand how terrible must have been the misery endured by the nation at this time to cause the conception and execution of such a measure. Can we picture to ourselves the scenes that must have occurred as the people converged into one gathering place? From the regions of the southern Andes the migrating hosts flowed together to Zarahemla and Bountiful, the lands selected as the temporary gathering place. They came with their flocks and herds, their grain and provisions, leaving nothing that would help to sustain the robber bands while they continued to wage their unhallowed war. (17 A.D.)

When the people reached the gathering place they fortified it so strongly that it became impregnable to their enemies. Under the instructions of Gidgiddoni, the Nephite Commander-in-Chief, they also made themselves strong armor and shields, as well as all kinds of weapons so that they might be fully prepared for the day of battle. Lachoneus, in the meantime, preached to them in great power, so much so that they feared his denunciations, forsook all their sins and turned to the Lord in great humility and devotion. The result was that when the robbers came against them the attacking force was driven back with great slaughter.

Game soon became so scarce in the wilderness that the Gadiantons began to suffer for food while besieging the Nephite stronghold. In addition to this the Nephites made frequent attacks upon them. Seeing his armies wasting away through famine and the sword, Zemnarihah, their commander, gave up all hope of success, withdrew from the siege and formed the design of marching his followers to the most distant parts of the land northward.

To permit the Gadianton Robbers to escape would have increased the difficulties under which the Nephites had so long suffered. Gidgiddoni, having learned of their purpose and knowing their weakness for want of food and because of the great

together in the land southward, because of the great curse which was upon the land northward.

25. And they did fortify themselves against their enemies; and they did dwell in one land, and in one body, and they did fear the words which had been spoken by Lachoneus, insomuch that they did repent of all their sins; and they did put up their prayers unto the Lord their God, that he would deliver them in the time that their enemies should come down against them to battle.

26. And they were exceedingly

slaughter made among them through the successful attacks of his own troops, sent his armies to cut off their retreat. During the night they got beyond the robbers who when they began their march on the morrow, found themselves between the armies of the Nephites. Many thousands surrendered and the remainder were slain. Zemnarihah was taken and hanged to the top of a tree; which, when he was dead the Nephites cut down. They then rejoiced and praised God for his mercies and blessings in delivering them; but it was not until five years later (26 A.D.) that the Nephites returned to and possessed their old homes.

The next year (27 A.D.) the laws were revised according to justice and equity. They had, doubtless, been greatly tampered with during the times that the Gadianton Robbers held control of the administration and elected the officers. Good order now prevailed throughout the whole land. Soon new cities were founded and built and many improvements made. Yet for all this the peace was short lived. Iniquity and dissension soon began to again raise their hideous heads and the prophets and servants of God were persecuted and illegally condemned to death.

We are not informed when Lachoneus died but in 30 A.D. another Lachoneus, probably his son, filled the judgment seat.

GIDGIDDONI

A Prophet-General of the Nephites, of the time of Christ; he was Commander-in-Chief of the armies of the commonwealth, in the days when Lachoneus, the elder, was Chief Judge and Governor and appears to a certain extent to have shared with that illustrious man the powers of the government. Besides being one of the ablest military commanders that ever led the Nephites to victory, he was also a great prophet and his inspired teachings, wise counsels and timely reproofs were as valuable in preserving that people from destruction as was his skill, strategy, resolution and courage as a general. Gidgiddoni was chosen commander of the Nephite forces the same year that Lachoneus decided, because of the imperiled condition of the Nephites from the ever-recurring attacks of the robbers, to gather all "unto one place." (16 A.D.) In this gigantic, almost unparalleled labor, Lachoneus was zealously supported by Gidgiddoni, under whose direction the assembled hosts fortified their land of refuge. It was not until the next year that all the people had assembled together, for it proved a slow and tedious work to bring thousands of people, many for thousands of miles, with all their movable substance and with a supply of seven years' provisions. In the latter part of the following year (18 A.D.) the robbers sallied out of their hiding places in the deserts and mountains and occupied the cities and lands temporarily deserted by the citizens. But they found no means of subsistence there and game soon grew scarce in the wilderness. Active warfare was their only resort, so Giddianhi, their leader, determined, if possible, to force his way into the country held by the Nephites. A desperate battle followed, Gidgiddoni acting on the defensive; the slaughter was more terrible than in any previous battle between the descendants of Lehi. Ultimately Giddianhi was slain,

sorrowful because of their enemy. And Gidgiddoni did cause that they should make weapons of war of every kind, and they should be strong with armor, and with shields, and with bucklers, after the manner of his instruction.

---

the robbers repulsed and pursued to the borders of the wilderness (19 A.D.). The robbers made no further attack the next year but having chosen one Zemnarihah as their chief, in 21 A.D., he so disposed his band as to surround the Nephites. His attempt was ineffectual. The region occupied by the Nephites was far too extended to admit of a siege being successful. The robbers also were short of food. Gidgiddoni perceived that this was his opportunity; time and again he made successful sorties, slaying tens of thousands of the enemy and harrassing by continual movements those who remained. At last the robbers determined to flee to the north and there concentrate in one region. Gidgiddoni, learning of their intentions and knowing their feeble bodily condition through lack of food, determined to intercept them. This he successfully accomplished, and thousands of the marauders were slain. Among the prisoners was Zemnarihah, who was afterwards hanged. The people continued in their gathered condition in Zarahemla and Bountiful until 26 A.D. Then, taking with them the provisions they had not consumed and their gold, silver and precious things, they returned to their old homes. A short period of prosperity followed, the great roads were repaired, old cities were rebuilt and new ones founded and many other improvements made for the benefit of the people, in all of which Gidgiddoni and Lachoneus were the leaders. His connection with these labors (28 A.D.) is the last reference made to Gidgiddoni in the Book of Mormon. The soldiers of Gidgiddoni succeeded in taking as prisoners all the robbers that were not killed. The word of God was preached to them and those who repented of their sins and covenanted to cease their evil practice were set at liberty. The remainder were condemned for their crimes and punished according to law. This entirely broke up these bands of murderers and robbers and peace and righteousness again prevailed.

CHAPTER 4

1. *The Robbers beaten and their leader slain.*

1. And it came to pass that in the latter end of the eighteenth year those armies of robbers had prepared for battle, and began to come down and to sally forth from the hills, and out of the mountains, and the wilderness, and their strongholds, and their secret places, and began to take possession of the lands, both which were in the land south and which were in the land north, and began to take possession of all the lands which had been deserted by the Nephites, and the cities which had been left desolate.

2. But behold, there were no wild beasts nor game in those lands which had been deserted by the Nephites, and there was no game for the robbers save it were in the wilderness.

3. And the robbers could not exist save it were in the wilderness, for the want of food; for the Nephites had left their lands desolate, and had gathered their flocks and their herds and all their substance, and they were in one body.

4. Therefore, there was no chance for the robbers to plunder and to obtain food, save it were to come up in open battle against the Nephites; and the Nephites being in one body, and having so great a number, and having reserved for themselves provisions, and horses and cattle, and flocks of every kind, that they might subsist for the space of seven years, in the which time they did hope to destroy the robbers from off the face of the land; and thus the eighteenth year did pass away.

5. And it came to pass that in the nineteenth year Giddianhi found that it was expedient that

---

VERSES 1-14. *There was no chance for the robbers to obtain food.* A little over a year had elapsed since the events recorded in the preceding chapter took place. Almost nineteen years had also passed away since the signs spoken of by Samuel, the Lamanite, concerning Christ's birth, appeared to the Nephites, both worthy and unworthy; they coming as a witness to the inhabitants of the western world that the Savior of mankind had taken up an abode among mortals. Nevertheless, the Gadiantons gave no heed to the words of the prophets, and fearing not that something or other would disrupt their well-laid plans, spent that time preparing for future invasions of Nephite possessions. When all was in readiness, the robbers, confident of success because of their overwhelming numbers, burst forth from their hiding places; they swarmed from their mountain retreats, and various strongholds, and took control of the deserted lands and the desolate villages and cities that had been temporarily abandoned by the Nephites.

However, the Gadianton Robbers neglected to provide for themselves one most important thing—food. In times past they relied upon plundering the possessions

he should go up to battle against the Nephites, for there was no way that they could subsist save it were to plunder and rob and murder.

6. And they durst not spread themselves upon the face of the land insomuch that they could raise grain, lest the Nephites should come upon them and slay them; therefore Giddianhi gave commandments unto his armies that in this year they should go up to battle against the Nephites.

7. And it came to pass that they did come up to battle; and it was in the sixth month; and behold, great and terrible was the day that they did come up to battle; and they were girded about after the manner of robbers; and they had a lamb-skin about their loins, and they were dyed in blood, and their heads were shorn, and they had headplates upon them; and great and terrible was the appearance of the armies of Giddianhi, because of their armor, and because of their being dyed in blood.

8. And it came to pass that the armies of the Nephites, when they saw the appearance of the army of Giddianhi, had all fallen to the earth, and did lift their cries to the Lord their God, that he would spare them and deliver them out of the hands of their enemies.

9. And it came to pass that when the armies of Giddianhi

of the Nephite farmers and stock raisers, who among the Nephites were in numbers, predominant. As a people, the Nephites were growers of barley and other grains for the use of man and beast; of the latter they had many. A raid upon the Nephite's fields and livestock often produced great stores of food for the invading hosts of robbers. Previously having given no thought to and totally unmindful of this great oversight on their part, they soon discovered that there were no cattle nor beasts of any kind that they could add to their quickly diminishing supply of food. Mormon says there "were no wild beasts nor game in those lands which had been deserted by the Nephites," and that only in the uninhabited parts of the wilderness was food to be obtained. Now only in these regions of wilderness could the robbers find sufficient food to sustain life, let alone not in any abundance, but on the other hand the Nephites had gathered together all their beasts of burden and those used for food and for raiment and had driven them to their place of refuge. "Therefore, there was no chance for the robbers to plunder and to obtain food." The Nephites, not to be found wanting for food and other necessary things of life had provided provisions to last them seven years, "in the which they did hope to destroy the robbers from off the face of the land."

It was only a short time until game became scarce in the wilderness, and the robbers began to suffer from hunger and the evils of starvation. Weakness from want of food overcame many of the robbers and thus they were unable to fight the battles which only strong men can endure.

The robbers were faced with dilemma after dilemma. In their dire need for food some thought to grow their own crops. This proposal was quickly abandoned for in doing so it would spread them out too thin for defense purposes, and an attack from Nephite sources would surely mean to them, disaster.

Thus pressed for want of food and a growing discontent within the ranks of his followers, Giddianhi, sensing that open warfare had become the robber's only resort, gave command to his armies to attack the Nephites. It was in the sixth month

saw this they began to shout with a loud voice, because of their joy, for they had supposed that the Nephites had fallen with fear because of the terror of their armies.

10. But in this thing they were disappointed, for the Nephites did not fear them; but they did fear their God and did supplicate him for protection; therefore, when the armies of Giddianhi did rush upon them they were prepared to meet them; yea, in the strength of the Lord they did receive them.

11. And the battle commenced in this the sixth month; and great and terrible was the battle thereof, yea, great and terrible was the slaughter thereof, insomuch that there never was known so great a slaughter among all the people of Lehi since he left Jerusalem.

12. And notwithstanding the threatenings and the oaths which Giddianhi had made, behold, the Nephites did beat them, insomuch that they did fall back from before them.

13. And it came to pass that Gidgiddoni commanded that his armies should pursue them as far as the borders of the wilderness, and that they should not spare any that should fall into their hands by the way; and thus they did pursue them and did slay them, to the borders of the wilderness, even until they had fulfilled the commandment of Gidgiddoni.

14. And it came to pass that Giddianhi, who had stood and fought with boldness, was pursued as he fled; and being weary because of his much fighting he was overtaken and slain. And thus was the end of Giddianhi the robber.

2. Giddianhi's successor, Zemnarihah, hanged.

15. And it came to pass that the armies of the Nephites did return again to their place of security. And it came to pass that this nineteenth year did pass away, and the robbers did not come again to battle; neither did they come again in the twentieth year.

16. And in the twenty and first

---

of their year (September, we presume) that this command was carried out. Terrible, we are told, was the appearance of the robber hosts. They wore a lamb-skin dyed in blood about their loins; their heads were shaven, but were covered with armor — headplates as they were called. When the Nephites perceived them coming they bowed to the earth in prayer unto the Lord. The robbers, seeing their actions in doing this, counted it as a sign of fear and set up a horrible shout and rushed upon them. A desperate battle followed; the Nephite armies were commanded by Gidgiddoni who acted on the defensive. The slaughter was more terrific than in any battle between the descendants of Lehi. Ultimately Giddianhi was slain, the robbers repulsed, and driven back into the wilderness.

VERSES 15-21. *The robbers came up on all sides of the Nephites to lay siege.* The robbers made no further attacks upon the Nephites during the next year, but they chose a ruthless leader from their ranks named Zemnarihah to replace their

year they did not come up to battle, but they came up on all sides to lay siege round about the people of Nephi; for they did suppose that if they should cut off the people of Nephi from their lands, and should hem them in on every side, and if they should cut them off from all their outward privileges, that they could cause them to yield themselves up according to their wishes.

17. Now they had appointed unto themselves another leader, whose name was Zemnarihah; therefore it was Zemnarihah that did cause that this siege should take place.

18. But behold, this was an advantage to the Nephites; for it was impossible for the robbers to lay siege sufficiently long to have any effect upon the Nephites, because of their much provision which they had laid up in store.

19. Because of the scantiness of provisions among the robbers —for behold, they had nothing save it were meat for their subsistence, which meat they did obtain in the wilderness;

20. And it came to pass that the wild game became scarce in the wilderness—insomuch that the robbers were about to perish with hunger.

21. And the Nephites were continually marching out by day and by night, and falling upon their armies, and cutting them off by thousands and by tens of thousands.

22. And thus it became the desire of the people of Zemnarihah to withdraw from their design, because of the great destruction which came upon them by night and by day.

23. And it came to pass that Zemnarihah did give command unto his people that they should withdraw themselves from the siege, and march into the furthermost parts of the land northward.

---

slain chief, Giddianhi (21 A.D.); he immediately ordered his bands to surround the Nephites, and to lay siege of them in an attempt to starve them into submission. To all purposes, this was ineffectual. The region occupied by the Nephites was too extended to admit of a siege being successful. The robbers were increasingly short of food while awaiting a possible surrender of the Nephite stronghold. Mormon, in making his abridgment of the record of these times, comments that "this was an advantage to the Nephites; for it was impossible for the robbers to lay siege sufficiently long to have any effect upon the Nephites, bcause of their much provision which they had laid up in store."

Gidgiddoni perceived that this was his opportunity; time and time again, he made successful sorties, slaying tens of thousands of the enemy, and harrassing, by continual movements, those who remained.

VERSES 22-23. *It became the desire of the people of Zemnarihah to withdraw from their design.* Because of the great losses his army had sustained in support of the siege he ordered, and also their increasing want of food to support their needs, Zemnarihah, seeing the futility of any further attempts to encroach upon the Nephite stronghold, finally and in desperation, gave into the wishes of his followers, and commanded them to flee to the north and there concentrate in one region far away from their present disastrous undertaking.

3. Gidgiddoni's military prowess.

24. And now, Gidgiddoni being aware of their design, and knowing of their weakness because of the want of food, and the great slaughter which had been made among them, therefore he did send out his armies in the nighttime, and did cut off the way of their retreat, and did place his armies in the way of their retreat.

25. And this did they do in the night-time, and got on their march beyond the robbers, so that on the morrow, when the robbers began their march, they were met by the armies of the Nephites both in their front and in their rear.

26. And the robbers who were on the south were also cut off in their places of retreat. And all these things were done by command of Gidgiddoni.

27. And there were many thousands who did yield themselves up prisoners unto the Nephites, and the remainder of them were slain.

28. And their leader, Zemnarihah, was taken and hanged upon a tree, yea, even upon the top thereof until he was dead. And when they had hanged him until he was dead they did fell the tree to the earth, and did cry with a loud voice, saying:

29. May the Lord preserve his people in righteousness and in holiness of heart, that they may cause to be felled to the earth all who shall seek to slay them because of power and secret combinations, even as this man hath been felled to the earth.

30. And they did rejoice and cry again with one voice, saying:

VERSES 24-28. *Gidgiddoni was aware of their design.* Gidgiddoni, being made aware of the robbers' intentions to flee the scene of their calamitous defeat, and knowing of their feeble bodily condition because of the lack of food, determined to intercept them. With masterly tact, he dispatched his troops in the darkness of night "and did cut off the way of their retreat, and did place his armies in the way of their retreat." In this way, Gidgiddoni, having headed the escaping robbers, had a substantial number of his soldiers both in the front and rear of the runaway Gadiantons. Nephite soldiers before and behind the frustrated robbers in their attempt to escape the Nephites' wrath, caught the robbers in a trap. Gidgiddoni's strategy had triumphed. Thousands of the marauders were slain; others in great numbers surrendered. Those remaining were taken prisoner. Among them was Zemnarihah, who "was taken and hanged upon a tree, yea, even the top thereof until he was dead." Afterward, when he was hanged until he was dead, the Nephites, as was their custom when the death penalty was exacted, cut down the tree upon which the hanging took place.

VERSES 29-33. *May the Lord preserve His people in righteousness.* The Nephites, after their victory over the robbers was thus assured, greatly rejoiced and praised God for His mercies and blessings in delivering them from their enemies. The Sacred Record says: "And it came to pass that they did break forth, all as one, in singing, and praising their God for the great thing which He had done for them, in preserving them from falling into the hands of their enemies . . . and they knew it was because of their repentance and their humility that they had been delivered from an everlasting destruction."

May the God of Abraham, and the God of Isaac, and the God of Jacob, protect this people in righteousness, so long as they shall call on the name of their God for protection.

31. And it came to pass that they did break forth, all as one, in singing, and praising their God for the great thing which he had done for them, in preserving them from falling into the hands of their enemies.

32. Yea, they did cry: Hosanna to the Most High God. And they did cry: Blessed be the name of the Lord God Almighty, the Most High God.

33. And their hearts were swollen with joy, unto the gushing out of many tears, because of the great goodness of God in delivering them out of the hands of their enemies; and they knew it was because of their repentance and their humility that they had been delivered from an everlasting destruction.

ZEMNARIHAH

A chief captain of the armies of the Gadianton Robbers who, in 21 A.D. came up on all sides in great force and laid siege to the people of Nephi. This system of warfare was, however, unsuccessful as the Nephites, who were gathered with their flocks, herds, provisions, etc., into one land, had laid up large stores of provisions while the robbers had to subsist upon the game they could kill in the wilderness. The Nephites, therefore, adopted a policy of constantly harrassing the robbers, making sorties by day and by night in unexpected places and inflicting great loss upon the forces of Zemnarihah. The results of this policy grew so disastrous that the robbers ultimately changed their tactics and made an effort to reach the land northward but being enfeebled by want of food they were not able to act with sufficient rapidity. The Nephite general, Gidgiddoni, being apprised of their intention, headed them off on the north and cut off their retreat on the south. Finding themselves hemmed in the robbers capitulated and those who did not do so were slain. Among the prisoners was Zemnarihah, whom the Nephites hung on the top of a tree until he was dead, after which the tree was felled to the earth. The robbers who had been captured were cast into prison and by and by the word of God was preached to them. Those who repented and covenanted to murder and rob no more were liberated while those who remained obdurate were punished according to their crimes.

CHAPTER 5

1. *Nephites Repent and Seek to End Works of Wickedness—2. Mormon's Account of Himself and of the Plates Kept by Him—3. Another Allusion to the Gathering of Israel.*

1. Nephites repent and seek to end works of wickedness.

1. And now behold, there was not a living soul among all the people of the Nephites who did doubt in the least the words of all the holy prophets who had spoken; for they knew that it must needs be that they must be fulfilled.

2. And they knew that it must be expedient that Christ had come, because of the many signs which had been given, according to the words of the prophets; and because of the things which had come to pass already they knew that it must needs be that all

---

VERSES 1-3. *The Nephites believed all the words of the holy prophets.* The rejoicing among the Nephites as recorded in Chapter 4, was, indeed, sincere. Together, they magnified the Lord and exalted His Holy Name. Their joy and gladness was not occasioned by a showing of material strength, in and of themselves, but they rejoiced in the Lord, they joyed in the God of their salvation because He, seeing their repentance and their humility, had, in His mercy and His righteousness, delivered them from "an everlasting destruction." Their thoughts, undoubtedly, were like those of the Psalmist, only King David spoke for the individual, they for the multitude: Create in us clean hearts, O God, and renew in us steadfast spirits. Cast us not away from Thy presence, and take not Thy Holy Spirit from us. Restore unto us the joy of Thy salvation, and hereafter let willing hearts uphold us. (*See,* Psalm 51:11-12)

The abridger of the Larger Plates of Nephi, Mormon, had many other records from which to draw his studied comments, because the Nephites kept many rather complete accounts of the happenings among their people. We refer particularly to Mormon's own words that are recorded in Helaman 3:13-16: "And now there are many records kept of the proceedings of this people, by many of this people, which are particular and very large, concerning them. But behold, a hundredth part of the proceedings of this people, yea, the account of the Lamanites and of the Nephites, and their wars, and contentions, and dissensions, and their preaching, and their prophecies, and their shipping and their building of ships, and their building of temples, and of synagogues and their sanctuaries, and their righteousness, and their wickedness, and their murders, and their robbings, and their plunderings, and all manner of abominations and whoredoms, cannot be contained in this work. But behold, there are many books and many records of every kind, and they have been kept chiefly by the Nephites. And they have been handed down from one generation to another by the Nephites. . . ." (*See,* verses 8-9)

Among the many other things of which records had been kept, Mormon notes were the *preaching and the prophecies* of the Nephites. A knowledge of things to come was had by all the people, and none of them doubted in the least that the words of "all the holy prophets" must be fulfilled. In making this important deduction, the Spirit of the Lord was with them and upon them. Many things contributed to the firmness of their belief. With their own eyes they had seen the deliverance

things should come to pass according to that which had been spoken.

3. Therefore they did forsake all their sins, and their abominations, and their whoredoms, and did serve God with all diligence day and night.

4. And now it came to pass that when they had taken all the robbers prisoners, insomuch that none did escape who were not slain, they did cast their prisoners into prison, and did cause the word of God to be preached unto them; and as many as would repent of their sins and enter into a covenant that they would murder no more were set at liberty.

5. But as many as there were who did not enter into a covenant, and who did still continue to have those secret murders in their hearts, yea, as many as were found breathing out threatenings against their brethren were condemned and punished according to the law.

6. And thus they did put an end to all those wicked, and secret, and abominable combinations, in the which there was so much wickedness, and so many murders committed.

---

of the Lord. Their own strength, they knew to be absolute weakness when compared to God's, their wisdom but foolishness. Together, all things presaged for them a glorious future, and unitedly, as with one voice, they proclaimed: "The Lord is God, and besides Him, there is none other." Only recently, Samuel the Lamanite, one of God's holy prophets, had foretold the coming of Jesus Christ, their Lord and God Who was actually the Son of the Eternal Father, to redeem all mankind. Of His coming, Samuel gave certain signs that would witness His birth. The Nephites had beheld these signs, so why not, they joyously pondered, should not all the words of the prophets likewise be fulfilled.

The faith of the Nephites in the words of the prophets, telling them of Jesus Christ, His birth, death, and resurrection, together with many blessings which God had vouchsafed them including His deliverance of them from destruction by the Gadianton Robbers, so melted their hard hearts, that they, as one, bowed before the *Majesty on High,* and, the Sacred Record says: "They did forsake all their sins, and their abominations, and their whoredoms, and did serve God with all diligence day and night."

VERSES 4-6. *They did put an end to all those . . . abominable combinations.* After Gidgiddoni's strategy had won, and righteousness had triumphed over wickedness, the good over evil, and the right over wrong, the Nephites took as prisoners all the robbers who were not slain. They cast them into prison, and there they preached the Word of God. Many repented of the course they had pursued, of the evil they had done, and expressed a determination to do them no more; these the Nephites set free upon them covenanting with their captors that they would "murder and rob no more."

But there were still some of the captives who, although beaten, cherished the thought of continuing their evil practices, perhaps when peace had again softened the hearts of the Nephites against iniquity, and when pride had once more robbed them of their faith in God. Any of the captives who expressed such a desire, and who, in addition, refused to enter into the prescribed covenant that they would rob and murder no more, and threatened their brethren with harm, "were condemned

7. And thus had the twenty and second year passed away, and the twenty and third year also, and the twenty and fourth, and the twenty and fifth; and thus had twenty and five years passed away.

8. And there had many things transpired which, in the eyes of some, would be great and marvelous; nevertheless, they cannot all be written in this book; yea, this book cannot contain even a hundredth part of what was done among so many people in the space of twenty and five years;

9. But behold there are records which do contain all the proceedings of this people; and a shorter but true account was given by Nephi.

10. Therefore I have made my record of these things according to the record of Nephi, which was engraven on the plates which were called the plates of Nephi.

11. And behold, I do make the record on plates which I have made with mine own hands.

2. Mormon's account of himself and the Plates kept by him.

12. And behold, I am called Mormon, being called after the land of Mormon, the land in which Alma did establish the church among the people, yea, the first church which was established among them after their transgression.

---

and punished according to the law." This entirely broke up these bands of murderers and robbers, and peace and righteousness again prevailed (21 A.D.), but it was not until five years later that the Nephites returned to and possessed their old homes.

VERSES 7-11. *I have made my record according to the records of Nephi.* Twenty-five years had now gone by since the signs given by Samuel that were to tell of Christ's birth were beheld by the Nephites both in the heavens and upon the earth. During that time many other great and marvelous things transpired which to many were wonderful to witness. But in the record Mormon was making, only a small part of them could be told. He noted, almost in the same words, certainly with the same intent, what he said about the Nephites who lived seventy-five years previously and which we quoted near the beginning of this chapter, 4, (Helaman 3:13-16). Many records were made of the events of this period, but Mormon informs us that all the knowledge from which his record is made, comes from the incidents recorded by the historians who wrote upon the *Plates of Nephi.* Their account of such occurrences is short and true, which fact he verifies. Therefore, he makes plain to all who read his abridgment that the information contained therein is engraven upon plates which he made with his own hands. Said information was material which was engraved upon the Plates of Nephi.

VERSES 12-16. *I am called Mormon.* The abridger of the Larger Plates of Nephi, Mormon, in these verses, gives a brief account of his calling, and testifies that it came of Jesus Christ, the Son of God, Whose disciple he was. The main purpose of this calling was, he declares, to preach Salvation and Eternal Life among his people, who were the people of the Lord God.

First, Mormon reveals the origin of his name, he being so called "after the Land of Mormon," the land in which Alma did establish the Church among the people. (Mosiah 18) His father's name was also Mormon. (Mormon 1:5) Very little is

13. Behold, I am a disciple of Jesus Christ, the Son of God. I have been called of him to declare his word among his people, that they might have everlasting life. 14. And it hath become expedient that I, according to the will of God, that the prayers of those

---

known concerning where the name, Mormon, came from, except the Sacred Record says it was the name given to a certain place near the City of Lehi-Nephi by the king; Zeniff, we presume.

MORMON

The Prophet Joseph Smith, in a letter published in the *Times and Seasons*, Nauvoo, May 15, 1843,[1] furnished the following explanation concerning the meaning of this word:

"It has been stated that this word was derived from the Greek word *mormo*. This is not the case. There was no Greek or Latin upon the plates from which I, through the grace of the Lord, translated the Book of Mormon."

Then he quotes from the Book of Mormon (Mormon 9:32-34), where we are told that the characters used were the "reformed Egyptian." He continues:

"Here, then the subject is put to silence, for 'none other people knoweth our language'; therefore, the Lord, and not man, had to interpret, after the people were all dead. And as Paul said, 'The world by wisdom knew not God'; so the world by speculation are destitute of revelation; and as God, in his superior wisdom, has always given his Saints, whenever he had any on the earth, the same spirit, and that spirit, as John says, is the true spirit of prophecy, which is the testimony of Jesus, I may safely say that the word *Mormon* stands independent of the learning and wisdom of this generation.

"Before I give a definition, however, of the word, let me say that the Bible, in its widest sense, means *good*; for the Savior says, according to the Gospel of John, "I am the Good Shepherd"; and it will not be beyond the common use of terms to say that *Good* is among the most important in use, and, though known by various names in different languages, still its meaning is the same, and is ever in opposition to *bad*."

The prophet further says:

"We say, from the Saxon, *good;* from the Dane, *god;* the Goth, *goda,* the German, *gut;* the Dutch, *goed;* the Latin, *bonus;* the Greek, *kalos;* the Hebrew, *tob,* and the Egyptian, *mon.* Hence, with the addition of *more,* or the contraction, *mor,* we have the word *Mormon,* which means literally, *more good.*"

Here we have the interesting information that the first part of the word is an abbreviation of the English adverb "more," and that the second part is the Egyptian adjective "mon." In other words, the prophet found, on the plates, as a proper noun, a compound word meaning, literally, "better," and, under the influence of the Holy Spirit, he solved the problem of transliterating it, by translating the first part into English and copying the second part, and making of the two, one word, half English and half Egyptian. This, I admit, is an unusual literary procedure, but we have an instance of it in our Bible, where a place called Maaleh-acrabbim (Joshua 15:3) is also called, "The Ascent of Akrabbim," (Numbers 34:4). Here half of the name is translated into English and the other half is a foreign word. See also, Genesis 23:2 and 35:27, where Hebron is called, in the first passage, Kirjath-Arba,

---

[1]The letter was revised by the Prophet, May 20, 1843. See *Documentary History of the Church,* under that date.

who have gone hence, who were the holy ones, should be fulfilled according to their faith, should | make a record of these things which have been done—
15. Yea, a small record of that

---

and in the second, "The City of Arbah," the first half of the name being translated into English and the second being left untranslated.[2] This, then, is how the word *Mormon* originated.

And it means "more good"; that is, "better."

The reference of the prophet, in this connection, to the Bible would indicate that the good expressed in the word is the same as that which we call "good news," or "gospel," and that "Mormon," therefore, means one who is the bearer of "good tidings."

It is probable that the *mon* in "Mormon" is akin to the *mon* or *men* in the Egyptian *Amon* or *Amen*. Dr. E. A. Wallis Budge, (*The Gods of the Egyptians*, Vol. 2, p. 2) says that Amen is from a root *men* "to abide, to be permanent, eternal." *Mon* or *men* (the vowel is indifferent) would, then, mean "good" in the sense of permanency, just as *nefer* means "good" in the sense of physical beauty. We gather this from what Champollin (*Precis du Systeme Hieroglyphique des Anciens Egyptiens*, p. 91) on the authority of Eusebius says, viz., that the divinity which takes the name Amen and Kneph or Noub, alternatively, was by the Greeks called *Agathodaimon*, and that Nero, when assuming a divine title, called himself *Neo-agathodaimon*. *Agathos* is, of course, the Greek word for "good," and it must have been suggested by the Egyptian *men* or *mon*.

It is a very interesting fact that many American languages, perhaps most of them, form their comparatives and superlatives by the use of the adverbs "more" and "most." In the Aztec, "better" is *ocachiqualli*, which means, literally, "more good." In the Otomi language "better" is *nra nho*, which means "more good." In the Maya, the comparative is formed by affixing the last vowel of the adjective with an "l" added or by simply affixing the particle *il*.

For instance, from *tibil*, a good thing, *utibil-il*, a better thing, is formed.

May we not ask, "What is the explanation of the singular fact that the Prophet Joseph Smith seems to have had a knowledge of how comparatives are formed in some of the principal American languages?"

Mormon was the last great Prophet-General of the Nephite race, but is better known to us as the custodian and compiler of the records of his people and the writer of the greater portion of the work named after him and known as the Book of Mormon. The father of Mormon, who was a descendant of Nephi, the son of the Patriarch Lehi, was born on the Northern Continent (311 A.D.), and when the younger Mormon was but eleven years of age, took him south to Zarahemla. Before his departure, he formed the acquaintance of Ammaron, the keeper of the Sacred Record, which, because of the iniquity of the people, he had hidden up in a hill called Antum. Ammaron informed Mormon, then a child ten years old, of what he had done, and placed the buried treasure in his charge. He instructed Mormon to go, when he was about twenty-four years old, to the hill where they were hidden and take the Plates of Nephi and to record thereon what he had observed concerning the people. The remainder of the records, etc., he was to leave where they were. Mormon was as great a religious teacher as he was a soldier. His annotations

---

[2]The familiar word Iroquois may possibly be another instance of this kind of word-building. The orators of that stock of Indians used to close their speeches by saying, *Hiro*, "I have spoken," very much as the Romans said, *Dixi*. Their sentinels had a cry of warning which sounded to the French something like *quai*. Out of these two words and a French ending, *ois*, the name Iroquois was composed.

which hath taken place from the time that Lehi left Jerusalem, even down until the present time. 16. Therefore I do make my | record from the accounts which have been given by those who were before me, until the commencement of my day;

---

throughout his compilation of the sacred records show this, as do also his instructions and epistles to his son, Moroni. Shortly before the great, final struggle near Cumorah, Mormon hid all the records that had been entrusted to his care in that hill, save the abridged records which he gave to his son.

To fulfill the promises of the Lord to the righteous of his brethren, Mormon noted that a record must be made available to the descendants of, or the seed of Joseph who shall live in times to come. For this reason, he found it necessary to make a small, yet a truly correct record of "these things which have been done." "Yea," he says, "a small record of that which hath taken place from the time that Lehi left Jerusalem, even down until the present time." Therefore, Mormon knowing that the things others before him had engraved upon the Plates of Nephi were true, and that in them was recorded the Gospel of Jesus Christ, he condensed their accounts and made them the principal component of his own work.

The promises of the Lord to the righteous Nephites of every generation that a knowledge of their forefathers should come to the remnants of the House of Israel who should dwell upon this continent was a covenant the Lord made with them, and its fulfillment was a treasure in which they rejoiced. We hereby refer the reader to such promises that the Lord made, and quote Enos' testimony as it was engraven upon the Smaller Plates of Nephi: "And after I, Enos, had heard these words, my faith began to be unshaken in the Lord; and I prayed unto Him with many long strugglings for my brethren, the Lamanites. And it came to pass that after I had prayed and labored with all diligence, the Lord said unto me: I will grant unto thee according to thy desires, because of thy faith. And now behold, this was the desire which I desired of Him — that if it should be, that my people, the Nephites, should fall into transgression, and by any means be destroyed, and the Lamanites should not be destroyed, that the Lord God would preserve a record of my people, the Nephites; even if it so be by the power of His holy arm, that it might be brought forth at some future day unto the Lamanites, that, perhaps, they might be brought unto salvation—For at the present our strugglings were vain in restoring them to the true faith. And they swore in their wrath that, if it were possible, they would destroy our records and us, and also all the traditions of our fathers. Therefore, I knowing that the Lord God was able to preserve our records, I cried unto Him continually, for He said unto me: Whatsoever thing ye shall ask in faith, believing that ye shall receive in the name of Christ, ye shall receive it. And I had faith, and I did cry unto God that He would preserve the records; and He covenanted with me that He would bring them forth unto the Lamanites in His own due time. And I, Enos, knew it would be according to the covenant which He had made; wherefore my heart did rest. And the Lord said unto me: Thy fathers have also required of Me this thing; and it shall be done unto them according to their faith; for their faith was like unto thine." (Enos 11-18; also See, I Nephi 13: 34ff; II Nephi 3:6-23; 26:16-17; 29:11; Mormon 5:12-13; 8:14-16; 8:25-32)

Mormon makes it plain that the source of all the accounts which he has incorporated into his work are the sacred historians who lived and wrote contemporaneous with each event they recorded. That they, he says, "were [lived] before me, until the coming of my day."

17. And then I do make a record of the things which I have seen with mine own eyes.

18. And I know the record which I make to be a just and a true record; nevertheless there are many things which, according to our language, we are not able to write.

19. And now I make an end of my saying, which is of myself, and proceed to give my account of the things which have been before me.

3. *Another Allusion to the Gathering of Israel.*

20. I am Mormon, and a pure descendant of Lehi. I have reason to bless my God and my Savior Jesus Christ, that he brought our

VERSES 17-19. *And then I make a record of the things which I have seen with mine own eyes.* After completing his abridgment of the accounts rendered by the historians of each period which were engraved on the Plates of Nephi, leaving them relatively with no part lacking and still retaining their proper sense, Mormon proposes to add thereto a record "of the things which I have seen with mine own eyes." Mormon, being an honorable and just man, the record of those things or happenings would be as he, honorable and just. But, he makes one apology, many things that happened among his people, because of a deficiency in their language, or because it lacked some quality necessary for completeness, he says, "We are not able to write." A fuller and freer conception of this defect in their writing, is made manifest to us by Mormon's son, Moroni, who was commanded of the Lord to include in the record he was making somewhat concerning the promises the righteous leaders of the Nephites had obtained from the Lord: that a *knowledge of Christ* should come unto his brethren, the Lamanites, a remnant of whom would still live for many generations upon the land which the Lord, Himself, had given them. Moroni did as he was commanded, but, nevertheless, he felt incapable of fully fulfilling the Lord's requirements. He sought the help of the Lord, and of his prayer to the Almighty, Moroni wrote: "And I said unto Him: Lord, the Gentiles will mock at these things, because of our weakness in writing; for Lord Thou hast made us mighty in word by faith, but Thou hast not made us mighty in writing; for Thou hast made all this people that they could speak much, because of the Holy Ghost which Thou hast given them. And Thou hast made us that we could write but little, because of the awkwardness of our hands. Behold, Thou hast not made us mighty in writing like unto the Brother of Jared, for Thou madest him that the things which he wrote were mighty even as Thou art, unto the overpowering of man to read them. Thou hast also made our words powerful and great, even that we cannot write them; wherefore, when we write we behold our weakness, and stumble because of the placing of our words; and I fear lest the Gentiles shall mock at our words." (Ether 12:23-25) In finishing the work which his father, Mormon, had commenced, Moroni also said: "Behold, I speak unto you as though I speak from the dead; for I know ye shall hear my words. Condemn me not because of mine imperfection, neither my father for his imperfection, neither them who have written before him; but rather give thanks unto God that He hath made manifest unto you our imperfections, that ye may learn to be more wise than we have been. (Mormon 9:30-31) "And whoso receiveth this record, and shall not condemn it because of the imperfections which are in it, the same shall know of greater things than these." (*Ibid.*, 8:12)

VERSES 20-23. *Surely He hath blessed the House of Jacob.* Mormon, in ecstasy, contemplated his descent from Father Lehi, and, in doing so, blessed Him Who rules

fathers out of the land of Jerusalem, (and no one knew it save
it were himself and those whom
he brought out of that land) and
that he hath given me and my
people so much knowledge unto
the salvation of our souls.

21. Surely he hath blessed the
house of Jacob, and hath been
merciful unto the seed of Joseph.

22. And insomuch as the children of Lehi have kept his commandments he hath blessed them
and prospered them according to
his word.

23. Yea, and surely shall he
again bring a remnant of the seed
of Joseph to the knowledge of the
Lord their God.

24. And as surely as the Lord
liveth, will he gather in from the
four quarters of the earth all the
remnant of the seed of Jacob, who
are scattered abroad upon all the
face of the earth.

25. And as he hath covenanted
with all the house of Jacob, even
so shall the covenant wherewith
he hath covenanted with the
house of Jacob be fulfilled in his

the lives of all men. A glorious paean in praise to God and His Son, Jesus Christ,
the Savior of the world, rose from Mormon's heart, and lifted him to unprecedented
heights of thanksgiving for Their divine goodness and mercies which They had
bestowed upon his people. The promise the Lord had given the Patriarch Lehi,
was that if his descendants would keep the commandments of God, they should be
blessed upon the land unto which he, Lehi, should be led. That promise was
fulfilled "according to His word." Not only did this promise extend to material
things, but in Mormon's own words: "He hath given my people so much knowledge
unto the Salvation of our souls." "Surely," he says, "He hath blessed the House of
Jacob, and hath been merciful unto the seed of Joseph," a remnant of which He will
bring to a "knowledge of the Lord their God." (This was written by Mormon
about 326 years after Christ.)

VERSES 24-26. *And then shall they know their Redeemer.* The Book of Mormon
has a message for all; for Jew and for Gentile. Every nation under heaven; every
kindred, tongue, and people who dwell upon the face of the Earth will hear its
voice, and "They shall know that I am He that doth speak." (*Jesus Christ,* III Nephi
20:39)

The promises of the Book of Mormon to the Gentiles are indeed great. To
them, it says that they shall be blessed upon this land, that is, Zion, the Land of
America; literally, the *Land of the King,* or the *Land of the Lord, our King.* "This
land shall be a land of liberty unto the Gentiles, and there shall be no king upon
this land . . . for I the Lord, the King of Heaven, will be their King, and I will be
a light unto them forever, that hear My words." (*II Nephi* 11:14)

To the Jew, its message and promise is contained in the verses we now have
under consideration. It is one of the greatest prophecies ever uttered, and its fulfillment
is being accomplished with an ever increasing rate of speed by some of the most
powerful forces on the Earth.

The Holy Land or Palestine, The Land of Jerusalem. "This is the land which
ye shall divide by lot unto the tribes of Israel for inheritance, and these are their
portion, saith the Lord God." (Ezekiel 47:13 to 48:29)

In connection with the prophecy of Ezekiel it is well to keep in mind the last
three verses of Chapter five, above noted.

The Holy Land would, some have estimated, extend from about 30 to 34 degrees
north latitude, and from 34 to 37 degrees east longitude. It would be about 280

own due time, unto the restoring all the house of Jacob unto the knowledge of the covenant that he hath covenanted with them. 26. And then shall they know their Redeemer, who is Jesus Christ, the Son of God; and then shall they be gathered in from the four quarters of the earth unto their own lands, from whence they have been dispersed; yea, as the Lord liveth so shall it be. Amen.

---

miles in length and 150 in width. It would be divided into twelve provinces, each named for one of the sons of Jacob and contain a strip of land 20 by 150 miles. Between Judah and Benjamin there would be a holy oblation. This reservation dedicated to the public service, would be about 50 by 150 miles, and the City of Jerusalem, with its suburbs would occupy an area in it 10 miles square.

The entire area of the Palestine of Ezekiel's vision is small, but it is only a beginning of a "Greater Palestine" which will, in all probability, extend from the River Euphrates in the north to the Red Sea, and from the Mediterranean to the Euphrates in the east. For the deserts will be made to blossom as the rose, just as has come to pass, by the power of God, where Israel has gathered on the American Continent. The country which the Lord promised to give to Abraham and his seed after him is, according to the divine Covenant, bounded by the River of Egypt and the Euphrates (Genesis 15:18), and Abraham's descendants will sometime come into possession of their inheritance.

Palestine will once more become the gathering place of the scattered Children of Judah, through the power of the Mighty One of Jacob, but He always accomplishes His purposes in human history through the instrumentality of His children. When Israel was to be brought out of Egyptian bondage, Moses was raised up and made the instrument through which their deliverance was made a reality. At the end of the Babylonian Captivity, Cyrus, the mighty prince of Persia, was moved upon to set the captives free and his successors continued to extend to them their protection while they were restoring their Temple and repairing the ruined walls of their city. In the same way, it is to be expected that, when the time comes for the last gathering and final restoration, the promises of the Lord will be fulfilled by means of natural agencies.

Cyrus was entrusted with power for the very purpose of enabling Israel to return to Palestine. For, about two hundred years before his birth, the Prophet Isaiah foretold his mission in these words: "Thus saith the Lord . . . that saith of Cyrus, He is My shepherd, and shall perform all My pleasure: even saying to Jerusalem, Thou shalt be built; and to the Temple, Thy foundation shall be laid." (Isaiah 44:24-28) Possibly this remarkable prediction was placed on record, by divine inspiration, for the effect it would naturally have on the Persian Ruler when his attention was called to it. He, himself, acknowledged his obligation to God and issued his famous decree as an expression of his gratitude for the success he had achieved. He says: "The Lord God of Heaven hath given me all the kingdoms of the Earth; and He hath charged me to build Him an house at Jerusalem, which is in Judah. Who is there among you of all His people? his God be with him, and let him go up to Jerusalem." (Ezra 1:2-3) That was a graceful act of acknowledgment of divine providence in the military and diplomatic achievements through which Cyrus had risen to eminence and power.

Is there, we may ask, a prophetic word by which we who live today may know by what human instrumentality the restoration of Palestine will be effected?

There is!

For the same prophet who indicated Cyrus as the deliverer from Babylonian captivity, directed us to look to the *real sovereign of Egypt* for the final restoration and deliverance of the Holy Land, when he placed on record the following word of the Lord: "For I am the Lord thy God, the Holy One of Israel, thy Saviour: *I gave Egypt for thy ransom.*" (Isaiah 43:3)

Has not God in our own day literally entrusted Egypt to the care of the great world powers? This is true notwithstanding the present turmoil which seems to confuse the vision of all who hope to see the fulfillment of Isaiah's prophecy.

Let us acknowledge the hand of the Lord in this, as in all further developments. He has given Egypt to them and, as He says through His prophet, as *a ransom for Israel.* It rests with these great powers, having accepted the price, to restore the property to the Lord.

There are indications that the thoughts of men are now being directed, as never before, toward the political necessity of restoring Palestine to its native glory, and the establishment there, in the City of David, of a kind of international court that will solve the problems that now divide and array nation against nation. Such an action would be due recognition of the interest all enlightened nations naturally have in the place where the cradle of their civilization stood.

The establishment of the independent state of *Israel* is an auspicious beginning that will yet grow until all the kingdoms of the Earth shall become the Kingdom of our Lord.

"Israel, youngest true democracy in the world, enters its seventh year amidst austerity, sacrifice, and violence. These elements are not new, historically, to young states nor to the indomitable people who carved their homeland out of the hostile desert. Achievements have been noteworthy since Israel was born in 1948. Not the least of these was the founding of a nation in an unproductive, ferment-ridden area. Thousands of persons, persecuted and discriminated against in other countries, hailed Israel as their own free country and flocked there in a historic migration. They set up truck farms and factories where jackals once roamed and nomads grazed their sheep. They made the desert blossom; they conquered disease where pestilence had made it unsafe for humans. They established compulsory education; they gave women the right to vote and other rights. They created a symbol of man's faith in himself and his great potentialities."

"Six years ago the United States was the first nation to recognize the Israeli Republic. Without this action and other friendly acts the state would not have survived its fight for life against the superior armies of its neighbors. Irrespective of what else we may consider necessary to compromise the thorny issues of the Middle East, the United States should make it abundantly clear to the Arabs and the world that we are resolved that Israel has come to stay. Recognition of Israel as an entity is the prerequisite to any formula for peace in this part of the globe." (*Salt Lake Tribune,* May 10, 1954)

The gathering of the Children of Israel and the rehabilitation of Palestine must be considered from the widest possible panoramic view. It is, by no means, a matter of sentiment. That measure would be the beginning of a regenerative movement affecting the entire world. Paul, in his letter to the Romans, takes this view, when he says: "For if the casting away of them (the Jews) be the reconciling of the world, what shall the receiving of them be, but life from the dead?" If, in the dispersed condition, they were an influence for good in the world, how much greater will that influence be when they are re-united and can take a place in the family of nations? That will be to the entire world, as "life from the dead."

There is no other salvation for the world than the establishment of that *Kingdom* of which the prophets have spoken from the beginning. All merely human governments have proved inadequate to the moral, spiritual, and physical needs of the children of men. No matter how well the machinery has worked to begin with, after a while it has become deranged, and, in many instances, unfit for the service for which it was intended. Therefore, God, Himself, will give to the world a form of government, perfect and adequate to all its needs. And this form of government will come from Zion and Jerusalem.

The race that has given to mankind such lawgivers and leaders as Moses and Ezra; such philosophers as Solomon and poets as David; and, in later years, such teachers as Miamonides and Mendelssohn, will yet bring forth the genius, the religious force, and the statesmanship necessary for the true solution of the moral, social, and political problems that cause trouble in the world today, and with this, the establishment of the *Universal Brotherhood of Man*. For that is the next stage to which our civilization must advance.

CHAPTER 6

1. *The People are Prospered*—2. *Pride, Wealth, and Class Distinction Follow*—3. *The Church Rent by Dissension*—4. *Deeds of Darkness.*

1. *The people are prospered.*

1. And now it came to pass that the people of the Nephites did all return to their own lands in the twenty and sixth year, every man, with his family, his flocks and his herds, his horses and his cattle, and all things whatsoever did belong unto them.

2. And it came to pass that they had not eaten up all their provisions; therefore they did take with them all that they had not devoured, of all their grain of every kind, and their gold, and their silver, and all their precious things, and they did return to their own lands and their posses-sions, both on the north and on the south, both on the land northward and on the land southward.

3. And they granted unto those robbers who had entered into a covenant to keep the peace, of the band who were desirous to remain Lamanites, lands, according to their numbers, that they might have, with their labors, wherewith to subsist upon; and thus they did establish peace in all the land.

4. And they began again to prosper and to wax great; and the twenty and sixth and seventh years passed away, and there was great order in the land; and they

---

VERSE 4. *And they began to prosper and to wax great.* As we have already noted, the soldiers of Gidgiddoni succeeded in taking as prisoners all the robbers who were not killed. The Word of God was preached to them, and those who repented and covenanted to cease their evil practices were set at liberty. In their magnanimity the Nephites gave them lands according to their numbers "that they might have, with their labors, wherewith to subsist upon." The remainder were condemned for their crimes, and punished according to the law. This entirely broke up the Gadianton bands of robbers and murderers, and peace and righteousness again prevailed. (21 A.D.)

However, it was not until five years later that the Nephites returned to their old homes, each man and his family taking with them their belongings, for there was much which they had gathered and not used during the years of their refuge into which they had gone for mutual protection against the repeated raids of the Gadiantons. Besides food which they had not eaten, their silver and gold and also other precious things, they returned with their flocks and herds, their cattle and horses; it seems reasonable to suppose that many of their livestock and beasts of burden had increased both in number and in fine condition during their sojourn in the Lands of Zarahemla and Bountiful, whereto their leaders had called them. Nevertheless and in spite of their dwelling in a place as temporary residents, they amassed while there a great store of worldly goods, and soon "they began again to prosper and to wax great." (verse 4)

The next year after the return of the Nephites to their own possessions the laws of the Republic were revised according to justice and equity. They had, doubtless,

had formed their laws according to equity and justice.

5. And now there was nothing in all the land to hinder the people from prospering continually, except they should fall into transgression.

6. And now it was Gidgiddoni, and the judge, Lachoneus, and those who had been appointed leaders, who had established this great peace in the land.

7. And it came to pass that there were many cities built anew, and there were many old cities repaired.

8. And there were many highways cast up, and many roads made, which led from city to city, and from land to land, and from place to place.

9. And thus passed away the twenty and eighth year, and the people had continual peace.

2. Pride, wealth, and class distinction follow.

10. But it came to pass in the twenty and ninth year there began to be some disputings among the people; and some were lifted up unto pride and boastings because of their exceeding great

been violently tampered with during the times that the Gadianton Robbers held control of the administration and elected the officers to conduct its affairs. Good order now prevailed throughout the whole land. Soon new cities were founded, old ones repaired, roads and other means of communication were built, and here the Sacred Record notes "now there was nothing in all the land to hinder the people from prospering continually, except they should fall into transgression." (verse 5)

Mormon, in his abridgment of the Larger Plates of Nephi, gives full credit for the "great peace" that was then established in the land to its two appointed leaders, Lachoneus, the Governor of the Land and also its Chief Judge, and Gidgiddoni, the righteous military Commander of its armed forces. Mormon meant to imply that it was by obedience to constituted authority that the people were blessed through God's grace, and that peace, His most precious gift, once again brought joy and happiness to the Nephite homes.

To acquaint the reader more fully with the leadership afforded the Nephite people, we quote Mormon's words concerning these two masterful guides: "And so great and marvelous were the words and prophecies of Lachoneus that they did cause fear to come upon all the people; and they did exert themselves in their might to do according to the words of Lachoneus. And it came to pass that Lachoneus did appoint chief captains over all the armies of the Nephites, to command them at the time that the robbers should come down out of the wilderness against them. Now the chiefest among all the captains and the great commander of the armies of the Nephites was appointed, and his name was Gidgiddoni. Now it was the custom among all the Nephites to appoint for their chief captains, (save it were in times of wickedness) some one that had the spirit of revelation and also prophecy; therefore, this Gidgiddoni was a great prophet among them, as also was the Chief Judge." (III Nephi 3:16-19)

VERSE 10. *Some were lifted up unto pride and boastings.* Yet in spite of God's deliverance of them from their enemies, and the peace that imbued them all, enabling them to see those things which brought them happiness and prosperity — which in the land wherein they lived abounded most plentifully — some of the people "were lifted up unto pride and boastings because of their exceeding great riches, yea, even

riches, yea, even unto great persecutions;

11. For there were many merchants in the land, and also many lawyers, and many officers.

12. And the people began to be distinguished by ranks, according to their riches and their chances for learning, yea, some were ignorant because of their poverty, and others did receive great learn-

ing because of their riches.

13. Some were lifted up in pride, and others were exceedingly humble; some did return railing for railing, while others would receive railing and persecution and all manner of afflictions, and would not turn and revile again, but were humble and penitent before God.

3. The Church rent by dissension.

14. And thus there became a great inequality in all the land, insomuch that the church began to be broken up; yea, insomuch that in the thirtieth year the church was broken up in all the land save it were among a few of the Lamanites who were convert-

---

unto great persecutions." We may not be surprised that peace was shortlived. Iniquity and dissension soon began again to raise their hideous heads, and the prophets and servants of God were persecuted and some illegally condemned to death.

As among all prosperous people where wealth and a desire for more worldly goods motivate their way of life, both material things and station therein, these things became common merchandise among the Nephites. There were many merchants going from place to place hawking their wares and exchanging anything that appealed to their customers' fancy or satisfied their whims. We may imagine that many made all the trouble they could because there were also many lawyers among them seeking fees. Officers in search of authority over their fellow men added a luster to the rapidly growing sense of superiority one had over the other. "And the people began to be distinguished by ranks, according to their riches and their chances for learning. . . ."

VERSE 13. *Some were humble and penitent before God.* Notwithstanding the blessings vouchsafed to them by the Lord, pride and angry passions molded the pattern offered in the lives of many Nephites of this period. Yet, there were others who because of deep spiritual understanding "were exceedingly humble." They refused to rail while others railed at them; neither did they revile the reviler, nor smite the smiter; they bore all manner of affliction remembering that God claims the righteous man as His own. To them He was The Majesty On High, and before Him, they were humble and penitent.

VERSE 14. *There became a great inequality in all the land, insomuch that the Church began to be broken up.* According to Nephite reckoning it was thirty years after the birth of Christ in faraway Judea that the events recorded of this period took place. Only a few years of peace had passed since the Gadianton Robbers were exterminated, yet in that short time many Nephites proved that their memories were still shorter. They entirely forgot the *Power* that had delivered them from the hands of wicked men, and abandoned themselves to their own strength, which, when compared to God's was absolute weakness. Their wisdom was likewise foolishness, and by it they knew not God. Their learning, which some received because it was the kind that could be bought (verse 12), led them down to depths they could not

ed unto the true faith; and they would not depart from it, for they were firm, and steadfast, and immovable, willing with all diligence to keep the commandments of the Lord.

15. Now the cause of this iniquity of the people was this—Satan had great power, unto the stirring up of the people to do all manner of iniquity, and to the puffing them up with pride, tempting them to seek for power, and authority, and riches, and the vain things of the world.

16. And thus Satan did lead away the hearts of the people to do all manner of iniquity; therefore they had enjoyed peace but a few years.

17. And thus, in the commencement of the thirtieth year —the people having been delivered up for the space of a long time to be carried about by the temptations of the devil whithersoever he desired to carry them, and to do whatsoever iniquity he desired they should—and thus in the commencement of this, the thirtieth year, they were in a state of awful wickedness.

18. Now they did not sin ignorantly, for they knew the will of God concerning them, for it had been taught unto them; therefore they did wilfully rebel against God.

---

fathom, and to heights they could not grasp. It was not long until the *Church of God*, its members enmeshed in the fabric of apostasy, ceased to exist except among a few worthy Lamanites "who were converted to the true faith; and they would not depart from it, for they were firm, and steadfast, and immovable, willing with all diligence to keep the commandments of the Lord." (verse 14)

VERSES 15-18. *Satan had great power, unto the stirring up of the people to do all manner of iniquity.* It is true, Satan has power over us only as we do his bidding. Little by little, in doing his will, we grant him sovereignty of our lives, and more and more he asserts dominion over us. In obeying him, honoring him, and sustaining him by our actions, we enter his kingdom and become *servants of evil*. At first our willingness to serve him may be evidenced by small matters, but in the end the final test is — small matters become large, and soon we excuse our actions, offer pretexts to assuage our remorse, and only apologize when we should *wear sackcloth*. Pride, we may conceive, is at first a small matter, but as it increases within us, our hearts are hardened, our efforts in establishing God's Kingdom upon the Earth are enfeebled, and our desires for the higher things of life are dulled. Only as we are firm, and steadfast, and immovable, and seek with all diligence to keep the Lord's commandments, can we thwart the plans of the evil one. Satan often begins his campaign of moral and mental, not forgetting physical, destruction by puffing up a people "with pride, tempting them to seek for power, and authority, and riches, and the vain things of the world." And thus, with the Nephites of this period, all thoughts of God were crowded from their hearts, and thus, "Satan did lead away the hearts of the people to do all manner of iniquity. . ." (verse 16) Mormon comments that "therefore they had enjoyed peace but a few years."

VERSE 18. *They did not sin ignorantly.* To rebel knowingly against the will of the Lord is an awful thing. The Nephites had been taught by holy men, men of God, all things concerning His will towards them, and in rejecting His Word, whether it came to them through the prophets of old, or the seers of their own time, and listening to the sophistry of the devil, they sinned knowingly, and not ignorantly. In fine, "They did wilfully rebel against God." (verse 18)

4. Deeds of Darkness.

19. And now it was in the days of Lachoneus, the son of Lachoneus, for Lachoneus did fill the seat of his father and did govern the people that year.

20. And there began to be men inspired from heaven and sent forth, standing among the people in all the land, preaching and testifying boldly of the sins and iniquities of the people, and testifying unto them concerning the redemption which the Lord would make for his people, or in other

---

VERSE 20. *Men, inspired from Heaven, stood among the people, preaching and testifying boldly of the sins and iniquities of the people.* Notwithstanding that the hearts and minds of the Nephite people had become diseased and depraved, the bounties of the earth continued to pour in upon them like a river of plenitude, making them rich in worldly goods and arrogant when dealing with their fellows. Pride ruled their hearts. The accumulation of material things imbued many with a false sense of security and safety against any enemy. Their chattles gave others a feeling of superiority over brother and sister. They were fast ripening for destruction. Their flocks and herds, their fields of yellow corn, their gold and silver, were gods that filled their hearts and to whom they paid homage. Day by day, they went their way unmindful of the *God of their Fathers* who had given them all these things. We repeat: *All thoughts of God were crowded from their hearts.*

At this crucial period in their history, which, too, was a turning point in their lives, Lachoneus, the son of the previous Chief Judge by the same name, "did fill the seat of his father and did govern the people that year," (verse 19) which was the thirtieth year of Nephite reckoning.

The Nephites, blessed as they were with a surplus of good things, which, as we have noted, were abundant in the land wherein they lived, nevertheless grew weary of well-doing; they forgot that "riches and honour are with Me; yea, durable riches and righteousness." (Proverbs 8:18) They "loved evil more than good; and lying rather than to speak righteousness.' (Psalm 52:3) We think of the faithful Priests of God's Church as they officiated in the rituals of the Law of Moses, and who took special heed to the words of King David which were written upon the Brass Plates of Laban: "Offer the sacrifices of righteousness, and put your trust in the Lord." (Psalm 4:5)

Although the Nephites of Lachoneus' time were apostate and openly rebelled against Him, the Lord's long-suffering and merciful kindness towards them endured yet another season.

The end to which all God's provinces are consecrated is the Salvation of His children. It seems to us that the poet's words are true: *Out of evil He still educes good;* God sends His children trials and tribulations that by overcoming them they become stronger, and also that they might remember Him. History shows in the experience of four thousand years that without occasions of distress and suffering to remind them of Him, *men know not God.* Distress! and suffering! Why? To what end? To the end, "That ye may remember, and do all My commandments, and be holy unto your God. . . ." (Numbers 15:40-41)

God knows men's weaknesses; *He will not forsake them, nor leave them in their grief.* He did not forsake the Nephites. And remember what is more, He does not desire the death of the transgressor, but that the sinner live and return unto Him. Therefore, and because the Nephites were of the House of Israel, men holding the Holy Priesthood — the Sacred Record says, "by Heaven inspired" — were sent forth

words, the resurrection of Christ; and they did testify boldly of his death and sufferings.

21. Now there were many of the people who were exceeding angry because of those who testified of these things; and those who were angry were chiefly the chief judges, and they who had been high priests and lawyers; yea, all those who were lawyers were angry with those who testified of these things.

22. Now there was no lawyer nor judge nor high priest that could have power to condemn any one to death save their condemnation was signed by the governor of the land.

23. Now there were many of those who testified of the things pertaining to Christ who testified boldly, who were taken and put to death secretly by the judges, that the knowledge of their death came not unto the governor of the land until after their death.

24. Now behold, this was contrary to the laws of the land, that any man should be put to death except they had power from the governor of the land—

25. Therefore a complaint came up unto the land of Zarahemla, to the governor of the land, against these judges who had condemned the prophets of the Lord unto death, not according to the law.

26. Now it came to pass that

---

to once again proclaim the grandeur that awaits the faithful and true. Throughout all the Lands of the Nephites they stood among the people and boldly testified as to their sins and iniquities; at the same time they preached repentance and "the Redemption the Lord would make for His people." (verse 20) The Resurrection of Christ was their message, and without any restraint except that offered by the people to whom they spoke, told of "His death and sufferings."

VERSE 21. *And those who were angry were chiefly the chief judges. . . .* The efforts of these evangelists and teachers to turn the people from their iniquitous ways did not result in the peace of righteous living to the strife-torn populace, but incited anger and resentment from the chief judges and apostate high priests against whom they had testified. While some scattered few were convinced of their evil practices and sought to make amends, the majority of the people became more bitter and malignant. Many lawyers, always ready for unrest, stirred them up to hatred and angry passions, even that some of the preachers of righteousness who came among them were put to death.

VERSES 22-23. *Many of those who testified . . . were secretly put to death.* No officer, according to Nephite law, had power to condemn a person to death without the authority of the governor, but many of the prophets were put to death secretly by the judges. The knowledge of such action was withheld from the proper authority until after the prophet's death.

VERSES 24-30. *A complaint came up to the governor.* A complaint against the lower judges for permitting such actions was made to the Chief Judge of the whole land at Zarahemla, and the offenders were tried according to the law. The wicked were strong because they were united in evil. But unity in evil is conspiracy, and that is just what happened among them. The kindred and friends of the offenders, with certain lawyers and high priests, entered into a secret agreement, or covenant to destroy the people who were in favor of law and order. This wicked covenant in turn

they were taken and brought up before the judge to be judged of the crime which they had done, according to the law which had been given by the people.

27. Now it came to pass that those judges had many friends and kindreds; and the remainder, yea, even almost all the lawyers and the high priests, did gather themselves together, and unite with the kindreds of those judges who were to be tried according to the law.

28. And they did enter into a covenant one with another, yea, even into that covenant which was given by them of old, which covenant was given and admin-istered by the devil, to combine against all righteousness.

29. Therefore they did combine against the people of the Lord, and enter into a covenant to destroy them, and to deliver those who were guilty of murder from the grasp of justice, which was about to be administered according to the law.

30. And they did set at defiance the law and the rights of their country; and they did covenant one with another to destroy the governor, and to establish a king over the land, that the land should no more be at liberty but should be subject unto kings.

---

destroyed justice; its aim was to save the guilty judges from the just penalty of their misdeeds. This was, in fact, the re-establishment of the order of Gadianton. They proposed to assassinate the governor, set up a king to rule the country, and destroy its liberties.

LACHONEUS, THE YOUNGER

The last of the Nephite judges, the son of the preceding judge, who bore the same name. He was assassinated in the year 30 A.D.

It is not entirely certain from the Sacred Record when Lachoneus, the younger, assumed the reins of government, but the idea seems to be conveyed that it was in the year 30 A.D. His dominion fell in perilous times. The people had ripened in iniquity and were ready for destruction. The prophets of God who raised their warning voices were slain by unjust judges and unscrupulous officers and the laws were perverted and trampled under foot. When these corrupt rulers were called to account by the supeme authority at the capital, they set the laws at defiance, refused to answer, broke out in open rebellion, endeavored to establish a monarchy and assassinated the Chief Judge.

CHAPTER 7

1. Chief Judge murdered and Government overthrown.

1. Now behold, I will show unto you that they did not establish a king over the land; but in this same year, yea, the thirtieth year, they did destroy upon the judgment-seat, yea, did murder the chief judge of the land.

2. Division into tribes.

2. And the people were divided one against another; and they did separate one from another into tribes, every man according to his family and his kindred and friends; and thus they did destroy the government of the land.

3. And every tribe did appoint a chief or a leader over them; and thus they became tribes and leaders of tribes.

4. Now behold, there was no man among them save he had much family and many kindreds and friends; therefore their tribes became exceeding great.

5. Now all this was done, and there were no wars as yet among them; and all this iniquity had come upon the people because

VERSE 1. *They did not establish a king over the land.* In spite of the fact that the rebellious overthrew the government, and caused that the Chief Judge be murdered while he sat upon the Judgment-Seat, they were unable, as they desired, to establish a kingship to rule over the land. In the spasmodic attempts by Nephite Royalists to place a king at the head of their government, they never succeeded to permanently change the form of its administrative powers. Although the Heaven-inspired laws of the Republic were sometimes perverted to meet the criminal tendencies of the wicked or feed their greed, they were not made subject to the despotic rule of a king. This was especially true at times when the Gadianton Robbers elected men to governmental offices, and forthwith proceeded to fulfil their unrighteous purposes.

VERSES 2-8. *The people were divided one against another.* The result of their uprising was not what the conspirators anticipated. More dissension and turmoil among the people caused even the wicked to retract their commitment given to support a king. Instead of a united front which alone could accomplish their designs, they divided into groups — the Sacred Record calls them tribes — every man with his family uniting with their kindred and friends. This completely disorganized the government, and also deranged the plans of the conspirators. Some men had large families and many friends and kindred, and their tribes were correspondingly large. Each tribe appointed its chief or leader, and it was his special duty to see that the laws they should thereafter adopt were properly carried out. (30 A.D.)

This really calamitous condition of the people came not upon them as the event of a day, or by sudden impact, but by their gradual apostasy from the Lord, and by yielding "themselves unto the power of Satan." Little by little they were

they did yield themselves unto the power of Satan.

6. And the regulations of the government were destroyed, because of the secret combination of the friends and kindreds of those who murdered the prophets.

7. And they did cause a great contention in the land, insomuch that the more righteous part of

the people had nearly all become wicked; yea, there were but few righteous men among them.

8. And thus six years had not passed away since the more part of the people had turned from their righteousness, like the dog to his vomit, or like the sow to her wallowing in the mire.

3. King Jacob.

9. Now this secret combination, which had brought so great iniquity upon the people, did gather themselves together, and did place at their head a man whom they did call Jacob;

10. And they did call him their king; therefore he became a king over this wicked band; and he was one of the chiefest who had given his voice against the prophets who testified of Jesus.

---

consumed with pride; little by little the temptations of the devil carried them farther and farther towards destruction, and soon "the more righteous part of the people had nearly all become wicked; yea, there were but few righteous men among them."

While these terrible social overturnings were taking place on the American Continent, how different were the events that were occurring in the midst of the House of Israel on the Eastern Continent! For it was in the year that Jesus, the Redeemer of the world, was baptized by John in the River Jordan, as Lehi, Nephi, and others of the ancient Nephite prophets had long before foretold. It was in this same year that Jesus commenced His public ministry and began to teach men the Law of His Gospel.

VERSES 9-14. *This secret combination placed Jacob at its head.*

We can easily see in the experience of the Nephites of this period why secret societies and clandestine combinations are not compatible with the ways of righteousness. If anything is good, it should be to the benefit of all. If it is not good, it is of evil and is of the devil. Unity in evil is conspiracy; unity without permanency of purpose is merely coalition; but unity that is lasting and real, comes from the Lord, and only that which is good endures to the end. Therefore, when men combine to foist upon others the will of the few; when they aggregate to themselves the power to live and let live; when they submerge all else to selfish and wanton practices, they open the flood-gates of iniquity, and in spite of *right*, make *might* the criterion, or test by which a thing is tried, or judged. It was just this sort of combination that brought misery to the Nephites. It was a secret society that destroyed them as a nation, and a *hidden motive* in their actions that brought down upon them the retribution of the *lie.* It was "the secret combination of the friends and kindreds of those who murdered the prophets" that was the cause of the Nephites' surrender to evil.

Now this combination which promised secrecy to its followers concerning each other's criminal acts, had a hidden purpose by which its adherents hoped to usurp both religious and political power. A combination of religious and political authority reposing in the hands of one, or a few men, would leave none to whom they need answer. With this end in view, the members of this diabolical organization assembled

11. And it came to pass that they were not so strong in number as the tribes of the people, who were united together save it were their leaders did establish their laws, every one according to his tribe; nevertheless they were enemies; notwithstanding they were not a righteous people, yet they were united in the hatred of those who had entered into a covenant to destroy the government.

12. Therefore, Jacob seeing that their enemies were more numerous than they, he being the king of the band, therefore he commanded his people that they should take their flight into the northernmost part of the land, and there build up unto themselves a kingdom, until they were joined by dissenters, (for he flat-tered them that there would be many dissenters) and they become sufficiently strong to contend with the tribes of the people; and they did so.

13. And so speedy was their march that it could not be impeded until they had gone forth out of the reach of the people. And thus ended the thirtieth year; and thus were the affairs of the people of Nephi.

14. And it came to pass in the thirty and first year that they were divided into tribes, every man according to his family, kindred and friends; nevertheless they had come to an agreement that they would not go to war one with another; but they were not united as to their laws, and their manner of government, for

together and chose one of their number as their leader whom they called *King*, and "he was one of the chiefest who had given his voice against the prophets who testified of Jesus."

VERSES 11-14. *Jacob commanded his people that they should take up their flight into the northernmost parts of the land.* Though the people comprising the different Nephite tribes were an aggregation of nondescripts, who in no particular way served the Lord, "yet, they were united in the hatred of those who had entered into a covenant to destroy the government." We observe that there was little else to unite them except their fear of the followers of Jacob, who were indeed the Gadianton Robbers. This appears to have led to a confederacy for purposes of defense. They agreed to keep the peace with one another, and to establish laws to prevent one tribe trespassing upon the rights of the others. The result was a multiplicity of laws; each tribe adopting measures which the leaders thereof thought would in the end inure to its own benefit.

Nevertheless, and in spite of their many laws to secure what they mistook for mutual concord, there hovered over them an uneasy peace. They wanted peace. That was the reason for their separation into tribes; to rid themselves of the tyranny of the few. There is one, and only one, real and lasting peace; that is the peace of righteousness. Of that they knew little. Any peace in opposition to righteousness, is all Peace! Peace! when there is no peace. (Jeremiah 6:14) "There is no peace, saith my God, to the wicked." (Isaiah 57:21) "And the work of righteousness shall be peace; and the effect of righteousness, quietness and assurance forever." (*Ibid.,* 32:17) We imagine that peace to them was as it is to us — the manner of our lives. We want peace as we have noted they did, but not every and any peace. We do not want the peace that is woven into treaties in the distant capitals of the world, nor the peace that is purchased on the field of battle. We do not want the peace that

to the minds of those who were their chiefs and their leaders. But they did establish very strict laws that one tribe should not trespass against another, insomuch that in some degree they had peace in the land; nevertheless, their hearts were turned from the Lord their God, and they did stone the prophets and did cast them out from among them.

4. Nephi's powerful ministry.

15. And it came to pass that Nephi—having been visited by angels and also the voice of the Lord, therefore having seen angels, and being eye-witness, and having had power given unto him that he might know concerning the ministry of Christ, and also being eye-witness to their quick return from righteousness unto their wickedness and abominations;

16. Therefore, being grieved for the hardness of their hearts and the blindness of their minds —went forth among them in that

---

is made in the committee room, or the peace of mere conventionalism; but what we do want is peace established on truth, upheld and sustained by the righteousness of God's children everywhere. Let us always remember, "Great peace have they which love Thy law. . . ." (Psalm 119:165); and in that day when all Israel shall be gathered into His fold and there shall be no more wickedness; then will the words of God's servant be fulfilled: ". . .all thy children shall be taught of the Lord; and great shall be the peace of thy children." (Isaiah 54:13; also quoted by Jesus Christ in a sermon to the Nephites, III Nephi 22:13)

An approximate count of the tribesmen, and the men of the secret combination, showed that the tribesmen were a majority. This, we may presume, angered Jacob, who had dreamed of power and great authority over all the people. In his impetuosity Jacob commanded his people to flee into the most northerly parts of the land where they could build up a kingdom to themselves. They carried out this plan, and their flight was too speedy to be intercepted. In the north they built a large city which they named Jacobugath.[1]

VERSES 15-16. *Nephi went forth boldly and did testify repentance and remission of sins through faith on the Lord Jesus Christ.* At this time of catastrophic happenings in the Nephite Commonwealth, Nephi, who afterwards became the chiefest of Christ's Disciples, was called by the voice of the Lord and the visitation of angels to labor diligently in Christ's ministry among the wicked people whose government had become so disarranged that it no longer functioned either religiously nor politically.

Being an eyewitness to their many follies, Nephi quickly sensed how quick the people were to forget God's goodness to them and to return "unto their wickedness and abominations." To sit idly by and lament their ways was not his part in the drama that was being enacted. Grieved unmeasurably because the great majority

---

[1]"And behold, that great City Jacobugath, which was inhabited by the people of King Jacob, have I caused to be burned with fire because of their sins and their wickedness, which was above all the wickedness of the whole earth, because of their secret murders and abominations; for it was they that did destroy the peace of My people and the government of the land; therefore I did cause them to be burned, to destroy them from before my face, that the blood of the prophets and the Saints should not come up unto Me any more against them." (III Nephi 9:9)

same year, and began to testify, boldly, repentance and remission of sins through faith on the Lord Jesus Christ.

17. And he did minister many things unto them; and all of them cannot be written, and a part of them would not suffice, therefore they are not written in this book. And Nephi did minister with power and with great authority.

---

of his people, by their actions, denied the Law of Moses which pointed to Christ, and which they had observed, he with courage and fortitude went forth and with boldness began to declare "repentance and remission of sins through faith on the Lord Jesus Christ." (verse 16)

VERSE 17. *Nephi did minister with power and great authority.* Going about every day doing good to his unfortunate people, and ministering to their wants, Nephi, however, performed his greatest service, as did all the prophets before him, in crying repentance and Salvation by reason of faith in Christ, and remission of sins.

We may conceive that Nephi not only preached the Gospel of Christ by word of mouth, but by alleviating his people's burdens and in ameliorating their sufferings. In many ways he administered aid in their wants. He brought succor to the oppressed and help to the helpless. He mourned with those who mourned, and rejoiced with them that saw in him the purposes of the Lord being accomplished. In many ways the power of God was manifest in his labors, but it must be remembered that an evil person often rejects divine intercession and refuses to accept God's providences. Thus the day of their affliction is prolonged. That is just what the Nephite tribesmen did; they spurned Nephi's ministrations because the Spirit of the Lord had left them; their hearts were hardened, and their minds, Mormon noted, were blinded by the craftiness of men. Nevertheless, Nephi was diligent in his divine commitment, and for three years "he did preach repentance and remission of sins."

On the plates Mormon had made, and on which he was attempting to engrave, in an abridged form, a full account of that which he found written upon other plates, there was not space to record his findings. He makes the comment that the many things in which Nephi ministered to his people therefore cannot be contained in the record he was making, "and a part of them would not suffice," (v. 17) but he adds this interesting observation: "And Nephi did minister with power and with great authority."[2]

Nephi's ministrations were attended with such showings of God's power that even the hard-hearted and stiff-necked were astonished at his words and could not disbelieve them. He spoke, convincing many of their wicked ways, yet they grew more and more angry with him because he was able to show them their need of repentance. In common parlance, he hit where it hurt them most. As a witness to them whereof he spoke, "In the Name of Jesus did he cast out devils and unclean spirits; and even his brother did he raise from the dead, after he had been stoned and suffered death by the people." (v. 19)[3]

---

[2]When Jesus ministered among the Jews, Matthew and Mark note that "They were astonished at His doctrine; for He taught them as one that had *authority,* and not as the scribes." (*See* Matthew 7:29, and Mark 1:22) Speaking of Jesus' ministry, Luke makes this significant observation, "Then He called His twelve disciples together, and gave them *power* and *authority* over all devils, and to cure diseases. And he sent them to preach the Kingdom of God, and to heal the sick." (Luke 9:1-2) The importance of authority is seen in Paul's charge to Titus, first Bishop of the Church of Cretians: "These things speak, and exhort, and rebuke with all *authority.* Let no man despise thee." (Titus 2:15)

[3]And it came to pass that on the morrow, when the multitude was gathered together, behold, Nephi and his brother whom he had raised from the dead, whose name was Timothy . . ." and ten others were named by the Savior as his disciples; "and it came to pass that they went forth and stood in the midst of the multitude." (III Nephi 19:4)

18. And it came to pass that they were angry with him, even because he had greater power than they, for it were not possible that they could disbelieve his words, for so great was his faith on the Lord Jesus Christ that angels did minister unto him daily.

19. And in the name of Jesus did he cast out devils and unclean spirits; and even his brother did he raise from the dead, after he had been stoned and suffered death by the people.

20. And the people saw it, and did witness of it, and were angry with him because of his power; and he did also do many more miracles, in the sight of the people, in the name of Jesus.

21. And it came to pass that the thirty and first year did pass away, and there were but few who were converted unto the Lord; but as many as were converted did truly signify unto the people that they had been visited by the power and Spirit of God, which was in Jesus Christ, in whom they believed.

22. And as many as had devils cast out from them, and were healed of their sicknesses and their infirmities, did truly manifest unto the people that they had been wrought upon by the Spirit of God, and had been healed; and they did show forth signs also and did do some miracles among the people.

23. Thus passed away the thirty and second year also. And Nephi did cry unto the people in

VERSES 18-20. *And the people saw it, and did witness it, and were angry with him because of his power.* Of all the passions, we already have noted, that occupy the human heart, the hatred of apostates for their former brethren is the most bitter and malignant. It is not a far step from anger to hatred; hatred for all that is good, anger for him that does good. With the apostate from God's holy Church the righteous man is berated because of his righteousness, and the evil one is held in repute. Well may we say with King David: "O ye that love the Lord, hate evil," (Psalm 97:10) and how often has history proved his former words to be true: "They that hate the righteous shall be desolate." (*Ibid.*, 34:21) The history of the Nephite tribesmen was one of desolation and destruction.

VERSES 21-22. *The thirty and first year did pass away, and there were but few who were converted unto the Lord.* Despite the untiring labors of Nephi in this part of the Lord's Vineyard, and his continuous ministry among its people, the thirty and first year of Nephite time-keeping passed away but only a few of the disgruntled Nephites were "converted unto the Lord." However, what few there were joined Nephi in the attempt to bring others to an understanding of Christ's mission. They bore testimony to the dissident of the Messiah Whose coming was foretold by Samuel, the Lamanite; and signified "unto the people that they had been visited by the power and Spirit of God, which was in Jesus Christ, in Whom they believed." (v. 21)

Not only did they mingle their cries with those of Nephi, but all who had been healed of any infirmities whatsoever unitedly praised the Lord, and as a witness to God's power that was in them, "did show forth signs also and did do some miracles among the people." (v. 22)

VERSES 23-26. *He did preach unto them repentance and remission of sins.* The thirty-second passed away as did the former year, but nevertheless Nephi and the

the commencement of the thirty and third year; and he did preach unto them repentance and remission of sins.

24. Now I would have you to remember also, that there were none who were brought unto repentance who were not baptized with water.

25. Therefore, there were ordained of Nephi, men unto this ministry, that all such as should come unto them should be baptized with water, and this as a witness and a testimony before God, and unto the people, that they had repented and received a remission of their sins.

26. And there were many in the commencement of this year that were baptized unto repentance; and thus the more part of the year did pass away.

---

faithful ones did not cease their entreaties in the hope that some few at least might forsake their sins and unite themselves with the Saints of God. Their labors were rewarded, for near the beginning of the thirty-third year many were baptized unto repentance.

Mormon makes it clear that *remission of sins* is an important and integral part of the Gospel Plan, and that all men who did repent thereof, and did forswear evil, were baptized with water. Men need repent of their sins, and then follows as logical and reasonable, a remission of their sins. He wants the reader to always keep in mind that *none save those who had been baptized with water were admitted into communion with the Saints and numbered among the people of God's Church.*[4]

To the end that the terms of the prayer many years later expressed by Moroni (*See*, footnote 4) be fulfilled, and that as a testimony to God and His children with whom they in the future should be in communion, Nephi ordained[5] male members of the Church to perform the sacred ordinance of baptism unto all who had repented of their sins, and who resolved to do them no more, their baptism being a witness to all that "they had repented and received a remission of their sins." (v. 25)

---

[4]"And after they had been received unto baptism, and were wrought upon and cleansed by the power of the Holy Ghost, they were numbered among the people of the Church of Christ; and their names were taken, that they might be remembered and nourished by the good word of God, to keep them in the right way, to keep them continually watchful unto prayer, relying alone upon the merits of Christ, Who was the Author and the Finisher of their faith." (Moroni 6:4))

Speaking of the errant one, listen to the words of Jesus Christ: "Nevertheless, ye shall not cast him out from among you, but ye shall minister unto him and pray for him unto the Father in My Name; and if it so be that he repenteth and is baptized in My Name, then shall ye receive him, and shall minister unto him of My flesh and blood. And if he repent not he shall not be numbered among My people, for behold I know My sheep, and they are numbered. Nevertheless, ye shall not cast him out of your synagogues, or your places of worship, for unto such shall ye continue to minister; for ye know not but what they will return and repent, and come unto Me with full purpose of heart, and I shall heal them; and ye shall be the means of bringing Salvation unto them." (III Nephi 30-32)

[5]*See*, Twelve Apostles ordained of God, I Nephi 20:7; Alma, the elder, ordained one priest to every fifty members, Mosiah 18:18; Priests and Elders ordained by Alma, Alma 6:1; Manner in which the Disciples ordained priests and teachers, Moroni, Chapter 3.

CHAPTER 8

1. Christ's Crucifixion Attested by Predicted Signs—2. Tempest and Earthquake, Whirlwind and Fire—3. A Great and Terrible Destruction—4. Three Days of Darkness.

1. Christ's crucifixion attested by predicted signs.

1. And now it came to pass that according to our record, and we know our record to be true, for behold, it was a just man who did keep the record—for he truly did many miracles in the name of Jesus; and there was not any man who could do a miracle in the name of Jesus save he were cleansed every whit from his iniquity—

2. And now it came to pass, if there was no mistake made by this man in the reckoning of our time, the thirty and third year had passed away;

3. And the people began to look with great earnestness for the sign which had been given by the prophet Samuel, the Lamanite, yea, for the time that there should be darkness for the space of three days over the face of the land.

4. And there began to be great doubtings and disputations among the people, notwithstanding so many signs had been given.

VERSES 1-4. *The people began to look for the sign that had been given by Samuel, the Lamanite.* During the turmoil and internecine strife that had beset the Nephite Republic in the years just passed, thereby destroying its capacity to govern and in like manner disarranging the affairs of the Church, there was one man who above all others was firm and steadfast in believing the words of the Lamanite Prophet, Samuel, concerning the death of the Savior. That man was Nephi, the Presiding High Priest of God's Church. According to the record of those times which he devoutly kept, and which he consecrated to the truth, he vowed that the thirty and third year of Nephite reckoning had passed away since the signs of Christ's birth had been given.

Nephi's record is true, Mormon attests, for Nephi was a "just man," he noted. Of the accuracy of that record, there can be no doubt. As a mark of Nephi's reliability, he was not false in any endeavor, the abridger of his record says. "For he truly did many miracles in the Name of Jesus; and there was not any man who could do a miracle in the Name of Jesus save he were cleansed every whit from his iniquity." (v. 1) So, logically, Mormon concluded that if Nephi made no calculable error, he was right in reckoning "the thirty and third year had passed away." (v. 2)

All the people in pursuit of their own happiness, and each walking in his own path, nevertheless, some fearful, others curious, and still others, in wonderment, "began to look with great earnestness for the sign which had been given by the Prophet Samuel, the Lamanite, yea, for the time that there should be darkness for the space of three days over the face of the land." (v. 3)

Notwithstanding the many predictions of the prophets already fulfilled, there was much doubt and uneasiness among the people concerning that which was in the future. They had not long to wait!

2. *Tempest and earthquake, whirlwind and fire.*

5. And it came to pass in the thirty and fourth year, in the first month, on the fourth day of the month, there arose a great storm, such an one as never had been known in all the land.

6. And there was also a great and terrible tempest; and there was terrible thunder, insomuch that it did shake the whole earth as if it was about to divide asunder.

7. And there were exceeding sharp lightnings, such as never had been known in all the land.

8. And the city of Zarahemla did take fire.

9. And the city of Moroni did sink into the depths of the sea, and the inhabitants thereof were drowned.

10. And the earth was carried up upon the city of Moronihah that in the place of the city there became a great mountain.

11. And there was a great and terrible destruction in the land southward.

12. But behold, there was a more great and terrible destruction in the land northward; for behold, the whole face of the land was changed, because of the tempest and the whirlwinds, and the thunderings and the lightnings, and the exceeding great quaking of the whole earth;

13. And the highways were broken up, and the level roads were spoiled, and many smooth places became rough.

14. And many great and notable cities were sunk, and many were burned, and many were shaken till the buildings thereof had fallen to the earth, and the inhabitants thereof were slain, and the places were left desolate.

15. And there were some cities which remained; but the damage thereof was exceeding great, and there were many of them who were slain.

16. And there were some who were carried away in the whirlwind; and whither they went no

---

VERSES 5-18. *There arose a great storm.* On the fourth day of the thirty-fourth Nephite year the promised signs of the Savior's crucifixion began. A horrible and devastating tempest burst upon the land. All that was ever told of the loudest thunder, and all that was ever seen of the most vivid lightning, would fail to picture the terrific visitation. The earth quivered and groaned and opened in wide, unfathomable chasms. Forests of gigantic trees were uprooted and carried high above the earth to meet in fearful shocks in the air and then driven down and shattered upon unyielding rocks. Mountains were riven and swallowed up in yawning gulfs, or were scattered into fragments and dispersed like hail before the tearing wind. Cattle were lifted from their feet and dashed over precipices, or were hurled before the blast to perish in the sea. Towers, temples, and homes, were torn up, shattered into fragments or crushed by falling rocks, and together with their inmates were ground to dust in the convulsion. Human beings were hurled high into the air and driven from point to point, until, at last, they found graves fathoms deep below the earth's surface. Blue and yellow flames burst from the edges of sinking rocks, blazed for a moment and then was the deepest darkness. Boiling springs gushed upwards from sulphurous caverns. Shrieks and howls from suffering animals, awful in them-man knoweth, save they know that they were carried away.

17. And thus the face of the whole earth became deformed, because of the tempests, and the thunderings, and the lightnings, and the quaking of the earth.

18. And behold, the rocks were rent in twain; they were broken up upon the face of the whole earth, insomuch that they were found in broken fragments, and in seams and in cracks, upon all the face of the land.

3. A great and terrible destruction.

19. And it came to pass that when the thunderings, and the lightnings, and the storm, and the tempest, and the quakings of the earth did cease—for behold, they did last for about the space of three hours; and it was said by some that the time was greater; nevertheless, all these great and terrible things were done in about the space of three hours—and then behold, there was darkness upon the face of the land.

4. Three days of darkness.

20. And it came to pass that there was thick darkness upon all the face of the land, insomuch that the inhabitants thereof who had not fallen could feel the vapor of darkness;

21. And there could be no light, because of the darkness, neither candles, neither torches; neither could there be fire kindled with their fine and exceedingly dry wood, so that there could not be any light at all;

22. And there was not any

---

selves, were drowned out in the overwhelming uproar. Rain poured down in torrents; cloudbursts, like floods, washed away all with which they came in contact, and pillars of steaming vapor seemed to unite the earth and sky.

This unparalleled storm raged throughout the land for three hours only — but to those who suffered through it, it seemed an age.

VERSE 19. *Darkness upon the face of the land.* During the short continuance of the storm the whole face of nature changed. Mountains sank, valleys rose, the sea swept over the plains, large stagnant pools of water usurped the place of flourishing cities; great chasms and precipices disfigured the face of the earth. Many cities were destroyed by earthquakes, fire, and the tumultuous overflow of the waters of the great seas.

We have noted that all these things, great and terrible, happened in three hours, and when at length they subsided, darkness "was upon all the face of the land."

VERSES 20-25. *Darkness did last for the space of three days.* When the storm had abated somewhat in its fury, and the earth quieted its pains; when the rain ceased its deluge, darkness, so dense that it could be felt, covered the land. There was not a ray of light to illumine its blackness. The Sacred Record says: "There was not any light seen, neither fire, nor glimmer, neither the Sun, nor the Moon, nor the stars, for so great were the mists of darkness which were upon the face of the land." (v. 22) It added despair and dismay, to the already distressed people.

For three days and three nights all was dark. To the inhabitants of this favored

light seen, neither fire, nor glimmer, neither the sun, nor the moon, nor the stars, for so great were the mists of darkness which were upon the face of the land.

23. And it came to pass that it did last for the space of three days that there was no light seen; and there was great mourning and howling and weeping among all the people continually; yea, great were the groanings of the people, because of the darkness and the great destruction which had come upon them.

24. And in one place they were heard to cry, saying: O that we had repented before this great

and terrible day, and then would our brethren have been spared, and they would not have been burned in that great city Zarahemla.

25. And in another place they were heard to cry and mourn, saying: O that we had repented before this great and terrible day, and had not killed and stoned the prophets, and cast them out; then would our mothers and our fair daughters, and our children have been spared, and not have been buried up in that great city Moronihah. And thus were the howlings of the people great and terrible.

land, who had not fallen victims of the overwhelming catastrophe, three days seemed endless. They mourned the loss of loved ones, and friends who vanished in the night. Despair and anguish took possession of their souls. They wept and howled.[1] It was the custom among oriental peoples, from whom the ancestors of the Nephites came, to wail, loudly and long because of the death of a loved one. They often hired mourners to howl, showing by the noise made, the extent of their grief.

VERSES 24-25. *O that we had repented before this great and terrible day.* Remorse, like a gnawing pain, excited by a sense of guilt, mingled with a repentant regret, took possession of each sufferer's conscience. An awareness of his own blameworthiness together with a feeling of obligation that if there was any future, to do only good, collectively lifted them out of the moral depths into which they had plunged, and restored in them the hopes expressed in the prophets' words which they had rejected. "And in one place," the Sacred Record says, "'they were heard to cry, saying: O that we had repented before this great and terrible day, and then would our brethren have been spared, and they would not have been burned in that great City Zarahemla." And still in another place the lamentations of the people, the cries of the fatherless and the widow, the sick and afflicted, mixed with the mournful dirge of the dead or the dying, prompted the awful conclusion: "O that we had repented before this great and terrible day, and not killed the prophets, and cast them out; then would our mothers and our fair daughters, and our children have been spared, and not have been buried up in that great City Moronihah. . . ." (v. 25) Thus there was a continuous round of mourning, weeping, and howling, heard throughout the whole land.

---

[1]"And it came to pass that when it was night they were weary, and retired to their camps; and after they had retired to their camps they took up a howling and a lamentation for the loss of the slain of their people; and so great were their cries, their howlings and lamentations, that they did rend the air exceedingly.

"And it came to pass that on the morrow they did go again to battle, and great and terrible was that day; nevertheless, they conquered not, and when the night came again they did rend the air with their cries, and their howlings, and their mournings, for the loss of the slain of their people." (Ether 15:16-17)

CHAPTER 9

1. *The Voice of God Proclaims the Extent of the Disaster and Declares the Cause Thereof*—2. *The Law of Moses Fulfilled*—3. *The Acceptable Sacrifice of a Broken Heart and a Contrite Spirit.*

1. *The Voice of God proclaims the extent of the disaster.*

1. And it came to pass that there was a voice heard among all the inhabitants of the earth, upon all the face of this land, crying:

2. Wo, wo, wo unto this people; wo unto the inhabitants of the whole earth except they shall repent; for the devil laugheth, and his angels rejoice, because of the slain of the fair sons and daughters of my people; and it is because of their iniquity and abominations that they are fallen!

3. Behold, that great city Zarahemla have I burned with fire, and the inhabitants thereof.

4. And behold, that great city Moroni have I caused to be sunk in the depths of the sea, and the inhabitants thereof to be drowned.

5. And behold, that great city Moronihah have I covered with earth, and the inhabitants thereof, to hide their iniquities and their abominations from before my face, that the blood of the prophets and the saints shall not come any more unto me against them.

6. And behold, the city of Gilgal have I caused to be sunk, and the inhabitants thereof to be buried up in the depths of the earth;

7. Yea, and the city of Onihah and the inhabitants thereof, and the city of Mocum and the inhabitants thereof, and the city of Jerusalem and the inhabitants thereof; and waters have I caused to come up in the stead thereof, to hide their wickedness and abominations from before my face, that the blood of the prophets and the saints shall not come up any more unto me against them.

8. And behold, the city of Gadiandi, and the city of Gadiomnah, and the city of Jacob, and the city of Gimgimno, all these have I caused to be sunk, and made hills and valleys in the places thereof;

VERSES 1-12. *There was a voice heard among all the inhabitants of . . . this land.* Out of the darkness, whence no one knew, the Voice of the Lord was heard by the affrighted people, proclaiming in their terrified ears the destruction that had taken place.

It was not a harsh Voice, although it was a *Voice of Warning*; it sounded repentance, and admonished righteousness. "The devil laugheth," said the Voice, "and his angels rejoice," because of their joyous satisfaction in seeing their faithful, but misguided, followers perish. The Nephites were a branch of the House of Israel, and the iniquity of its fair sons and daughters was a triumph of evil. To save them from the errors of their way they were destroyed. Wherefore, were these things done.

and the inhabitants thereof have I buried up in the depths of the earth, to hide their wickedness and abominations from before my face, that the blood of the prophets and the saints should not come up any more unto me against them.

9. And behold, that great city Jacobugath, which was inhabited by the people of king Jacob, have I caused to be burned with fire because of their sins and their wickedness, which was above all the wickedness of the whole earth, because of their secret murders and combinations; for it was they that did destroy the peace of my people and the government of the land; therefore I did cause them to be burned, to destroy them from before my face, that the blood of the prophets and the saints should not come up unto me any more against them.

10. And behold, the city of Laman, and the city of Josh, and the city of Gad, and the city of Kishkumen, have I caused to be burned with fire, and the inhabitants thereof, because of their wickedness in casting out the prophets, and stoning those whom I did send to declare unto them concerning their wickedness and their abominations.

11. And because they did cast them all out, that there were none righteous among them, I did send down fire and destroy them, that their wickedness and abominations might be hid from before my face, that the blood of the prophets and the saints whom I sent among them might not cry unto me from the ground against them.

12. And many great destructions have I caused to come upon this land, and upon this people, because of their wickedness and their abominations.

In pronouncing Wo, wo, wo, unto all the inhabitants of the earth who do wickedly, and not repent thereof, the Voice foretold that a miserable and sorrowful state awaits all them who will not heed the words of the prophets; Their words are My words, we conceive the Voice of the Lord saying, "For I am He Who speaketh." (Ether 4:8)

Terrible was the catalogue of woes that this Heavenly Voice rehearsed. The great City of Zarahemla and its inhabitants, God had caused to be burned with fire. Moroni was sunken in the depths of the sea and her iniquitous children had been drowned. Gilgal had been swallowed up in an earthquake, and her people were entombed in the bowels of the earth. Onihah, Mocum, and Jerusalem had disappeared, and waters overflowed the places where they so lately stood. Gadiandi, Gadiomnah, Jacob, and Gimgimno, were all overthrown, and desolation where new hills and valleys occupied their places, while their inhabitants were buried deep in the earth. Jacobugath, Laman, Josh, Gad, and Kishkumen, had all been burned, most likely by lightnings from heaven. The desolation was almost complete; the face of the earth was changed, and tens of thousands, probably more, of souls had been suddenly called to meet the reward of their sinful lives. For their destruction came upon them so that their wickedness and abominations might be hid from Heaven, and that the blood of the prophets and the Saints whom the wicked had slain might not come up any more in appeal unto God against them.

VERSE 12. *And many great destructions have I caused to come upon this land, and upon this people, because of their wickedness and abominations.* This land, both North and South America, is the Land of Zion. The land in the north is called by the Book of Mormon the *Land of Mulek.* We call it *America.* Translated, it means *The Land of the King,* or *The Land of the Lord, our King.* That is *The Land of Zion.*[1] It is a choice land,[2] and all who dwell thereon, under the penalty of God's displeasure if they do not, shall serve Him. He has appointed us to do His bidding. If we do so, blessings await us; if we do not, justice will be ours. The blessing God promised the fathers of the Nephite and Lamanite races — Lehi and his sons, that those who live in this land and are firm and steadfast in keeping the commandments of the Lord shall be prospered and otherwise blessed — is a promise to us who live here now and those who ever shall, even as it was to the seed of Lehi and Nephi. The Lord does not forget His promises!

GENERAL NOTES

VERSE 12

This Land — THE LAND OF ZION (*See,* Chapter 20:14)
THE NAME AMERICA — THE ACCEPTED THEORY OF ITS ORIGIN—
THE MORE PROBABLE THEORY

AMERICA. We have already seen, under *Mulek,* that, according to Prof. Jules Marcou, *America* is an American name, and the suggestion was offered that the root of the word is the same as that of *Mulek.* It remains to consider, briefly, the accepted theory of the origin of the name. (*See,* Volume III, COMMENTARY ON THE BOOK OF MORMON, p. 328ff)

"The naming of the Western Continent which has since been known as America took its rise from a voyage made in 1499 by Amerigo Vespucci, a distinguished Florentine navigator. Vespucci wrote a number of letters in Latin to Lorenzo de Medici, one of which was printed in 1505, and was the first of his narratives published. On September 4, 1504, he wrote a letter from Lisbon to Rene, Duke of Lorraine, in which he claimed to have discovered the mainland in 1497. As Vespucci was a man of superior learning and intelligence, and his name was thus publicly connected with the New World, as the discoverer of the continent—although he was not the first to reach *Terra Firma*—Columbus, Cabot, and others having preceded him—the well known cosmographer, Martin Waldseemuller, of Fribourg, patronized by Renè, decided in 1507 to give the New World the name of America."[3]

This is a concise and correct statement of the popular theory concerning the origin of the glorious name of our Country and Continent. But does it really rest on facts?

MEANING OF AMERIGO. As to the meaning of the name, Prof. Fiske informs us that *Amerigo* "is an Italianized form of the old German *Amalrich* which in medieval French became *Amaury,*" and that it means *the steadfast.*[4]

---

[1]*See Mulek,* Volume II, p. 328, COMMENTARY ON THE BOOK OF MORMON, Also, *See* General Notes at end of this Chapter.

[2]"And inasmuch as ye shall keep My commandments, ye shall prosper, and shall be led to a land of promise; yea, even a land which I have prepared for you; a land which is choice above all other lands." (I Nephi 2:20)

"Wherefore, I will consecrate this land unto thy seed, and them who shall be numbered among thy seed, forever, for the land of their inheritance; for it is a choice land, saith God unto me, above all other lands, wherefore I will have all men that dwell thereon that they shall worship Me, saith God." (II Nephi 10:19)

"And the Lord would not suffer that they should stop beyond the sea in the wilderness, but He would that they should come forth even unto the Land of Promise, which was choice above all other lands, which the Lord God had preserved for a righteous people." (Ether 2:7)

"And thus the Lord did pour out His blessings upon this land, which was choice above all other lands; and He commanded that whoso should possess the land should possess it unto the Lord, or they should be destroyed when they were ripened in iniquity; for upon such, saith the Lord: I will pour out the fulness of My wrath." (Ether 9:20)

[3]*The United States,* edited by Edwin Wiley, M.A., Ph.D., of the Library of Congress; and Irving E. Rimes; Vol. 1, p. 113.

[4]*Discovery of America,* Vol. 2, p. 24.

THE ORTHODOX THEORY NOT UNDISPUTED. Most readers of history take it for granted that the naming of America after Vespucci is an indisputable and undisputed historic fact. But this is far from the truth. The Amerigo-theory has been under fire of controversy ever since its first appearance in the realm of letters. It has been pointed out, in the first place, that Vespucci was not the discoverer of America at all, Columbus, and Cabot, and others having preceded him; in the second place, that the country could not, consistently, have been named after him, because he never was the commander of an expedition to the New World. It is not the custom to name a new land, or sea, or river, after the mate or the pilot or any other subordinate officer. It is the commander who is the discoverer, not the pilot. Sanch Ruiz, the pilot of Columbus, would never be mentioned as the discoverer of the West Indies. Nor would Estevan Gomez be regarded as the discoverer of the Straits of Magellan, although he was the pilot of the ill-fated sailor. Why, then, should we be required to believe that an absurd exception has been made in favor of Vespucci?

The story of the Florentine in 1497 is, and always has been, disputed, because of lack of evidence. Mr. Bancroft presents the arguments on both sides,[5] and then sums up the case thus: "To me the proofs seem conclusive that Vespucci made no voyage to South America prior to 1499, when he accompanied Alonzo de Ojeda. Against a North American expedition the evidence, if less conclusive, is still very strong since the most that can be claimed in its favor is a probability that the Central American coast was visited by some navigator before 1502, and a possibility, though certainly a slim one, that Vespucci accompanied such navigator."

In other words, in the opinion of Mr. Bancroft, there is no evidence that Vespucci made an American voyage in 1497, either to North or South America. Emerson was almost vehement in his denunciation of the Amerigo-theory. He gave vent to his feelings thus: "Strange that broad America must wear the name of a thief! Amerigo Vespucci, the pickle-dealer at Seville, who went out in 1499, a subaltern with Ojeda, and whose highest naval rank was boatswain's mate in an expedition that never sailed, managed in this lying world to supplant Columbus and baptize half the earth with his own dishonest name."[6]

PROF. MARCOU'S OBJECTIONS. Prof. Jules Marcou, whose article in the *Atlantic Monthly* for March, 1875, goes into the subject thoroughly, points out that the first name is never used in geography, to honor a person, except in the case of royalty. We say, Louisiana, Carolina, Maryland, Victoria, etc., in honor of crowned heads; but the Straits of Magellan, Vancouver's Island, Tasmania, Van Dieman's Land, etc., after common mortals. According to this rule, our country ought to be called Vesputia, or some such name, in honor of Vespucci. In our judgment this argument is unanswerable.[7] There is no doubt a blunder was committed, both historical and philological, when the conclusion was jumped at that *America* somehow was derived from *Amerigo*, or *Albericus* which was the name Waldseemuller knew. It is more probable that *America* was coined after *Amerique* or *Maraca*—indigenous American words—than that *America* was invented in honor of *Albericus*. Somehow the cart has been put before the horse in this instance.

MONTESINOS' SPELLING. Montesinos always wrote *Hamerica* intead of *America*. The odd explanation of that peculiarity is that he wanted letters enough to make the anagram *hec Maria* out of the name. But that seems to be far-fetched. It is

[5]*The History of Central America*, Vol. 6, pp. 100-106.

[6]*English Traits*, 1856, (p. 148, Riverside Ed. 1883); quoted by Fiske, *Discovery of America*, Vol. 2, p. 162.

[7]Students of this interesting subject are no longer as sure as they used to be that *America* was really named after or in honor of Amerigo. In August, 1922, the house in which Waldseemuller—as is supposed—wrote the pamphlet in which the two names were, erroneously, connected, was sold at auction. The press dispatch announcing this event was dated Paris, France, August 12, 1922, and began thus: "That Amerigo Vespucci's name should have suggested the appelation of the new continent discovered by Columbus was an historical blunder that has been consecrated by time." On the 12th of March, the same year, a press dispatch from Berlin, Germany, characterized Vespucci as a *swindler*, who never saw America. But that dispatch added, "It would be a pity to explode the bubble of his fame after a lapse of more than four hundred years, during which he has held an honored place in the annals of his native city of Florence, side by side with her other illustrious sons, such as Dante and Michelangelo."

more probable that, during his many years of residence and travel in America, he had heard the name pronounced with an *h*. That would seem to him a justification for regarding it as an anagram of the name of the Virgin. If he had added the *h* himself, it would have been no argument for his favorite theory. But his supposition that the name was made up of the letters in the name of Mary proves that he, at least, did not accept the Amerigo-theory.[8]

AMERICA AND AMALEKI. In the article previously referred to, we have made the statement that *America* is, both in form and meaning, identical with the Book of Mormon names *Amaleki* and *Amalickiah*. These words consist of three parts, *a*, which is the same as the Hebrew definite article,[9] *the; malek*, or *malick*, which mean *king;* and *i*, or *iah*, which mean *Jehovah*. Compare A-meric-a with *Amaleki*, or *Amalickiah*, and note how close the resemblance is. The only difference is that between the *r* and the *l*, but that is a difference in appearance only, not in reality.

This statement may need further explanation.

Franz Boaz, in his *Handbook of American Indian Languages*,[10] gives us this information.

"Certain sounds that occur in American languages are interpreted by observers sometimes as one European sound, sometimes as another. Thus the Pawnee language contains a sound which may be heard more or less distinctly sometimes as an *l*, sometimes as an *r*, sometimes as *n*, and again *d*, which, however, without any doubt, is throughout the same sound, although modified to a certain extent by its position in the word, and by surrounding sounds. It is an exceedingly weak *r*, made by trilling with the tip of the tongue at a point a little behind the roots of the incisors, and in which the tongue hardly leaves the palate, the trill being produced by the lateral part of the tongue adjoining the tip. As soon as the trill is heard more strongly we receive the impression of an *r*. When the lateral movement prevails and the tip of the tongue does not seem to leave the palate, the impression of an *l* is strongest."

Mr. Boaz also says that the *r*-sound is rare in the languages of the American Indians, and that the trill of it is so weak it merges into *l, d, n*, or *y*, as the case may be.

The conclusion from this is that the *l-sound*, in all probability, is the original sound, and that the *r*-sound is a secondary linguistic acquisition; that, in other words, the *l*-sound in Am-aleki was first in point of time, and that the *r*-sound in A-merica is, virtually, the same sound, or the latter variant of it. In some Indian dialects the *l* is retained in *America*. The Choctaws, for instance, call our country, *Miliki*.[11] For king their word is *Minko*, in which the *l* in Mulek has merged into a sort of nasal sound instead of one represented by our *r*.

Garcilasso de la Vega, speaking of the *Quichua*, the Cusco dialect, says, it lacks six letters used in the Spanish alphabet, one of which is *l*. *R*, he says, "Takes its place," as *peru* for *pelu; Rimac*, "he who speaks," as an oracle, for *Lima*, etc. That accounts for the change of *Amalek* to *Amarek*. A conspicuous change from *l* to *r* in North America is found in the word *Oregon* from *Oligon-unk*, which Rafinesque says means *hollow mountain*.[12]

This peculiarity is, by no means, confined to the American languages. According to Champollion the Egyptian hieroglyph for *l*, the *lion couche*, was the equivalent of the Hebrew *lamed*, but in Greek and Latin proper nouns it was rendered by an *r*.[13] The old Latin *tellus*, earth, or ground, has become *terra*, in later Latin, and tlalli in the old Mexican.[14]

---

[8]*Memorias Antiguas Historiales del Peru*, Hakluyt Society, London, 1920, p. 2.

[9]The article was originally *hal*. This became *ha* in Hebrew and *al* in the Arabic, and, probably, *a* in some of the American languages; a soft aspirant like the Hebrew *aleph*.

[10]*Bulletin 40*, Smithsonian Institute. Inst. Part I, pp. 16-17.

[11]*Choctaw Dictionary*, Cyrus Byington, Smithsonian Institution, Bulletin 46, Washington, D. C., 1915.

[12]*The American Nations*, Vol. 1, p. 154.

[13]*Precis du Systeme Hieroglyphique des Anciens Egyptiens*, Paris, France, 1824, pp. 59 and 63.

[14]*The Primitive Aryans in America*, Denison, p. 45. Just as Malcolm of the Hebrews became Marcus among the Romans.

AMERICA AND MULEK. From all this, the evolution of the name of America is as plain as the transformation of any word the origin of which is supposed to be known. The first Aryan roots *mol-ik* became *molouk* in Egyptian and *melech* in Hebrew. Among the descendants of Lehi in this part of the world it became *Mulek*, and from this stem, the words *Amaleki, Amalickiah*, and others branched out. These names became *marca, Americ, Amerique*, and finally, *America*.

There is less difference between *America*, and the root words *mol-ik* than there is between some of the familiar Old Testament names, as written in other records. Compare the following, which are the same names in two languages:

Hebrew	Egyptian
Zerah (II Chron. 14:9)	Usahkon
Shishak (I Kings 11:40)	Sheshenq
Hittite	Khati
Jerusalem, or Jerushalaim	Ourousalimou
Joseph	Joshoupilu
Hebrew	Apouriou (?)

Compare, further, Amraphel (Genesis 14:1) with Hammurabi (or with Amara-pal); Noph (Isaiah 19:13) with Memphis; the Hebrew Jochanan (or Johana) with our name John, or its various modern forms, such as Johannes, Johan, Janne, Juan, Jean, Ivan, etc. This will help us to realize that the suggestions made now and the preceding ones, are well within the laws by which the evolution of words is governed.

THE N(ME FOUND IN NICARAGUA. Under *Mulek* it is stated that the name *America*, or, which is the same, *Amerique*, or *Amerrique* was found by the noted English traveler and scientist, Thomas Belt, to be an Indian name of a mountain range, and that he so states in his *Naturalist in Nicaragua*.

The Pan-American offices in Washington, D. C., has kindly furnished us with a copy of this famous work, and from it we are able to produce a copy of the passage we refer to:

"We gradually ascended the range that separates the watershed of the Lake of Nicaragua from that of the Blewfields River, passing over grassy savannahs. About two leagues from Libertad there are many old Indian graves, covered with mounds of earth and stones. A well-educated Englishman, Mr. Fairbairn, has taken up his abode at this place, and is growing maize and rearing cattle. There are many evidences of a large Indian population having lived at this spot, and their pottery and fragments of their stones for bruising maize have been found in some graves that have been opened. Mr. Fairbairn got me several of these curiosities, amongst them are imitations of the heads of armadillos, and other animals. Some of these had formed the feet of urns, others were rattles, containing small balls of baked clay. The old Indians used these rattles in their solemn religious dances, and the custom is probably not yet quite obsolete, for as late as 1823 Mr. W. Bullock saw, in Mexico, Indian women dancing in a masque representing the court of Montesuma, and holding rattles in their right hands, to the noise of which they accompanied their motions. Several stone axes have been found, which are called 'thunderbolts' by the natives, who have no idea that they are artificial, although it is less than four hundred years ago since their forefathers used them. Like most of the ancient Indian towns, the place is a very picturesque one. At a short distance to the west, rise great perpendicular cliffs, and huge isolated rocks and pinnacles. The name of this range gives us a clue to the race of the ancient inhabitants. In the highlands of Honduras, as has been noted by Squier, the termination of *tique* or *rique* is of frequent occurrence in the names of places as *Chaparristique, Lepaterique, Llotique, Ajuterique*, and others. The race that inhabited this region were the Lenca Indians, often mentioned in the accounts given by the missionaries of their early expeditions into Honduras. I think that the Lenca Indians were the ancient inhabitants of Chontales, that they were the 'Chontals' of the Nahuatls or Aztecs of the Pacific side of the country, and that they were partly conquered, and their territories encroached upon by the latter before the arrival of the Spaniards, as some of the Aztec names of Places in Nicaragua do not appear to be such as could be given originally by the first inhabitants; thus Juigalpa, pronounced Hueygalpa, is southern Aztec for 'Big Town.' "—Thomas Belt, F.C.S., *The Naturalist in Nicaragua*, Chapter 9, p. 154.

"The site of Juigalpa is beautifully chosen, as is usual with the old Indian towns. It is on a level, dry piece of land, about three hundred feet above the river. A rocky brook behind the town supplies the water for drinking and cooking purposes. The large square or plaza has the church at one end; on the other three sides are red-tiled adobe houses and stores, with floors of clay or red bricks. Streets branch off at right angles from the square, and are crossed by others. The best houses are those nearest the square. Those on the outskirts are mere thatched hovels, with open sides of bamboo poles. The house I stayed at was at the corner of one of the square blocks, and from the angle the view extended in four directions along the level roads. Each way the prospect was bounded by hills in the distance, northeast were the white cliffs of the *Amerrique* range, mantled with dark woods. The intervening country could not be seen, and only a small portion of the range itself; framed in, as it were, by the sides of the street. It looked close at hand, like a piece of artificial rockery, or the grey walls of a castle covered with ivy. The range to the southwest is several miles distant; and is called San Miguelito by the Spaniards, but I could not learn its Indian name."—*Ibid.*, Chapter 10, p. 176.

"Having finished our business in Juigalpa, we arranged to start on our return early the next morning, Velasquez going round by Acoyapo whilst Rito accompanied me to the mines. I had a fowl cooked overnight to take with us, and set off at six o'clock. I shall make some remarks on the road on points not touched on in my account of the journey out. After leaving Juigalpa, we descended to the river by a rocky and steep path, crossed it, and then passed over alluvial plains, interesected by a few nearly dry river beds, to the foot of the southwestern side of the *Amerrique* hills, then gradually ascended the range that separates the Juigalpa district from that of Libertad. The ground was gravelly and dry, with stony hillocks covered with low trees and bushes."—*Ibid.*, Chapter 10, p. 178.

"At last we reached the summit of the range, which is probably not less than three thousand feet above the sea, and entered on the district of Libertad. Rounded boggy hills covered with grass, sedgy plants and stunted trees, replaced the dry gravelly soil of the Juigalpa district."—*Ibid.*, Chapter 10, p. 183.

"Our road, now lay over the damp grassy hills of the Libertad district. It edged away from the *Amerrique* range on our right. To our left, about three miles distant, rose the dark sinuous line of the great forest of the Atlantic slope. Only a fringe of dark-foliaged trees in the foreground was visible, the higher ground behind was shrouded in a sombre pall of thick clouds that never lifted, but seemed to cover a gloomy and mysterious country beyond. Though I had dived into the recesses of these mountains again and again, and knew that they were covered with beautiful vegetation and full of animal life, yet the sight of that leaden-colored barrier of cloud resting on the forest tops, whilst the savannahs were bathed in sunshine, ever raised in my mind vague sensations of the unknown and the unfathomable. Our course was nearly parallel to this gloomy forest, but we gradually approached it. The line that separates it from the grassy savannahs is sinuous and irregular. In some places a dark promontory of trees juts out into the savannahs, in others a green grassy hill is seen almost surrounded by forest."—*Ibid.*, Chapter 10, p. 184.

"As we rode on, the grass increased, there were swampy places in the hollows, and now and then very muddy spots on the road. On every side the prospect was bounded by long ranges of hills—some of them precipitous, others covered to the summits with dark foliaged trees, looking nearly black in the distance. About noon we came in sight of the Amerrique range, which I recognized at once, and know that we had reached the Juigalpa district, though still several leagues distant from the town."—*Ibid.*, Chapter 17, p. 324.

We have italicized the name Amerrique.

In connection with this the following information, secured from authentic sources at Washington, is important and interesting:

In the book entitled *Nicaragua*, by E. G. Squier, published in Boston, 1860, the orographic system to which the highlands in question belong is thus described:

2. The Law of Moses fulfilled.

13. O all ye that are spared because ye were more righteous than they, will ye not now return unto me, and repent of your sins, and be converted, that I may heal you?

"The second or principal mountain range, the great backbone of the continent and the true Cordilleras, enters the state from Honduras in the Department of Nueva Segovia and extends due southeast until it strikes the San Juan River at a point about fifty miles above its mouth. It sends out numerous spurs or dependent ranges towards the Atlantic, between which flow down the many considerable streams that intersect what is called the Mosquito Shore."

Another reference to these mountains is found in a book by the French traveler, Paul Levy, published in Paris, 1873. Levy designates this range as the "Honduran-Nicaraguan Range," following the authority of the German geographer, Berghaus (*Physikalischen Atlas*, Dresden, 1838).

Felix Belly, another French explorer, uses the same general denomination in his work *A travers l'Amerique Centrale,* Paris, 1867.

La Republica de Nicaragua, an official guide published by the Nicaraguan government in 1900, gives a description of the orography of the country which follows the terminology of Berghaus.

In a letter to the writers from the staff of the Nicaraguan government in Washington, D. C., we quote the following:

"The work of the celebrated English scientist, Thomas Belt, entitled *The Naturalist in Nicaragua,* and first published in London in 1873, is the one in which the name 'Amerrique' is given to the highlands between Juigalpa and la Libertad. Mr. Belt lived in the province of Chontales from 1868 to 1872 and was employed as Superintendent of the Chontales Gold Mining Company. He traveled extensively through Nicaragua and while his assertion regarding this name is not confirmed by other travelers and geographers, this fact will only prove that the use of such name was or is restricted to a small and somewhat isolated region of the country. The authority of Mr. Belt as a keen observer and an accurate writer is very high and there is no possibility of error in statements of this kind, contained in a book recognized as a classic among the literature of natural history. A copy of the passages from the book where the name 'Amerrique' appears is enclosed."

It is, then, an indisputable fact that the name *America* is an original American word, much older than both Vespucci and Waldseemuller. It is, perhaps, still applied to the mountain region described by Mr. Belt, and in its several variations it is found practically all over the American continents.

Mr. Belt's discovery is of special interest to readers of the Book of Mormon, as an indication of a Mulekite origin of the name of the mountain district he describes.

Prof. Marcou was of the opinion that *America* is the accepted form of the old Indian *Americ* or *Amerique,* and not, as generally held, a name coined in glorification of Amerigo Vespucci. If this view is correct, *America* is, both in form and meaning, identical with the Book of Mormon names, *Amaleki* and *Amalickiah,* the meaning of which is, "The King of Jehovah," and, as applied to the country, "The Land of the King of Jehovah"; that is to say, in other words, *The Land of Zion.*

VERSES 13-18. *In Me is the Law of Moses fulfilled.* When the heavenly Voice had finished the recital of the calamities that had befallen the land and its inhabitants, the Speaker commenced an appeal to those who yet lived, and revealed to them Who He was.

VERSE 13. *That I may heal you.* The solemn benediction pronounced by the heavenly Voice upon the "fear-becrazed" survivors of the great catastrophe that had engulfed the entire Nephite Land, gave hope and courage to its distraught people who were about to despair. The Lord, seeing their distress, pitied them, and said: "Whosoever will come, him will I receive; and blessed are those who come unto

14. Yea, verily I say unto you, if ye will come unto me ye shall have eternal life. Behold, mine arm of mercy is extended towards you, and whosoever will come, him will I receive; and blessed are those who come unto me.

15. Behold, I am Jesus Christ the Son of God. I created the heavens and the earth, and all things that in them are. I was with the Father from the beginning. I am in the Father, and the Father in me; and in me hath the Father glorified his name.

Me." (v. 14) Strongly marked with Heaven's gracious command, were other blessings the Voice proclaimed, chiefest among these was the promise "that I may heal you." (v. 13) Repentance was the condition thereof, "and a return unto Me," the price. We understand the phrase, "that I may heal you," means, make whole from any and all afflictions whatsoever, especially, those of the spirit.

VERSE 14. *Come unto Me.* This verse seems to indicate that of all human achievements, to gain Eternal Life in God's Kingdom is the greatest of any. Eternal Life is God's most precious gift to His children. The gracious invitation of the giver of that divine utterance, "Come unto Me," made His request more alluring by Himself offering aid to the weak and weary, to the helpless and those who have no helper but the Lord. We are strongly reminded of a story that Jesus told His disciples in Old Jerusalem. In the *Parable of the Lost Sheep* He likens His followers to sheep, and Himself to their Shepherd. As a Good Shepherd He watches over His flock continually, and when in want, gives His sheep succor according to the hour and the power of their need. In this verse He says: "*My arm of mercy is extended towards you.*" He is the Helper, the Shepherd! The poor, stray sheep may be lost in the woods, hunted by the wolf, fallen over the precipice, hungry, helpless, and cold. But the Good Shepherd is on His way, and is looking for it, and will find it, and will take it in His arms, and will carry it to the fold, and with his friends and neighbors will rejoice that the lost is found and the dead is again alive. While the words, "Come unto Me," are an expression of divine hope, still we must remember, "Thy word, O God, is my law."

VERSES 15-18. *Behold, I am Jesus Christ the Son of God.* With great power the Voice declared: "I am Jesus Christ the Son of God," thereby witnessing to all who heard that the owner thereof was high in the Councils of Heaven, and had unquestioned authority to declare its blessings. "I created the heavens and the earth, and all that in them are," the Voice again declared; so we ask, "Why should not the elements from which they are made obey His will?"[15] All things obey His will. The infirmities of the flesh, the imposts life lays, the burdens carried to the grave, are often blessings coming from Him to us in disguise, and that in healing these afflictions the Lord rebukes the destroyer, and places the repentant sinner beyond the power of evil. "That," the Prophet Joseph Smith said, "is Eternal Life." "If ye will come unto Me ye shall have Eternal Life." (v. 14)

I was with the Father from the beginning. Jesus Christ, the Son of God, alone, is the *Only-Begotten of the Father,* but He also was the *First* born to God in the World of Spirits. That was the beginning of which Christ speaks in verse 15. He was with His Father in all the works accomplished by His Father. The grand Creation was done under His Father's supervision.

---

[15]"Behold, by the power of His word man came upon the face of the earth, which earth was created by the power of His word. Wherefore, if God being able to speak and the world was, and to speak and man was created, O then, why not able to command the earth, or the workmanship of His hands upon the face of it, according to His will and pleasure?" (Jacob 4:9)

I am in the Father, and the Father in Me. This is not a difficult passage. It means that the desire of one, is the desire of the other; Their purpose is the same, to bring about the Salvation and Eternal Life of man. Their aim, that for which They strive, is mutual. No dissensions, no disagreement in opinion, no discord between Them; They are alike in manner, form, and degree.

Christ, Himself, when He ministered to the Nephites in the Land Bountiful, chose Twelve Disciples to minister for Him after He was gone, and the prayer He offered to His Father in Heaven, thanking Him for them, is a full and complete explanation of the sentiment He expressed in this verse (15): "Father, thou hast given them the Holy Ghost because they believe in Me; and Thou seest that they believe in Me because Thou hearest them, and they pray unto Me; and they pray unto Me because I am with them. And now Father, I pray unto Thee for them, and also for all those who shall believe their words, that they may believe in Me, that I may be in them as Thou, Father, art in Me, that we may be one." (III Nephi 19:22-23)

Shortly before Christ left the Nephites in the care of the Twelve He had chosen, He granted to each of them the desire of his heart. To three of them whose desire was the same as what His beloved Disciple, John, desired when He ministered among the Jews,[16] He gave the same blessing. Then Jesus, among other blessings, said to the Three of His Nephite Disciples: "And for this cause ye shall have fulness of joy; and ye shall sit down in the Kingdom of My Father; yea, your joy shall be full, even as the Father hath given Me fulness of joy; and ye shall be even as I am, and I am even as the Father; and the Father and I are one." (III Nephi 28:10)

In Me hath the Father glorified His Name. In substituting Himself in the place of sinners, and therein offering Himself as a Ransom to atone for the sins of the world, Jesus Christ, the Eternal Son of God, brought us Redemption. By His grace in doing so, He did what is most for our good and greatest for the glory of our Father Who is in Heaven. By the expression, *His grace,* we mean His doing something for us which we could not do for ourselves. By the Transgression of Adam, death came into the world; by the atoning Sacrifice of Christ, Everlasting Life in the Realm of our Father is now the portion of all His children. "He died," that is our Elder Brother, Jesus Christ, the Great Jehovah, "that we might live."

---

[16]*Revelation given to Joseph Smith the Prophet, and Oliver Cowdery, at Harmony, Pennsylvania, April, 1829, when they inquired through the Urim and Thummim as to whether John, the beloved Disciple, tarried in the flesh or had died. The Revelation is the translated version of the record made on parchment by John and hidden up by himself.* SEE, HISTORY OF THE CHURCH, *Vol. I, pp. 35-36.*

1. And the Lord said unto me: John, My beloved, what desireth thou? For if ye shall ask what you will, it shall be granted unto you.

2. And I said unto Him: Lord, give unto me power over death, that I may live and bring souls unto Thee.

3. And the Lord said unto me: Verily, verily, I say unto thee, because thou desireth this thou shalt tarry until I come in My glory, and shalt prophesy before nations, kindreds, tongues and people.

4. And for this cause the Lord said unto Peter: If I will that he tarry till I come, what is that to thee? For he desired of Me that he might bring souls unto Me, but thou desiredst that thou mightest speedily come unto Me in My Kingdom.

5. I say unto thee, Peter, this was a good desire; but My beloved has desired that he might do more, or a greater work yet among men than what he has before done.

6. Yea, he has undertaken a greater work; therefore I will make him as flaming fire and a ministering angel; he shall minister for those who shall be heirs of Salvation who dwell on the earth.

7. And I will make thee to minister for him and for thy brother, James; and unto you, ye shall both have according to your desires, for ye both joy in that which ye have desired." (Section 7, *Doctrine and Covenants.*)

That the Son of God was taken by wicked men and put to death to satisfy the demands of ignorance and infatuation, is true. Also it is true that the ways of evil men are often turned to God's glory. The poet says it this way: "Out of evil still educing good." Out of the iniquity of a selfish few came the Redemption of all. Redemption from what? From sin! Thus from out of the darkness that covered the land, the Voice of Jesus came to the startled Nephites: "I have come unto the world to bring Redemption unto the world, to save the world from sin."[17]

To add to the glory that is Christ's, and thereby is the Name of the Father glorified, the *Last and Great Sacrifice* was a voluntary one.[18] It was a part of the Plan of Salvation. Christ willingly laid down His life as a sacrifice for sin. "Therefore doth My Father love Me, because I lay down My life, that I might take it again. No man taketh it from Me, but I lay it down of Myself. I have power to lay it down, and I have power to take it again. This commandment have I received of My Father." (John 10-17-18)

We may get a fuller and freer understanding of the sentiment spoken by Jesus, "In Me hath the Father glorified His Name," when we remember that all evil came into the world through the Transgression of Adam. Through him all men became "carnal, sensual, and devilish."[19] *Carnal* means fleshy, or of the flesh; that is "a state of nature." (Alma 41:11) All mortal men "are in the gall of bitterness and in the bonds of iniquity; they are without God in this world, and they have gone contrary

---

17"For behold, I say unto you, this is not all. For how beautiful upon the mountains are the feet of Him that bringeth good tidings, that is the founder of peace, yea, even the Lord, Who has redeemed His people; yea, Him Who has granted Salvation unto His people;

"For were it not for the Redemption which He hath made for His people, which was prepared from the foundation of the world, I say unto you, were it not for this, all mankind must have perished.

"But, behold, the Bands of Death shall be broken, and the Son reigneth, and hath power over the dead; therefore, He bringeth to pass the Resurrection of the dead.

"And there cometh a Resurrection, even a First Resurrection; yea, even a Resurrection of those who have been, and those who are, and who shall be, even until the Resurrection of Christ—for so shall He be called.

"And now, the resurrection of all the prophets, and all those who have kept the commandments of God, shall come forth in the First Resurrection; therefore, they are the First Resurrection.

"They are raised to dwell with God Who has redeemed them; thus they have Eternal Life through Christ, Who has broken the Bands of Death. (Mosiah 15:18-23)

Redeem means, (1) To buy again something that has been sold, by paying back the price that bought it; (Lev. 25:25) (2) To deliver and bring out of bondage those who have been kept prisoners by their enemies. (Deut. 7:5; 32:6) As an example: Jerusalem had been sold, figuratively speaking, by the apostate Jews. They had perverted the ways of the Lord, and, too, they had abandoned the Covenant their fathers had made with the Lord at Mt. Sinai. The Land of Jerusalem was the land of their inheritance. The Mosaic Law provided that land which had been sold could be redeemed. However, a price was demanded for its redemption. What was that price? Jerusalem had not been bartered away for gold or for silver, nor was it sold as common merchandise. There was only One Who could meet the prescribed terms. That One was their King! Isaiah said: "He hath redeemed Jerusalem"; not with money or with the might of a great army. But He hath redeemed it with the blood which was shed on Mt. Calvary; the Redemption brought about by Jesus of Nazareth, the King of the Jews.

When Isaiah says, "Jerusalem," we may interpret it as meaning the whole Earth and all mankind. "The earth is the Lord's and the fulness thereof; the world and they that dwell therein." (Psalm 24:1) The Salvation of His children is the great purpose to which all of God's providences are consecrated, and in them, all the people of the earth will behold His Redemption.

18"And now, behold, I will testify unto you of myself that these things are true. Behold, I say unto you, that I do know that Christ shall come among the children of men, to take upon him the transgressions of his people, and that he shall atone for the sins of the world; for the Lord God hath spoken it.

to the nature of God; therefore, they are in a state contrary to the nature of happiness." (*Ibid.*)

Evil things are unclean things; evil thoughts are unclean thoughts. No unclean thing can enter into the Kingdom of Heaven.[20] Heaven is that place where God and the angels dwell, and where God is, no evil may come. As we have noted, mankind in his carnal state is the victim of evil; his joys are of the flesh, and his pleasures, sensual. Many of his hopes are of the devil, devilish. Death itself is of the devil. But even at death man cannot return to that place where he once was, or where his Father lives. The Father and His children are parted—separated. This is where the Plan of Salvation is best understood; this is where it may be said that the *Way has been prepared and the Pathway marked out* whereby a return to that ineffable Home may be attained by mortals. The Father and His children must be reunited. The Father's glory is the Salvation and Exaltation of His children. A *reconciliation* between them must be had. That reconciliation has been accomplished by Him Who is King of kings and Lord of lords. A return to his Father's House is the reward of the repentant sinner who endures to the end; and that reward is through Jesus Christ, the Eternal Son of God, the Great Mediator between God and man. "In Me hath the Father glorified His Name." (v. 15)

And here, let us not forget that we, too, may glorify the Name of our Father

---

"For it is expedient that an atonement should be made; for according to the great plan of the Eternal God there must be an atonement made, or else all mankind must unavoidably perish; yea, all are hardened; yea, all are fallen and are lost, and must perish except it be through the atonement which it is expedient should be made.

"For it is expedient that there should be a great and last sacrifice; yea, not a sacrifice of man, neither of beast, neither of any manner of fowl; for it shall not be a human sacrifice; but it must be an infinite and eternal sacrifice.

"Now there is not any man that can sacrifice his own blood which will atone for the sins of another. Now, if a man murdereth, behold will our law, which is just, take the life of his brother? I say unto you, Nay.

"But the law requireth the life of him who hath murdered; therefore there can be nothing which is short of an infinite atonement which will suffice for the sins of the world.

"Therefore, it is expedient that there should be a great and last sacrifice; and then shall there be, or it is expedient there should be, a stop to the shedding of blood; then shall the law of Moses be fulfilled, every jot and tittle, and none shall have passed away.

"And behold, this is the whole meaning of the law, every whit pointing to that great and last sacrifice; and that great and last sacrifice will be the Son of God, yea, infinite and eternal.

"And thus he shall bring salvation to all those who shall believe on his name; this being the intent of this last sacrifice, to bring about the bowels of mercy, which overpowereth justice, and bringeth about means unto men that they may have faith unto repentance.

"And thus mercy can satisfy the demands of justice, and encircles them in the arms of safety, while he that exercises no faith unto repentance is exposed to the whole law of the demands of justice; therefore only unto him that has faith unto repentance is brought about the great and eternal plan of redemption. (Amulek, *Alma* 34:8-16)

[19]"For they are carnal and devilish, and the devil has power over them; yea, even that old serpent that did beguile our first parents, which was the cause of their fall; which was the cause of all mankind becoming carnal, sensual, devilish, knowing evil from good, subjecting themselves to the devil." (Mosiah 16:3)

"Therefore, as they had become carnal, sensual, and devilish, by nature, this probationary state became a state for them to prepare; it became a preparatory state." (Alma 42:10)

[20]"But behold, I say unto you, the Kingdom of God is not filthy, and there cannot any unclean thing enter into the Kingdom of God. . . ." (I Nephi 15:34)

"And He doth not dwell in unholy temples; neither can filthiness or anything which is unclean be received into the Kingdom of God. . . ." (Alma 7:21)

"And I say unto you again that He cannot save them in their sins; for I cannot deny His word, and He hath said that no unclean thing can inherit the Kingdom of Heaven; therefore, how can ye be saved, except ye inherit the Kingdom of Heaven? Therefore, ye cannot be saved in your sins." (Alma 11:37)

"And no unclean thing can enter into His Kingdom; therefore nothing entereth into His rest save it be those who have washed their garments in My blood, because of their faith, and the repentance of all their sins, and their faithfulness unto the end." (III Nephi 27:19)

16. I came unto my own, and my own received me not. And the | scriptures concerning my coming are fulfilled.

---

by serving Him as did Christ by His serving His Father's children, and by us diligently keeping His commandments. To serve God means among many other things a constant sacrifice on our part of all selfish longings. To minister to the needs of His children is but a "thank-offering" to God for the blessings we receive from Him; in serving others we put to their highest use the things He has entrusted to our care. We thus become His servants; we do His will. In all ages God's servants served His children. It is good to remember that none were ever overcome who put their trust in the Great Father of us all by ministering to His children, our fellows. The service we render to God is measured by the same rod, and in the same terms with which we serve one another. We should always keep in our minds, that to serve Him in perfect freedom, and to worship Him is life's greatest happiness and its true satisfaction. King Benjamin, one of the great Prophet-Kings of the Nephites, said: "In my days of service to you . . . I have only been in the service of God." In serving God's children we may become poorer in the things of the world, but we will be richer in heavenly treasures; and always remember, "Better is little with the fear of the Lord than great treasure and trouble (turmoil) therewith." (Proverbs 15:16)

In the Gospel Plan no lessons are more boldly proclaimed than the lesson of service. The conclusion is not to be escaped that we serve God best by sharing with the needy the gifts we constantly receive from His bounteous hands, by showing compassion for the distressed, by upholding the falling, by loosing the bound. Truly, we can ennoble our lives no more graciously than by serving God with deeds of loving-kindness to our fellowmen. Yes, indeed, we can glorify the Name of our Father in thus doing.

In reading the magnificent and profound sentiments expressed by the Voice as they are recorded in Verse 15, we feel constrained to repeat the fervent prayer offered by the Jews of this day:

"May the time not be distant, O God, when Thy Name shall be worshiped in all the earth, when unbelief shall disappear and error be no more. We fervently pray that the day may come when all men shall invoke Thy name, when corruption and evil shall give way to purity and goodness, when superstition shall no longer enslave the mind, nor idolatry blind the eye, when all inhabitants of the earth shall know that to Thee alone every knee must bend and every tongue give homage. O may all created in Thine image recognize that they are brethren, so that, one in spirit and one in fellowship, they may be forever united before Thee. Then shall Thy Kingdom be established on earth and the word of Thine ancient seer be fulfilled: 'The Lord will reign for ever and ever.'"

Truly, the wonderful gift bought for us on Calvary's Hill inspires us to greater deeds of love and helpfulness to our fellow men, and we ourselves pray: "O Heavenly Father, put into our hearts the love and fear of Thee, that we may consecrate our lives to Thy service and glorify Thy Name in the eyes of all men."

In ending our discussion of Verse 15, may we do so by repeating the last verse of the 65th Section of the *Book of Doctrine and Covenants*: "Wherefore, may the Kingdom of God go forth, that the Kingdom of Heaven may come, that Thou, O God, mayest be glorified in Heaven so on Earth, that Thine enemies may be subdued; for Thine is the honor, power and glory, forever and ever. Amen."

VERSE 16. *My Own received Me not.* For ages the wise men and the poets of the Jews had foretold the coming of a King, one Who would lead them into battle, which in every case would be victorious, and would enthrone Jerusalem above the nations of the earth. But when He came and was crucified in their Capitol; when they found that His emissaries were not princes and nobles but poor fishermen of Galilee, their hard hearts became like granite; their hatred intense, their spite was keen and inexhaustible, and they left no stone untouched or unturned that they might throw at the bulwarks and battlements of the Christian Church.

When the day would come in which He would reign, all Judah's foes would be subdued. Jerusalem, the beloved City of the Jews, would be the Capitol of the World, and they would rule the nations of the earth in regal splendor. He would be their King, and they His loyal subjects. He was to be of noble parentage, a Son of King David, of a family whose great name was "like unto the name of the great men that are in the earth." (II Samuel 7:9)

But when Christ was born in Bethlehem, He was of a family whose home was with the despised inhabitants of the Roman Province of Galilee. His father was a carpenter, and most of His relations were fishermen. He was born in a manger, the only lodging available in the City where Joseph went to pay taxes. Jesus' birth, however, brought to pass a prophecy uttered many hundreds of years before: "But, thou, Bethlehem, Ephratah, though thou be little among the thousands of Judah, yet out of thee shall He come forth unto Me That is to be ruler in Israel; Whose goings forth have been from of old, from everlasting." (Micah 5:2)

The humble birth of Jesus was not what the Jews expected of their King. And Nazareth, by the blue waters of Galilee, where, as a child, He played, grew to manhood, and studied, was of so little repute that when Philip told Nathaniel: "We have found Him, of Whom Moses in the Law, and the prophets did write, Jesus of Nazareth, the son of Joseph," Nathaniel replied, "Can there any good thing come out of Nazareth?" (John 1:45-46)

Truly, Christ's forefathers were of the kingly and illustrious "House of David," but when He came, its glory had departed, and its splendor was remembered only in song.

"And there shall come forth a rod out of the stem of Jesse, and a branch shall grow out of its roots." (Isaiah 11:1) Jesse was the father of King David, but when the fruit of his loins (Acts 2:30), Christ, was raised up to sit on David's throne, the age of prophecy had passed. The Jews had rejected any new word coming from God; many of His servants were slain, and the laws given by Him, through Moses, had been changed to meet the ambitious purposes of priests and kings. As a nation, the Jews were apostate. There appeared to be a famine in the land ". . . not a famine of bread, nor a thirst for water, but of hearing the words of the Lord." (Amos 8:18) The voice of God's holy prophets had been stilled. The Jews roamed in the twilight of a brilliant past. When compared to the time of David, when Christ was born, all was changed. A story we tell softly and in the spirit of holiness is: On an occasion a huge throng was assembled in Pilate's Council Chamber. The Son of God, Jesus, the King of the Jews, the Creator of the Heavens and the Earth, stood amid scorn before the judgment bar of man, rejected, condemned; *His Own received Him not.* As was the custom at this holiday time of each year, the Judge, a Roman Procurator, offered to release to the people one who was accused of crime. Pilate, seeing no evil in Jesus, offered to them His release, or that of Barabbas, a well-known culprit. To this suggestion they shouted: "Not this man, but Barabbas." "What then," said Pilate, "shall I do with Him Who you call *King of the Jews?*" And in their ignorance and infatuation they again shouted: "Crucify Him; Crucify Him." "My own received Me not." (v. 16)

17. And as many as have received me, to them have I given to become the sons of God; and even so will I to as many as shall believe on my name, for behold, by me redemption cometh, and in me is the law of Moses fulfilled.

VERSE 17. *In Me is the Law of Moses fulfilled.* Out of seventy souls, including the eleven sons of the Patriarch Jacob, who went down into Egypt at the behest of Joseph, another son who was already there, there grew a people who "increased abundantly, and multiplied, and waxed exceeding mighty"; and filled the whole land with a goodly offspring. This caused a great fear to come upon Pharaoh, the King of that Land, who was new there and did not know Joseph. Pharaoh appealed to his people, saying: "Behold, the people of the Children of Israel are more and mightier than we: Come on, let us deal wisely with them; lest they multiply . . . Therefore they did set over them taskmasters to afflict them with their burdens . . . But the more they afflicted them, the more they multiplied and grew. And they were grieved because of the Children of Israel. And the Egyptians made the Children of Israel to serve with rigor. And they made their lives bitter with hard bondage, in mortar, and in brick, and in all manner of service in the field: all their service, wherein they made them serve, was with rigor." (Exodus 1:7-14)

Many harsh measures were heaped upon the backs of God's children, increasing their labor far beyond the possibility of its completion, thereby adding to their suffering and mental anguish. Even it was decreed by Pharaoh that all male children born of Israelitish parents should be cast into the River Nile.

"And it came to pass in process of time, that the King of Egypt died: and the Children of Israel sighed by reason of the bondage, and they cried, and their cry came up unto God by reason of the bondage. And God heard their groaning, and God remembered His covenant with Abraham, with Isaac, and with Jacob. And God looked upon the Children of Israel, and God had respect unto them." (Exodus 2:23-25)

God called Moses to be an instrument in His hands for their deliverance. Both Moses and his brother, Aaron, at God's command, presented themselves before Pharaoh many times, demanding that the Children of Israel be set free from bondage, that thereby they might worship, or serve, the God of their Fathers. Pharaoh hardened his heart and would not that they should go. Many times penalties, the most severe, settled upon the land and upon its inhabitants because of his refusal. At length, when other, what are called *plagues*, failed to soften his heart, or cause him to relent, the death of all first-born of both man and beast in all the Kingdom, including those from Pharaoh down to the captive that was "in the dungeon," together with the first-born of all cattle, caused him to yield. Fear came upon the Egyptians for they said: "We be all dead men," so they urged haste in the Israelites' departure. Pharaoh, too, was anxious that they depart quickly, "And he called for Moses and Aaron by night, and said: 'Rise up, and get you forth from among my people, both ye and the Children of Israel; and go, serve the Lord, as ye have said. And also take your flocks and your herds, as ye have said, and be gone; . . ." (Exodus 12:31-32)

"Now the sojourning of the Children of Israel, who dwelt in Egypt, was four hundred and thirty years. And it came to pass at the end of the four hundred and thirty years, even the selfsame day it came to pass, that all the hosts of the Lord went out from the Land of Egypt." (Exodus 12:40-41) In all there were more than 600,000 numbered among the Israelites besides women and children. (*Ibid.*, 12:37)

It was a heterogeneous mass of humanity that made up the numbers of the Children of Israel; there were old and young. There were both male and female, infirm and whole; there were farmers and stockraisers who brought along with them their flocks and herds; there were fishermen who had plied their trade along the banks of the River Nile; there were makers of brick, and workers in brick and stone; there were carpenters and laborers of every kind. Altogether, in one grand effort, they formed the Army of Israel which was the *Army of the Lord.*

However, they were not united in their purpose as an army should be. Some sought glory; some for advantage over their fellows; some adventure, but most sought freedom to serve the God of their fathers, Abraham, Isaac, and Jacob. Their different objectives disarranged their orderly advance. Notwithstanding that the power of God and His goodness in their behalf was manifested to them, they, at times, openly rebelled against Him. (Witness the incident of the Golden Calf.) Even some wanted to return to Egypt and to their former bondage. (Numbers 14:4) We must remember that during their years of bondage to the Egyptians, many of the Children of Israel had forgotten the God of their Fathers and had adopted the customs and habits of their bondmasters. They toiled, as did their taskmasters, on the day the Lord had set apart as a day of rest and one in which to think of Him. They took great oaths as did the Egyptians, and they made for themselves gods of wood and gods of stone and of precious metals. To these they bowed down and worshiped. Their roots were deeply imbedded in Egyptian soil. It became necessary, and God also commanded it, that Moses, to preserve what discipline and unity there was among them, appointed captains from their numbers to drill and marshal them into an army, (Exodus 18:25; Deut. 1:15) and to be to them righteous judges. Their unity was the discipline of the rod, not the inspiration of their hearts.

The story of the famous Exodus of the Children of Israel has been told thousands of times, and thousands of times has God's goodness to them and His watchful care over them been extolled. It reminds us of the 114th Psalm of King David wherein is accounted how the Lord prepared their way: "When Israel went out of Egypt, the House of Jacob from a people of strange language; Judah was His sanctuary, and Israel His dominion. The sea saw it, and fled: Jordan was driven back. The mountains skipped like rams, and the hills like lambs. What ailed thee, O thou sea, that thou fleddest? thou Jordan, that thou wast driven back? Ye mountains, that ye skipped like rams; and ye little hills, like lambs? Tremble, thou earth, at the presence of the Lord, at the presence of the God of Jacob; Which turned the rock into a standing water, the flint into a fountain of waters." (*See,* Numbers 20:8-11; Deut. 8:15)

Now, as we have noted, that from the very first, Israel was an obstinate and stiff-necked people. Often it refused to walk in the Lord's path which had been shown to it, but chose different ways that led it along the road to degradation and sorrow. It was so imbued with the ideas and sympathies of the Egyptians that it could not shake itself free from its habits and customs. Only a few of the people could live the Gospel of Christ with its high moral standards. They understood not its spirit of love.

". . . It was expedient that there should be a law given to the Children of Israel, yea, even a very strict law; for they were a stiffnecked people, quick to do iniquity, and slow to remember the Lord their God. Therefore there was a law give them, yea, a law of performances and of ordinances, a law which they were to observe strictly from day to day, to keep them in remembrance of God and their duty towards Him. But I say unto you, that all these things were types of things to come.

"And now, did they understand the Law? I say unto you, Nay, they did not all understand the Law; and this because of the hardness of their hearts; for they understood not that there could not any man be saved except through the Redemption of God. For behold, did not Moses prophesy unto them concerning the coming of the Messiah, and that God should redeem His people? Yea, and even all the prophets who have prophesied ever since the world began—have they not spoken more or less concerning these things?

"Have they not said that God Himself should come down among the children of men, and take upon Him the form of man, and go forth in mighty power upon the face of the earth? Yea, and have they not said also that He should bring to pass the resurrection of the dead, and that He, Himself, should be oppressed and afflicted? (*Abinadi,* Mosiah 13:29-35)

"And the Lord God hath sent His holy prophets among all the children of men, to declare these things to every kindred, nation, and tongue, that thereby whosoever should believe that Christ should come, the same might receive remission of their sins, and rejoice with exceeding great joy, even as though He had already come among them. Yet the Lord saw that His people were a stiffnecked people, and He appointed unto them a Law, even the Law of Moses. And many signs, and wonders, and types, and shadows, showed He unto them, concerning His coming; and also holy prophets spake unto them concerning His coming; and yet they hardened their hearts, and understood not that the Law of Moses availeth nothing, except it were through the Atonement of His blood." (*King Benjamin,* Mosiah 3:13-15)

The Law of Moses was, we may say, prophetic. It commanded sacrifice, which was indicative of the great Sacrifice that was to be made. Its performances and ordinances were visible signs of the Messiah, Whose coming they foretold.

The Nephites were of Israel. All Israelites of ancient times were taught to accept the Law as their guide. It was emblematic of things to come. It pointed out the way to Christ, the Messiah, Whose coming they awaited. By faith they saw these things as though they had already happened. The Law thus promised Salvation to everyone who looked to Christ for Redemption. Faith in that which is to come is not unusual, nor is it strange. There is no doubt that faith imposes burdens, but its rewards are sure. All things are done by the power of faith. Israel, in the days of Moses, as now, walked by faith. Ancient Israel looked forward to His coming; we look back. Both visions are equally efficacious.

Passages from the Book of Mormon, showing the purpose for which the Law of Moses was given and its fulfillment, are made particularly clear by the following: "Behold, my soul delighteth in proving unto my people the truth of the coming of Christ; for, for this end hath the Law of Moses been given; and all things which have been given of God from the beginning of the world, unto man, are the typifying of Him." (II Nephi 11:4)

"And notwithstanding we believe in Christ, we keep the Law of Moses, and look forward with steadfastness unto Christ, until the Law be fulfilled." (II Nephi 25:24)

"For, for this intent have we written these things, that they may know that we knew of Christ, and we had a hope of His glory many hundred years before His coming; and not only we ourselves had a hope of His glory, but also all the holy prophets which were before us. Behold, they believed in Christ and worshiped the Father in His Name, and also we worship the Father in His Name. And for this intent we keep the Law of Moses, it pointing our souls to Him; and for this cause it is sanctified unto us for righteousness. . ." (Jacob 4:4-5)

"And they also took of the firstlings of their flocks, that they might offer sacrifice and burnt offerings according to the Law of Moses." (Mosiah 2:3)

"Yea, and they did keep the Law of Moses; for it was expedient that they should keep the Law of Moses as yet, for it was not all fulfilled. But notwithstanding the Law of Moses, they did look forward to the coming of Christ, considering that the Law of Moses was a type of His coming, and believing that they must keep those outward performances until the time that He should be revealed unto them. Now they did not suppose that Salvation came by the Law of Moses; but the Law of Moses did serve to strengthen their faith in Christ; and thus they did retain a hope through faith, unto Salvation, relying upon the spirit of prophecy, which spake of things to come." (Alma 25:15-16)

As many as have received Me, to them have I given to become the sons of God. In spite of the fact that He was rejected by His Own, and was crucified by them notwithstanding He sought only their good, Christ foretold of no retaliation for His evil reception by the Jewish hierarchy, but promised all who shall believe on His Name that they would *become the sons of God.*

John, in his Gospel, says: "But as many as received Him, to them gave He power to become the sons of God, even to them that believe on His Name." (John 1:12) Bible commentators on this important subject say that Christ gave to them that should believe on His name the *right,* or *privilege,* to become the sons of God. That is true. But not all the meaning of Christ's promise is therein expressed. Words too often, somehow or other, fail to reveal the real meaning of a thought; they do not fully elucidate and explain it. They hide the sense they intend to convey under a mass of verbiage just as a beautiful flower is sometimes hidden underneath a growth of rank grass. This promise of our Lord is one of the fair and fragrant flowers of Christianity. It blossoms in our hearts. We not only have the privilege to become one among the sons of God, but also through the Atonement of Christ we have restored to us, and that literally, our rightful inheritance in His Kingdom as a son or daughter of our Heavenly Father, Who is God.

When we read the above-mentioned statement of John's, we remember that the *power* Christ gave to those who believed on His Name was not like the power of a priest who can make an ecclesiastic, or the power of man that can make a just and an upright person, but that only a divine power from Heaven above, can make of a mortal one who is worthy to be called *a son of God.*

The best comments on this wonderful theme are those made by the Savior Himself, and some of His inspired servants. In the *Doctrine and Covenants* we read: "I am Jesus Christ, the Son of God, Who was crucified for the sins of the world, even as many as will believe on My Name, that they may become the sons of God, even one in Me as I am one in the Father, as the Father is one in Me, that we may be one." (D. & C. 35:2)

LAW OF MOSES—

1 Nephi	4:15	According to the law of H., save they
	17:22	All his commandments according to the law of M.
2 Nephi	5:10	In all things, according to the law of M.
	11:4	For this end hath the law of M. been
	25:24	We believe in Christ, we keep the law of M.
Jacob	4:5	For this intent we keep the law of M.
	7:7	Keep not the law of M., which is the
	7	Convert the law of M., into the worship
Jarom	1:5	They observed to keep the law of M.
	11	Teaching the law of M., and the intent
Mosiah	2:3	Burnt offerings, according to the law of M.
	3:14	Appointed unto them a law, even the law of M.
	15	That the law of M. availeth nothing
	12:28	They said, We teach the law of M.
	29	If ye teach the law of M. why do ye
	31	Ye have said that ye teach the law of M.
	12:31	What know ye concerning the law of M.?
	31	Doth salvation come by the law of M.?

18. I am the light and the life of the world. I am Alpha and | Omega, the beginning and the end.

	32	Said, That salvation did come by the law of M.
	13:27	Salvation cometh by the law of M.
	27	Ye should keep the law of M. as yet
	27	Shall no more be expedient to keep the law of M.
	28	Unavoidably perish, notwithstanding the law of M.
	16:14	Therefore, if ye teach the law of M.
	24:5	Teach them anything . . . neither the law of M.
Alma	25:15	And they did keep the law of M.
	15	It was expedient that they should keep the law of M.
	15	But notwithstanding the law of M.
	15	The law of M. was a type of his coming
	16	Not suppose that salvation came by the law of M.
	16	The law of M. did serve to strengthen
	30:3	The ordinances of God, according to the law of M.
	3	They were taught to keep the law of M.
	31:9	And his statutes, according to the law of M.
	34:13	Then shall the law of M. be fulfilled
Helaman	13:1	Commandments of God, according to the law of M.
	15:5	And his judgments according to the law of M.
3 Nephi	1:24	No more expedient to observe the law of M.
	9:17	And in me is the law of M. fulfilled
	15:2	Wondered what he would concerning the law of M.
	25:4	Remember ye the law of M. my servant
4 Nephi	1:12	The performances and ordinances of the law of M.
Ether	12:11	By faith, was the law of M. given

VERSE 18. *I am the Light and the Life of the world.* "Verily, thus saith the Lord . . . I am the true Light that lighteth every man that cometh into the world." (D. & C. 93:1-2) The Prophet Abinadi, in preaching to the wicked priests of King Noah, said of Christ: "He is the Light and the Life of the world; yea, a light that is endless, that can never be darkened; yea, also a life which is endless, that there can be no more death." (Mosiah 16:9) In Christ is that Life which is Eternal. His atoning Blood, shed for us on Calvary's Hill, is the Ransom He paid that we might live. To Him, and to none other, be the honor and the glory; the might, majesty, and dominion, forever; for, for us, by His grace and by His free-will Offering He broke the bands of death, and thereby brought immortality to man. "Surely, He hath borne our grief, and carried our sorrows. . . ." (Isaiah 53:4) *Our grief* is death, brought about by the Fall of Adam; and *our sorrows,* the incidents of carnal existence. Instead of death, Christ brought *Life Everlasting;* instead of sorrow, He brought *joy.*

We find no better place than here to record our thanksgiving to the Lord God Who is Jesus Christ for the blessing of Life Everlasting, and this by repeating the words of Ammon, son of King Mosiah, spoken to his brethren at the close of their wonderful mission to the Lamanites about a hundred years previous to the events recorded in these verses: "Therefore, let us glory, we will glory in the Lord; yea, we will rejoice, for our joy is full; yea, we will praise our God forever. Behold, who can glory too much in the Lord? Yea, who can say too much of His great power, and of His mercy, and His long-suffering towards the children of men? . . ." (Alma 26:25) ". . . for this is my life and my light, my joy and my Salvation, and my Redemption from everlasting wo. Yea, blessed is the Name of my God. . . ." (*Ibid.,* 26:36)

19. And ye shall offer up unto me no more the shedding of blood; yea, your sacrifices and your burnt offerings shall be done away, for I will accept none of your sacrifices and your burnt offerings.

3. The acceptable sacrifice of a broken heart and a contrite spirit.

20. And ye shall offer for a sacrifice unto me a broken heart and a contrite spirit. And whoso cometh unto me with a broken heart and a contrite spirit, him will I baptize with fire and with the Holy Ghost, even as the Lamanites, because of their faith in me at the time of their conversion, were baptized with fire and with the Holy Ghost, and they knew it not.

The Light of the world. In every dispensation of the Gospel, God's inspired servants and teachers have likened truth to light, and have compared error to darkness. "For you shall live by every word that proceedeth forth from the mouth of God. For the word of the Lord is truth, and *whatsoever is truth is light,* and whatsoever is light is Spirit, even the Spirit of Jesus Christ. And the Spirit giveth light to every man that cometh into the world; and the Spirit enlighteneth every man through the world, that hearkeneth to the voice of the Spirit." (D. & C. 84:44-46) Wherefore, the Lord said: "I will be a light unto them forever, that hear My words." (II Nephi 10:14) To hear the words of the Lord, or to hear His voice, is to obey Him. Whether those words come directly from Him, or through His servants, they are His; He says: ". . . I am He that doth speak." (III Nephi 20:39)

To recognize truth when we hear it is a gift of the Spirit. "For the Spirit speaketh the truth and lieth not." (Jacob 4:13) As but one speaking for many we may say: "Like a Lamp unto my feet, the Lord lighteth the way before me." At this point we are constrained to ask with Isaiah: "Who is among you that feareth the Lord, that obeyeth the voice of His servant, that walketh in darkness and hath no light?" (II Nephi 7:10) And again we are constrained to repeat Isaiah's admonition: "O House of Jacob, come ye and let us walk in the light of the Lord . . ." (II Nephi 12:5) And with this thought in mind, we will remember the words of the ancient Hebrew brethren: "For with Thee is the fountain of life: in Thy light shall we see light." (Psalm 36:9)

I am Alpha and Omega. The first and last letters in the Greek Alphabet. They mean the beginning and the end, the first and last. Alpha (A) is a symbol used variously, as in astronomy to describe or to designate the chief or brightest star of a constellation. Christ is the *Chiefest and Brightest Star* in the firmament of heaven. He was in the beginning and will remain throughout all eternities; He is endless.

Christ is called *Alpha and Omega* to denote that He is the beginning and the ending: the Author, Preserver, and Upholder, of all things, and His glory is their end. "Thou art worthy, O Lord, to receive glory and honor and power, for Thou hast created all things, and for Thy pleasure they are and were created." (Rev. 4:11)

VERSE 19. *And ye shall offer up unto Me no more the shedding of blood.* (See Chapter 15:2-8)

VERSE 20. *Ye shall offer for a sacrifice unto Me a broken heart and a contrite spirit.* (See Helaman 5:45) The Lord does not delight in a blood sacrifice; He has no pleasure in burnt offerings; if so, we would offer them. The sacrifices of the Lord are a broken heart and a contrite spirit. Them, He will not despise.

21. Behold, I have come unto the world to bring redemption unto the world, to save the world from sin.

22. Therefore, whoso repenteth and cometh unto me as a little child, him will I receive, for of such is the kingdom of God. Behold, for such I have laid down my life, and have taken it up again; therefore repent, and come unto me ye ends of the earth, and be saved.

"Create in me a clean heart, O God, and renew a steadfast spirit within me. Cast me not away from Thy presence; and take not Thy holy Spirit from me. Restore unto me the joy of Thy Salvation, and let a willing spirit uphold me." (Jewish Union *Prayer Book*)

VERSE 22. *Whoso repenteth and cometh unto Me as a little child, him will I receive.* (See III Nephi 11:37-38)

CHAPTER 10

1. Silence in the Land—2. Again the Voice from Heaven—3. The Darkness Disperses—4. Only the More Righteous of the People are Spared.

1. Silence in the land.

1. And now behold, it came to pass that all the people of the land did hear these sayings, and did witness of it. And after these sayings there was silence in the land for the space of many hours;

2. For so great was the astonishment of the people that they did cease lamenting and howling for the loss of their kindred which had been slain; therefore there was silence in all the land for the space of many hours.

2. Again the Voice from Heaven.

3. And it came to pass that there came a voice again unto the people, and all the people did hear and did witness of it, saying:

4. O ye people of these great cities which have fallen, who are descendants of Jacob, yea, who are of the house of Israel, how

---

VERSES 1-2. *There was silence in the land for the space of many hours.* After the people had heard this glad message of forgiveness, they ceased their mourning and howling for their kindred who had been lost in the great destruction that had visited the land, and there was a thoughtful silence among them for many hours. They meditated on the scene presented before them, and wondered at its severity.

Howling was a part of funeral services to all orientals, and it seems the custom of doing so continued down from generation to generation among the Nephites whose fathers were from the orient. Among the near-Easterners, sadness was best expressed by the more noise they made. It was measured in the same ratio. To lament in a loud manner caused many professional mourners to offer their services that the added wails they gave would impress the general public with the importance of the deceased person. In a modified form this custom persisted with the descendants of Lehi.

Another evidence of this custom, showing that it was of long standing, the Jaredites gave vent to this same practice. At the final and great battle in which the Jaredites were all slain save it were Coriantumr and the Prophet Ether, the people set up a cry that "did rend the air exceedingly." It is recorded of them thus: "And it came to pass that when it was night they were weary, and retired to their camps; and after they had retired to their camps they took up a howling and a lamentation for the loss of the slain of their people; and so great were their cries, their howlings and lamentations, that they did rend the air exceedingly. And it came to pass that on the morrow they did go again to battle, and great and terrible was that day; nevertheless, they conquered not, and when the night came again they did rend the air with their cries, and their howlings, and their mournings, for the loss of the slain of their people." (Ether 15:16-17)

VERSES 3-8. *There came a Voice again unto the people.* The Voice of Jesus was again heard recounting how oft He had sought to gather together the House of

oft have I gathered you as a hen gathereth her chickens under her wings, and have nourished you.

5. And again, how oft would I have gathered you as a hen gathereth her chickens under her wings, yea, O ye people of the house of Israel, who have fallen; yea, O ye people of the house of Israel, ye that dwell at Jerusalem, as ye that have fallen; yea, how oft would I have gathered you as a hen gathereth her chickens, and ye would not.

6. O ye house of Israel whom I have spared, how oft will I

gather you as a hen gathereth her chickens under her wings, if ye will repent and return unto me with full purpose of heart.

7. But if not, O house of Israel, the places of your dwellings shall become desolate until the time of the fulfilling of the covenant to your fathers.

8. And now it came to pass that after the people had heard these words, behold, they began to weep and howl again because of the loss of their kindred and friends.

3. The darkness disperses.

9. And it came to pass that thus did the three days pass away. And it was in the morning, and the darkness dispersed from off the face of the land, and the earth did cease to tremble, and the rocks did cease to rend, and the dreadful groanings did cease, and all the tumultuous noises did pass away.

10. And the earth did cleave

Israel, but just as often they had refused His pleadings. He then promised that again He would seek to gather them even as a hen gathereth her chickens, under His protecting care. The Nephites were of Israel and entitled to the same blessings as promised to all God's covenant people. These blessings were predicated upon righteousness, and were promised by the Savior "If ye will repent and return unto Me with full purpose of heart," (v. 6) but if they would not heed Him, He said that the places of their dwellings should become desolate until the time of the fulfilling of God's covenant with their fathers. When the people heard this awful prophecy, they began again to weep and howl because of the loss of their kindred and friends.

VERSES 9-11. *After three days the darkness dispersed from off the face of the land.* Three days had passed in darkness, in terror, and in woe, when the thick mist rolled off the face of the land, revealing to the astonished eyes of the survivors how great had been the convulsions that had shaken the earth. When the darkness passed away the earth ceased to tremble, the rocks were no longer rent, the dreadful groanings ceased, and the tumultuous noises ended. Then nature was again at peace, and peace filled the hearts of the living; their mourning was turned to praise, and their joy was in Christ, their Deliverer.

Mormon here notes that thus far "were the Scriptures fulfilled which had been spoken by the prophets." Consider the following: In the vision had by Nephi, son of Lehi, in which the future appearing of the Risen Redeemer to his seed was unfolded to the prophet, he records it thus: "And it came to pass that I saw a mist of darkness on the face of the Land of Promise; and I saw lightnings, and I heard thunderings, and earthquakes, and all manner of tumultuous noises; and I saw the earth and the rocks, that they rent; and I saw mountains tumbling into

together again, that it stood; and the mourning, and the weeping, and the wailing of the people who were spared alive did cease; and their mourning was turned into joy, and their lamentations into the praise and thanksgiving unto the Lord Jesus Christ, their Redeemer.

11. And thus far were the scriptures fulfilled which had been spoken by the prophets.

---

pieces; and I saw the plains of the earth, that they were broken up; and I saw many cities that they were sunk; and I saw many that they were burned with fire; and I saw many that did tumble to the earth, because of the quaking thereof. And it came to pass after I saw these things, I saw the vapor of darkness, that it passed from the face of the earth; and behold, I saw multitudes who had fallen because of the great and terrible judgments of the Lord. And I saw the Heavens open, and the Lamb of God descending out of Heaven; and He came down and showed Himself unto them." (I Nephi 12:4-6)

Another marvelous prophecy uttered by Nephi, and recorded by him upon the Smaller Plates: "And the God of our fathers, who were led out of Egypt, out of bondage, and also were preserved in the wilderness by Him, yea, the God of Abraham, and of Isaac, and the God of Jacob, yieldeth Himself, according to the words of the angel, as a man, into the hands of wicked men, to be lifted up, according to the words of Zenock, and to be crucified, according to the words of Neum, and to be buried in a sepulchre, according to the words of Zenos, which he spake concerning the three days of darkness, which should be a sign given to those who should inhabit the isles of the sea, more especially given to those who are of the House of Israel. For thus spake the prophet: The Lord God surely shall visit all the House of Israel at that day, some with His voice, because of their righteousness, unto their great joy and salvation, and others with the thunderings and the lightnings of His power, by tempest, by fire, and by smoke, and vapor of darkness, and by the opening of the earth, and by mountains which shall be carried up. And all these things must surely come, saith the Prophet Zenos. And the rocks of the earth must rend; and because of the groanings of the earth, many of the kings of the Isles of the Sea shall be wrought upon by the Spirit of God, to exclaim: The God of nature suffers." (I Nephi 19:10-12)

The Lamanite Prophet, Samuel, whose words of prophecy concerning these awful times were fulfilled in their entirety, and which the Savior commanded that they be written in the Nephite Records, foretold the darkness and the destruction that should accompany the Lord's death: (III Nephi 23:8-10) "But behold, as I said unto you concerning another sign, a sign of His death, behold, in that day that He shall suffer death the sun shall be darkened and refuse to give his light unto you; and also the moon and the stars; and there shall be no light upon the face of this land, even from the time that He shall suffer death, for the space of three days, to the time that He shall rise again from the dead. Yea, at the time that He shall yield up the ghost there shall be thunderings and lightnings for the space of many hours, and the earth shall shake and tremble; and the rocks which are upon the face of this earth, which are both above the earth and beneath, which ye know at this time are solid, or the most part of it is one solid mass, shall be broken up; Yea, and they shall be rent in twain, and shall ever after be found in seams and in cracks, and in broken fragments upon the face of the whole earth, yea, both above the earth and beneath. And behold, there shall be great tempests, and there shall be many mountains laid low, like unto a valley, and there shall be many places which are now called valleys which shall become mountains, whose height is great. And many highways shall be broken up, and many cities shall become desolate. (See, Helaman 14)

4. Only the more righteous of the people are spared.

12. And it was the more righteous part of the people who were saved, and it was they who received the prophets and stoned them not; and it was they who had not shed the blood of the saints, who were spared—

13. And they were spared and were not sunk and buried up in the earth; and they were not drowned in the depths of the sea; and they were not burned by fire, neither were they fallen upon and crushed to death; and they were

---

VERSES 12-13. *It was the more righteous part of the people who were saved.* Mormon seeks in these verses to impress upon those unto whom his work will come that it was because of their desire unto righteousness that the more righteous were saved. Those who were delivered from untimely death and also destruction, were "they who received the prophets, and stoned them not; and it was they who had not shed the blood of the Saints." Let us not forget that not only were the righteous among them, delivered from physical destruction, and their annals corroborate this fact, but they were all of that generation emancipated from sin. It is recorded of them, "For none of them are lost." The Savior's own words confirm this: "And now, behold, My joy is great, even unto fulness, because of you, and also of this generation; yea, and even the Father rejoiceth, and also all the holy angels, because of you and this generation; for none of them are lost. (III Nephi 27:30)

Mormon now appeals to the reader of his abridgment of the times herein spoken, to search the Scriptures, and find out for themselves whether or not the fire, and smoke, the tempests and whirlwinds, the opening of the earth's crust to receive the wicked, "and all these things were not unto the fulfilling of the prophecies of many of the holy prophets." (v. 14) We quote fully the fifteenth verse that the point Mormon seeks to make, is definitely understood: "Behold, I say unto you, Yea, many have testified of these things at the coming of Christ, and were slain because they testified of these things." (*See*, Helaman 14)

Among the many prophets who Mormon said had testified concerning the great convulsions of the earth and the terrible experiences of the inhabitants living in the Western Hemisphere during the time of the Savior's death and while His body lay in its tomb, he mentioned as noteworthy the Prophets Zenock and Zenos. Mormon was especially purposeful in naming these two, because, he said, "They testified particularly concerning us, who are a remnant of their seed." (v. 16)

Zenock was a Prophet of Israel, but of his personal history, or to what age he belonged, we know nothing. His writings were familiar to the Nephites as he was quoted by Nephi (I Nephi 19:10); Alma (Alma 33:15); Amulek (Alma 34:7); Nephi (Helaman 8:20), and Mormon.

Zenos was a Hebrew Prophet who was also quoted by the Nephite servants of God. All we are told of his personal history is that he was slain because he testified boldly of what God had revealed to him. That he was a man greatly blessed of the Lord with the spirit of prophecy is shown in that wonderful and almost incomparable *Parable of the Tame Olive Tree* given at length by Jacob (Jacob 5). His prophecies were quoted by Nephi (I Nephi 19:10, 12, 16); Alma (Alma 33:3, 13, 15); Amulek (Alma 34:7); Samuel, the Lamanite, (Helaman 15:11), and by Mormon.

Not only did Zenos and Zenock testify that the Nephites were of the House of Israel, calling them a remnant of Jacob's seed, but Jacob himself, the father of all Israel, testified "concerning a remnant of the seed of Joseph," his son. "And behold,

not carried away in the whirl-wind; neither were they over-powered by the vapor of smoke and of darkness.

14. And now, whoso readeth, let him understand; he that hath the scriptures, let him search them, and see and behold if all these deaths and destructions by fire, and by smoke, and by tempests, and by whirlwinds, and by the opening of the earth to receive them, and all these things are not unto the fulfilling of the prophecies of many of the holy prophets.

15. Behold, I say unto you, Yea, many have testified of these things at the coming of Christ, and were slain because they testified of these things.

16. Yea, the prophet Zenos did testify of these things, and also Zenock spake concerning these things, because they testified par-ticularly concerning us, who are the remnant of their seed.

17. Behold, our father Jacob also testified concerning a rem-nant of the seed of Joseph. And behold, are not we a remnant of the seed of Joseph? And these things which testify of us, are they not written upon the plates of brass which our father Lehi brought out of Jerusalem?

18. And it came to pass that in the ending of the thirty and fourth year, behold, I will show unto you that the people of Nephi who were spared, and also those who had been called Lamanites, who had been spared, did have great favors shown unto them, and great blessings poured out upon their heads, insomuch that soon after the ascension of Christ into heaven he did truly manifest himself unto them—

19. Showing his body unto

are not we a remnant of the seed of Joseph? And these things which testify of us, are they not written upon the *Plates of Brass* which our father Lehi brought out of Jerusalem?"

That the Nephites were of Israel, and a remnant of Joseph's seed — that same Joseph who was sold into Egypt — is attested by the words of Moroni, the leader of the Nephite armies over a hundred years previously: "Yea, let us preserve our liberty as a remnant of Joseph; yea, let us remember the words of Jacob, before his death, for behold, he saw that a part of the remnant of the coat of Joseph was preserved and had not decayed. And he said — Even as this remnant of garment of my son hath been preserved, so shall a remnant of the seed of my son be pre-served by the hand of God, and be taken unto Himself, while the remainder of the seed of Joseph shall perish, even as the remnant of this garment." (Alma 46:24)

VERSES 18-19. *The people of Nephi who were spared . . . Christ . . . did truly manifest Himself unto them.* These two verses are what we may call a preface to Mormon's account of Christ's ministry among the Nephites. It was then the "thirty and fourth year" after the birth of the Savior in far-away Judea that these things took place of which he gives only a brief summary, which we know as *Mormon's Abridgment.* He tells us very plainly that not a hundredth part of the things he found written upon the *Plates of Nephi* could be contained in the record he was making. Later on we will read: "And now there cannot be written in this book even a hundredth part of the things which Jesus did truly teach unto the people." (III Nephi 26:6)

them, and ministering unto them; and an account of his ministry shall be given hereafter. There- | fore for this time I make an end of my sayings.

However, we are told by Mormon that the Nephites and also the Lamanites who were spared the awful destruction that had ravaged the whole land wherein they lived, were shown many great favors, and had blessings innumerable poured out upon their heads. These great rewards for their righteousness were culminated by the greatest blessing of all — the Savior of Mankind, the great Messiah for whose coming they had awaited, Jesus Christ, the Eternal Son of God, "did truly manifest Himself unto them — showing His body unto them, and ministering unto them; and an account of His ministry shall be given hereafter."

THE BIRTH OF CHRIST

Luke, the Evangelist, who had his information from eyewitnesses to the historical beginning of Christianity, and who records incidents which only Mary, the Mother of Jesus, herself, could have told him, gives us a more detailed account of that epoch-making event than any other writer from that time.

One of his most precious bits of history is the well-known narrative of the experiences of the shepherds. They were keeping watch over their flocks during the night, at Bethlehem. Perhaps they were passing the time conversing about the Messiah and His Kingdom, which were burning questions at that time. Suddenly they were surrounded by a bright light. They became frightened. In the light an angel appeared, who told them not to be afraid. He had come, he said, with tidings of great joy: "For unto you is born this day in the City of David a Savior, which is Christ the Lord." He also gave them a sign by which they would know the truth of this announcement: "Ye shall find the babe wrapped in swaddling clothes lying in a manger." (Luke 2:8-12) And suddenly a heavenly choir was heard praising God: "Glory to God in the highest, and on earth peace, good will toward men."

The Angel who first appeared was, probably, Gabriel, the Angel of the annunciation. (*Ibid.*, 1:26-27) Gabriel, we are told, is Noah, the second ancestor of the human race, who seems to have had a special mission at the time of the introduction of the Dispensation of the Meridian of Time, just as the Angel Moroni had in connection with the beginning of the Dispensation in which we live.

CLOTHES SIGNIFICANT

The "swaddling clothes," by which the shepherds would know the Babe Whose birth had been announced, were perhaps not the common covering in use at that time. There, probably, were many babes in the overcrowded inn, resting in convenient mangers.

Mme. Lydia Von Finkelstein Mountford, a Christian Jewess, herself born in the Holy Land, in her little book on *Jesus in His Homeland,* tells us that the baby clothes which were wrapped around the Babe Jesus, were the same which had belonged to the family of David. There was, she says, a garment of white silk with blue stripes, indicating royalty. There was a red garment, that betokened the House of Boaz. There also was a garment of "many colors," indicating that the Child Jesus was to be the Savior of the entire world. This garment of "many colors," proclaimed Him not only of David and Boaz, but of every branch of the House of Jacob. It was similar to the multicolored coat which Jacob gave to his son, Joseph, who proved to be a savior of Egypt, and of his father's whole family. This is all very probable. For, only if the garments—swaddling clothes— meant something great to the shepherds, could they be a sign to them of the birth of the Messiah.

AND NOW WE TURN TO THE BOOK OF MORMON

Shortly after the arrival of Lehi and his little company in the Valley of Lemuel, near the Red Sea, Nephi had a remarkable vision. An angel came and stood before him and said, "Nephi, what beholdest thou?"

He said: "A Virgin, most beautiful and fair."

The Angel then asked: "Knowest thou the condescension of God?"

Nephi seemed puzzled about this question. Condescension, of course, means the act of descending to a lower level. Paul uses the word in that sense when he says: "Mind not high things, but condescend to men of lower estate. Be not wise in your own conceits." (Romans 12:16) But how could the vision of the Virgin suggest the "Condescension of God?" That was not clear to Nephi. Wherefore he answered rather evasively: "I know that He loveth His children; nevertheless, I do not know the meaning of all things."

The Angel then gave the explanation: "Behold the Virgin whom thou seest is the mother of the Son of God, after the manner of the flesh."

This indeed was a revelation on the condescension of God.

The Virgin now was carried away in the spirit "for the space of a time." Then she reappeared in the vision "bearing a Child in her arms," and the Angel said, "Behold the Lamb of God, yea, even the Son of the Eternal Father!"

Never was a more important revelation than this given to the world. The incarnation of God in Jesus! The Lamb of God, the

Son of the Eternal Father, manifested to destroy the works of the adversary.

WORLD IN CONFUSION

If we look around us in the world today, we see a great deal of confusion. For many years most of the nations of the earth have been in battle array. Great sums of money have been expended every year to expedite war, and make it appear inevitable. Reason has lost its footing; sanity has upset its throne. Men in vast numbers are leaving the beliefs and traditions of their fathers; great nations openly proclaim a disbelief in God. The teachings of the Savior, for ages the vanguard of our civilization, are now declared to be foolishness. Waters from the stinking springs of iniquity have flooded the earth, deep as an ocean, with their impurities. Hatred is burning in many camps, and no one knows when the fires will be beyond control. All this is the work of the adversary.

The outlook might be discouraging but for the fact that the Lord is the Head of the human family, and will gain the victory just as surely as He conquered death by His resurrection. St. Paul tells us: "So Christ was once offered to bear the sins of many; and unto them that look for Him shall He appear the second time without sin unto Salvation." (Hebrews 9:28) That is to conquer sin, as well as death.

Let us remember that this land (America) is dedicated to God. Let us remember the truly solemn occasion when Moroni, the Commander-in-Chief of the Nephite Armies, B.C. 73, made a banner of his mantle and on it wrote: "In memory of our God, our religion, and freedom, and our peace, our wives, and our children." (Alma 46:12) Moroni fastened it to a pole and called it *The Title of Liberty*. God and religion first, for without these there will be no freedom, neither peace.

But Jesus Christ is the God of this land in a special sense, as we read in Ether 2:12: "Behold this is a choice land, and whatsoever nation shall possess it shall be free from bondage, and from captivity, and from all other nations under heaven, if they will but serve the God of the land, who is Jesus Christ, who hath been manifest by the things we have written."

This is the daily message of the Gospel of Jesus Christ which shall be heard in every home in this much favored land, so highly blessed by the Lord.

JESUS CHRIST
PROPHECIES CONCERNING CHRIST, HIS ADVENT, MINISTRY, DEATH AND RESURRECTION

One of the most remarkable things connected with the history of the Nephites is the great plainness and detail with which the coming of the Redeemer and the events of His life in Judæa were revealed through their prophets, many of whom lived before the time of His advent. Among other things it was declared that:

God, Himself, should come down from Heaven among the children of men and should redeem His people. (Mosiah 15:1)

He should take upon Himself flesh and blood. (Mosiah 15:1)

He would be born in the land of their fathers, the Land of Jerusalem. (Alma 7:10)

His mother's name should be Mary. (Mosiah 3:8; Alma 7:10)

She should be a Virgin of the City of Nazareth, very beautiful and fair, a precious and chosen vessel. (I Nephi 11:13)

She should be overshadowed and conceive by the power of the Holy Ghost. (Alma 7:10)

He should be called Jesus Christ, the Son of God. (Mosiah 3:8)

At His birth a new star should appear in the heavens. (Helaman 14:5)

He should be baptized by John at Bethabara, beyond Jordan. (I Nephi 10:9)

John would testify that he had baptized the Lamb of God. (I Nephi 10:10)

After His baptism, the Holy Ghost should come down upon Him in the form of a dove. (I Nephi 11:27; II Nephi 31:8)

He should call twelve men as His special witnesses, to minister in His name. (I Nephi 12:8)

He should go forth among the people ministering in power and great glory, casting out devils, healing the sick, raising the dead and performing many mighty miracles. (Mosiah 3:5)

He should take upon Himself the infirmities of His people. (Alma 7:12)

He should suffer temptation, pain of body, hunger, thirst and fatigue; blood should come from every pore of His body by reason of His anguish because of the abominations of His people. (Mosiah 3:7, 9)

He should be lifted upon the cross and slain for the sins of the world. (I Nephi 19:10)

He should be buried in a sepulchre, where He would remain for three days. (Mosiah 3:10)

After He was slain He should rise from the dead and should make Himself manifest by the power of the Holy Ghost unto the Gentiles. (I Nephi 10:11)

He should lay down His life according to the flesh and take it up again by the power of the Spirit, that He might bring to pass the resurrection of the dead; He being the first who should arise. At His resurrection many graves should be opened and should yield up their dead. These would be Saints who had beforetime passed away and they would appear to the living. (Helaman 14:15-25)

He should redeem all mankind who would believe on His name. (Helaman 14:2)

In the above we have not mentioned the sayings of Isaiah and other Jewish prophets which are inserted in the Book of Mormon but which also appear in the Bible.

VISITS OF JESUS BEFORE HIS ADVENT

On this continent, as on the Eastern, Jesus manifested Himself from time to time to some of His faithful servants, before His coming in the flesh. He was the guide of His people, the guardian of the Church and the revealer of the mind and will of the Godhead. He went before the people of Jared in their journey, instructing them and covenanting with them. Few events recorded in the Book of Mormon are more widely known than His appearance in the body of His Spirit to the Brother of Jared. His statements with regard to Himself then were: "I am He who was prepared from the foundation of the world to redeem My people. Behold, I am Jesus Christ, . . . and even as I appear unto thee to be in the spirit, will I appear unto My people in the flesh." (Ether 3:8-16)

In later centuries, when making known the *Divine Will* to the elder Alma regarding the discipline of His Church, He declares: "It is I that taketh upon Me the sins of the world; for it is I that hath created them; and it is I that granteth unto him that believeth unto the end, a place at my right hand."

Not only were the Nephites very familiar with the details of the earthly life of the Redeemer but they also were made acquainted by their prophets, from Lehi to Samuel, the Lamanite, with the fact that after His resurrection He would visit them. This was shown in a vision to Nephi (I Nephi 12:6) and Nephi taught it to his people. (II Nephi 26:1-9) It so continued to be taught by the Priesthood throughout all their generations. (Alma 16:20)

The time of His birth at Bethlehem was also declared by the prophets with great exactness. Nephi states that His birth should take place 600 years from the time his father left Jerusalem and this prophecy was known to all his descendants. (See, I Nephi 10:4; 19:8;

II Nephi 25:19) We quote the last: "For according to the words of the prophets, the Messiah cometh in six hundred years from the time that my father left Jerusalem; and according to the words of the prophets, and also the word of the angel of God, His name shall be Jesus Christ, the Son of God."

In the year B.C. 6, Samuel, the Lamanite, prophesied that on this continent, at the time of the Savior's birth, there should be great lights in the heavens, so that there should be a day, a night and another day without darkness; a new star should rise and many signs and wonders should be seen in the heavens. Again at the time of the Redeemer's death, the sun should be darkened and refuse to give its light and also the stars; and there should be no light upon the face of this land from the time He died until the time that He rose again from the dead. At His death there should be mighty thunderings and lightnings for many hours and the earth should shake and tremble and the rocks which are upon its face should be broken up and there should be great tempests and many mountains should be laid low and valleys should become mountains of great height and many cities become desolate. Then many graves should yield up their dead and many Saints who would then be resurrected, should appear to the living.

SIGNS OF HIS BIRTH

When six hundred years had passed from the time Lehi left Jerusalem, the time arrived of which Samuel, the Lamanite, and other prophets had borne testimony, when the phenomena should appear to bear witness of the birth of the Son of God. As the day drew near, signs and miracles increased among the people. But the hardened in heart began to circulate the idea that the time had passed and the prophecies had failed. They even went so far as to appoint a day when all who believed in the coming of the Savior should be slain, except the sign be first given.

This gross wickedness caused Nephi, the High Priest, great sorrow. Before God, in mighty prayer, he bowed all the day long. At last the comforting word came; the Anointed One said: "On this night shall the sign be given, and on the morrow come I into the world, to show unto the world that I will fulfill all that which I have caused to be spoken by the mouth of my holy prophets." (III Nephi 1:13) As it was thus declared, so was it fulfilled. At the going down of the sun, it was as light as daytime and so continued until the morning, when the sun again rose in its usual course. A new star had also appeared in the heavens. Then the faithful rejoiced. They knew that their Redeemer was born and that the great Plan of Salvation had entered its most glorious phase; but the wicked quaked with awful dread; they realized the extent of their iniquity, they also knew they were murderers at heart, for they had planned and plotted to take the lives of the righteous and in the fear and terror that this overwhelming sense of their piteous condition wrought, they sank to the earth as though they were dead.

Many now believed who previously had scorned the divine messages that the prophets bore; but others, inspired of Satan, as soon as they recovered from the fright which the appearance of the promised signs had produced, began to explain them away and by various lying rumors endeavored to nullify the good that had been done in the hearts of many. Others commenced to teach that it was no longer expedient to observe the Law of Moses, or to offer sacrifices, not comprehending that the infinite Sacrifice had not yet been made.

SIGNS OF THE DEATH OF CHRIST

On the fourth day of the thirty-fourth Nephite year after Christ's birth, the promised sign of the Savior's crucifixion began. A terrible and devastating tempest burst upon the land. The earth quivered and groaned and opened in wide, unfathomable depths and chasms. Mountains were riven and swallowed up in yawning gulfs or were shattered into fragments and dispersed like hail before the tearing wind. Towers, temples, houses, were torn up, scattered in pieces or crushed by falling rocks and together with their inmates were lost and ground to dust in the convulsion. Blue and yellow flames burst from the edges of sinking rocks, blazed for a moment and then all was the deepest darkness. Rain poured down in torrents, cloudbursts, like floods washed away all with which they came in contact and pillars of steaming vapor seemed to unite earth and sky. This unparalleled storm raged throughout the land for three hours only, but during its short continuance the whole face of nature was changed. Mountains sank, valleys rose, the sea swept over the plains, large stagnant pools of water usurped the place of flourishing cities, great chasms, rents and precipices disfigured the face of the earth.

Three days of unnatural and impenetrable darkness followed the horrors of the tempest and from the heavens a voice was heard by the affrighted people proclaiming in their terrified ears the destruction that had taken place.

Terrible was the catalogue of the woes which that heavenly voice rehearsed. Nearly all their cities, great and small, had been destroyed by flood or fire, by earthquake or hurricane. The desolation was complete, the face of the earth was changed, tens of thousands, probably millions, of their neighbors had suddenly been called to meet the reward of their sinful lives; for this destruction came upon them that their wickedness and abominations might be hid from the face of Heaven and that the blood of the prophets and Saints they had slain might not come up any more in appeal unto God against them.

When the heavenly voice had finished the recital of the calamities that had befallen the land and its inhabitants, the speaker appealed to those who yet lived to repent of their sins and return unto Him and that they should have Eternal Life and He then revealed to them who He was. He declared unto them that:

> I am Jesus Christ, the Son of God. I created the heavens and the earth and all things that in them are. I was with the Father from the beginning. I am in the Father and the Father in Me and in Me hath the Father glorified His name.
>
> I came unto My own and My own received Me not. And the Scriptures concerning My coming are fulfilled.
>
> And as many as have received Me, to them have I given to become the sons of God and even so will I to as many as shall believe on My name, for behold, by Me redemption cometh and in Me is the law of Moses fulfilled.
>
> I am the light and the life of the world. I am Alpha and Omega, the beginning and the end. (III Nephi 9:18)

After the people had heard this glad message they ceased mourning for their dead relatives and there was silence in the land for the space of many hours. Then again was the voice of Jesus heard recounting how often He had sought to gather His children but they would not and promising in the future that He would again gather them if they would listen to Him. But if they would not heed Him the places of their dwellings should become desolate until the time of the fulfilling of God's covenant with their fathers. When the people heard this awful prophecy they began to weep and howl again because of the loss of their kindred and friends.

As on the Eastern Continent, so on this; at the time of Christ's Resurrection, numbers of the Saints who were dead arose from their graves and were seen and known by many of the living.

Three days had passed in darkness, in terror and in woe, when the thick mist rolled off the face of the land, revealing to the astonished eyes of the survivors how great had been the convulsions that had shaken the earth. As the darkness passed away the earth ceased to tremble, the rocks were no longer rent and the tumultuous noises ended. Nature was again at peace and peace filled the hearts of the living; their mourning was turned into praise and their joy was in Christ, their Deliverer.

CHRIST MINISTERS TO THE NEPHITES

Some time after the terrible events which denoted His death, exactly how long we know not, a multitude assembled near the temple which was in the Land Bountiful. Possibly many of those holding the High Priesthood had gone there to call upon the Lord and to officiate in the duties of their calling. The multitude spake one to another with regard to the Savior, of whose death the three days of unexampled, impenetrable darkness had been a sign.

While thus engaged a strange, sweet voice fell upon their ears, yet it pierced them to the centre, so that their whole frames trembled. At first they knew not what it said or whence it came, nor even when the words were again spoken did they understand. But when those words came a third time they understood their glorious import and knew that it was the voice of God. He said unto them: "Behold, My Beloved Son, in Whom I am well pleased, in whom I have glorified My name—hear ye Him." (III Nephi 11:7) Obedient to this heavenly voice they cast their eyes upward and to their joyous astonishment beheld the Messiah, clothed in a white robe, coming out of heaven.

Even yet they did not comprehend who He was but thought Him an angel. As He descended to the earth and stood in their midst their wondering eyes were all turned towards Him but for awe not a mouth was opened nor a limb moved. Then the Redeemer stretched forth His hand and said to the multitude: "Behold, I am Jesus Christ, whom the prophets testified shall come into the world. And behold, I am the light and life of the world; and I have drunk out of that bitter cup which the Father hath given Me, and have glorified the Father in taking upon Me the sins of the world, in the which I have suffered the will of the Father in all things from the beginning." (III Nephi 11:10-11)

Then the whole multitude fell to the earth. They remembered the sayings of the prophets; they realized that their God stood in the midst of them.

Again the Risen Redeemer spake: "Arise," said He, "and come forth unto Me, that ye may thrust your hands into My side, and also that ye may feel the prints of the nails in My hands and in My feet, that ye may know that I am the God of Israel, and the God of the whole earth, and have been slain for the sins of the world." (III Nephi 11:14)

Now they who heard Him from the first to the last went forth and assured themselves that it was He of Whom the prophets had spoken. Then with shouts of praise they cried: "Hosanna! blessed be the name of the Most High God." (III Nephi 11:17) And they fell down at His feet and worshiped Him.

Jesus next called Nephi to Him, then eleven others and gave them authority to baptize the people, at the same time strictly charging them as to the manner in which they should perform this ordinance, that all disputes on this point might cease among the believers.

After Jesus had chosen the Twelve Disciples, He commenced to teach the people the principles of the fullness of the Gospel. Step by step He led them over the same precious ground of universal truth as He had done to His followers in Galilee, Judæa and Samaria. Sometimes, though, the difference of the inspired translation of the Book of Mormon and the worldly-wise one of the Bible, a slight difference is noticeable in the wording of the instructions but as a rule these differences are trivial, the advantage being with the Nephites, whose greater faith drew from the Savior deeper truths than Judah had received, or caused Him to display greater manifestations of His omnipotence and boundless love. From the believers He would turn to the Twelve, and give them special instructions as His ministers; then again He would shed forth His words of mercy, truth and divine wisdom upon the multitude and by and by again address the Disciples. So He continued day by day until all was revealed, either to the multitude or to the Twelve, that was necessary for the Eternal Salvation of the obedient. Then He left them to the care and ministry of the chosen Disciples.

Some have wondered why Jesus should have given so many of His teachings to the Nephites in the same manner and words as He did to the Jews. The reason is that those teachings were perfect and could not be improved. They were universal, that is, they were adapted to the wants of all peoples, whether of Israel or of the Gentiles, whether of Judah or Joseph. Among the teachings that He gave the Nephites which do not appear in the Bible account of His ministrations to the Jews are His references to the "Ten Lost Tribes," His explanations of the prophecies of Malachi and of the Prophet Isaiah, His statements regarding the then future history of the peoples on this continent, particularly drawing attention to those events that would concern and be connected with the remnant of the House of Lehi and His declarations regarding the name by which His Church should be known.

The miracles that attended His ministry on this land were, many of them, of the same character as the wondrous works He performed among the Jews; only frequently more marvelous and more glorious, on account of the greater faith of the Nephites. He healed the sick, cast out devils, raised the dead in Bountiful as He did in Judæa and Galilee. But there were other manifestations that were somewhat different. In the Land of Jerusalem, Jesus miraculously fed five thousand by increasing the store of loaves and fishes that had been provided; in Bountiful He administered the Emblems of His body and blood when neither the Disciples nor the multitude had brought either bread or wine. Angels ministered to men during His labors among the Jews; they did so more abundantly during

His visits to the Nephites. Again, though we are told in the Bible
of the Holy Redeemer blessing little children, we are nowhere to
read therein of the glorious manifestations, the outpourings of the
Spirit, the ministry of angels, the baptism of fire that took place when
the Risen Redeemer condescended to bless the little ones of the
Nephites.

NAMES AND TITLES GIVEN TO JESUS CHRIST
IN THE BOOK OF MORMON

Among the names and titles given to Christ in the Book of
Mormon are: Mediator, Messiah, Redeemer, Great and True Shep-
herd, Lamb, Lamb of God, Son of God, Son of Righteousness, Son of
the Eternal Father, Only Begotten of the Father, Creator, The
Eternal Father of Heaven and Earth, King, King of all the Earth, God
of Israel, God of the whole Earth, Most High God, Lord Omnipotent,
Mighty God, Holy One, Holy One of Israel, Mighty One of Jacob,
Wonderful Counselor, Prince of Peace and several others.

Jesus Christ did show Himself unto the people of Nephi, as the multitude were gathered together in the Land Bountiful, and did minister unto them; and on this wise did He show Himself unto them.

CHAPTER 11

Jesus Christ in the Land Bountiful. III Nephi, Chapters 11-26, is a record of the ministry of Jesus among the People of Nephi in the Land Bountiful, shortly after His resurrection. It is the minutes of a conference held for three days on the Temple Grounds in Bountiful. It contains the fulness of the Gospel.

1. *The Eternal Father Proclaims the Christ*—2. *The Resurrected Christ Appears*—3. *The Multitude Permitted to Feel His Wounds*—4. *Mode of Baptism Prescribed*—5. *Contention and Disputations Forbidden*—6. *Christ the Rock.*

1. *The Eternal Father proclaims the Christ.*

2. *The Resurrected Christ appears.*

Some time after the tribulations that marked the Sacrifice of the Lord of life and glory, exactly how long we know not, a multitude assembled near the Temple which was in the Land Bountiful. The sacred building, it seems, was not destroyed in the late devastating convulsions. Possibly many of those holding the High Priesthood had assembled there to call upon the Lord, and to officiate in the duties of their calling. At any rate, those whom Jesus deemed worthy to be His Twelve Disciples, by some inspiration, gathered there. With the rest of the multitude they conversed on the marvelous changes that had been wrought by the desolating earthquakes and their attendant horrors. They also spake one to another with regard to the Savior, of Whose death the three days of unexampled, impenetrable, darkness had been a sign.

While thus engaged, a strange, sweet, voice fell upon their ears, yet it pierced them to the center, causing their whole frames to tremble. At first they wist not what it said or whence it came; nor even when the words were again repeated did they understand. But when they came a third time they understood their glorious import, and knew that it was the voice of God. He said unto them, "Behold My Beloved Son, in Whom I am well pleased, in Whom I have glorified My Name; Hear ye Him." Obedient to this heavenly voice they cast their eyes upward, and to their joyous astonishment beheld the Messiah, clothed in a white robe, descending out of Heaven.

Even yet they did not comprehend Who it was, but thought Him an angel. As He descended to the Earth and stood in their midst, their wondering eyes were all turned toward Him, but for awe not a mouth was opened nor was a limb moved. Then the Redeemer stretched forth His hand and said unto the multitude, "Behold I am Jesus Christ, Whom the prophets testified should come into the world; and behold, I am the Life and Light of the world; and I have drunk out of the bitter cup which the Father hath given to Me, and have glorified the Father in taking upon Me the sins of the world, in the which I have suffered the will of the Father in all things from the beginning."

Then the whole multitude fell to the earth, they remembered the sayings of the prophets; they realized that their God stood in the midst of them.

Again the Redeemer spake: "Arise, said He, and come forth unto Me, that you may thrust your hands into My side, and also that ye may feel the prints of the nails in My hands and in My feet, that ye may know that I am the God of Israel and the God of the whole Earth, and have been slain for the sins of the world."

Now they who heard Him, even from the first to the last, went forth and assured themselves that it was He of Whom the prophets had spoken. Then with shouts of joy, and with praises to God, the Father, they cried: "Hosanna! blessed be the Name of the Most High God." And they all fell down at His feet and worshiped Him.

---

1. And now it came to pass that there were a great multitude gathered together, of the people of Nephi, round about the temple which was in the land Bountiful; and they were marveling and wondering one with another, and were showing one to another the great and marvelous change which had taken place.

2. And they were also conversing about this Jesus Christ, of whom the sign had been given concerning his death.

3. And it came to pass that while they were thus conversing one with another, they heard a voice as if it came out of heaven; and they cast their eyes round about, for they understood not the voice which they heard; and it was not a harsh voice, neither was it a loud voice; nevertheless, and notwithstanding it being a small voice it did pierce them that did hear to the center, insomuch that there was no part of their frame that it did not cause to quake; yea, it did pierce them to the very soul, and did cause their hearts to burn.

4. And it came to pass that again they heard the voice, and they understood it not.

5. And again the third time they did hear the voice, and did open their ears to hear it; and their eyes were towards the sound thereof; and they did look steadfastly into heaven, from whence the sound came.

6. And behold, the third time they did understand the voice which they heard; and it said unto them:

7. Behold my Beloved Son, in whom I am well pleased, in whom I have glorified my name—hear ye him.

8. And it came to pass, as they understood they cast their eyes up again towards heaven; and behold, they saw a Man descending out of heaven; and he was clothed

---

VERSES 1-11. *Jesus appears.* A great multitude of Nephites were gathered together on the Temple Grounds in Bountiful. They were conversing about the destruction wrought by the recent storms and earthquakes, of which news had reached them (III Nephi 8:5-25), also of the darkness that had followed. While thus conversing they heard a voice, a sound that pierced their very souls; but it

in a white robe; and he came down and stood in the midst of them; and the eyes of the whole multitude were turned upon him, and they durst not open their mouths, even one to another, and wist not what it meant, for they thought it was an angel that had appeared unto them.

9. And it came to pass that he stretched forth his hand and spake unto the people, saying:

10. Behold, I am Jesus Christ, whom the prophets testified shall come into the world.

11. And behold, I am the light and the life of the world; and I have drunk out of that bitter cup which the Father hath given me, and have glorified the Father in taking upon me the sins of the world, in the which I have suffered the will of the Father in all things from the beginning.

3. *The multitude permitted to feel His wounds.*

12. And it came to pass that when Jesus had spoken these words the whole multitude fell to the earth; for they remembered that it had been prophesied among them that Christ should show himself unto them after his ascension into heaven.

13. And it came to pass that the Lord spake unto them saying:

14. Arise and come forth unto me, that ye may thrust your hands into my side, and also that ye may feel the prints of the nails in my hands and in my feet, that ye may know that I am the God of Israel, and the God of the whole earth, and have been slain for the sins of the world.

15. And it came to pass that the multitude went forth, and thrust their hands into his side, and did feel the prints of the nails in his hands and in his feet; and this they did do, going forth one by one until they had all gone forth, and did see with their eyes and did feel with their hands, and did know of a surety and did bear record, that it was he, of whom it was written by the prophets, that should come.

16. And when they had all gone forth and had witnessed for themselves, they did cry out with one accord, saying:

17. Hosanna! Blessed be the name of the Most High God! And they did fall down at the feet of Jesus, and did worship him.

---

was not understood. Again and again, that voice came. As they heard it a third time, they became aware of its meaning. It said: "Behold, My beloved Son, in Whom I am well pleased, in Whom I have glorified My Name. Hear ye Him."

As they looked towards the source from which that voice came, they saw a heavenly Being descending. He was clothed in white robes. As He stood among them, they thought He was an angel. But He spoke to them saying: "Behold, I am Jesus Christ."

VERSES 12-17. *Preliminaries of the meeting.* The multitude, naturally, on hearing Jesus speak, fell down to worship Him. But Jesus bade them arise and convince

THE FIRST DAY

4. *Mode of Baptism prescribed.*

18. And it came to pass that he spake unto Nephi (for Nephi was among the multitude) and he commanded him that he should come forth.

19. And Nephi arose and went forth, and bowed himself before the Lord and did kiss his feet.

20. And the Lord commanded him that he should rise. And he arose and stood before him.

21. And the Lord said unto him: I give unto you power that ye shall baptize this people when I am again ascended into heaven.

5. *Contention forbidden.*

22. And again the Lord called others, and said unto them likewise; and he gave unto them power to baptize. And he said unto them: On this wise shall ye baptize; and there shall be no disputations among you.

23. Verily I say unto you, that whoso repenteth of his sins through your words and desireth

---

themselves of His Divinity. They were permitted to touch His pierced side and His hands and feet. They had seen Him descending, but that was not proof of His identity. Another being from the other side might have impersonated Him. But when they gently contacted the marks of His Atonement on the cross, they had a personal experience that could not be successfully contradicted. Then they burst forth in song: "Hosanna! Blessed be the Name of the Most High God!"

"Hosanna" is a salutation, and also it is a prayer, "Save Now!" In verse 14, Jesus is called "The God of Israel, and the God of the whole Earth." Here He is called, "The Most High God." The Hebrew, "El Elyone," is a name applied to the Supreme and All-Glorious Ruler of the Universe.

Again the multitude fell down to pray. This time our Lord did not restrain them; instead He began to instruct them.

Verses 18-21. *Jesus commands Nephi to come forth.* After the preliminaries occasioned by His unexpected visit were cared for, Jesus began the impromptu meeting by calling Nephi and others to come forward, and He gave them authority to perform baptisms.

Nephi was the grandson of Helaman and the custodian of the Plates of Brass and other sacred things. (III Nephi 1:2-3) He was one of the multitude. (v. 18) When Jesus called him, he rose immediately, came forward and fell down before our Lord and kissed His feet; an act of complete submission of his body to the power and authority of the Savior. Jesus commanded him to arise, and when Nephi stood up before Him, He said: "I give unto you power that ye shall baptize this people when I am again ascended into Heaven." Thus, Jesus conferred authority upon Nephi to officiate in the ordinance of baptism among the Nephites.

to be baptized in my name, on this wise shall ye baptize them— Behold, ye shall go down and stand in the water, and in my name shall ye baptize them.

24. And now behold, these are the words which ye shall say, calling them by name, saying:

25. Having authority given me of Jesus Christ, I baptize you in the name of the Father, and of the Son, and of the Holy Ghost. Amen.

26. And then shall ye immerse them in the water, and come forth again out of the water.

27. And after this manner shall ye baptize in my name; for behold, verily I say unto you, that the Father, and the Son, and the Holy Ghost are one; and I am in the Father, and the Father in me, and the Father and I are one.

28. And according as I have commanded you thus shall ye baptize. And there shall be no disputations among you, as there have hitherto been; neither shall there be disputations among you concerning the points of my doctrine, as there have hitherto been.

29. For verily, verily I say unto you, he that hath the spirit of contention is not of me, but is of the devil, who is the father of contention, and he stirreth up the hearts of men to contend with anger, one with another.

30. Behold, this is not my doctrine, to stir up the hearts of men with anger, one against another; but this is my doctrine, that such things should be done away.

31. Behold, verily, verily, I say unto you, I will declare unto you my doctrine.

32. And this is my doctrine, and it is the doctrine which the Father hath given unto me; and I bear record of the Father and the Father beareth record of me, and the Holy Ghost beareth record of the Father and me; and I bear record that the Father commandeth all men, everywhere, to repent and believe in me.

VERSE 22. *The Lord called others.* Others were called and received the same authority. Their names are given in III Nephi 19:4. They were instructed regarding the ordinance of Baptism, so as to prevent, beforehand, different opinions and any discussions concerning this "gate by which ye shall enter."

VERSE 23. *Whom to baptize.* "Whoso repenteth of his sins through your words and desireth to be baptized in My Name."

VERSES 23 (cont.)-26. *How to baptize.* "Behold, ye shall go down and stand in the water, and in My Name shall ye baptize them." "And then shall ye immerse them in the water, and come forth again out of the water." *The baptismal formula:* "These are the words which ye shall say, calling them by name, saying: Having authority given me of Jesus Christ, I baptize you in the Name of the Father, and of the Son, and of the Holy Ghost, Amen."

VERSE 27. *The Divine Trinity.* Three persons in the Godhead are mentioned in this formula. The reason is this: "For behold, verily I say unto you, that the Father, and the Son, and the Holy Ghost are one; and I am in the Father, and

33. And whoso believeth in me, and is baptized, the same shall be saved; and they are they who shall inherit the kingdom of God.

34. And whoso believeth not in me, and is not baptized, shall be damned.

35. Verily, verily, I say unto you, that this is my doctrine, and I bear record of it from the Father; and whoso believeth in me believeth in the Father also; and unto him will the Father bear record of me, for he will visit him with fire and with the Holy Ghost.

36. And thus will the Father bear record of me, and the Holy Ghost will bear record unto him of the Father and me; for the Father, and I, and the Holy Ghost are one.

37. And again I say unto you, ye must repent, and become as a little child, and be baptized in my name, or ye can in nowise receive these things.

38. And again I say unto you, ye must repent, and be baptized in my name, and become as a little child, or ye can in nowise inherit the kingdom of God.

6. *Christ the Rock.*

39. Verily, verily, I say unto you, that this is my doctrine, and whoso buildeth upon this buildeth upon my rock, and the gates of hell shall not prevail against them.

40. And whoso shall declare more or less than this, and estab-

---

the Father in Me, and the Father and I are one. *They are one governing body.* Again, "Whoso believeth in Me believeth in the Father also; and unto him will the Father bear record of Me, for He will visit him with fire and the Holy Ghost. For the Father and I and the Holy Ghost are one." (*See,* vv. 35-36)

VERSES 37-38. *Ye must repent, and become as a little child.* Our Lord, next, tells Nephi and the other disciples, and He repeats it by way of emphasis, that repentance, a childlike disposition and baptism, are three conditions without which none can inherit the Kingdom of God.

Why childlike? The normal little child is willing to learn. It is content with the arrangements of its father or mother, its teachers, its lawful governors, to whom it is bound by love, admiration and respect. Because of that disposition it fits perfectly in its place in the family, the school or the society. It is so with those who have experienced repentance, been "born again" and become as a little child, childlike, and have proved their willingness to obey the Lord; they are they who can have a useful place in God's Kingdom. They are never rebellious. In other words, they are as a stone laid in its proper place in the structure reared on the Eternal Rock, which Rock is Jesus Christ.[1]

---

[1]The corner stone, or the head stone of the corner (Psalm 118:22), is that stone put as the angle of a building usually at the foundation thereof, and is of fundamental importance. It is often used metaphorically. Jesus Christ is the Corner Stone which was rejected by the Jews, but It however became the Corner Stone of the Church.

As Christ, the Head, is called the Corner Stone, so also His followers, true believers, who are built upon that Stone, and derive spiritual strength from that Stone which is the foundation of the Church, are called stones. (I Peter 2:5)

lish it for my doctrine, the same cometh of evil, and is not built upon my rock; but he buildeth upon a sandy foundation, and the gates of hell stand open to receive such when the floods come and the winds beat upon them.

41. Therefore, go forth unto this people, and declare the words which I have spoken, unto the ends of the earth.

VERSES 39-40. *Eternal Rock.* This expression seems to be one application of that familiar Christian theological term, "And who shall declare more or less than this, and establish it for My doctrine, the same cometh of evil, and is not built upon My rock. (verses 37-40) Our Lord here explains the meaning of the "rock" upon which His Church stands. *It is the doctrine of Christ concerning Repentance and Baptism.* "This," He says, "is My doctrine," My rock. (Compare Matthew 16:18; III Nephi 18:12-13) It is the doctrine of Christ that is the "Rock" and not the Apostle Peter as some declare. The expression "the rock" is used in the scriptures with different meanings that must be interpreted according to the context. There are times when it refers to the gospel and other times when the reference is to revelation and again to the Church. The Apostle Paul says, in speaking of the Children of Israel when they journeyed in the Wilderness of Arabia: "And did all drink the same spiritual drink: for they drank of that spiritual Rock that followed them: and *that Rock was Christ.*" (I Corinthians 10:4)

The Lord did not call Peter a stone, which in meaning is the same as *rock,* upon which He would build His Church. The Savior recognized that Peter was steadfast, and could be relied upon to carry forth the work of the ministry to which he was to be assigned. Peter was immovable, firm, and unwavering in keeping the commandments of God. *The Lord called him a stone in that sense.*

Nowhere in the Standard Works of the Church is *revelation* directly called a rock. It is a means whereby a truth is made known and is not that truth itself. Christ told Peter that the knowledge Peter had that "Thou are the Christ, the Son of the living God," was given (revealed) to him by "My Father which is in Heaven," and upon this truth, that is (this Rock) that I am Christ, will I build My Church. (Matthew 16:18) "The Church is built upon My Gospel"; (III Nephi 27:10) this is My Gospel . . . that I came into the world to do the will of My Father, because My Father sent Me." (*Ibid.,* 27:10; *See,* particularly verse 40)

The Hebrew language contains many words the meaning of which is determined by that to which they refer. The *Rock of Horeb* which Moses struck with his staff, and from which water burst forth to slake the thirst of the Children of Israel on an occasion as they wandered in the Arabian Desert is a perfect example. Rock here refers to a solid mass of stony material, or to a mass of concreted pebbles, sometimes called a conglomerate. Also, "The Lord is my Rock," refers to something entirely different. (Psalm 18:2) Further on in the same *Song* of King David, we read: "For who is God save the Lord? or who is a rock save our God?" The first sentence of the Hebrew Scriptures is what we have said before, perhaps the most sublime words ever written: "In the beginning God (the Hebrew Rock) created the Heaven and the Earth." (Genesis 1:1) Rock, here, refers to the Creator. Certainly, the Savior did not refer to Peter as the Creator. Yet, in fine, that is just what some people would have them believe who do not understand the Gospel in its fulness.

Nothing with כ *and* פ *in the dictionary to indicate any solid ground.*	To force ⸻ כָּפֹה, כְּפָא,
	Top, Summit ⸻ כִּפָּה,
	Universe ⸻ כִּפָּה,
	Governing the Universe ⸻ מֶלֶךְ בְּכִפָּה

Stone ⸻	אֶבֶן, מַצֵּבָה,
Rock ⸻	צוּר, סֶלַע,
Flint, Pebbly boulder ⸻	חַלָּמִישׁ,

Targum Unkalos

	אַבְנָא	אֵ׳
Gen. 28:22 ⸻	קָמָה	בֵּ׳
Exod. 33:23 ⸻	טִנָּרָא	טִ׳
Num. 28:8-10 ⸻	כֵּיפָא *	בֵּ׳
Num. 23:9 ⸻	טוּרַיָּא,	Mountains ⸻ אֵ׳
Num. 24:21 ⸻	תִּקְפָּא	Stronghold ⸻ תָּ׳
Deut. 8:15; 32:4, 15, 18, 30, 37 תִּקְפָּא	Referring to the Creator	אֵלָ׳

---

* כֵּיפָא *Targum[2] translates these words according to what they refer to. He uses the*
in Numbers 28:8-10, where Moses hit the rock and brought forth water.
Thus St. John did not state that the Savior called Simon צוּר, *for* צוּר *in general*
refers to the Creator, or Most Powerful: as Moses in his farewell song referred to
God, but He compared Peter to a stone כֵּיפָא *which in Hebrew means* סֶלַע .

Now: St. Matthew 16:18.

וְגַם אֲנִי אוֹמֵר לָךְ כִּי כֵיפָא (סֶלַע) אָתָּה, וְעַל הַצּוּר הַזֶּה הִנְנִי אֶבְנֶה קְהִלָּתִי, וְשַׁעֲרֵי הַשַּׁחַת
לֹא יָכוֹלוּ נֶגְדָּהּ :

וְאַף אֲנָא מֵימַר לָךְ אֲרֵי כֵיפָא אַתְּ, וְעַל תִּקְפָּא הָדֵין אֲנָא כ) אַבְנָא כְּנִשְׁתָּאִי, וּתְרָעֵי
דַחֲבָלָא לָא מֵיכְלוּ קֳבֵלֵיהּ :

2See footnote on following page.

The thoughtful student will gain much knowledge by studying the accompanying plate which was prepared especially to illustrate the fact which is here advanced.

The Gates of Hell. The gate and gateway of an ancient city were important parts of every community. There, the people gathered to hear the news. (Genesis 19:1; 23:10; 34:20) There, justice was administered. (Deuteronomy 21:19; 25:7; Joshua 20:4; Ruth 4:1-11) There, ambassadors were received. (Judges 9:35; Job 29:7-10; Jeremiah 17:19) On account of the importance of the gate the term sometimes referred to the entire city, as in Genesis 4:60; or to the people of the city, as in Samuel 15:2. In Assyria the gates were elaborate architectural works of art; lofty, magnificent, and guarded by symbolical figures. The *Gates of Hell* means the entire powers of Sheol.

Baptism anciently. Perhaps here we may remark that baptism is a sacred ordinance, or a rite, as old as the Gospel, itself. An illustration or two of this must suffice.

Adam, our venerated ancestor, was baptized. He asked the Lord for information concerning repentance and baptism, and received the light asked for. Then, "He was caught away by the Spirit of the Lord, and was carried down into the water, and was brought forth out of the water." By this means he received the Holy Ghost, and became, it seems, a High Priest, for we read, "And thou art after the order of Him Who was without beginning of days or end of years, from all eternity to all eternity." (*Pearl of Great Price,* Moses 6:52-68) The order of *Him* Who was without beginning of days or end of years, is, of course, the Order of Melchizedek, which is the Order of the Son of God.

The Waters of Mormon. Alma, about 147 years before our Lord, baptized in a clear spring called the *Waters of Mormon.* The significance of the baptism Alma administered was that the recipient was willing to serve God and keep His commandments during this life. The baptism was performed thus: "Alma took Helem, he being one of the first, and went and stood forth in the water, and cried, saying, O Lord, pour out Thy Spirit upon Thy servant, that he may do this work with holiness of heart. And when he had said these words, the Spirit of the Lord was upon him, and he said, Helem, I baptize thee, having authority from Almighty God, as a testimony that you have entered into a covenant to serve Him until you are dead as to the mortal body. And after Alma had said these words, both Alma and Helem came forth out of the water rejoicing, being filled with the Spirit." (Mosiah 18:5-17) This was a covenant for this life, but the reward of it would be *Life Everlasting.*

---

[2]*Targum,* the translation of the Old Testament Scriptures into Aramaic. This version originated at a time when Hebrew had given way to Aramaic as the popular language of the Jews. The need of explaining the Old Testament Scriptures to the people after their subjugation by the Persians is suggested by Nehemiah 8:8, where we read that Ezra read the Law to the people, while it was interpreted by his assistants, interpreters—Meturgemans—as they were called. As the Targum was not committed to writing, little of it has survived. There are, indeed, three Targums of the Pentateuch and one of the Prophets, as well as of the Psalms, Job, Proverbs, the Song of Songs, Ruth, Lamentations, Esther, and Ecclesiastes. The Targum is not of much critical value, but throws considerable light on the life of the Jews at the time it was composed. (*Encyclopedia Americana,* 1952)

CHAPTER 12

1. *The Savior's teachings to the Nephites.*

2. *He calls and commissions the Twelve Disciples.*

Jesus next called Nephi to Him, then eleven others, and gave them authority to baptize the people, at the same time strictly charging them as to the manner in which the ordinance was to be performed, to the end that all disputes on this point might not occur among the believers. The names of the Twelve whom the Savior chose were: Nephi, his brother Timothy, whom he had beforetime raised from the dead, also his son, Jonas, and Mathoni, Mathonihah, Kumen, Kumenonhi, Jeremiah, Shemnon, Jonas, Zedekiah, and Isaiah. These Twelve are to sit in the great Day of Judgment as the Judges of the seed of Lehi, and be themselves judged by the Twelve Apostles whom Jesus had called from among the Jews.

After Jesus had chosen the Twelve, he commenced to teach the people the principles of the fulness of the Gospel. Step by step he led them over the same precious ground of universal truth as he had his followers in the temple at Jerusalem, by the shore of the Sea of Galilee, and on the hillsides of Judea and Samaria. Sometimes, through the difference of the inspired translation of the Book of Mormon from the worldly-wise one of the Bible, a slight difference is noticeable in the wording of the instructions, but as a rule these differences are trivial, the advantage being with the Nephites, whose greater faith drew from the Savior deeper truths than Judah had received, or caused him to display greater manifestations of His omnipotence and boundless love. From the believers He would turn to the Twelve, and give them special instructions as His ministers, then again He would shed forth His words of mercy, truth and divine wisdom upon the multitude; and by and by again address the disciples. So He continued day by day until all was revealed, either to the multitude or to the Twelve, that was necessary for the eternal salvation of the obedient.

Some have wondered why Jesus should have given so many of the same teachings to the Nephites as He did to the Jews. The reason is that those teachings were perfect and could not be improved. They were universal, that is, they were adapted to the wants of all peoples, whether of Israel or of the Gentiles, whether of Judah or Joseph. They were a portion of the everlasting gospel and had to be preached to all the world as a witness, to those who dwelt in America as well as those of Asia, Africa and Europe. Thus we find in the teachings given to the Nephites what we term the first principles of the gospel — faith, repentance and baptism; we also find those divine lessons of love, truth, humility and duty that glorified the Savior's "Sermon on the Mount." These we shall not reproduce but will draw attention to other teachings of the Savior not recorded by the Four Evangelists; that is they are not to be found in their writings as at present contained in the New Testament.

1. And it came to pass that when Jesus had spoken these words unto Nephi, and to those who had been called, (now the number of them who had been called, and received power and authority to baptize, was twelve) and behold, he stretched forth his hand unto the multitude, and cried unto them, saying: Blessed are ye if ye shall give heed unto the words of these twelve whom I have chosen from among you to minister unto you, and to be your servants; and unto them I have given power that they may baptize you with water; and after that ye are baptized with water, behold, I will baptize you with fire and with the Holy Ghost; therefore blessed are ye if ye shall believe in me and be baptized, after that ye have seen me and know that I am.

2. And again, more blessed are they who shall believe in your words because that ye shall testify that ye have seen me, and that ye know that I am. Yea, blessed are they who shall believe in your words, and come down into the depths of humility and be baptized, for they shall be visited with fire and with the Holy Ghost, and shall receive a remission of their sins.

3. *His words to the multitude.*

3. Yea, blessed are the poor in spirit who come unto me, for theirs is the kingdom of heaven.

4. And again, blessed are all they that mourn, for they shall be comforted.

VERSES 1-2. *The Holy Ghost promised.* The instructions noted above were given to Nephi and the Disciples whom Jesus had chosen to preach and baptize. To the multitude, Jesus said, "Blessed are ye, if ye shall heed unto the words of these whom I have chosen from among you to minister unto you, and be your servants." The Savior promised them the Holy Ghost on condition of faith and baptism, after that ye have Me and know that I am. Seeing and knowing should produce faith.

THE LAW OF LAWS

Having instructed the Twelve Disciples regarding baptism, and authorized them to teach and baptize, our Lord delivered the discourse recorded in this Chapter. (12) It was mainly directed to the Disciples, and parts of it were intended for them, but it was spoken in the hearing of the assembled throng.

VERSES 2-20. *The Law of the Gospel.* The first part of this Chapter is the fundamental Law of the Kingdom of God. Concerning this we read as the word of the Lord, "Whoso remembereth these sayings of Mine and doeth them, him will I raise up at the Last Day," or as Alma expresses the same divine promise, "Whosoever putteth his trust in Him, the same shall be lifted up at the Last Day." (Mosiah 23:22) For, to trust in Him is to keep His commandments.

4. *The Sermon on the Mount.* Compare Matthew 5.

5. And blessed are the meek, for they shall inherit the earth.

6. And blessed are all they who do hunger and thirst after righteousness, for they shall be filled with the Holy Ghost.

7. And blessed are the merciful, for they shall obtain mercy.

8. And blessed are all the pure in heart, for they shall see God.

9. And blessed are all the peacemakers, for they shall be called the children of God.

10. And blessed are all they who are persecuted for my name's sake, for theirs is the kingdom of heaven.

11. And blessed are ye when men shall revile you and persecute, and shall say all manner of evil against you falsely, for my sake;

12. For ye shall have great joy and be exceeding glad, for great shall be your reward in heaven; for so persecuted they the prophets who were before you.

THE BEATITUDES

The Preface to the Law of Christ is the so-called *Beatitudes* which indicate the true nature of the citizen in the *Kingdom of God.*

VERSE 3. *Blessed are the poor in spirit who come unto me.* That is, who come unto Me conscious of their imperfections and destitution, and are therefore humble. "For theirs is the Kingdom of Heaven."

VERSE 4. *Blessed are all they that mourn.* Levity does not become a follower of Christ. (*See, Doctrine and Covenants* 88:121) But those who mourn for their fellow men "Shall be comforted."

VERSE 5. *Blessed are the meek.* That is those who have the humility that consists in complete dependence on God. "For they shall inherit the Earth," not as conquering invaders, but as children and heirs of Him, Who is Ruler of all.

VERSE 6. *Blessed are all they who do hunger and thirst after righteousness.* Those who feel the same need in their souls of righteousness as they do in their bodies for food; "For they shall be filled with the Holy Ghost," Who will keep them in the way of righteousness.

VERSE 7. *Blessed are the merciful.* Those who feel compassion with their fellow men; "For they shall obtain mercy."

VERSE 8. *Blessed are the pure in heart.* Those whose hearts are cleansed of evil thoughts and designs can see God in all things, and therefore be happy whatever betides, in life or in death.

VERSE 9. *Blessed are all the peacemakers.* All who make it their object in life to plant peace and love. "They shall be called," or recognized as "the children of God." Because in that respect they are following Him Who is, as are they, a child of the King—the *Prince of Peace.*

VERSES 10-12. *Blessed are ye when men shall revile you and persecute and shall say all manner of evil against you falsely, for My sake.* To suffer persecution as a follower of Christ is a privilege, "For great shall be your reward in Heaven." Persecution on Earth for the sake of the Lamb, entitles one to association with the innumerable company of glorious martyrs in Heaven.

13. Verily, verily, I say unto you, I give unto you to be the salt of the earth; but if the salt shall lose its savor wherewith shall the earth be salted? The salt shall be thenceforth good for nothing, but to be cast out and to be trodden under foot of men.

14. Verily, verily, I say unto you, I give unto you to be the light of this people. A city that is set on a hill cannot be hid.

15. Behold, do men light a candle and put it under a bushel? Nay, but on a candlestick, and it giveth light to all that are in the house;

16. Therefore let your light so shine before this people, that they may see your good works and glorify your Father who is in heaven.

17. Think not that I am come to destroy the law or the prophets. I am not come to destroy but to fulfil;

18. For verily I say unto you, one jot nor one tittle hath not passed away from the law, but in me it hath all been fulfilled.

19. And behold, I have given you the law and the commandments of my Father, that ye shall believe in me, and that ye shall repent of your sins, and come unto me with a broken heart and a contrite spirit. Behold, ye have the commandments before you, and the law is fulfilled.

20. Therefore come unto me and be ye saved; for verily I say unto you, that except ye shall keep my commandments, which I have commanded you at this time, ye shall in no case enter into the kingdom of heaven.

21. Ye have heard that it hath been said by them of old time, and it is also written before you, that thou shalt not kill, and whosoever shall kill shall be in danger of the judgment of God;

VERSE 13. *Jesus next reminds His followers that they are to be the salt of the Earth.* Through their moral qualities they were to preserve the world from moral decay. Salt is a great preservator that keeps and upholds the wholesome condition of animal life. But if the salt should lose its savor, it would be useless, except as gravel on the road, to be trodden under foot of men. Jesus uses the simile to impress upon the minds of His hearers their obligation to sustain and support the *Kingdom* by keeping His commandments. Savor means *taste, tang, zest, property* or *quality.*

VERSES 14-20. *Behold, do men light a candle and put it under a bushel?* They were also to be a light unto this people. In answer to the foregoing question which He, Himself, asks, He says, "Nay, but on a candlestick, and it giveth light to all that are in the house." But if it goes out in darkness, it is still more useless. Under a bushel this cover might become even a stumbling block in the darkness. Hence the necessity of keeping the commandments.

But they must be kept as the Lord interprets them, and not men. And so, our Lord, in this discourse, gives us his explanation concerning them.

VERSES 21-26. *Murder.* Our Lord teaches that the once common view, according to which only the actual slayer of a fellow being stands in danger of the judgment of God, is too narrow. One who is angry with his brother is in the same danger. One who shall say to his brother, "Raca" (which means literally, "empty-

22. But I say unto you, that whosoever is angry with his brother shall be in danger of his judgment. And whosoever shall say to his brother, Raca, shall be in danger of the council; and whosoever shall say, Thou fool, shall be in danger of hell fire.

23. Therefore, if ye shall come unto me, or shall desire to come unto me, and rememberest that thy brother hath aught against thee—

24. Go thy way unto thy brother, and first be reconciled to thy brother, and then come unto me with full purpose of heart, and I will receive you.

25. Agree with thine adversary quickly while thou art in the way with him, lest at any time he shall get thee, and thou shalt be cast into prison.

26. Verily, verily, I say unto thee, thou shalt by no means come out thence until thou hast paid the uttermost senine. And while ye are in prison can ye pay even one senine? Verily, verily, I say unto you, Nay.

27. Behold, it is written by them of old time, that thou shalt not commit adultery;

28. But I say unto you, that whosoever looketh on a woman, to lust after her, hath committed adultery already in his heart.

29. Behold, I give unto you a commandment, that ye suffer none of these things to enter into your heart;

30. For it is better that ye should deny yourselves of these things, wherein ye will take up your cross, than that ye should be cast into hell.

31. It hath been written, that whosoever shall put away his wife, let him give her a writing of divorcement.

32. Verily, verily, I say unto you, that whosoever shall put away his wife, saving for the cause of fornication, causeth her to

head") stands in danger of a trial before the ecclesiastical council. Similarly, one who begins by calling his brother a "fool," stands in danger of finally landing in "hell" fire, as an outcast. For the road downward is easy. Our Lord counsels His hearers to be reconciled to each other, to forgive each other, before they engage in worship. Anger and devotion to God do not mix. They are like fire and water. "I, the Lord, will forgive all men." (D. & C. 64:10) Be reconciled to thy brother, and then come to me.

VERSES 27-30. *Adultery.* The view that adultery is only the actual transgression of the Seventh Commandment, when a married woman is concerned, our Lord corrects. The transgression begins in the heart. "Whosoever looketh on a woman"; that is, whosoever views one of the opposite sex for the deliberate purpose of awakening impure lusts, has "Committed adultery already in his heart." "It is better," he says, "that ye should deny yourselves of these things, wherein ye will take up your cross, than that ye should be cast into hell."

VERSES 31-32. *Divorce.* This suggests the question of divorce. Our Lord's teaching here seems to be that even a written letter of divorcement does not in fact dissolve a marriage union, except when fornication—the Evangelists say adultery—is the cause of it. Such a bill, barely permitted by the Mosaic Law, may release the parties from living together in this life, but their status is nevertheless such

commit adultery; and whoso shall marry her who is divorced committeth adultery.

33. And again it is written, thou shalt not forswear thyself, but shall perform unto the Lord thine oaths;

34. But verily, verily, I say unto you, swear not at all; neither by heaven, for it is God's throne;

35. Nor by the earth, for it is his footstool;

36. Neither shalt thou swear by the head, because thou canst not make one hair black or white;

37. But let your communication be Yea, yea; Nay, nay; for whatsoever cometh of more than these is evil.

38. And behold, it is written, an eye for an eye, and a tooth for a tooth;

39. But I say unto you, that ye shall not resist evil, but whosoever shall smite thee on thy right cheek, turn to him the other also;

40. And if any man will sue thee at the law and take away thy coat, let him have thy cloak also;

41. And whosoever shall compel thee to go a mile, go with him twain.

42. Give to him that asketh thee, and from him that would borrow of thee turn thou not away.

43. And behold it is written also, that thou shalt love thy neighbor and hate thine enemy;

44. But behold I say unto you, love your enemies, bless them that curse you, do good to them that hate you, and pray for them

---

that if the woman join another man, she becomes an adulteress, and the man, an adulterer. This must necessarily apply to a marriage union formed by divine authority, where the two by the Almighty, have been made "one flesh." "What therefore God hath joined together, let no man put asunder." (Matthew 19:6) A genuine marriage union is not to be tied and untied as dictated by human whims. What God has done, must be left for God to undo.

VERSES 33-37. *Perjury.* The old time law was, "Thou shalt not forswear thyself." Our Lord says, "Swear not at all." Man has nothing to swear by, nothing to offer as a pledge for his veracity. Neither heaven nor earth, neither his head nor even his hair belongs to him. "Let your communication be Yea, yea; Nay, nay." More than that is evil.

VERSES 38-41. *Retaliation.* "It is written, an eye for an eye, and a tooth for a tooth." This is the formula for perfect justice. An eye for an eye, a tooth for a tooth, but no more. This is far in advance of even modern ideas of retaliation that call for punishment "with a vengeance." But the ideal of our Lord is still higher: "Ye shall not resist evil, but whosoever shall smite thee on thy right cheek, turn to him the other also."

That non-resistance is a mighty force for good is shown in the history of the Christian Church during the first centuries, when it conquered the world by the "rod of its mouth and the breath of its lips." (Isaiah 11:4) Also in the story of the people of Anti-Nephi-Lehi. (Alma 24:6-27)

VERSES 42-48. *Giving and lending.* Both are duties, according to ability, "For the sake of retaining a remission of your sins from day to day." (Mosiah 4:26)

who despitefully use you and persecute you;

45. That ye may be the children of your Father who is in heaven; for he maketh his sun to rise on the evil and on the good.

46. Therefore those things which were of old time, which were under the law, in me are all fulfilled.

47. Old things are done away, and all things have become new.

48. Therefore I would that ye should be perfect even as I, or your Father who is in heaven is perfect.

It is required to feed the hungry, clothe the naked, visit the sick, etc. "And see that all these things are done in wisdom and order." (*Ibid.*, v. 27)

As for borrowing, God says, "Remember that whosoever among you borroweth of his neighbor should return the thing that he borroweth, according as he doth agree, or else thou shalt commit sin also." (Mosiah 4:28) This really restricts the duty of lending to articles that can be used and returned, such as a cloak, a book, a loaf of bread, even if the same loaf cannot be returned, or, as an exception, a piece of money, the equivalent of which can be returned when earned.

But, as a rule, to lend money is not a matter of charity, although it is called lending. It is a cold business proposition. Generally the borrower obligates himself to pay dearly for the use of his neighbor's money, and often he cannot do it, and the lender, if he is not adequately secured, becomes the loser. Frequently the result is estrangement and ill feelings between those who should be friends and brethren, and often leads to apostasy. It is a wise rule not to borrow or lend money under such conditions. The Lord does not place his disciples under obligation to engage in business transactions for which they are not equipped, even if requested as loans.

CHAPTER 13

Compare Matthew 6

1. The Savior's sermon to the Nephites continued.

1. Verily, verily, I say that I would that ye should do alms unto the poor; but take heed that ye do not your alms before men to be seen of them; otherwise ye have no reward of your Father who is in heaven.

2. Therefore, when ye shall do your alms do not sound a trumpet before you, as will hypocrites do in the synagogues and in the streets, that they may have glory of men. Verily I say unto you, they have their reward.

3. But when thou doest alms let not thy left hand know what thy right hand doeth;

4. That thine alms may be in secret; and thy Father who seeth in secret, himself shall reward thee openly.

5. And when thou prayest thou shalt not do as the hypocrites, for they love to pray, standing in the synagogues and in the corners of the streets, that they may be seen of men. Verily I say unto you, they have their reward.

6. But thou, when thou prayest, enter into thy closet, and when thou hast shut thy door, pray to thy Father who is in secret; and thy Father, who seeth in secret, shall reward thee openly.

7. But when ye pray, use not vain repetitions, as the heathen, for they think that they shall be heard for their much speaking.

8. Be not ye therefore like unto them, for your Father knoweth what things ye have need of before ye ask him.

9. After this manner therefore

VERSES 1-4. *I would that ye should do alms unto the poor.* To do alms unto the poor is an important duty, but the Lord warns against charity with ostentation. "Let not thy left hand know what thy right hand doeth."

THE LORD'S PRAYER

Our Father who art in Heaven, hallowed by Thy Name. Thy will be done on Earth as it is in Heaven. And forgive us our debts, as we forgive our debtors. And lead us not into temptation, but deliver us from evil. For Thine is the Kingdom, and the power, and the glory, forever. Amen.

VERSES 5-13. What is called the Lord's Prayer is incorporated in the discourse here. It is a model for prayer in all ages.

pray ye: Our Father who art in heaven, hallowed be thy name.

10. Thy will be done on earth as it is in heaven.

11. And forgive us our debts, as we forgive our debtors.

12. And lead us not into temptation, but deliver us from evil.

13. For thine is the kingdom, and the power, and the glory, forever. Amen.

14. For, if ye forgive men their trespasses your heavenly Father will also forgive you;

15. But if ye forgive not men their trespasses neither will your Father forgive your trespasses.

16. Moreover, when ye fast be not as the hypocrites, of a sad countenance, for they disfigure their faces that they may appear unto men to fast. Verily I say unto you, they have their reward.

17. But thou, when thou fastest, anoint thy head, and wash thy face;

18. That thou appear not unto men to fast, but unto thy Father,

---

VERSE 9. *Our Father Who art in Heaven.* To Him our prayers should be directed, in the name of the Son, Jesus Christ. (Mosiah 15:2-4) *Hallowed be Thy Name.* A petition for preservation from doing anything that might dishonor the ineffable Name, particularly in times of persecution.

VERSE 10. *Thy will be done on Earth as it is in Heaven.* The short petition, *Thy Kingdom come* is not part of this version of the Prayer as it is in the New Testament, but it may be assumed that when the will of God is being done on Earth as it is in Heaven, then His Kingdom is established among men.

VERSE 11. *And forgive us our debts, as we forgive our debtors.* The meaning is obvious. The author of Ecclesiasticus well says: "He that revengeth shall find vengeance from the Lord, and He will surely keep his sins (in remembrance). Forgive thy neighbor the hurt that he hath done unto thee, so shall thy sins also be forgiven when thou prayest." (Eccl. 28:1-5)

VERSE 12. *And lead us not into temptation.* This means, keep us from too strong trials, least we should fall. *But deliver us from evil.* From sin and from Satan.

VERSE 13. *For Thine is the Kingdom, and the power, and the glory, forever.* This is a shorter form of the Doxology of David as recorded in Chron. 29:10-12.

VERSES 16-18. *Fasting.* To *Fast* has always been a religious observance, whether prescribed by regulations, or voluntary. In our Church, as is well known, one day a month, formerly the first Thursday, now the first Sunday, in the month is designated *Fast Day.* According to President Brigham Young, the observance of it was originally made necessary for the taking care of the poor. They came, he says, to the Prophet Joseph Smith in Kirtland, before the Law of Tithing had been revealed, and from him wanted assistance. It was decided upon setting aside one day monthly for the poor. The intention was to carry all the flour, meat, butter, fruit, etc., that ordinarily would be eaten on that day to someone selected to distribute it among the needy Saints.

Among the Jews, fasting became a frequent observance. It was considered an expression of penitence, in connection with prayer, or as a sacrifice and a sign of mourning, or great piety. The Lord condemns all ostentation on such occasions as hypocrisy. He says, "When thou fasteth, anoint your head and wash thy face." That is, make it an occasion of joy and gladness. Do not disfigure your faces with

who is in secret; and thy Father, who seeth in secret, shall reward thee openly.

19. Lay not up for yourselves treasures upon earth, where moth and rust doth corrupt, and thieves break through and steal;

20. But lay up for yourselves treasures in heaven, where neither moth nor rust doth corrupt, and where thieves do not break through nor steal.

21. For where your treasure is, there will your heart be also.

22. The light of the body is the eye; if, therefore, thine eye be single, thy whole body shall be full of light.

23. But if thine eye be evil, thy whole body shall be full of darkness. If, therefore, the light that is in thee be darkness, how great is that darkness!

24. No man can serve two masters; for either he will hate the one and love the other, or else he will hold to the one and despise the other. Ye cannot serve God and Mammon.

2. The Savior's Commandments to the Twelve.

25. And now it came to pass that when Jesus had spoken these words he looked upon the twelve whom he had chosen, and said unto them: Remember the words which I have spoken. For behold, ye are they whom I have chosen to minister unto this people.

Therefore I say unto you, take no thought for your life, what ye shall eat, or what ye shall drink; nor yet for your body, what ye shall put on. Is not the life more than meat, and the body than raiment?

26. Behold the fowls of the air,

---

dust and ashes, as the hypocrites do. Then, "thy Father, Who seeth in secret, shall reward thee openly."

The Prophet Isaiah, with whose writings the Nephites were familiar, says, "Is it such a fast that I have chosen? A day for a man to afflict his soul? Is it to bow down his head as a bulrush, and to spread sackcloth and ashes under him? Wilt thou call this a fast, and an acceptable day to the Lord? . . . Is it not to deal thy bread to the hungry, and that thou bring the poor that are cast out, to thine house? When thou seest the naked, that thou cover him; and that thou hide not thyself from thine own flesh. (Isaiah 58:5-7)

VERSES 19-24. *Ye cannot serve God and Mammon.* Our Lord closes this part of His sermon with the solemn assurance that in His service there is no divided allegiance. There is not such a condition as both God and Mammon. It must be, either, or, "No man can serve two masters . . . Ye cannot serve God and Mammon" — both God and Greed.

VERSES 25-34. *But seek ye first the Kingdom of God.* These verses contain a brief version of the Savior's address to the Twelve. The Twelve are exhorted to remember what the Lord had spoken, for He says, "Ye are they whom I have chosen to minister to this people." They were His servants, His messengers. As such, they were to devote their whole time to the work of the ministry and to His interests. God, Who feeds the birds and clothes the lilies would also clothe them. "Take no thought of the morrow." This is not, as some have assumed, a general license

for they sow not, neither do they reap nor gather into barns; yet your heavenly Father feedeth them. Are ye not much better than they?

27. Which of you by taking thought can add one cubit unto his stature?

28. And why take ye thought for raiment? Consider the lilies of the field how they grow; they toil not, neither do they spin;

29. And yet I say unto you, that even Solomon, in all his glory, was not arrayed like one of these.

30. Wherefore, if God so clothe the grass of the field, which today is, and tomorrow is cast into the oven, even so will he clothe you, if ye are not of little faith.

31. Therefore take no thought, saying, What shall we eat? or, What shall we drink? or, Wherewithal shall we be clothed?

32. For your heavenly Father knoweth that ye have need of all these things.

33. But seek ye first the kingdom of God and his righteousness, and all these things shall be added unto you.

34. Take therefore no thought for the morrow, for the morrow shall take thought for the things of itself. Sufficient is the day unto the evil thereof.

---

to live a thoughtless life in idle waste of time; it is the assurance of the Master that God will provide His faithful servants with what they need if they will fulfill the mission to which He has called them, as He did when He sent the Twelve Apostles in Palestine on their mission. Immediately before His suffering in the Garden, He asked them, "When I sent you without purse, and scrip, and shoes, lacked ye anything?" And they answered, "Nothing."

Our Lord could, therefore say to the Twelve here, as to those on the former occasion, "Take no thought for the morrow."

CHAPTER 14

1. The Savior's Sermon Continued—2. Further Instructions to the Multitude—3. Compare Matthew 7.

1. *The Lord again turns to the Multitude with Instructions and Admonitions.*

1. And now it came to pass that when Jesus had spoken these words he turned again to the multitude, and did open his mouth unto them again, saying: Verily, verily, I say unto you, Judge not, that ye be not judged.

2. For with what judgment ye judge, ye shall be judged; and with what measure ye mete, it shall be measured to you again.

3. And why beholdest thou the mote that is in thy brother's eye, but considerest not the beam that is in thine own eye?

4. Or how wilt thou say to thy brother: Let me pull the mote out of thine eye—and behold, a beam is in thine own eye?

5. Thou hypocrite, first cast the beam out of thine own eye; and then shalt thou see clearly to cast the mote out of thy brother's eye.

6. Give not that which is holy unto the dogs, neither cast ye your pearls before swine, lest they trample them under their feet, and turn again and rend you.

2. *Further Instructions to the Multitude.*

7. Ask, and it shall be given unto you; seek, and ye shall find; knock, and it shall be opened unto you.

8. For every one that asketh, receiveth; and he that seeketh, findeth; and to him that knocketh, it shall be opened.

VERSES 1-2. *Judge not. For as ye judge, ye will be judged.*

VERSES 3-5. *The "mote and the beam."* Do not approach thy brother in order to remove the mote from his eye, as long as you have a beam in your own eye. The beam will prevent you from coming near him; also from seeing what you are doing.

"A person who would say another is not a Latter-day Saint, for some trifling affair in human life, proves that he does not possess the Spirit of God. . . . If I judge my brethren and sisters, unless it is by revelations of Jesus Christ, I have not the Spirit of Christ, if I had, I should judge no man."—President Brigham Young.

VERSES 7-11. *Prayer.* Our Lord says, "Ask, and it shall be given unto you; seek, and ye shall find; knock, and it shall be opened unto you."

With these words Christ summons His people to prayer. And more especially to prayer in the private closet. That is the beginning and continuation of spiritual progress. Prayer is the secret of success, from a spiritual point of view, in every human undertaking. The Church, itself, is the answer to a prayer, and every im-

9. Or what man is there of you, who, if his son ask bread, will give him a stone?

10. Or if he ask a fish, will he give him a serpent?

11. If ye then, being evil, know how to give good gifts unto your children, how much more shall your Father who is in heaven give good things to them that ask him?

12. Therefore, all things whatsoever ye would that men should do to you, do ye even so to them, for this is the law and the prophets.

13. Enter ye in at the strait gate; for wide is the gate, and broad is the way, which leadeth to destruction, and many there be who go in thereat;

14. Because strait is the gate, and narrow is the way, which leadeth unto life, and few there be that find it.

15. Beware of false prophets, who come to you in sheep's clothing, but inwardly they are ravening wolves.

16. Ye shall know them by their fruits. Do men gather grapes of thorns, or figs of thistles?

17. Even so every good tree bringeth forth good fruit; but a corrupt tree bringeth forth evil fruit.

18. A good tree cannot bring forth evil fruit, neither a corrupt tree bring forth good fruit.

19. Every tree that bringeth not forth good fruit is hewn down, and cast into the fire.

20. Wherefore, by their fruits ye shall know them.

21. Not every one that saith unto me, Lord, Lord, shall enter

---

portant revelation has come through minds prepared to receive them by communion with the Father. It was only after Elijah had been "hidden" as it were, with God, that he had the power to combat the paganism of his day. Moses, too, emerged from his association with God in the desert as one of the greatest of law givers and prophets. Prayer, public and private, is more important than preaching. Both, in order to be effective, must be dictated by the Holy Spirit.

In answer to prayer. "Latter-day Saints have individually almost without exception been given testimonies of the divine mission of the Prophet Joseph Smith. Hundreds of thousands of people who have never lived in a Stake of Zion, who have never gathered to Zion, from the midnight sun country of Scandinavia to South Africa, have been blessed with individual testimonies in answer to earnest prayer, that God lives and that Jesus Christ is in very deed His Son, also that Joseph Smith is a prophet of God."—President Heber J. Grant.

VERSE 12. *The Golden Rule.* In the experience of a disciple of the Master, the question may at times arise as to what his duties are to his fellow men. The *Golden Rule* is the infallible answer to that question: "All things whatsoever ye would that men should do to you, do ye even so to them. For this," the Lord says, "is the law and the prophets." And, perhaps, we may reverently add, the Gospel, too! For this rule embodies the entire moral code of the Gospel of Christ and the Kingdom of God, equally binding upon nations and associations, as in individuals.

In Tobit 4:15, we read, "Do that to no man, which thou hatest"; but the precept, as delivered by the Savior, enjoins us not only to avoid harming our brother, but to do that which benefits him.

into the kingdom of heaven; but he that doeth the will of my Father who is in heaven.

22. Many will say to me in that day: Lord, Lord, have we not prophesied in thy name, and in thy name have cast out devils, and in thy name done many wonderful works?

23. And then will I profess unto them: I never knew you; depart from me, ye that work iniquity.

24. Therefore, whoso heareth these sayings of mine and doeth them, I will liken him unto a wise man, who built his house upon a rock—

25. And the rain descended, and the floods came, and the winds blew, and beat upon that house; and it fell not, for it was founded upon a rock.

26. And every one that heareth these sayings of mine and doeth them not shall be likened unto a foolish man, who built his house upon the sand—

27. And the rain descended, and the floods came, and the winds blew, and beat upon that house; and it fell, and great was the fall of it.

VERSES 15-23. *Beware of false prophets.* Jesus adds a warning against *false prophets*, stating that, "Ye shall know them by their fruits." If their work is, or results in unrighteousness, then they are false prophets.

CHAPTER 15

1. The Law of Moses Superseded—2. The Giver of the Law—3. The Sheep of Another Fold.

1. *The Law of Moses superseded.*

1. And now it came to pass that when Jesus had ended these sayings he cast his eyes round about on the multitude, and said unto them: Behold, ye have heard the things which I taught before I ascended to my Father; therefore, whoso remembereth these sayings of mine and doeth them, him will I raise up at the last day.

2. And it came to pass that when Jesus had said these words he perceived that there were some among them who marveled, and wondered what he would concerning the law of Moses; for they understood not the saying that old things had passed away, and that all things had become new.

3. And he said unto them: Marvel not that I said unto you that old things had passed away, and that all things had become new.

4. Behold, I say unto you that the law is fulfilled that was given unto Moses.

2. *The Giver of the Law fulfills the Law.*

5. Behold, I am he that gave the law, and I am he who covenanted with my people Israel; therefore, the law in me is fulfilled, for I have come to fulfil the law; therefore it hath an end.

6. Behold, I do not destroy the prophets, for as many as have not been fulfilled in me, verily I say unto you, shall all be fulfilled.

7. And because I said unto you that old things have passed away,

---

VERSES 1-4. *The Law of Moses.* When Jesus had reached a point in His teachings wherein He told the people that old things had passed away, and that all things had become new, He perceived that some of His hearers were wondering about the meaning of what He said.

Among the Jews, anciently, it was customary during the discourses of the masters to ask questions concerning matters not clearly understood by them. It seems that the Nephites had perpetuated that course of action, for, at this particular time in His address Jesus became aware, possibly through their questions, that some of His hearers did not understand what He said about old and new things. (III Nephi 12:46-47) This gave Him occasion to explain this important subject — "The Law is fulfilled that was given unto Moses." (v. 4) Jesus said unto them: "Marvel not that I said unto you, that old things had passed away, and that all things had become new.

VERSES 5-10. *The Law in Me is fulfilled.* According to the explanation given by our Lord this does not mean that a truth revealed during the Old Covenant is

I do not destroy that which hath been spoken concerning things which are to come.

8. For behold, the covenant which I have made with my people is not all fulfilled; but the law which was given unto Moses hath an end in me.

9. Behold, I am the law, and the light. Look unto me, and endure to the end, and ye shall live; for unto him that endureth to the end will I give eternal life.

10. Behold, I have given unto you the commandments; therefore keep my commandments. And this is the law and the prophets, for they truly testified of me.

---

no longer true; nor that the fundamental principles of righteousness are changed. It means this:

The Old Covenant had numerous ceremonies and contained many institutions, all of which were types of Christ, intended to teach the children of God the Plan of Salvation. By the sacrifices God demonstrated the awful consequences of sin; the holiness of God was seen in the separation of His sanctuary from the things of the world; the necessity of repentance, the Atonement, and the duties of the Priesthood, etc., were all typified. But the life and Person of Christ were the fulfillment of all such types and typical institutions. Consequently, we now look to Him for the precepts and examples which before His advent were foreshadowed in the services under the Mosaic Law. In that sense the Law of Moses was set aside for His more perfect demonstrations. It is the mode, not the subject, of instruction that has been done away with.

The Apostle Paul says: "But before faith," that is, the Gospel of Jesus, "come, we were kept under the Law, shut up unto the faith which should afterwards be revealed. Wherefore the Law was our schoolmaster to bring us to Christ, that we might be justified by faith. But after that faith [the Gospel] is come, we are no longer under a schoolmaster. For we are all the children of God by faith in Jesus Christ." (Galatians 3:23-26)

Continuing, Jesus said, "Behold I say unto you, that the Law is fulfilled that was given unto Moses. Behold, I am He that gave the Law, and I am He Who covenanted with My people, Israel: therefore, the Law in Me is fulfilled, for I have come to fulfill the Law; therefore it hath an end. Behold, I do not destroy the prophets, for as many as have not been fulfilled in Me, verily I say unto you, shall all be fulfilled. And because I said unto you, that old things hath passed away, I do not destroy that which hath been spoken concerning things which are to come. For behold, the covenant which I have made with My people is not all fulfilled; but the law which was given unto Moses hath an end in Me. Behold, I am the Law, and the Light; look unto Me, and endure to the end, and ye shall live, for unto him that endureth to the end, will I give Eternal Life. Behold, I have given unto you the commandments, therefore keep My commandments. And this is the Law and the prophets, for they truly testified of Me."

How simple, yet how grand, how plain and how comprehensive are these teachings, both in regard to Himself and to the Law which He had given to the forefathers of the Jews and to the Nephites! If men would receive these instructions in the plainness in which they were given, how much controversy would have an end, how much dissension would never have had an existence!

3. *The sheep of another fold.*

11. And now it came to pass that when Jesus had spoken these words, he said unto those twelve whom he had chosen:

12. Ye are my disciples; and ye are a light unto this people, who are a remnant of the house of Joseph.

13. And behold, this is the land of your inheritance; and the Father hath given it unto you.

14. And not at any time hath the Father given me commandment that I should tell it unto your brethren at Jerusalem.

15. Neither at any time hath the Father given me commandment that I should tell unto them concerning the other tribes of the house of Israel, whom the Father hath led away out of the land.

16. This much did the Father command me, that I should tell unto them:

17. That other sheep I have which are not of this fold; them also I must bring, and they shall hear my voice; and there shall be one fold, and one shepherd.

18. And now, because of stiffneckedness and unbelief they understood not my word; therefore I was commanded to say no more of the Father concerning this thing unto them.

19. But, verily, I say unto you that the Father hath commanded me, and I tell it unto you, that ye were separated from among them because of their iniquity; therefore it is because of their iniquity that they know not of you.

20. And verily, I say unto you again that the other tribes hath the Father separated from them; and it is because of their iniquity that they know not of them.

21. And verily I say unto you, that ye are they of whom I said: Other sheep I have which are not of this fold; them also I must bring, and they shall hear my voice; and there shall be one fold, and one shepherd.

22. And they understood me not, for they supposed it had been the Gentiles; for they understood not that the Gentiles should be converted through their preaching.

23. And they understood me not that I said they shall hear my voice; and they understood me not that the Gentiles should not at any time hear my voice—that

VERSES 11-24. *Jesus said to those Twelve whom He had chosen.* After having given these explanations to the multitude gathered about Him, Jesus again turned to the Twelve Disciples whom He had chosen and told them the meaning of the words He spoke unto the Jews when He was ministering among them in Jerusalem: "Other sheep I have which are not of this fold; them also I must bring, and they shall hear my voice; and there shall be one fold and one shepherd."

These other sheep of which Jesus spoke were the Nephites themselves, He said, who had separated from the Jews because of the latter's iniquity; and because of their continued evil doing and lack of faith, the knowledge of the existence of Lehi's family on the American Continent had been withheld from them. But, what was still more, Jesus had yet other sheep, which were neither of the Jews nor of the

I should not manifest myself unto them save it were by the Holy Ghost.

24. But behold, ye have both heard my voice and seen me; and ye are my sheep, and ye are numbered among those whom the Father hath given me.

Nephites, nor of the lands in which they dwelt. They were a people whom He had not yet visited and who had not yet heard His voice; but He had received a commandment from the Father to visit them, to show Himself unto them, and teach them, and then they would all be of the one fold and He would be Shepherd to them all.

The other sheep of which the Savior spoke, neither the Jews nor the Nephites, we understand to be the Ten Tribes of Israel who were carried away into captivity, but who unlike the House of Judah, never returned to their homes in the Promised Land. We are told that they were led away by the power of the Lord to a land of which no one knows anything, only that which is revealed.

CHAPTER 16

1. Yet Another Fold to Hear the Savior—2. Blessings Upon the Believing Gentiles—3. The State of Those Who Reject the Gospel—4. The Prophet Isaiah Cited.

1. *Yet another fold to hear the Savior.*

1. And verily, verily, I say unto you that I have other sheep, which are not of this land, neither of the land of Jerusalem, neither in any parts of that land round about whither I have been to minister.

2. For they of whom I speak are they who have not as yet heard my voice; neither have I at any time manifested myself unto them.

3. But I have received a commandment of the Father that I shall go unto them, and that they shall hear my voice, and shall be

---

VERSES 1-3. *Verily, verily,* means, in very truth; beyond question; certainly; truly; confidently. This phrase was used very often by the prophets of old. *I have other sheep which are not of this land, neither of the Land of Jerusalem.* Still other sheep, who have not yet heard His voice, but to whom He is about to go and manifest Himself.

Scattered abroad throughout the whole Earth, and also among all those of our brethren who ever have lived thereon, are sheep of Christ's Fold. Even the departed who dwell in the World of Spirits, and who in the flesh never heard of Him, Christ is their Shepherd Whose watchfulness is ever over them. Although His sheep, wherever they may be, are widely separated, He knows each one and loves them all.

In Ancient America the Nephites were numbered among His sheep. Many Jews in Old Jerusalem likewise were of His Fold, and in them He took great delight. But, however, He has other sheep, and of them Christ told the Nephites: ". . . they . . . have not as yet heard My voice; neither have I at any time manifested Myself unto them." (v. 2) Christ does not here even suggest they belong to the Twelve Tribes.

The Great Father of all, through His prescience, loving care, and guidance, so that in the end all His children might receive His blessings, commanded Our Lord, His Only Begotten Son, the Good Shepherd, to go unto them, that they might see Him, and "that they shall hear My voice, and shall be numbered among My sheep, that there may be one Fold and one Shepherd; therefore I go to show Myself unto them." (v. 3)

The question has been asked: "Who are these sheep of whom the Savior spoke?" In answer several suggestions have been made. Which one may be right, we do not know. All may be wrong. If the Good Shepherd thought it was important that the Nephites should know their whereabouts, He undoubtedly would have told them. Sufficient unto His purpose was His mere statement. However, that our opinion may not go by default in that it is not stated, we venture the following answer to the query.

These "other sheep" are good and just men who dwell in the Spirit World. Surely, the Lord, the Good Shepherd, has sheep there as well as here. Death does not destroy the fact of being followers of Christ; that is of being His sheep. We

numbered among my sheep, that there may be one fold and one shepherd; therefore I go to show myself unto them.

4. And I command you that ye shall write these sayings after I am gone, that if it so be that my people at Jerusalem, they who have seen me and been with me in my ministry, do not ask the Father in my name, that they may receive a knowledge of you by the Holy Ghost, and also of the other tribes whom they know not of, that these sayings which ye shall write shall be kept and

shall be manifested unto the Gentiles, that through the fulness of the Gentiles, the remnant of their seed, who shall be scattered forth upon the face of the earth because of their unbelief, may be brought in, or may be brought to a knowledge of me, their Redeemer.

5. And then will I gather them in from the four quarters of the earth; and then will I fulfil the covenant which the Father hath made unto all the people of the house of Israel.

2. Blessings upon the Believing Gentiles.

6. And blessed are the Gentiles, because of their belief in me, in and of the Holy Ghost, which witnesses unto them of me and of the Father.

7. Behold, because of their be-

---

are the same—living or dead. That little corridor that divides the living and the dead is so small that mentally and spiritually there is little difference between them. Less than a minute sometimes spells our physical change. Death does not rob one of being a follower of Jesus. A follower of Christ here, will no doubt be a follower of Him over there. Death is but an incident of life.

We give this as our opinion only. We have no documentary evidence to substantiate our conclusion, but after much consideration, we are willing to make the aforesaid reasoned judgment. We remember the words of Peter: "For Christ also hath once suffered for sins, the just for the unjust, that He might bring us to God, being put to death in the flesh, but quickened by the Spirit: By which also He went and preached unto the spirits in prison." (I Peter 3:18-19)

These sheep may not be the ones of whom the Savior spoke, but certainly He has sheep in the Great Beyond just as He has here.

Concerning the last two of the flocks mentioned by our Lord, He stated these important facts:

VERSE 4. *They may be brought to a knowledge of Me, their Redeemer.* They will be found dispersed upon all the face of the Earth, because of their unbelief; but they will receive knowledge of their Redeemer through Gentile sources, who have accepted the Book of Mormon.

VERSE 5. *They will be gathered in from the "four quarters of the Earth."* And then, the Covenant of God which He made with all the House of Israel — all three flocks — will be fulfilled.

VERSES 6-10. *Blessed are the Gentiles.* The Gentiles, who, believe in the Son, Jesus Christ, and in the Holy Ghost, as well as the Father, will be blessed and will receive the truth. But those who reject Them, will be judged.

lief in me, saith the Father, and because of the unbelief of you, O house of Israel, in the latter day shall the truth come unto the Gentiles, that the fulness of these things shall be made known unto them.

8. But wo, saith the Father, unto the unbelieving of the Gentiles—for notwithstanding they have come forth upon the face of this land, and have scattered my people who are of the house of Israel; and my people who are of the house of Israel have been cast out from among them, and have been trodden under feet by them;

9. And because of the mercies of the Father unto the Gentiles, and also the judgments of the Father upon my people who are of the house of Israel, verily, verily, I say unto you, that after all this, and I have caused my people who are of the house of Israel to be smitten, and to be afflicted, and to be slain, and to be cast out from among them, and to become hated by them, and to become a hiss and a byword among them—

10. And thus commandeth the Father that I should say unto you: At that day when the Gentiles shall sin against my gospel, and shall be lifted up in the pride of their hearts above all nations, and above all the people of the whole earth, and shall be filled with all manner of lyings, and of deceits, and of mischiefs, and all manner of hypocrisy, and murders, and priestcrafts, and whoredoms, and of secret abominations; and if they shall do all those things, and shall reject the fulness of my gospel, behold, saith the Father, I will bring the fulness of my gospel from among them.

11. And then will I remember my covenant which I have made unto my people, O house of Israel, and I will bring my gospel unto them.

12. And I will show unto thee, O house of Israel, that the Gentiles shall not have power over you; but I will remember my covenant unto you, O house of Israel, and ye shall come unto the knowledge of the fulness of my gospel.

13. But if the Gentiles will repent and return unto me, saith the Father, behold they shall be numbered among my people, O house of Israel.

14. And I will not suffer my people, who are of the house of Israel, to go through among them, and tread them down, saith the Father.

15. But if they will not turn unto me, and hearken unto my voice, I will suffer them, yea, I will suffer my people, O house of Israel, that they shall go through

---

VERSES 11-13. *I will remember My Covenant unto you.* Then the Gospel will be preached to all the House of Israel.

VERSES 14-16. *I should give unto this people this land for their inheritance.* The final outcome will be that "this land" will be given to "this people," that is, the descendants of Lehi, for an inheritance; not as the spoils of war. And then the

among them, and shall tread them down, and they shall be as salt that hath lost its savor, which is thenceforth good for nothing but to be cast out, and to be trodden under foot of my people, O house of Israel.

16. Verily, verily, I say unto you, thus hath the Father commanded me—that I should give unto this people this land for their inheritance.

3. The state of those who reject the Gospel.

17. And then the words of the prophet Isaiah shall be fulfilled, which say:

18. Thy watchmen shall lift up the voice; with the voice together shall they sing, for they shall see eye to eye when the Lord shall bring again Zion.

---

words of Isaiah (Isaiah 52:8-10) will be fulfilled: "The Lord hath made bare His holy arm in the eyes of all nations; and all the ends of the Earth shall see the salvation of God."

VERSES 17-20. *And then the words of the Prophet Isaiah shall be fulfilled, which say:*

Thy watchmen shall lift up the voice. (See, Isaiah 52:8-10; *also*, III Nephi 20: 29-35) This prophecy uttered by Isaiah does not refer to the watchmen who were set about Jerusalem in the towers of its walls to warn of approaching enemies, but to all the holy prophets who in times past have raised their voices to declare the coming of the Lord, the Messiah, and like *watchmen* notify the people of Jerusalem of the wonderful reception due Him Who is their King, and to warn them of the error of His rejection.

"Who," we may ask, "were the first to see the King?" The prophets, whom Isaiah calls *watchmen*. The King had sent them as His emissaries to warn the inhabitants of Jerusalem and to prepare them for things that were to come. They never slept; they relied upon the Lord for their strength. The words of the Psalmist were ever with them: "Except the Lord keep the city, the watchmen waketh in vain." When the watchmen behold the King's glorious appearance and hear His triumphant shout, they unite themselves in His joyful march, at the same time they bid everyone to join in the exultant cry, "Behold, the King! Our God reigneth!" They see eye to eye with Him; their united purpose is the Redemption of Zion. Their joy is serving the King; their gladness is praising Him.

Watchmen. The inspired teachers of God's children; the watchmen set out to guide and comfort them are like keepers of sheep. They work for only one Master. They lead His flock to pleasant places; they guide them along the right paths to where the Good Shepherd awaits their coming. He knows them all, and calls them by name. He loves each one. Some have fallen by the way; some are lost; some are hunted by the wolf; others are hungry, helpless, and cold. All need His care. "Therefore, O ye shepherds, hear the word of the Lord; . . . Behold I, even I, will both search My sheep, and seek them out. . . . I will strengthen the sick, and will bind up that which was broken. . . . I will feed them in a good pasture, and upon the high mountains of Israel shall their fold be. . . . I will feed my flock. . . ." (See, Ezekiel, Chapter 34) Great comfort to ancient Judah was the promise of His coming. I will "seek them out," are the words of the Lord. We will rejoice with them because we are assured "He will find them, and will take them in His arms, and will carry them to His fold," and will rejoice with them, for, "Together they shall sing . . . when the Lord shall bring again Zion." (Isaiah 52:8) (*The Targum* renders it, "When He shall bring back His Shekinah (Spirit) to Zion." The Dead Sea Scroll ends the last line by adding, "in mercy.")

See eye to eye, means here, that the prophets shall see with their own eyes the return of the Lord's people to the Land of Zion. It may also mean that there will be no difference of opinion among the *watchmen* as to that. It will be evident to all.

Break forth into joy. This verse expresses what is known as *Prophetic Perfect.* That is, things are spoken of as past, those things which are yet to come.

4. *The Prophet Isaiah cited.*

To understand more clearly Isaiah's prophecy to which the Savior referred, we reprint our comments which we caused to be made in Volume II, COMMENTARY ON THE BOOK OF MORMON, p. 128ff.

How beautiful upon the mountains are the feet of him that bringeth good tidings. The magnificent and stately language used by Isaiah in proclaiming this great event of prophecy, sets it apart, making more bright and beautiful the exalted and majestic picture he here presents. "How beautiful upon the mountains" expresses his jubilation as Isaiah proclaims the coming of Him, who is King. Not any king, but the *King* of kings. The term *mountains,* or *mountain,* is used throughout the Scriptures, and usually means, when not referring to a particular mountain, the *glory,* or the *power,* or the *Temple of God.* The whole earth is God's Temple; its Holy of Holies is in our hearts. It is that place where we bring our prayers, and our praise, and our offerings of homage to Him. It is a temple, not made with hands. It is a "mighty fortress of our God," whose parapets shine with the burnished armour of His servants. (*See* Isaiah 52:7)

These words of Isaiah's are beautiful, and form one of the most meaningful of his inspired predictions. It has, however, caused many divergent interpretations by commentators of the Bible. They appear confused as to whom it refers, and the message it bears. One writer says one thing; another, something else. To many the passage portrays a messenger from the field of battle heralding the good tidings of victory. To others, it means the return of the captive Jews from their long exile. Still others see in it the coming back to Jerusalem of the king who had left his sacred city to battle the common enemy, and, who, in regal splendor returns and jubilantly proclaims peace through victory and salvation from woe. The people of Jerusalem had, many times in their history, awaited anxiously and almost impatiently for the watchmen on its ruined walls to proclaim, with almost exultant voices, the sounding of such good tidings. (*See* II Samuel 18:25-26) In spite of the great learning evinced by some of these scholars, and the piety that guides them in their research, we say, definitely, their conclusions are wrong! The one spoken of is the Lord, the Mighty King of Heaven and Earth. The Salvation He proclaims is the Salvation of the human soul, not the cessation of tribulation for which the Jews, for many years, had hoped. The Lord publishes "Peace, good will toward men," or as some interpret it, "Peace to men of good will." The majesty of His coming, the glory of His approach, is not understood by those who see in it only the advent of an earthly potentate who sometime before had departed to conquer and vanquish the foes of Jerusalem.

The words of the Psalmist find fulfillment here: "Honor and majesty are before Him: strength and beauty are in His sanctuary." (Psalm 96:6)

As Jerusalem was centered with mountains round about, the Jews, conscious of the mighty defense these mountains afforded their beloved city, making it a citadel, understood the words of the prophet. The imagery created by Isaiah's lofty comparison appealed to the subtle and discerning minds of those who had waited the coming of Him Whom the prophets had long foretold. He was their King, and to them, a Messenger of Salvation, their Rock and their Redeemer. He, they had been told for ages, would lead them into battle and would bring them peace through victory over their enemies. Jerusalem would be enthroned above all the nations of the earth. Their praise of Him was bounded only by their hopes in Him, and by the vision of His glorious appearing which Isaiah announced anew.

Thy God reigneth. This is the grand and jubilant message their King proclaims. All the others are subordinated. Peace, good tidings of man's Redemption are published by Him whom they see approaching on the distant mountains. They watch Him as He draws nearer; His feet are like stars; His raiment, new, like the dawn of day; His voice is like thunder, the reverberations of which shake the earth. He declares His message, "Thy God reigneth." Not, "Thy God will reign," or "He will be King," but "He is King," now and forever. Yesterday, today, and tomorrow, He is the same; our King, our Deliverer, our All. They see the King, they hear His voice. "Peace, God's most precious gift to man," is now declared to be his portion. The Jews remembered the words of the Psalmist, "The Lord will give strength unto His people; the Lord will bless His people with peace." (Psalm 29:11)

Break forth into joy. The glorious appearance of the King and His royal entourage brought forth shouts of joy that swelled into a mighty "Hosanna." Isaiah now bids all, "Break forth into joy." (Lit. "Break forth, sing together.") All ye who have grown weary waiting for the King to come, also, ye who are become withered like an unwatered garden, ye, too, that love the Law of the Lord, "who wait for Him more than the watchmen wait for the morning, Sing together." The Lord has not forgotten His people, neither will He see them perish. He hath redeemed Zion. Great is our King! Who is our King, but the Lord? And, who is the Lord, save He is God! "Let the heavens be glad, and the earth rejoice; let the fields exult, and all that is therein!" (Jewish Adage. See I Chronicles 16:31-32) The Lord hath comforted His people. Sing aloud! Isaiah knew the strength of song.

Singing was an important part of Israel's worship. Music was heard throughout the land. Songs of praise to God lifted the most menial of tasks to His service. The vine, the fruitful field, the harvest, the flocks, doves, lilies, sorrow, delight, and victory — all were remembered in songs of memorial to His goodness. Israel sought comfort in song. "When my cares are many within me, songs in Thy praise delight my soul." (Hebrew proverb) "For the Lord will comfort Zion: He will comfort all her waste places and will make her wilderness like Eden, and her desert like the garden of the Lord; joy and gladness shall be found therein, thanksgiving, and the voice of melody." (Isaiah 51:3) In weakness, as in strength; in failure, as in success, they sang songs of joy and thanksgiving. In them, they expressed their innermost thoughts. "O sing unto the Lord, a new song: sing unto the Lord, all the earth. Sing unto the Lord; bless His name; proclaim His salvation from day to day." (Psalm 96:1-2. *Jewish rendition*)

A good conception of the influence singing the songs of Zion had upon ancient Judah may be obtained by reading the first four verses of the 137th Psalm. Words of poetry memorializing this sorrowful experience in Israel's history are, today, sung by both Jews and their Christian brethren. These words are found in the Hymn Book of the Church of Jesus Christ of Latter-day Saints. They not only express Judah's sorrow in her Babylonian captivity, but also, as is pointed out in the King James Translation of the Bible, her "constancy under captivity."

19. Break forth into joy, sing together, ye waste places of Jerusalem; for the Lord hath comforted his people, he hath redeemed Jerusalem.

20. The Lord hath made bare his holy arm in the eye of all the nations; and all the ends of the earth shall see the salvation of God.

Down by the river's verdant side,
Low by the solitary tide,
There, while the peaceful waters slept,
We pensively sat down and wept,
And on the bending willows hung
Our silent harps through grief unstrung.

For they who wasted Zion's bowers
And laid in dust her ruined towers
In scorn their weary slaves desire
To strike the chords of Israel's lyre,
And in their impious ears to sing
The sacred songs to Zion's king.

How shall we tune those lofty strains
On Babylon's polluted plains,
When low in ruin on the earth
Remains the place that gave us birth,
And stern destruction's iron hand
Still sways our desolated land.

O never shall our harps awake,
Laid in the dust for Zion's sake,
For ever on the willows hung,
Their music hushed; their chords un-strung;
Lost Zion! city of our God,
While groaning 'neath the tyrant's rod.

And while we toil through wretched life
And drink the bitter cup of strife,
Until we yield our weary breath,
And sleep released from woe in death,
Will Zion in our memory stand —
Our lost, our ruined native land.

Still mold'ring lie thy leveled walls
And ruin stalks along thy halls.
And brooding o'er thy ruined towers
Such desolation sternly lowers,
That when we muse upon thy woe,
The gushing tears of sorrow flow!

VERSE 19. *He hath redeemed Jerusalem. Redeem means,* (1) To buy again something that has been sold, by paying back the price that bought it. (Lev. 25:25; 27:20) (2) To deliver and bring out of bondage those who were kept prisoners by their enemies. (Deut. 7:5; 32:6) *Cruden's Concordance of the Bible.* Jerusalem had been sold, figuratively speaking, by the apostate Jews. They had perverted the ways of the Lord, and, too, they had abandoned the covenant their fathers had made with the Lord at Mount Sinai. The land of Jerusalem was the land of their inheritance. The Mosaic Law provided that land which had been sold, among other things, could be redeemed. However, a price was demanded for its redemption. What was the price? Jerusalem had not been bartered away for gold or for silver, nor was it sold as common merchandise. There was only One who could meet the prescribed terms. That One was their King! Isaiah said, "He hath redeemed Jerusalem"; not with money nor with the might of a great army, but He hath Redeemed it with the blood that was shed on Mount Calvary; the Redemption brought about by Jesus of Nazareth, the King of the Jews.

VERSE 20. *The Lord hath made bare His holy arm.* The power and authority of God, often referred to as *His holy arm,* is, in the Redemption of Jerusalem, made manifest to all nations. When Isaiah says, "Jerusalem," we may interpret it as meaning the entire *earth* and *all mankind.* "The earth is the Lord's and the fulness thereof; the world, and they that dwell therein." (Psalm 24:1) The welfare of His children is the great purpose to which all God's providences are consecrated, and in them, all the people of the earth will behold His Salvation.

GENERAL NOTES

The whereabouts and identity of the so-called "lost tribes has often been discussed. As seen in this section of the Book of Mormon, they are in a place where Jesus could visit and minister to them at the time of His death; that is, they or at least part of them, were dwelling together. That place is called the "North Countries" in the *Doctrine and Covenants* (Section 133:26). That might refer to the northern parts of Europe, and also America, and even Asia. The traditions related by Esdras (2 Es. 13) is, that the Ten Tribes were carried over the waters (the Euphrates and the Tigris, perhaps), and so came into another land. But some of them decided to flee to another place, "where never mankind dwelt," and they "entered into the Euphrates by the narrow passages of the river, and from there they traveled a year and a half to a place called, *Arsareth,*" where they were to dwell until the time of their restoration. If the events predicted in the *Doctrine and Covenants,* Section 133, are to take place consecutively, their complete restoration will not take place until immediately after the second advent of our Lord. The Icelandic sagas and myths, and the traditions of Aztecs and Mayas might profitably be studied in this connection. They, too, tell about wonderful journeys on land and sea.

CHAPTER 17

1. *The Savior heals the sick.*

1. Behold, now it came to pass that when Jesus had spoken these words he looked round about again on the multitude, and he said unto them: Behold, my time is at hand.

2. I perceive that ye are weak, that ye cannot understand all my words which I am commanded of the Father to speak unto you at this time.

3. Therefore, go ye unto your homes, and ponder upon the things which I have said, and ask of the Father, in my name, that ye may understand, and prepare your minds for the morrow, and I come unto you again.

4. But now I go unto the Father, and also to show myself unto the lost tribes of Israel, for they are not lost unto the Father, for he knoweth whither he hath taken them.

5. And it came to pass that when Jesus had thus spoken, he cast his eyes round about again on the multitude, and beheld they were in tears, and did look steadfastly upon him as if they would ask him to tarry a little longer with them.

6. And he said unto them: Behold, my bowels are filled with compassion towards you.

7. Have ye any that are sick among you? Bring them hither. Have ye any that are lame, or blind, or halt, or maimed, or leprous, or that are withered, or that are deaf, or that are afflicted in any manner? Bring them hither

---

VERSES 1-10. *Prepare your minds for the morrow.* By this time, the day was, probably, advanced, and the multitude showed signs of weariness, wherefore Jesus observed that their minds were not prepared, at this time, to receive any more of the word of the Lord, so He told them to go to their homes and prepare their minds, by prayerful pondering, the things He had said unto them that day, when on the morrow He promised to return unto them again.

But as He gazed upon them He noticed that they were in tears, and in their distress they looked beseechingly upon Him as if they would ask Him to tarry a little longer with them.

These mute entreaties prevailed with Him, His bowels were filled with compassion towards them; and, the Sacred Record tells us that He said to them: 'Have ye any that are sick among you? Bring them hither. Have ye any that are lame, or blind, or halt, or maimed, or leprous, or that are withered, or that are deaf, or that are afflicted in any manner? Bring them hither and I will heal them, for I have compassion upon you; My bowels are filled with mercy. For I perceive that ye desire that I should show unto you what I have done unto your brethren at Jerusalem, for I see that your faith is sufficient that I should heal you. And it came

and I will heal them, for I have compassion upon you; my bowels are filled with mercy.

8. For I perceive that ye desire that I should show unto you what I have done unto your brethren at Jerusalem, for I see that your faith is sufficient that I should heal you.

9. And it came to pass that when he had thus spoken, all the multitude, with one accord, did go forth with their sick and their afflicted, and their lame, and with

their blind, and with their dumb, and with all them that were afflicted in any manner; and he did heal them every one as they were brought forth unto him.

10. And they did all, both they who had been healed and they who were whole, bow down at his feet, and did worship him; and as many as could come for the multitude did kiss his feet, insomuch that they did bathe his feet with their tears.

2. He blesses the little children of the Nephites.

11. And it came to pass that he commanded that their little children should be brought.

12. So they brought their little children and set them down upon the ground round about him, and Jesus stood in the midst; and the multitude gave way till they had all been brought unto him.

13. And it came to pass that when they had all been brought, and Jesus stood in the midst, he commanded the multitude that

they should kneel down upon the ground.

14. And it came to pass that when they had knelt upon the ground, Jesus groaned within himself, and said: Father, I am troubled because of the wickedness of the people of the house of Israel.

15. And when he had said these words, he himself also knelt upon the earth; and behold he prayed unto the Father, and the

---

to pass that when He had thus spoken, all the multitude, with one accord, did go forth with their sick and their afflicted, and their lame, and with their blind, and with their dumb, and with all them that were afflicted in any manner; and He did heal them every one as they were brought forth unto Him. And they did all, both they who had been healed and they who were whole, bow down at His feet, and did worship Him; and as many as could come for the multitude did kiss His feet, insomuch that they did bathe His feet with their tears."

VERSES 11-23. *He commanded that their little children should be brought.* Next Jesus commanded them to bring unto Him their little children. So the people brought them and set them down upon the ground round about Him, and the multitude gave way till they had all been brought as the Savior had commanded. And when they all had been brought, Jesus stood in their midst and commanded further that the multitude kneel down upon the ground. And when they had done so, Jesus sighed and began to pray. He offered a pitiful exclamation of sorrow; Father, He said, "I am troubled because of the wickedness of the people of the House of Israel." He saw what was to come upon them in a future gen-

things which he prayed cannot be written, and the multitude did bear record who heard him.

16. And after this manner do they bear record: The eye hath never seen, neither hath the ear heard, before, so great and marvelous things as we saw and heard Jesus speak unto the Father;

17. And no tongue can speak, neither can there be written by any man, neither can the hearts of men conceive so great and marvelous things as we both saw and heard Jesus speak; and no one can conceive of the joy which filled our souls at the time we heard him pray for us unto the Father.

18. And it came to pass that when Jesus had made an end of praying unto the Father, he arose; but so great was the joy of the multitude that they were overcome.

19. And it came to pass that Jesus spake unto them, and bade them arise.

20. And they arose from the earth, and he said unto them: Blessed are ye because of your faith. And now behold, my joy is full.

21. And when he had said these words, he wept, and the multitude bare record of it, and he took their little children, one by one, and blessed them, and prayed unto the Father for them.

3. *Angels minister unto the children.*

22. And when he had done this he wept again;

23. And he spake unto the multitude, and said unto them: Behold your little ones.

24. And as they looked to be-

hold they cast their eyes towards heaven, and they saw the heavens open, and they saw angels descending out of heaven as it were in the midst of fire; and they came down and encircled those

---

eration. And when He had said these words, He, Himself knelt; and He prayed unto the Father and the things which He prayed could not be written, but the multitude who heard Him bore record: That eye had never seen, neither had ear heard, before, so great and marvelous things as they saw and heard Jesus speak unto the Father. When Jesus had made an end of praying, He arose, but so great was the joy of the multitude that they were overcome. But Jesus bade them arise. Then they arose, and He said unto them, "Blessed are ye because of your faith. And now behold, My joy is full." And when He had said these words, He wept; "and He took their little children, one by one, and blessed them, and prayed unto the Father for them." "And when He had done this He wept again." And then the Resurrected Lord said unto the multitude, "Behold your little ones."

Angels minister to the children, a marvelous and touching scene. As the fathers and mothers, brothers and sisters, of the little children cast their eyes upward they saw the heavens open, and numerous angels descending out therefrom as it were in the midst of fire; and they came down and encircled the little ones round about, and the multitude saw that they were surrounded by the flames thereof, yet were not burned. Intensely they watched as the angels ministered to the children.

little ones about, and they were encircled about with fire; and the angels did minister unto them.

25. And the multitude did see and hear and bear record; and they know that their record is true for they all of them did see and hear, every man for himself; and they were in number about two thousand and five hundred souls; and they did consist of men, women, and children.

And the throng who saw these glorious things numbered 2,500 men, women, and children, and they all bore record of the wonderful things of which they had seen, heard, and partaken.

Can we imagine anything more lovely, more touching, and more glorious, than this scene must have been? Can we conceive the joy that must have filled the hearts of these Nephites as they beheld the angels of Heaven descending from the *Courts of Glory* and ministering to their little ones? How deep must have been their love for the Savior Who had brought these blessings to them? How strong must have grown their faith in Him? We cannot recall a circumstance in recorded history that draws Earth nearer to Heaven than this, or that seems to bind the ties so strongly that unite the *Powers of Eternity* with the children of mortality.

CHAPTER 18

1. The Sacrament Administered—2. The Savior's Teachings Regarding It—3. He confers on His Disciples the power to give the Holy Ghost—4. He Ascends into Heaven.

1. *The Sacrament administered.*

1. And it came to pass that Jesus commanded his disciples that they should bring forth some bread and wine unto him.

2. And while they were gone for bread and wine, he commanded the multitude that they should sit themselves down upon the earth.

3. And when the disciples had come with bread and wine, he took of the bread and brake and blessed it; and he gave unto the disciples and commanded that they should eat.

4. And when they had eaten and were filled, he commanded that they should give unto the multitude.

5. And when the multitude had eaten and were filled, he said unto the disciples: Behold there shall one be ordained among you, and to him will I give power that he shall break bread and bless it and give it unto the people of my church, unto all those who shall believe and be baptized in my name.

2. *The Savior's teachings regarding it.*

6. And this shall ye always observe to do, even as I have done, even as I have broken bread and blessed it and given it unto you.

7. And this shall ye do in remembrance of my body, which I have shown unto you. And it shall be a testimony unto the Father that ye do always remember me. And if ye do always remember me ye shall have my Spirit to be with you.

VERSES 1-5. *Jesus commanded His Disciples that they should bring forth bread and wine.* Jesus next commanded His Disciples to bring him some bread and wine, and while they were gone to obtain them, He caused the multitude to sit down upon the ground. When the Disciples returned, He took of the bread and brake and blessed it. This He gave to the Disciples to eat and they were then filled with the Holy Spirit. He then commanded them to give it to the people of the multitude. When they had eaten and were likewise filled with the Spirit, Jesus told His Disciples that He would give one of them authority, by ordination, to break bread and bless it, as He had done, and to give it to the members of the Church.

VERSES 6-7. *This shall ye always observe to do.* When the people had eaten and were rejoicing in the blessings they were then receiving, Jesus began to instruct them in regard to the meaning of the bread they had just partaken of. This, He said, was to be done in remembrance of His body, as a testimony to the Father "that ye do always remember Me."

8. And it came to pass that when he said these words, he commanded his disciples that they should take of the wine of the cup and drink of it, and that they should also give unto the multitude that they might drink of it.

9. And it came to pass that they did so, and did drink of it and were filled; and they gave unto the multitude, and they did drink, and they were filled.

10. And when the disciples had done this, Jesus said unto them: Blessed are ye for this thing which ye have done, for this is fulfilling my commandments, and this doth witness unto the Father that ye are willing to do that which I have commanded you.

11. And this shall ye always do to those who repent and are baptized in my name; and ye shall do it in remembrance of my blood, which I have shed for you, that ye may witness unto the Father that ye do always remember me. And if ye do always remember me ye shall have my Spirit to be with you.

12. And I give unto you a commandment that ye shall do these things. And if ye shall always do

these things blessed are ye, for ye are built upon my rock.

13. But whoso among you shall do more or less than these are not built upon my rock, but are built upon a sandy foundation; and when the rain descends, and the floods come, and the winds blow, and beat upon them, they shall fall, and the gates of hell are ready open to receive them.

14. Therefore blessed are ye if ye shall keep my commandments, which the Father hath commanded me that I should give unto you.

15. Verily, verily, I say unto you, ye must watch and pray always, lest ye be tempted by the devil, and ye be led away captive by him.

16. And as I have prayed among you even so shall ye pray in my church, among my people who do repent and are baptized in my name. Behold I am the light; I have set an example for you.

17. And it came to pass that when Jesus had spoken these words unto his disciples, he turned again unto the multitude and said unto them:

18. Behold, verily, verily, I say

VERSES 8-14. *Drink of the wine.* After explaining the purpose of the *Broken Bread*, He gave, to His Disciples, the cup of wine. After they drank thereof, He directed them to give it to the people. Having done this the Lord pronounced a blessing upon them. "For," said He, "this is fulfilling My commandments, and this does witness unto the Father that ye are willing to do that which I have commanded you."

Not Intoxicating Wine. It might be proper to note here that the wine mentioned was certainly not the intoxicating kind. In the Hebrew language there are many words or terms, translated *wine.* Most of them stand for harmless grape-juice, or preserves, or even vinegar. The wine that was made inebriating by fermentation or by the addition of drugs, such as myrrh, mandragora, or opiates, was not used for sacred purposes.

unto you, ye must watch and pray always lest ye enter into temptation; for Satan desireth to have you, that he may sift you as wheat.

19. Therefore ye must always pray unto the Father in my name;

20. And whatsoever ye shall ask the Father in my name, which is right, believing that ye shall receive, behold it shall be given unto you.

21. Pray in your families unto the Father, always in my name, that your wives and your children may be blessed.

22. And behold ye shall meet together oft; and ye shall not forbid any man from coming unto you when ye shall meet together, but suffer them that they may come unto you and forbid them not;

23. But ye shall pray for them, and shall not cast them out; and if it so be that they come unto you oft ye shall pray for them unto the Father, in my name.

24. Therefore, hold up your light that it may shine unto the world. Behold I am the light which ye shall hold up—that which ye have seen me do. Behold ye see that I have prayed unto the Father, and ye all have witnessed.

25. And ye see that I have commanded that none of you should go away, but rather have commanded that ye should come unto me, that ye might feel and see; even so shall ye do unto the world; and whosoever breaketh this commandment suffereth himself to be led into temptation.

26. And now it came to pass that when Jesus had spoken these words, he turned his eyes again upon the disciples whom he had chosen, and said unto them:

27. Behold, verily, verily, I say unto you, I give unto you another commandment, and then I must go unto my Father that I may fulfil other commandments which he hath given me.

28. And now behold, this is the commandment which I give unto you, that ye shall not suffer any one knowingly to partake of my

After having administered the Sacrament, our Lord admonished the people to pray always. To watch and to pray is a shield against temptation. He also warned them against neglecting their public meetings, and against forbidding anyone to attend those gatherings. He told them to hold up their light that it might shine unto all the world. And then He added the exceedingly important observation, "Behold, I am the light which ye shall hold up — that which ye have seen me do." In other words, they were to preach Christ, His life and death; not themselves. There is no other Light.

VERSES 27-34. *Not to Eat and Drink Unworthily.* Christ then turned to His Disciples and instructed them not knowingly to permit anyone to partake of the Emblems of the Sacrament unworthily; for to do so is to eat and drink damnation to one's own soul.

Saint Paul similarly warns the Saints: "For he that eateth and drinketh, unworthily, eateth and drinketh damnation to himself, not discerning the Lord's body." (1 Cor. 11:29) He adds, "For this cause many among you are weak and sickly, and not a few sleep." (In death.)

flesh and blood unworthily, when ye shall minister it;

29. For whoso eateth and drinketh my flesh and blood unworthily eateth and drinketh damnation to his soul; therefore if ye know that a man is unworthy to eat and drink of my flesh and blood ye shall forbid him.

30. Nevertheless, ye shall not cast him out from among you, but ye shall minister unto him and shall pray for him unto the Father, in my name; and if it so be that he repenteth and is baptized in my name, then shall ye receive him, and shall minister unto him of my flesh and blood.

31. But if he repent not he shall not be numbered among my people, that he may not destroy my people, for behold I know my sheep, and they are numbered.

32. Nevertheless, ye shall not cast him out of your synagogues, or your places of worship, for unto such shall ye continue to minister; for ye know not but what they will return and repent, and come unto me with full purpose of heart, and I shall heal them; and ye shall be the means of bringing salvation unto them.

33. Therefore, keep these sayings which I have commanded you that ye come not under condemnation; for wo unto him whom the Father condemneth.

34. And I give you these commandments because of the disputations which have been among you. And blessed are ye if ye have no disputations among you.

He confers upon His Disciples the Power to give the Holy Ghost.

35. And now I go unto the Father, because it is expedient that I should go unto the Father for your sakes.

36. And it came to pass that when Jesus had made an end of these sayings, he touched with his hand the disciples whom he had chosen, one by one, even until he had touched them all, and spake unto them as he touched them.

37. And the multitude heard not the words which he spake, therefore they did not bear record; but the disciples bare record that he gave them power to give the Holy Ghost. And I will show unto you hereafter that this record is true.

Paul further says, "But let a man examine himself, and so let him eat of that bread, and drink of that cup." (*Ibid.*, 28) If any Saint is fearful and trembling, thinking that, perhaps, he is partaking of the Emblems unworthily, because of human weakness, let him, or her, consider that the Lord does not require impossible perfection but honest willingness to keep His commandments. He who comes to the Lord's table and can truthfully testify that he is willing to do what is right, is welcome, and he will find there, strength to overcome temptations and evil influences.

VERSES 35-37. *He Touched with His Hand the Disciples He had Chosen.* When Jesus had made an end to His sayings, He touched with His hand each one of the

4. *He ascends into heaven.*

38. And it came to pass that when Jesus had touched them all, there came a cloud and overshadowed the multitude that they could not see Jesus.

39. And while they were overshadowed he departed from them, and ascended into heaven. And the disciples saw and did bear record that he ascended again into heaven.

Disciples whom He had chosen, one by one. As He touched them he spoke, giving them power to give the Holy Ghost.

VERSES 38-39. *He Ascended into Heaven.* When He had given the Disciples power to impart the Holy Ghost, a cloud overshadowed the multitude, and they saw Jesus no more that day; but the Disciples saw Him, and bore record that He ascended into Heaven.

And thus ended conference the first day.

CHAPTER 19

SECOND DAY

1. Names of the Nephite Twelve—2. Their Baptism—3. The Holy Ghost Given—4. The Savior's Second Visitation.

1. *Names of the Nephite Twelve.*

1. And now it came to pass that when Jesus had ascended into heaven, the multitude did disperse, and every man did take his wife and his children and did return to his own home.

2. And it was noised abroad among the people immediately, before it was yet dark, that the multitude had seen Jesus, and that he had ministered unto them, and that he would also show himself on the morrow unto the multitude.

3. Yea, and even all the night it was noised abroad concerning Jesus; and insomuch did they send forth unto the people that there were many, yea, an exceeding great number, did labor exceedingly all that night, that they might be on the morrow in the place where Jesus should show himself unto the multitude.

4. And it came to pass that on the morrow, when the multitude was gathered together, behold, Nephi and his brother whom he had raised from the dead, whose name was Timothy, and also his son, whose name was Jonas, and also Mathoni, and Mathonihah, his brother, and Kumen, and Kumenonhi, and Jeremiah, and Shemnon, and Jonas, and Zedekiah, and Isaiah—now these were the names of the disciples whom Jesus had chosen—and it came to pass that they went forth and stood in the midst of the multitude.

Verses 1-3. *Did labor exceedingly all that night.* Before dismissing the multitude at the close of the first day's conference session, Jesus promised the assembled throng that He would return the following day. (III Nephi 17:3) And when He ascended into Heaven the multitude dispersed, every one returning home. All that night the news that Christ had come spread from mouth to mouth. Many were too excited to sleep and labored diligently spreading the news far and wide, so that when the morning came, the whole populace was astir wending their way to the place where Jesus was expected to appear.

When the multitude had gathered together, their number was found to be so great that the Disciples divided them into twelve congregations, and one of them taught each of these large bodies.

Verse 4. *Names of the Twelve Disciples.* The names of the twelve Disciples who had been chosen by the Savior are given in this verse.

5. And behold, the multitude was so great that they did cause that they should be separated into twelve bodies.

6. And the twelve did teach the multitude; and behold, they did cause that the multitude should kneel down upon the face of the earth, and should pray unto the Father in the name of Jesus.

7. And the disciples did pray unto the Father also in the name of Jesus. And it came to pass that they arose and ministered unto the people.

8. And when they had ministered those same words which Jesus had spoken—nothing varying from the words which Jesus had spoken—behold, they knelt again and prayed to the Father in the name of Jesus.

9. And they did pray for that which they most desired; and they desired that the Holy Ghost should be given unto them.

2. *The baptism of the Twelve.*

3. *The Holy Spirit is given.*

4. *The Savior's second visitation.*

10. And when they had thus prayed they went down unto the water's edge, and the multitude followed them.

11. And it came to pass that Nephi went down into the water and was baptized.

12. And he came up out of the water and began to baptize. And he baptized all those whom Jesus had chosen.

13. And it came to pass when they were all baptized and had come up out of the water, the Holy Ghost did fall upon them, and they were filled with the Holy Ghost and with fire.

14. And behold, they were encircled about as if it were by fire; and it came down from heaven, and the multitude did witness it, and did bear record; and angels did come down out of heaven and did minister unto them.

15. And it came to pass that while the angels were ministering unto the disciples, behold, Jesus came and stood in the midst and ministered unto them.

16. And it came to pass that

VERSES 7-8. *Prayer.* The conference opened with prayer. Then followed faithful reports of the proceedings of the previous day's worship. They were evidently dictated by the Spirit, for, it is said, they were "nothing varying from the words which Jesus had spoken."

VERSE 9. A special prayer was now offered up for the Holy Ghost, that It might be given unto them.

VERSES 10-18. *Jesus came and stood in the midst of them.* The conference then adjourned to the water's edge. First, Nephi went into the water and was baptized, and thereupon he baptized all "those whom Jesus had chosen." Then the fervent petitions that the Holy Ghost be given them, was answered, for they, the Disciples, were filled with the Spirit as with fire, and what is more, sacred flames encircled them about, and angels from Heaven came and ministered to them.

he spake unto the multitude, and commanded them that they should kneel down again upon the earth, and also that his disciples should kneel down upon the earth.

17. And it came to pass that when they had all knelt down upon the earth, he commanded his disciples that they should pray.

18. And behold, they began to pray; and they did pray unto Jesus, calling him their Lord and their God.

19. And it came to pass that Jesus departed out of the midst of them, and went a little way off from them and bowed himself to the earth, and he said:

20. Father, I thank thee that thou hast given the Holy Ghost unto these whom I have chosen; and it is because of their belief in me that I have chosen them out of the world.

21. Father, I pray thee that thou wilt give the Holy Ghost unto all them that shall believe in their words.

22. Father, thou hast given them the Holy Ghost because they believe in me; and thou seest that they believe in me because thou hearest them, and they pray unto me; and they pray unto me because I am with them.

23. And now Father, I pray unto thee for them, and also for all those who shall believe on their words, that they may believe in me, that I may be in them as thou, Father, art in me, that we may be one.

24. And it came to pass that when Jesus had thus prayed unto the Father, he came unto his disciples, and behold, they did still continue, without ceasing, to pray unto him; and they did not multiply many words, for it was given unto them what they should pray, and they were filled with desire.

25. And it came to pass that Jesus blessed them as they did pray unto him; and his countenance did smile upon them, and the light of his countenance did shine upon them, and behold they were as white as the countenance and also the garments of Jesus; and behold the whiteness thereof did exceed all the whiteness, yea, even there could be nothing upon earth so white as the whiteness thereof.

26. And Jesus said unto them: Pray on; nevertheless they did not cease to pray.

27. And he turned from them again, and went a little way off and bowed himself to the earth; and he prayed again unto the Father, saying:

28. Father, I thank thee that thou hast purified those whom I have chosen, because of their faith, and I pray for them, and also for them who shall believe

---

By and by, Jesus, Himself, came and stood in the midst of His Disciples, and taught them more of the Plan of Salvation. He commanded them all, the people and the Twelve, to again kneel upon the earth, and the Disciples He instructed to pray. And they prayed unto Jesus, calling Him their Lord and their God.

on their words, that they may be purified in me, through faith on their words, even as they are purified in me.

29. Father, I pray not for the world, but for those whom thou hast given me out of the world, because of their faith, that they may be purified in me, that I may be in them as thou, Father, art in me, that we may be one, that I may be glorified in them.

30. And when Jesus had spoken these words he came again unto his disciples; and behold they did pray steadfastly, without ceasing, unto him; and he did smile upon them again; and behold they were white, even as Jesus.

VERSES 19-36. *Jesus also prayed.* When Jesus heard these prayers, He went a little way off, bowed Himself to the earth and said: "Father, I thank Thee that Thou hast given the Holy Ghost unto these whom I have chosen; and it is because of their belief in Me that I have chosen them out of the world. Father, I pray Thee that Thou wilt give the Holy Ghost unto all them that shall believe in their words. Father, Thou hast given them the Holy Ghost because they believe in Me; and Thou seest that they believe in Me because Thou hearest them, and they pray unto Me because I am with them. And now Father, I pray unto Thee for them, and also for all those who shall believe on their words, that they may believe in Me, that I may be in them as Thou, Father, art in Me, that we may be one."

When our Savior had ended this prayer He returned to His Disciples. He found them still praying. Then He blessed them, and smiled upon them. When He smiled, the light of His countenance shone upon them, and in the reflection of His brightness they became as white as the face or the garments of Jesus; — the whiteness of which there was nothing upon this Earth.

Jesus, in joy, once again retired a short distance away to commune with His Father in Heaven. He prayed thus:

"Father, I thank Thee that Thou hast purified those whom I have chosen, because of their faith, and I pray for them who shall believe on their words, that they may be purified in Me, through faith on their words, even as they are purified in Me. Father, I pray not for the world, but for those whom Thou hast given Me out of the world, because of their faith, that they may be purified in Me, that I may be in them as Thou, Father, art in Me, that we may be one, that I may be glorified in them."

It was thus that both the Speaker, the Son of God, Himself, and the audience were prepared for the sermon that was to follow. And so fervent were their supplications that the supplicants became transfigured. (v. 25)

Prayer is an exceedingly important function in the private and public life of man. It is the medium by means of which spiritual light and power are conveyed to him. It is the never-failing *radio* connection between him and his pristine, glorious, Celestial Home.

Again, we have repeated word for word, Jesus' prayer on this occasion. It is so beautiful that to comment on it would be like painting the lily, or seeking to improve the work of a master: "And it came to pass that He went again a little way off and prayed unto the Father; And tongue cannot speak the words which He prayed, neither can be written by man the words which He prayed. And the multitude did hear and do bear record; and their hearts were open and they did understand in their hearts the words which He prayed. Nevertheless, so great and

THE THIRD BOOK OF NEPHI

31. And it came to pass that he went again a little way off and prayed unto the Father;

32. And tongue cannot speak the words which he prayed, neither can be written by man the words which he prayed.

33. And the multitude did hear and do bear record; and their hearts were open and they did understand in their hearts the words which he prayed.

34. Nevertheless, so great and marvelous were the words which he prayed that they cannot be written, neither can they be uttered by man.

35. And it came to pass that when Jesus had made an end of praying he came again to the disciples, and said unto them: So great faith have I never seen

---

marvelous were the words which He prayed that they cannot be written, neither can they be uttered by man."

"And it came to pass that when Jesus had made an end of praying He came again to His Disciples, and said unto them: So great faith have I never seen among all the Jews; wherefore I could not show unto them so great miracles, because of their unbelief. Verily, I say unto you, there are none of them that have seen so great things as ye have seen; neither have they heard so great things as ye have heard."

THE TWELVE DISCIPLES

When the Risen Redeemer appeared to the Nephites in the Land Bountiful (34 A.D.) He chose twelve men as His Disciples, to whom He gave authority to perform the rite of baptism and administer the Sacrament and other ordinances of the Gospel. On these Twelve, who are always called Disciples in the Book of Mormon, never apostles, was conferred the power to judge the descendants of Lehi at the final Judgment Day, as they, themselves, were to be judged by the Twelve Apostles chosen by the Lord from amongst the Jews. The names of the Twelve Nephite Disciples were: Nephi, his brother Timothy and his son Jonas, Mathoni, Mathonihah, Kumen, Kumenonhi, Jeremiah, Shemnon, Jonas, Zedekiah and Isaiah. To these Twelve our Savior gave many instructions which He withheld from the multitude.

On one occasion, toward the close of His ministrations, He asked them, one by one, "What is it ye desire of Me, after that I am gone to the Father?" (III Nephi 28:1) Then nine of them said, "We desire, after we have lived unto the age of man, that our ministry, wherein Thou hast called us, may have an end, that we may speedily come unto Thee in Thy kingdom." (Ibid., 28:2) And He said unto them, "Blessed are ye, because ye desired this thing of Me; therefore, after that ye are seventy and two years old ye may come unto Me in My kingdom; and with Me ye shall find rest." (Ibid., 28:3)

Then He turned to the three who had not answered, and again asked them what they would have Him do for them. But they faltered in their reply; their wish was such a peculiar one, that they were afraid to express it. Then He told them He knew their thoughts, that they had desired that they might bring souls to Him, while the world stood. And because of the purity and disinterestedness of their desire He promised the three Disciples that they should never taste of death but when He should come in His glory they should be changed in the twinkling of an eye from mortality to immortality and should sit down in the Kingdom of the Father and their joy should be full. And further, that while in the flesh, they

among all the Jews; wherefore I could not show unto them so great miracles, because of their unbelief.

36. Verily I say unto you, there are none of them that have seen so great things as ye have seen; neither have they heard so great things as ye have heard.

---

would not suffer pain, nor experience sorrow, save it were for the sins of the world. Then Jesus, with His finger touched the nine who were to die but the three who were to live He did not touch and then He departed. Afterwards the heavens were opened and the three were caught up into heaven and a change was wrought upon their mortal natures. But, Mormon says, (III Nephi 28:39-40) "This change was not equal to that which shall take place at the last day; but there was a change wrought upon them, insomuch that Satan could have no power over them, that he could not tempt them; and they were sanctified in the flesh, that they were holy, and that the powers of the earth could not hold them. And in this state they were to remain until the Judgment Day of Christ; and at that day they were to receive a greater change, and to be received into the Kingdom of the Father, to go out no more, but to dwell with God eternally in the Heavens." They also saw unspeakable things, which they were forbidden to utter; in fact, the power to tell these mysteries was withheld from them.

The sacred record gives no information as to who the three were who were not to taste of death. Mormon was about to write their names but the Lord forbade him.

After the final ascension of the Savior, the Twelve labored zealously in proclaiming His word. Theirs was a most happy task, for all the people heeded their sayings; in a short time every soul on both continents had accepted the message they bore. It was now their joy to lead the people upward in all the laws of the everlasting Gospel, bringing them nearer to Heaven and to God each succeeding day. In His glorious ministry and with these delightful and most peaceful surroundings, nine continued to labor until they passed away to the realms of the blessed. The other three continued their Godlike labors, year after year, until a change began to come over the spirit of the people. Little by little, but ever at an increasing rate, iniquity grew in their midst. By and by, schismatic churches arose, dissenting sects multiplied, infidels abounded. As the decades rolled by, the people waxed greatly in iniquity and in impurity of life. After a time they began to persecute the more faithful and humble — even the Three Disciples were not spared from their malignant hate. They were shut up in prison, but the walls of the prison were rent in twain by the power of God; they were cast into fiery furnaces, but the flames burned them not; they were thrown into dens of wild beasts, but they played with the savage inmates, as a child does with a lamb and they received no harm. Death had no power over them; swords would not slay them; fire would not burn them; prisons could not hold them; chains could not bind them; the grave could not entomb them; the earth could not conceal them for they had passed through a glorious change which freed them from earthly pain, suffering and death. The age in which they ministered was a peculiar one. Under ordinary circumstances the superhuman powers shown by them would have brought the wicked to repentance. But the happy age of peace and innocence that followed the Savior's ministry was fast passing away; the people were hardening their hearts; they were relapsing into iniquity with their eyes open and were sinning knowingly and understandingly. It is most likely that angels from heaven could not have converted them; they had given themselves up to Satan and every manifestation of the power of God in behalf of his servants only made them more angry and more determined upon the destruction of those who sounded in their ears the unwelcome Message of divine wrath. The hurricane might demolish the dungeon; the earthquake overthrow the walls of the prison; the earth refuse to close when the Disciples were cast into it; these protests of nature simply caused their hardened hearts to conjure up fresh methods of torture and devise new means to destroy those whom they so intensely and yet so unwarrantably hated. But they ever failed; the Three Nephites still lived. Encountering thus the rage and cruelty of the wicked, they gradually withdrew; their ministrations grew more infrequent; until at last they ceased to visit the haunts of men altogether. Moroni states that he and his father, Mormon, had seen them and had been ministered to by them; and these, the last two prophets of their race, were, in all probability, the last of that dispensation who were favored with a visit from these Three Nephites. They have also been seen by numbers of the faithful in this dispensation.

CHAPTER 20

1. Bread and wine, miraculously provided.

1. And it came to pass that he commanded the multitude that they should cease to pray, and also his disciples. And he commanded them that they should not cease to pray in their hearts.

2. And he commanded them that they should arise and stand up upon their feet. And they arose up and stood upon their feet.

3. And it came to pass that he brake bread again and blessed it, and gave to the disciples to eat.

4. And when they had eaten he commanded them that they should break bread, and give unto the multitude.

5. And when they had given unto the multitude he also gave them wine to drink, and commanded them that they should give unto the multitude.

6. Now, there had been no bread, neither wine, brought by the disciples, neither by the multitude;

7. But he truly gave unto them bread to eat, and also wine to drink.

8. And he said unto them: He

VERSES 1-7. *He brake bread again and blessed it.* And it came to pass that when Jesus had made an end of praying He came again to the Disciples, and said unto them: So great faith have I never seen among all the Jews; wherefore I could not show unto them so great miracles, because of their unbelief." (III Nephi 19:35)

The Lord Jesus then commanded all to cease from praying, nevertheless He admonished them to continue to pray in their hearts at all times and under all conditions.

He next directed them to arise; and at His word they stood upon their feet. Then He administered unto them bread and wine, the emblems of His body and of His blood which He had given as a ransom for their sins and the sins of the whole world. It is to be noted that neither the Disciples nor any one of the multitude had brought the bread and wine, but that both were supplied by an unseen hand. Whoever brought them, their presence was a manifestation of the power of the Master.

VERSE 8. *Shall be filled.* On this occasion our Lord uttered the memorable words found in this verse: "He that eateth this bread eateth of My body to his soul; and he that drinketh of this wine drinketh of My blood to his soul; and his soul shall never hunger nor thirst, but shall be filled."

When the multitude had eaten and had drunk the bread and wine, they were filled with the Holy Spirit, and with one voice gave glory to Jesus, Whom they both saw and heard.

A controversy settled. Our Lord, it will be observed, settles here by anticipation the age-long controversy concerning the nature of the Holy Emblems. There is

that eateth this bread eateth of my body to his soul; and he that drinketh of this wine drinketh of my blood to his soul; and his soul shall never hunger nor thirst, but shall be filled.

9. Now, when the multitude had all eaten and drunk, behold, they were filled with the Spirit; and they did cry out with one voice, and gave glory to Jesus, whom they both saw and heard.

10. And it came to pass that when they had all given glory unto Jesus, he said unto them: Behold now I finish the commandment which the Father hath commanded me concerning this people, who are a remnant of the house of Israel.

11. Ye remember that I spake unto you, and said that when the words of Isaiah should be fulfilled —behold they are written, ye have them before you, therefore search

2. The Remnant of Jacob.

16. Then shall ye, who are a remnant of the house of Jacob, go forth among them; and ye shall be in the midst of them who shall

them—

12. And verily, verily, I say unto you, that when they shall be fulfilled then is the fulfilling of the covenant which the Father hath made unto his people, O house of Israel.

13. And then shall the remnants, which shall be scattered abroad upon the face of the earth, be gathered in from the east and from the west, and from the south and from the north; and they shall be brought to the knowledge of the Lord their God, who hath redeemed them.

14. And the Father hath commanded me that I should give unto you this land, for your inheritance.

15. And I say unto you, that if the Gentiles do not repent after the blessing which they shall receive, after they have scattered my people—

be many; and ye shall be among them as a lion among the beasts of the forest, and as a young lion among the flocks of sheep, who, if

---

neither *Transubstantiation,* nor *Consubstantiation.* The Emblems remain bread and wine—or water. They are eaten as such. But by partaking worthily of them, the soul draws spiritual nourishment from the Atoning Sacrifice of our Lord, the Lamb of God, just as the body of flesh and blood receives physical life and vigor from the material elements. It is a spiritual function — an eating and drinking "to the soul."

A Pauline doctrine. The Apostle Paul, in Corinthians 10;16, expresses the same thought, when he says that the bread we break is a communion, a *koinonia,* of the body of Christ, and that the cup we bless is a *participation* of His blood. He sees the Church as a divine corporation, the common asset of which is the Atonement of Christ, in which each individual member has an equal share.

The Sacrament is, further, a sermon, or a short dramatic sketch, of the death of our Lord, as a sacrifice for the sins of the world. "As often as ye eat this bread and drink this cup ye do show the Lord's death till he come." (Cor. 11:26)

he goeth through both treadeth down and teareth in pieces, and none can deliver.

17. Thy hand shall be lifted up upon thine adversaries, and all thine enemies shall be cut off.

18. And I will gather my people together as a man gathereth his sheaves into the floor.

19. For I will make my people with whom the Father hath covenanted, yea, I will make thy horn iron, and I will make thy hoofs brass. And thou shalt beat in pieces many people; and I will consecrate their gain unto the Lord, and their substance unto the Lord of the whole earth. And behold, I am he who doeth it.

20. And it shall come to pass, saith the Father, that the sword of my justice shall hang over them at that day; and except they repent it shall fall upon them, saith the Father, yea, even upon all the nations of the Gentiles.

21. And it shall come to pass that I will establish my people, O house of Israel.

22. And behold, this people will I establish in this land, unto the fulfilling of the covenant which I made with your father Jacob; and it shall be a New Jerusalem. And the powers of heaven shall be in the midst of this people; yea, even I will be in the midst of you.

3. *The Savior proclaims Himself to the Prophet.*

23. Behold, I am he of whom Moses spake, saying, A prophet shall the Lord your God raise up unto you of your brethren, like unto me; him shall ye hear in all things whatsoever he shall say unto you. And it shall come to pass that every soul who will not hear that prophet shall be cut off from among the people.

4. *Many prophets cited.*

24. Verily I say unto you, yea, and all the prophets from Samuel and those that follow after, as many as have spoken, have testified of me.

25. And behold, ye are the children of the prophets; and ye are of the house of Israel; and ye are of the covenant which the Father made with your fathers, say-

---

It is shown as vicarious, as it was represented by the sacrifices in the Old Testament. It is therefore, a most solemn and impressive proclamation of the atoning death of the Lamb of God, highly needed when unbelief and infidelity in various forms threaten to overflow the world.

Three great monuments. The Church owns three historical monuments which all stand as unimpeachable witnesses to Christ's work as the Savior of the world. These are: (1) the Sacrament of the Lord's Supper in memory of His Death upon the Cross; (2) Baptism, in memory of His Burial, and (3) the Lord's Day, in memory of His Resurrection from the dead. If we understand the significance and importance of these monuments, we will treasure them for ourselves and our children, and never neglect them.

ing unto Abraham: And in thy seed shall all the kindreds of the earth be blessed.

26. The Father having raised me up unto you first, and sent me to bless you in turning away every one of you from his iniquities; and this because ye are the children of the covenant—

27. And after that ye were blessed then fulfilleth the Father the covenant which he made with Abraham, saying: In thy seed shall all the kindreds of the earth be blessed—unto the pouring out of the Holy Ghost through me upon the Gentiles, which blessing upon the Gentiles shall make them mighty above all, unto the scattering of my people, O house of Israel.

28. And they shall be a scourge unto the people of this land. Nevertheless, when they shall have received the fulness of my gospel, then if they shall harden their hearts against me I will return their iniquities upon their own heads, saith the Father.

29. And I will remember the covenant which I have made with my people; and I have covenanted with them that I would gather them together in mine own due time, that I would give unto them again the land of their fathers for their inheritance, which is the land of Jerusalem, which is the promised land unto them forever, saith the Father.

30. And it shall come to pass that the time cometh, when the fulness of my gospel shall be preached unto them;

31. And they shall believe in me, that I am Jesus Christ, the Son of God, and shall pray unto the Father in my name.

32. Then shall their watchmen lift up their voice, and with the voice together shall they sing; for they shall see eye to eye.

33. Then will the Father gather them together again, and give unto them Jerusalem for the land of their inheritance.

34. Then shall they break forth into joy—Sing together, ye waste places of Jerusalem; for the Father hath comforted his people, he hath redeemed Jerusalem.

35. The Father hath made bare his holy arm in the eyes of all the nations; and all the ends of the earth shall see the salvation of the Father; and the Father and I are one.

36. And then shall be brought to pass that which is written: Awake, awake again, and put on thy strength, O Zion; put on thy beautiful garments, O Jerusalem, the holy city, for henceforth there shall no more come into thee the

---

VERSES 10-25. After the administration of the Sacrament, our Lord delivers the address recorded in these verses, which is a continuation of the sermon begun the previous day on the subject of the gathering of the remnants of His Covenant People. (III Nephi 15:11-20)

VERSE 14. *This Land.* (*See,* General notes, p. 102; The Land of Zion—America)

uncircumcised and the unclean.

37. Shake thyself from the dust; arise, sit down, O Jerusalem; loose thyself from the bands of thy neck, O captive daughter of Zion.

38. For thus saith the Lord: Ye have sold yourselves for naught, and ye shall be redeemed without money.

39. Verily, verily, I say unto you, that my people shall know my name; yea, in that day they shall know that I am he that doth speak.

40. And then shall they say: How beautiful upon the mountains are the feet of him that bringeth good tidings unto them, that publisheth peace; that bringeth good tidings unto them of good, that publisheth salvation; that saith unto Zion: Thy God reigneth!

41. And then shall a cry go forth: Depart ye, depart ye, go ye out from thence, touch not that which is unclean; go ye out of the midst of her; be ye clean that bear the vessels of the Lord.

42. For ye shall not go out with haste nor go by flight; for the Lord will go before you, and the God of Israel shall be your rearward.

43. Behold, my servant shall deal prudently; he shall be exalted and extolled and be very high.

44. As many were astonished at thee—his visage was so marred, more than any man, and his form more than the sons of men—

45. So shall he sprinkle many nations; the kings shall shut their mouths at him, for that which had not been told them shall they see; and that which they had not heard shall they consider.

46. Verily, verily, I say unto you, all these things shall surely come, even as the Father hath commanded me. Then shall this covenant which the Father hath covenanted with his people be fulfilled; and then shall Jerusalem be inhabited again with my people, and it shall be the land of their inheritance.

VERSES 10-46. *This land belongs to the Remnant of Jacob.* Our Lord begins His address by the assurance that the scattered remnants of the House of Jacob would be gathered in from the east and the west, from the north and the south, and that "The Father hath commanded Me that I should give unto you this land for your inheritance." He next promised that He would establish them in this land, unto the fulfilling of the covenant which I made with your father, Jacob. The Remnant of Jacob, He said, would be among the unrepentant Gentiles, as a lion in the forest or among a flock of sheep.

The Jews will also be gathered. In due time, Jesus says, He will also remember the other scattered remnants of His people, and gather them in the land of their fathers, the Land of Jerusalem. They will receive the Gospel, and then their watchmen will lift up their voices and sing together. Then, He says, shall Jerusalem be inhabited again by My people, and it shall be as the land of their inheritance.

CHAPTER 21

1. *Sign of the Father's Work.*

1. And verily I say unto you, I give unto you a sign, that ye may know the time when these things shall be about to take place—that I shall gather in, from their long dispersion, my people, O house of Israel, and shall establish again among them my Zion;

2. And behold, this is the thing which I will give unto you for a sign—for verily I say unto you that when these things which I declare unto you, and which I shall declare unto you hereafter of myself, and by the power of the Holy Ghost which shall be given unto you of the Father, shall be made known unto the Gentiles that they may know concerning this people who are a remnant of the house of Jacob, and concerning this my people who shall be scattered with them;

3. Verily, verily, I say unto you, when these things shall be made known unto them of the Father, and shall come forth of the Father, from them unto you;

4. For it is wisdom in the Father that they should be established in this land, and be set up as a free people by the power of the Father, that these things might come forth from them unto a remnant of your seed, that the covenant of the Father may be fulfilled which he hath covenanted with his people, O house of Israel;

5. Therefore, when these works and the works which shall be wrought among you hereafter shall come forth from the Gentiles, unto your seed which shall dwindle in unbelief because of iniquity;

6. For thus it behooveth the Father that it should come forth from the Gentiles, that he may show forth his power unto the Gentiles, for this cause that the Gentiles, if they will not harden their hearts, that they may repent and come unto me and be baptized in my name and know of the true points of my doctrine, that they may be numbered among my people, O house of Israel;

7. And when these things come to pass that thy seed shall begin to know these things—it shall be

---

VERSES 1-7. *I will give unto you a sign.* The Lord, next, reveals the sign by which the observer may know that the gathering of the dispersed remnants is about to commence. He says that when the revelations now received and others still future, should come to the knowledge of the Gentiles, and through them to the remnant of Jacob, then they might know "that the work of the Father hath

a sign unto them, that they may know that the work of the Father hath already commenced unto the fulfilling of the covenant which he hath made unto the people who are of the house of Israel.

8. And when that day shall come, it shall come to pass that kings shall shut their mouths; for that which had not been told them shall they see; and that which they had not heard shall they consider.

9. For in that day, for my sake shall the Father work a work, which shall be a great and a marvelous work among them; and there shall be among them those who will not believe it, although a man shall declare it unto them.

10. But behold, the life of my servant shall be in my hand;

therefore they shall not hurt him, although he shall be marred because of them. Yet I will heal him, for I will show unto them that my wisdom is greater than the cunning of the devil.

11. Therefore it shall come to pass that whosoever will not believe in my words, who am Jesus Christ, which the Father shall cause him to bring forth unto the Gentiles, and shall give unto him power that he shall bring them forth unto the Gentiles, (it shall be done even as Moses said) they shall be cut off from among my people who are of the covenant.

12. And my people who are a remnant of Jacob shall be among the Gentiles, yea, in the midst of them as a lion among the beasts of the forest, as a young lion

---

already commenced unto the fulfilling of the covenant with the people who are of the House of Israel." This is also to be a time of extraordinary commotion, both political and religious.

VERSES 8-10. *Kings shall shut their mouths.* In that day the Father, for the sake of the Son, will do a work that shall be great and marvelous among them and to such a degree that kings will stand silent in awe and wonderment.

A man shall be raised up to declare that work, but some will not believe his message. (v. 9) The Lord's "servant" will be persecuted and "marred" but not killed, for His life will be in the hand of God, who will heal Him. (v. 10)

VERSE 11. *Whosoever will not believe on my words.* And then it will come to pass that those who refuse to believe in the words of Christ (proclaimed by the messenger mentioned in verse 9) will be cut off from the covenant people.

The "Servant." It may be said, in passing, that the poems concerning the "servant" (v. 10) may be best understood to refer, in the first place, to Israel as a nation (Isaiah 49:1-6) with a special mission among the Gentiles; and in the second place, to the Messiah, the Savior of all. In the case of Israel, as in the case of the greatest of her sons, the road to exaltation has been laid over Calvary.

And therefore, we read, that, it shall come to pass that whosoever will not believe in the words of Jesus Christ, which the Father will cause Him to bring forth unto the Gentiles, shall be cast off from the covenant people. (*Compare* II Nephi 3:11-13; III Nephi 20:23)

VERSES 12-13. *The Remnant of Jacob among the Gentiles.* At that time the remnant of Jacob shall be among the Gentiles as a lion among beasts of the forest, or among sheep.

among the flocks of sheep, who, if he go through both treadeth down and teareth in pieces, and none can deliver.

13. Their hand shall be lifted up upon their adversaries, and all their enemies shall be cut off.

2. *Glorious Destiny of Repentant Gentiles.*

3. *Condemnation Predicted for the Impenitent.*

14. Yea, wo be unto the Gentiles except they repent; for it shall come to pass in that day, saith the Father, that I will cut off thy horses out of the midst of thee, and I will destroy thy chariots;

15. And I will cut off the cities of thy land, and throw down all thy strongholds;

16. And I will cut off witchcrafts out of thy land, and thou shalt have no more soothsayers;

17. Thy graven images I will also cut off, and thy standing images out of the midst of thee, and thou shalt no more worship the works of thy hands;

18. And I will pluck up thy groves out of the midst of thee; so will I destroy thy cities.

19. And it shall come to pass that all lyings, and deceivings, and envyings, and strifes, and priestcrafts, and whoredoms, shall be done away.

20. For it shall come to pass, saith the Father, that at that day whosoever will not repent and come unto my Beloved Son, them will I cut off from among my people, O house of Israel;

21. And I will execute vengeance and fury upon them, even as upon the heathen, such as they have not heard.

This seems to point to a time when the aborigines of America will cause trouble. Or, has, perhaps, the prophecy been fulfilled, at least as far as the United States is concerned, in the Indian wars already fought?

There are at present, as estimated, about 523,591 Indians in the United States. They have about 40,000,000 acres of land between them. An increasing number frequent public schools. Inter-marriages with Caucasians are also increasing in frequency. On the whole their standard of civilization is rapidly improving.

In some other American countries the Indian element is much larger. In Mexico, for instance, it is estimated that there are almost 5,000,000 Indians and twice that many "Mestizos." In countries where the aboriginal element is so large, disturbances may occur, however, in that case, the blame is largely with the Gentiles.

The Gentiles to blame. Our Lord here teaches:

VERSE 14. If the Gentiles do not repent, their horses and wagons will be destroyed. Armies, navies or aircraft will not avail.

VERSE 15. Their cities will be laid to waste, no matter how big they may be.

VERSES 16-21. Their superstitions and false objects of worship will be cut off.

On the other hand, if they repent, then,

22. But if they will repent and hearken unto my words, and harden not their hearts, I will establish my church among them, and they shall come in unto the covenant and be numbered among this the remnant of Jacob, unto whom I have given this land for their inheritance;

23. And they shall assist my people, the remnant of Jacob, and also as many of the house of Israel as shall come, that they may build a city, which shall be called the New Jerusalem.

4. The New Jerusalem.

24. And then shall they assist my people that they may be gathered in, who are scattered upon all the face of the land, in unto the New Jerusalem.

25. And then shall the power of heaven come down among them; and I also will be in the midst.

26. And then shall the work of the Father commence at that day, even when this gospel shall be preached among the remnant of this people. Verily I say unto you, at that day shall the work of the Father commence among all the dispersed of my people, yea, even the tribes which have been lost, which the Father hath led away out of Jerusalem.

27. Yea, the work shall commence among all the dispersed of my people, with the Father, to prepare the way whereby they may come unto me, that they may call on the Father in my name.

28. Yea, and then shall the work commence, with the Father, among all nations, in preparing the way whereby his people may be gathered home to the land of their inheritance.

29. And they shall go out from all nations; and they shall not go out in haste, nor go by flight, for I will go before them, saith the Father, and I will be their rearward.

VERSE 22. God will establish His Church among them and they will be numbered among the remnant of Jacob.

VERSE 23. They will cooperate in the building of the New Jerusalem.

VERSE 24. They will assist in the gathering into the New Jerusalem of those who are scattered upon the face of the land.

VERSE 25. The power of heaven shall come down and He will be amongst them.

VERSES 26-29. And then shall the work of the Father commence, even when this Gospel shall be preached among the remnant of "this people."

At that day also shall the work of the Father commence among all the dispersed of His people, even among the Lost Tribes from Jerusalem. Also, at that day, shall this work commence among all nations in preparing the *way* for the return of His people to the land of their inheritance.

We take this to mean that the first proclamation of the Gospel to the

GOSPEL

My Gospel—

I Nephi	13:34	I will bring forth . . . much of my G.
	36	In them shall be written my G.
III Nephi	16:10	When the Gentiles shall sin against my G.
	10	And shall reject the fulness of my G.
	10	I will bring the fulness of my G. from
	11	And I will bring my G. unto them
	12	The knowledge of the fulness of my G.
	20:28	Shall have received the fulness of my G.
	30	When the fulness of my G. shall be preached unto
	27:8	If it so be that ye are built upon my G.
	9	Ye are built upon my G.; therefore ye
	10	Be that the Church is built upon my G.
	11	But if it be not built upon my G.
	13	I have given unto you my G.
	21	Verily, I say unto you, this is my G.
Ether	4:18	Come unto me, and believe my G.

Gospel

I Nephi	10:11	The G. which should be preached among
	14	Gentiles had received the fulness of the G.
	13:24	It contained the plainness of the G. of
	26	Have taken away from the G. of the Lamb
	29	Are taken away from the G. of the Lamb
	32	Most precious parts of the G. of the Lamb
	34	And precious parts of the G. of the Lamb
	15:13	The fulness of the G. of the Messiah
	14	The knowledge of the G. of their Redeemer
	22:11	In bringing about his covenants and his G.
II Nephi	30:5	The G. of Jesus Christ shall be declared
Jacob	7:6	That which ye call the G. . . . of Christ
III Nephi	21:26	When this G. shall be preached among
	27:13	This is the G. which I have given
	28:23	Did preach the G. of Christ unto all
IV Nephi	1:38	They who rejected the G., were called Lamanites,
	38	Wilfully rebel against the G. of Christ
Mormon	3:21	That ye may believe the G. of Christ
	5:15	People may more fully believe his G.
	7:8	And lay hold of the G. of Christ
	9:8	Denieth . . . knoweth not the G. of Christ
	22	And preach the G. to every creature
Ether	4:3	And they have rejected the G. of Christ

Indians was the beginning of the mighty work of gathering of all the remnants of the covenant people, and the final manifestation of the glory of God on earth.*

*If this view is correct, the missionary journey of Oliver Cowdery, Peter Whitmer Jr., Ziba Peterson and Parley P. Pratt, in the fall of 1830, was the beginning of the work of Gathering.

CHAPTER 22

1. The Savior further Quotes the Prophecies of Isaiah. Compare Isaiah 54.

1. And then shall that which is written come to pass: Sing, O barren, thou that didst not bear; break forth into singing, and cry aloud, thou that didst not travail with child; for more are the children of the desolate than the children of the married wife, saith the Lord.

2. Enlarge the place of thy tent, and let them stretch forth the curtains of thy habitations; spare not, lengthen thy cords and strengthen thy stakes;

3. For thou shalt break forth on the right hand and on the left, and thy seed shall inherit the Gentiles and make the desolate cities to be inhabited.

4. Fear not, for thou shalt not be ashamed; neither be thou confounded, for thou shalt not be put to shame; for thou shalt forget the shame of thy youth, and shalt not remember the reproach of thy youth, and shalt not remember the reproach of thy widowhood any more.

5. For thy maker, thy husband, the Lord of Hosts is his name; and thy Redeemer, the Holy One of Israel—the God of the whole earth shall he be called.

6. For the Lord hath called thee as a woman forsaken and grieved in spirit, and a wife of youth, when thou wast refused, saith thy God.

7. For a small moment have I forsaken thee, but with great mercies will I gather thee.

8. In a little wrath I hid my face from thee for a moment, but with everlasting kindness will I have mercy on thee, saith the Lord thy Redeemer.

9. For this, the waters of Noah unto me, for as I have sworn that the waters of Noah should no more go over the earth, so have I sworn that I would not be wroth with thee.

10. For the mountains shall depart and the hills be removed, but my kindness shall not depart from thee, neither shall the covenant of my people be removed, saith the Lord that hath mercy on thee.

11. O thou afflicted, tossed with tempest, and not comforted! Behold, I will lay thy stones with fair colors, and lay thy foundations with sapphires.

12. And I will make thy windows of agates, and thy gates of carbuncles, and all thy borders of pleasant stones.

13. And all thy children shall be taught of the Lord; and great

---

Verses 1-17. *Isaiah quoted.* The Savior then commenced to explain to the multitude many of the sayings of the ancient prophets, more especially Isaiah. He dwelt on the great events of the latter days that should precede His second coming, drawing particular attention to those that would concern and be connected with

shall be the peace of thy children.

14. In righteousness shalt thou be established; thou shalt be far from oppression for thou shalt not fear, and from terror for it shall not come near thee.

15. Behold, they shall surely gather together against thee, not by me; whosoever shall gather together against thee shall fall for thy sake.

16. Behold, I have created the smith that bloweth the coals in the fire, and that bringeth forth an instrument for his work; and I have created the waster to destroy.

17. No weapon that is formed against thee shall prosper; and every tongue that shall rise against thee in judgment thou shalt condemn. This is the heritage of the servants of the Lord, and their righteousness is of me, saith the Lord.

---

the remnants of the House of Lehi, and in which they would be partakers. From His words we learn that in the latter times the everlasting Gospel will be preached in their midst; that many will receive it; that they will take a prominent part in the building of the New Jerusalem, and in many of the other events that will herald the near approach of that blessed day when the reign of Christ and the triumph of truth and righteousness shall extend from pole to pole, over the whole of this globe.

CHAPTER 23

1. And now, behold, I say unto you, that ye ought to search these things. Yea, a commandment I give unto you that ye search these things diligently; for great are the words of Isaiah.

2. For surely he spake as touching all things concerning my people which are of the house of Israel; therefore it must needs be that he must speak also to the Gentiles.

3. And all things that he spake have been and shall be, even according to the words which he spake.

4. Therefore give heed to my words; write the things which I have told you; and according to the time and the will of the Father they shall go forth unto the Gentiles.

5. And whosoever will hearken unto my words and repenteth and is baptized, the same shall be saved. Search the prophets, for many there be that testify of these things.

1. *The Savior Commands that Omissions from Nephite Records be Supplied.*

6. And now it came to pass that when Jesus had said these words he said unto them again, after he had expounded all the scriptures unto them which they had received, he said unto them: Behold, other scriptures I would that ye should write, that ye have not.

7. And it came to pass that he said unto Nephi: Bring forth the record which ye have kept.

8. And when Nephi had brought forth the records, and laid them before him, he cast his eyes upon them and said:

9. Verily I say unto you, I commanded my servant Samuel, the Lamanite, that he should testify unto this people, that at the day

---

VERSES 1-5. *Ye ought to search these things.* The Savior urged, even commanded, the people to search the things of which Isaiah had spoken, for He said that great are his words. He also urged them to be baptized after they had repented, saying, "The same shall be saved." "Search the prophets, for many there be that testify of these things."

VERSES 7-14. *Other Scriptures.* Jesus now turned to Nephi and requested to be shown his records. Observing that the Nephite records did not contain the prophecy of Samuel, the Lamanite, concerning the resurrection of Saints at the time of Christ's rising from the dead, He asked them, "Was it not so?" And they said, "Yea, Lord, Samuel did prophesy according to Thy words, and they were all fulfilled." The Savior thereupon instructed Nephi to add that important item to his record.

that the Father should glorify his name in me that there were many saints who should arise from the dead, and should appear unto many, and should minister unto them. And he said unto them: Was it not so?

10. And his disciples answered him and said: Yea, Lord, Samuel did prophesy according to thy words, and they were all fulfilled.

11. And Jesus said unto them: How be it that ye have not written this thing, that many saints did arise and appear unto many and did minister unto them?

12. And it came to pass that Nephi remembered that this thing had not been written.

13. And it came to pass that Jesus commanded that it should be written; therefore it was written according as he commanded.

14. And now it came to pass that when Jesus had expounded all the scriptures in one, which they had written, he commanded them that they should teach the things which he had expounded unto them.

The doctrine of the Resurrection is the foundation of the Christian faith. For, in the language of St. Paul, "If there be no resurrection of the dead, then is Christ not risen, and your faith is also in vain . . . ye are yet in your sins. Then they also which are fallen asleep in Christ are perished." (1 Corinthians 15:13-18) This being so, the testimony of eyewitnesses to the appearance of resurrected beings is of tremendous value. (See, Matthew 27:52-53)

2. Prophecy of Samuel the Lamanite.

The Prophecy of Samuel, the Lamanite, was that Christ would die in order that Salvation might come; "Yea," he said, "it behooveth Him and becometh expedient that He dieth, to bring to pass the resurrection of the dead, that thereby men may be brought into the presence of the Lord." (Helaman 14:15-17) That His death actually brought about resurrection is a fact attested by eyewitnesses, and not merely a theory.

All men, at some time, must stand in their resurrected bodies before the Judgment Seat of Christ. All nations, too, must be judged at the second advent of our Lord. (Matthew 25:31-46)

CHAPTER 24

1. Malachi's Words Given to the Nephites—2. The Law of Tithes and Offerings.
Compare Malachi 3 (*See,* Chapter 25)

1. *Malachi's words given to the Nephites.*

1. And it came to pass that he commanded them that they should write the words which the Father had given unto Malachi, which he should tell unto them. And it came to pass that after they were written he expounded them. And these are the words which he did tell unto them, saying: Thus said the Father unto Malachi—Behold, I will send my messenger, and he shall prepare the way before me, and the Lord whom ye seek shall suddenly come to his temple, even the messenger of the covenant, whom ye delight in; behold, he shall come, saith the Lord of Hosts.

2. But who may abide the day of his coming, and who shall stand when he appeareth? For he is like a refiner's fire, and like fuller's soap.

3. And he shall sit as a refiner and purifier of silver; and he shall purify the sons of Levi, and purge them as gold and silver, that they may offer unto the Lord an offering in righteousness.

4. Then shall the offering of

VERSES 1-6. *Behold, I will send My Messenger.* The Risen Lord continued to instruct the eager Nephites, and, in their sacred records, He commanded them to write the words of the Prophet Malachi which He would tell unto them. He waited while they were written; He then expounded their meaning, which caused the assembled throng to rejoice in the eternal purposes of God.

Malachi was the last of the great Hebrew prophets of whom we have any record who ministered unto the Jews. He labored among them about 200 years after Lehi left Jerusalem, or B.C. 397. The Nephites, therefore, had no knowledge of his prophecies, but received them with joy from the mouth of the Savior, Himself.

Of Malachi's prophecies which the Risen Lord repeated to the astonished Nephites one remains with us the inspiriting and inspiring prelude to greater things which will usher in Christ's Reign on Earth.

For nearly 2000 years the people of the earth have been told that their Lord and Savior, Jesus Christ, would suddenly come to His Temple, and there reign in glory as King of kings and Lord of lords. The day by prophets long foretold would be a happy day. He would be their King, and they would be His loyal subjects. The coming of that day had been long deferred. Waiting for it had filled many hearts with despair. Hopelessness had taken the place of gladness.

When it was pointed out to them that there was no Temple on all the Earth to which the Lord could come, and when they heard the rant and rantings of those who awaited His coming, a sort of disappointed pride mocked their joyous expectations. They looked for what they saw not, and searched for that which they could not find.

Malachi's prophecy which the Savior quoted and therein testified of its divine origin, was repeated by Him, thus:

"Behold, I will send My messenger, and he shall prepare the way before Me,

Judah and Jerusalem be pleasant unto the Lord, as in the days of old, and as in former years.

5. And I will come near to you to judgment; and I will be a swift witness against the sorcerers, and against the adulterers, and against false swearers, and against those that oppress the hireling in his wages, the widow and the father-

and the Lord Whom ye seek shall suddenly come to His Temple, even the *Messenger of the Covenant*,[1] whom ye delight in; behold, He shall come, saith the Lord of Hosts." (Malachi 3:1; III Nephi 24:1)

That glorious promise is known unto all Christian believers; it is their hope and stay. But, alas, when the King, the Lord Jesus Christ, sent His messenger, the Prophet Joseph Smith, they would not hear his words. From him they turned away. Instead, they looked for a royal entourage, and there found that the Kings' emissaries were not princes and nobles but poor tillers of the soil. They found that the men whom they had so recently scourged and cast out were, indeed, the ambassadors of that King, sent to prepare His way.

It was then that their hard hearts became like granite; their spite was keen and inexhaustible, and they let the angry passions that filled their hearts become the sole judge of their rising hate. And of all the passions that occupy the human heart, theirs was the most bitter and malignant.

They mocked, they ridiculed, they spat upon, all those who believed and who took upon themselves the hated name, *Mormon*. But, the faithful, like the Nephites in the days of Amos, neither reviled at the reviler, nor did they smite the smiter. They bore all these things with courage and fortitude, remembering the pains of their Redeemer.

As we have said, Malachi lived about 400 years B.C., less than 140 years after the Babylonian captivity. During that comparatively short period, the people had sunk very low, morally. Malachi censored those who, to all appearances, held the Priesthood, for profane and mercenary transactions in the performance of the ritualistic service in the Law of Moses. They offered unclean sacrifices on the *Altar of Jehovah,* because they could acquire the ceremonially proffered animals or birds at a lower price. (Malachi 1:7-10) He condemned the people for marrying idolaters and multiplying divorces. (*Ibid.,* 2:11-16) Then Malachi predicted the coming of a day of reckoning with the advent of the Messiah, who is to be preceded by a messenger with the mission to prepare the way of the Lord's coming. (*Ibid.,* 3 and 4)

Now the Nephites knew nothing of Malachi, so for their comfort and instruction, Jesus rehearsed to them the important things which God had revealed through Malachi. In fact, Mormon says, "He did expound all things, even from the beginning until the time that He should come in His glory." (III Nephi 26:3)

Chapters 3 and 4 of the writings of Malachi is the portion of Malachi's

[1]*Messenger of the Covenant.* Septuagint, Latin, septuaginta meaning seventy. The pre-Christian Greek version of the Old Testament still in use in the Eastern Church; so called from the legend that the translation was made by seventy emissaries from Jerusalem for Ptolemy II, about B.C. 270.

This is the version reputed to have been used by the Savior and His Apostles. It translated Isaiah 9:6, thus:

"For a little child is born unto us; and a son is given unto us, whose dominion is on his shoulder; and his name shall be called: *Messenger of the Great Council,* Wonderful Counselor, Strong Mighty One; Ruler of Peace, Father of the Coming Age."

The first mentioned Name is not given in the *King James Authorized Version,* but the Son mentioned was surely, if He was anything, the *Messenger of the Great Council, or Covenant.* (See, COMMENTARY ON THE BOOK OF MORMON, Volume II, p. 165)

less, and that turn aside the stranger, and fear not me, saith the Lord of Hosts.

6. For I am the Lord, I change not; therefore ye sons of Jacob are not consumed.

2. *The Law of Tithes and Offerings.*

7. Even from the days of your fathers ye are gone away from mine ordinances, and have not kept them. Return unto me and I will return unto you, saith the Lord of Hosts. But ye say, Wherein shall we return?

8. Will a man rob God? Yet ye have robbed me. But ye say: Wherein have we robbed thee? In tithes and offerings.

9. Ye are cursed with a curse, for ye have robbed me, even this whole nation.

10. Bring ye all the tithes into the storehouse, that there may be meat in my house; and prove me now herewith, saith the Lord of Hosts, if I will not open you the windows of heaven, and pour you out a blessing that there shall not be room enough to receive it.

---

prophecy that Jesus recited to the assembled Nephites, and which is incorporated in the Book of Mormon. (III Nephi 24-25)

In this section, we learn:

a. That a messenger would be sent to prepare the way for the Messiah.

b. Some suppose that the Lord spoke of John the Baptist. That John was a messenger who as a fact was sent to prepare the way of our Lord when first He was born to Mary cannot be doubted. (See, Matthew 11:10; 17:12; Mark 1:2; 9-12-13; Luke 1:17) Of that there can be no question.

But our Lord in His discourse to the Nephites was speaking particularly of the gathering of His people in the Last Days, and His Own Second Coming. The Prophecy of Malachi must therefore be one in regard to these times. And it is! It has reference to the *Everlasting Covenant* as established through the instrumentality of the Prophet Joseph Smith and his successors. There can be no doubt about that, either. For the Lord says: "And even so I have sent Mine *Everlasting Covenant* into the world, to be a light to the world, and to be a standard for My people and for the Gentiles to seek to it, *and to be a messenger before My face to prepare the way before Me.*" (*Doctrine and Covenants* 45:9. Italics are the Editor's.)

Previous to the time of the last quotation, He says: "Wherefore I the Lord, knowing the calamity which should come upon the inhabitants of the earth, called upon My servant Joseph Smith, Jun., and spake unto him from Heaven, and gave him commandments; . . . that Mine Everlasting Covenants might be established; that the fulness of My Gospel might be proclaimed by the weak and the simple unto the ends of the world, and before kings and rulers." (*Ibid.*, 1:17-23)

The Messenger of whom the Savior spoke, has come, and the Lord will again come to His Temple, suddenly.

c. We learn also that when He comes, He will separate the dross from the precious metal.

Verses 7-18. *Wherein shall we return?*

d. That not to keep the ordinances of God, is to *rob* Him.

The Prophet Malachi exhorts the people to return to God, and teaches that their first sign of true repentance ought to be the payment of an honest tithing. The whole nation, he says, is under a curse, because the people have been robbing God.

11. And I will rebuke the devourer for your sakes, and he shall not destroy the fruits of your ground; neither shall your vine cast her fruit before the time in the fields, saith the Lord of Hosts.

12. And all nations shall call you blessed, for ye shall be a delightsome land, saith the Lord of Hosts.

13. Your words have been stout against me, saith the Lord. Yet ye say: What have we spoken against thee?

14. Ye have said: It is vain to serve God, and what doth it profit that we have kept his ordinances and that we have walked mournfully before the Lord of Hosts?

15. And now we call the proud happy; yea, they that work wickedness are set up; yea, they that tempt God are even delivered.

16. Then they that feared the Lord spake often one to another, and the Lord hearkened and heard; and a book of remembrance was written before him for them that feared the Lord, and that thought upon his name.

17. And they shall be mine, saith the Lord of Hosts, in that day when I make up my jewels; and I will spare them as a man spareth his own son that serveth him.

18. Then shall ye return and discern between the righteous and the wicked, between him that serveth God and him that serveth him not.

Now bring all the tithes into the storehouse . . . prove Me herewith, saith the Lord of Hosts, if I will not open you the windows of Heaven, and pour out a blessing . . . and all nations shall call you blessed. (See, vv. 10-12)

This is reasonable. If a man repents to the extent that love of God prompts him to return an honest tithe to his Maker, he is not likely to break, wittingly, any other commandment. To pay an honest tithe to his Maker is not all. But the paying of this tribute is a good indication, generally speaking, of the spiritual condition of a Church member.

CHAPTER 25

1. Elijah and His Mission—2. The Great and Dreadful Day of the Lord.
(Compare Malachi 4)

1. Elijah and his mission.

2. The great and dreadful day of the Lord.

1. For behold, the day cometh that shall burn as an oven; and all the proud, yea, and all that do wickedly, shall be stubble; and the day that cometh shall burn them up, saith the Lord of Hosts, that it shall leave them neither root nor branch.

2. But unto you that fear my name, shall the Son of Righteousness arise with healing in his wings; and ye shall go forth and grow up as calves in the stall.

3. And ye shall tread down the wicked; for they shall be ashes under the soles of your feet in the day that I shall do this, saith the Lord of Hosts.

4. Remember ye the law of Moses, my servant, which I commanded unto him in Horeb for all Israel, with the statutes and judgments.

5. Behold, I will send you

VERSES 1-6. *The day cometh that shall burn as an oven.* This chapter is a recording of Christ's words as He repeated to the Nephites more of the Prophet Malachi's divinely inspired utterances. Malachi's prophecy is also found in the Hebrew Scriptures, and by repeating them the Risen Redeemer gave them His approval.

From them we learn that before the great and dreadful day of the Lord, Elijah, the Prophet, would be sent unto mortals with the mission of turning the heart of the fathers to the children, and the heart of the children to their fathers, "Lest," the Lord says, "I come and smite the earth with a curse." (v. 6)

This promise was fulfilled on April 3, 1836, when the Prophet Elijah appeared to Joseph, the Prophet of this Dispensation, and to Oliver Cowdery, in the Kirtland Temple, and said: "Behold, the time has fully come, which was spoken of by the mouth of Malachi—testifying that he (Elijah) should be sent before the great and dreadful day of the Lord come—To turn the hearts of the fathers to the children, and the children to the fathers, lest the whole earth be smitten with a curse— Therefore, the keys of this dispensation are committed into your hands; and by this ye may know that the great and dreadful day of the Lord is near, even at the doors." (*Doctrine and Covenants* 110:14-16)

A careful reading of the Revelation on wars (*Doctrine and Covenants*, Section 87) leads us to the conclusion that the "great and dreadful day of the Lord" actually dawned upon the world with that shot that was fired on Fort Sumter in Charleston Harbor, January 9, 1866, and of which it is said: "It was heard around the world." The revelation predicts the Civil War (*Ibid.*, 1), and further predicts that it is only the beginning of greater catastrophies that are yet to follow. "Then," it says, "war shall be poured out upon all nations." (v. 3) Section 87 also foretells of labor disputes and Indian uprisings, sword and bloodshed, famine, plague,

Elijah the prophet before the coming of the great and dreadful day of the Lord;

6. And he shall turn the heart of the fathers to the children, and the heart of the children to their fathers, lest I come and smite the earth with a curse.

---

earthquakes, thunder and lightnings, until the consummation decreed shall have made an end of all nations — all human governments. "Wherefore," the Lord says, "stand ye in holy places, and be not moved, until the day of the Lord come." That is, until all these things take place; "For, behold it cometh quickly, saith the Lord." (v. 8)

CHAPTER 26

THE THIRD DAY

1. The Savior Expounds all Things from the Beginning—2. Marvelous Words Spoken by the Mouths of Babes—3. The Work of the Disciples.

1. *The Savior expounds all things from the beginning.*

2. *Marvelous words spoken by the mouths of babes.*

1. And now it came to pass that when Jesus had told these things he expounded them unto the multitude; and he did expound all things unto them, both great and small.

2. And he saith: These scriptures, which ye had not with you, the Father commanded that I should give unto you; for it was wisdom in him that they should be given unto future generations.

3. And he did expound all things, even from the beginning until the time that he should come in his glory—yea, even all things which should come upon the face of the earth, even until the elements should melt with fervent heat, and the earth should be wrapt together as a scroll, and the heavens and the earth should pass away;

4. And even unto the great and last day, when all people, and all kindreds, and all nations and tongues shall stand before God, to be judged of their works, whether they be good or whether they be evil—

5. If they be good, to the resurrection of everlasting life; and if they be evil, to the resurrection of damnation; being on a parallel, the one on the one hand and the other on the other hand, according to the mercy, and the justice, and the holiness which is in Christ, who was before the world began.

6. And now there cannot be written in this book even a hundreth part of the things which Jesus did truly teach unto the people;

7. But behold the plates of Nephi do contain the more part of the things which he taught the people.

VERSES 1-16. *Expounded all things.* The conference lasted for three days, but the minutes of only two are given in detail. In explanation, the Prophet Mormon, who abridged the record that was made at the time of the Savior's visit, informs us that the Lord, after having quoted the Scriptures, expounded all things from the beginning, and that even a hundredth part of the teachings of Jesus during these days of heavenly guidance could not be recorded or be reproduced in his relatively short summary. Christ's words of solace and His benedictions given in explication of the Gospel Plan caused, as we have said, the multitude of Nephites to rejoice in the eternal purposes of God. They were all written down on the Plates of Nephi, but Mormon was not permitted to copy it in detail. The full minutes of the Third Day of the Conference are therefore eliminated, and the general statement is made,

8. And these things have I written, which are a lesser part of the things which he taught the people; and I have written them to the intent that they may be brought again unto this people, from the Gentiles, according to the words which Jesus hath spoken.

9. And when they shall have received this, which is expedient that they should have first, to try their faith, and if it shall so be that they shall believe these things then shall the greater things be made manifest unto them.

10. And if it so be that they will not believe these things, then shall the greater things be withheld from them, unto their condemnation.

11. Behold, I was about to write them, all which were engraven upon the plates of Nephi, but the Lord forbade it, saying: I will try the faith of my people.

12. Therefore I, Mormon, do write the things which have been commanded me of the Lord. And now I, Mormon, make an end of my sayings, and proceed to write the things which have been commanded me.

13. Therefore, I would that ye should behold that the Lord truly did teach the people, for the space of three days; and after that he did show himself unto them oft, and did break bread oft, and bless it, and give it unto them.

14. And it came to pass that he did teach and minister unto the children of the multitude of whom hath been spoken, and he did loose their tongues, and they did speak unto their fathers great and marvelous things, even greater than he had revealed unto the people; and he loosed their tongues that they could utter.

15. And it came to pass that after he had ascended into heaven—the second time that he showed himself unto them, and had gone unto the Father, after having healed all their sick, and their lame, and opened the eyes of their blind and unstopped the ears of the deaf, and even had done all manner of cures among them, and raised a man from the dead, and had shown forth his

---

that, after the second ascension—which would be the third day—the multitude saw and heard the little children of the Nephites "Open their mouths and utter marvelous things; and the things which they did utter were forbidden that there should not any man write them." (v. 16)

In summing up the information contained in verses 1-13, let us say this: For three days did the Savior mingle with the Nephites, and did instruct them; and even after that, He met with them often and with them, partook of the Sacrament of the Lord's Supper.

VERSE 14. *The Savior teaches and ministers to the children of the Nephites.* More than this, He ministered to and blessed the children of the Nephites. He loosed the tongues of these little ones, that they spoke great and marvelous things to their parents, even, we are told, greater things than Jesus had revealed to the people.

power unto them, and has ascended unto the Father—

16. Behold, it came to pass on the morrow that the multitude gathered themselves together, and they both saw and heard these children; yea, even babes did open their mouths and utter marvelous things; and the things which they did utter were forbidden that there should not any man write them.

3. The work of the Disciples.

17. And it came to pass that the disciples whom Jesus had chosen began from that time forth to baptize and to teach as many as did come unto them; and as many as were baptized in the name of Jesus were filled with the Holy Ghost.

18. And many of them saw and heard unspeakable things, which are not lawful to be written.

19. And they taught, and did minister one to another; and they had all things common among them, every man dealing justly, one with another.

Jesus also healed all their sick. The lame, the blind, the deaf, were made whole, and one man He raised from the dead.

VERSES 17-21. *The Disciples then began to baptize and to teach.* Upheld by the power of the Priesthood which the Savior had conferred upon them, the "Disciples whom Jesus had chosen" immediately went forth and began to baptize and teach all who came unto them. We can imagine the zeal with which they labored. Just fresh from the instructions they had received from the mouth of the Savior, Himself, they could not rest from the duty which they knew devolved upon them. Soon converts were raised up on every hand, and prayers were offered to the Father in the Name of Jesus Crucified, whom they had both seen and heard. As a crown resting upon the brow of the worthy, the Holy Ghost of Whom the Savior had testified, filled every heart and illumined every soul who was baptized in the Name of Jesus, and "Many of them saw and heard unspeakable things, which are not lawful to be written." (v. 17)

Great were the efforts of Christ's Nephite Disciples to spread the Gospel truths, and also great was the response of the people. In vast numbers they sought baptism, and it was not long until the Church of Christ included every Nephite in the land — there were no Lamanites — through baptism all the inhabitants of this vast continent took upon themselves the Name of Christ and were added to His Church.

Like a lamp unto their feet, the Spirit of Christ lighted the way before them, and as meat to the hungry and drink to those who were athirst, God's Gospel Plan was to them a feast spread upon the *Table of our Lord.* When mortals alone are considered, we may say that the *Perfect Law of Heaven* for once was enthroned among men. As did the early Christian Saints in old Jerusalem, they "had all things common among them (v. 19; *See*, Acts 2); there was no pride of wealth, and no poverty. Neighbors dealt justly with one another and none there were who felt the pangs of unrighteous condemnation.

All entered the Gate to God's Kingdom whereunto the Straight and Narrow Way led; it is recorded that not one of the Nephites who lived in this happy, holy, state of divine and brotherly love was lost. Mormon, in his summary of the events of this period, states that, (and now we only consider the beginning thereof) "And it came to pass that there was no contention in the land, because of the love of God which did dwell in the hearts of the people. And there were no envyings, nor

20. And it came to pass that they did do all things even as Jesus had commanded them.

21. And they who were baptized in the name of Jesus were called the church of Christ.

strifes, nor tumults, nor whoredoms, nor lyings, nor murders, nor any manner of lasciviousness; and surely there could not be a happier people among all the people who had been created by the hand of God. There were no robbers, nor murderers, neither were there Lamanites, nor any manner of -ites; but they were in one, the children of Christ, and heirs to the Kingdom of God." (IV Nephi 15-17)

CHAPTER 27

1. Jesus Christ Names His Church—2. All Things are Written by the Father—
3. Men are to be Judged by What is Written in the Books.

1. *Jesus Christ names His Church.*

1. And it came to pass that as the disciples of Jesus were journeying and were preaching the things which they had both heard and seen, and were baptizing in the name of Jesus, it came to pass that the disciples were gathered together and were united in mighty prayer and fasting.

2. And Jesus again showed

VERSES 1-7. *Ye shall call the Church in My Name.* On one occasion as the Twelve Disciples whom Jesus had chosen, were traveling about as He had commanded, preaching the Gospel and baptizing in His Name all those who came unto them desiring to have that sacred ordinance performed, they united together in mighty prayer. The subject about which they prayed most earnestly was, "What should be the name of the Church?" for its members were not united on this matter.

While they were thus engaged, Jesus again showed Himself unto them. They were praying to the Father in Jesus' Name, and He perceiving their perplexity, said unto them: "What will ye that I shall give unto you?" Their answer was quick and deliberate: "We will that Thou wouldst tell us the Name whereby we shall call this Church."

After a gentle reprimand to those who disputed because of what Name the Church should be called, Jesus pointed to the Scriptures in which an answer to this query could easily be found.

"Have you not read the Scriptures," He asked, "which say ye must take upon you the *Name of Christ,* which is My Name? For by this Name shall ye be called at the Last Day. And whoso taketh upon him My Name, and endureth to the end, the same shall be saved at the Last Day. Therefore, whatsoever ye shall do, ye shall do it in My Name; *therefore ye shall call the Church in My Name. . . .*" (v. 7)

Christ further told them that it could not be His Church if it were not called by His Name. If they called the Church by the name of a man, it would be that man's church, and if by the name of Moses, it would be Moses' church; but being His Church it should be called by His Holy Name, provided, the Lord said: "if it so be that they are built upon My Gospel."

Let us digress for a moment, and consider the present Name of Christ's Church, the *Church of Jesus Christ of Latter-day Saints.* Let us begin with what is called the *Dark Ages.* We herein reprint what we have said previously:

There are many passages of Scripture that relate to the Dark Ages. It is a section in the story of mankind that is little understood. How man plunged into such depths of depravity, while at the same time he created unexcelled works of art and architecture, has not been explained. It is a mystery. It can only be likened to the downfall of classic Greece, there, when the arts were in their highest glory, the wickedness and abandonment of that people reached its maximum.

Surely darkness covered the earth. There was scarcely a ray of light to illumine the darkness. One is bewildered by the lack of moral and spiritual light, the darkness of which hung like a cloud over all Europe.

Well might the prophet exclaim:

himself unto them, for they were praying unto the Father in his name; and Jesus came and stood in the midst of them, and said unto them: What will ye that I shall give unto you?

3. And they said unto him: Lord, we will that thou wouldst tell us the name whereby we shall call this church; for there are disputations among the people concerning this matter.

"Therefore night shall be unto you, that ye shall not have a vision; and it shall be dark unto you, that ye shall not divine; and the Sun shall go down over the prophets, and the day shall be dark over them." (Micah 3:6)

Just as the earth in rotating turns from the great Sun into darkness, just so did the people of the earth turn from the *Son of Righteousness*. For centuries there was no light; God did not reveal Himself to those who claimed to be His vicegerents here on earth.

In medieval darkness, ignorance and superstition were almost universal. It was a crime to read God's Holy Word, and a heresy to worship Him according to one's own conscience. The annals of those times trace, indelibly, the course of the human heart when evil and error take the lead. The chosen leaders of the Church, the guardians of its purity, the watchmen in its towers appointed to defend and to guide, became its corruptors, and the Church, itself, was made a vehicle upon which unworthy priests rode to positions of prominence and power. The highest positions in the Church were bought and sold as common merchandise. Men became the servants of evil; in the name of that which is most holy, they excused themselves in doing that which is most to be eschewed.

Priest-ridden, by fraud maintained, with error throughout, the Church of Jesus Christ ceased to exist upon the earth. In the words of Doctor D. D. Cummin, a student of those times and a clergyman of the Church of England:

"Deadly errors grew up like rank grass; deception, the most revolting, outraged the whole church; blasphemous assumptions and what Paul calls 'doctrines of devils' heaped power and affluence upon the clergy, until they were, in the words of the Apostle, 'exalted above all that is called God.' The doctrines of the church were arrayed in robes the most grotesque and ridiculous, and all Christendom was decked in the habiliments of absolute apostasy."

We think it not necessary nor wise to enter here into any prolonged exposition of the awful events recorded of the Middle Ages of Europe, but we deem it important to say that during that long night all succession in the Priesthood of God was broken, and what was left was merely a sham, a fraud, which led like "the blind leading the blind" along "slippery ways of darkness." Their unseeing eyes failed to behold "the Light that shines in the dark," "the Light of the world," the "Son of Righteousness."

It is not our purpose to denounce any church, nor to condemn its adherents for their beliefs. Each church has some truth in it, but they do not have the *Priesthood of God*. With their different forms of idolatry and their many creeds, their charms, deceptions, rosaries, amulets, cannons of law, etc., etc., they proclaim themselves to be, not the Church of Jesus Christ, but the "great and abominable church" which Nephi saw in a vision and which was referred to by the Apostle Paul as the "Mystery of Iniquity," the apostate church, "BABYLON THE GREAT." (Revelation 17:5)

It is here where the true Church of Christ, represented by *Mormonism*, can be said to be the Voice of Israel's Shepherd calling His sheep from the wood, from the mountain tops, from the moor. Mormonism declares the majestic truth that the night of spiritual darkness has passed, that the morning twilight is here, that the

4. And the Lord said unto them: Verily, verily, I say unto you, why is it that the people should murmur and dispute because of this thing?

5. Have they not read the scriptures, which say ye must take upon you the name of Christ, which is my name? For by this name shall ye be called at the last day;

6. And whoso taketh upon him my name, and endureth to the end, the same shall be saved at the last day.

7. Therefore, whatsoever ye shall do, ye shall do it in my name; therefore ye shall call the church in my name; and ye shall call upon the Father in my name that he will bless the church for my sake.

8. And how be it my church save it be called in my name? For if a church be called in Moses' name then it be Moses'

Voice of our Father has again been heard to speak, and again is preached that glorious proclamation, *"Prepare ye the Way of the Lord."*

Mormonism declares, emphatically and without equivocation, that the Priesthood of God has again been entrusted into the hands of men here upon the earth, and that the same gifts, powers, and blessings of old are again "signs that shall follow them that believe."

Let the Prophet Joseph Smith, himself, tell us concerning events that occurred at this time:

We [Joseph Smith and Oliver Cowdery] continued the work of translation [the Book of Mormon] when, in the ensuing month (May 1829), we on a certain day went into the woods to pray and inquire of the Lord respecting baptism for the remission of sins, that we found mentioned in the translation of the plates. While we were thus employed, praying and calling upon the Lord, a messenger from Heaven descended in a cloud of light, and having laid his hands upon us, he ordained us saying:

"Upon you, my fellow servants, in the Name of Messiah, I confer the Priesthood of Aaron, which holds the keys of the ministering of angels, and of the Gospel of repentance, and of baptism by immersion for the remission of sins; and this shall never be taken again from the Earth, until the sons of Levi do offer again an offering unto the Lord in righteousness."

He said this Aaronic Priesthood had not the power of laying on hands for the gift of the Holy Ghost, but that this should be conferred on us hereafter, and he gave us directions that I should baptize Oliver Cowdery, and that afterwards he should baptize me.

Accordingly we went and were baptized. I baptized him first, and afterward he baptized me . . . after which I laid my hands upon his head and ordained him to the Aaronic Priesthood, afterwards he laid his hands on me and ordained me to the same Priesthood . . . for so we were commanded.

The messenger who visited us on this occasion and conferred this Priesthood upon us, said that his name was John, the same that is called John the Baptist in the New Testament; and that he acted under the direction of Peter, James and John, who held the keys of the Priesthood of Melchizedek, which Priesthood, he said, would in due time be conferred on us, and that I should be called the First Elder of the Church, and he (Oliver Cowdery) the second. It was the fifteenth day of May, 1829, that we were ordained under the hand of this messenger, and baptized.

Immediately on our coming up out of the water after we had been baptized, we experienced great and glorious blessings from our Heavenly Father. No sooner had I baptized Oliver Cowdery, than the Holy Ghost fell upon him, and he stood up and prophesied many things which should shortly come to pass. And again, so soon as I had been baptized by him, I also had the spirit of prophecy, when, standing

church; or if it be called in the name of a man then it be the church of a man; but if it be called in my name then it is my church, if it so be that they are built upon my gospel.

9. Verily I say unto you, that ye are built upon my gospel; therefore ye shall call whatsoever things ye do call, in my name; therefore if ye call upon the Father, for the church, if it be in my name the Father will hear you;

10. And if it so be that the church is built upon my gospel then will the Father show forth his own works in it.

11. But if it be not built upon my gospel, and is built upon the works of men, or upon the works of the devil, verily I say unto you they have joy in their works for a season, and by and by the end

---

up, I prophesied many things which should shortly come to pass. And again, so with the Church, and this generation of the children of men. We were filled with the Holy Ghost, and rejoiced in the God of our Salvation. (Taken from a little pamphlet, *Joseph Smith Tells His Own Story.*)

Many of those to whom this thing had been declared have asked: "What, then, did the Reformation of the Sixteenth Century mean?" How about all those good men, Luther, Knox, Calvin, John Wesley? Surely they were not deluded, much less impostors. No, we admit that, just as the stars in the sky on a dark night after the great Sun has gone down, there is still some light, thank God; but notwithstanding all this, we deny that the true Church of Jesus Christ exists or has existed in any one of the many creeds of the world since the Seventh Century.

We do not disclaim that position, we proclaim it!

Although the Glorious Reformation did much to raise mankind, and although it banished, we hope forever, many of the abuses to which the Church was subjected, still it was powerless to bring back the true Church.

When the great Reformers commenced their fight against what they called "The desecration of the church and the perversion of its teachings," the *Church of Christ was then upon the earth, or it was not.* There can be no question as to that. If it was, they should have, under no circumstance, made one to oppose it; if it was not, they could not have created it. If they made a church, then it was their church and had no power to save. *Christ, and Christ only,* is the Author of our Salvation, the Founder and Head of our Church, the Church of Jesus Christ, and there is no other.

VERSES 9-12. *Ye are built upon My Gospel. Gospel,* means Good Tidings, especially the good news concerning Christ, the Kingdom of God, and Salvation; hence the teachings of Christ.

For our purpose here, this definition, though a brief one, is ample. Christ says that if the Church is built upon *My Gospel,* that is, if it is built upon *My teachings,* I will recognize it as *My Church.* And further He says, "If ye call upon the Father, for the Church, if it be in My Name the Father will hear you; And if it so be that the Church is built upon My Gospel then will the Father show forth His own works in it." (vv. 9-10)

But on the other hand, if a church is *built upon the works of men, or upon the works of the devil,* that church may bring its workmen joy for a short season, a sort of personal gratification that feeds the hunger of greed and infatuation, but however, as unchangeable as is the rising Sun, the events of time await only the grace of God. Therefore, all their works "shall be as the morning cloud, and as the early dew that passeth away . . . and as the smoke out of the chimney." (Hosea 13:3)

cometh, and they are hewn down and cast into the fire, from whence there is no return.

12. For their works do follow them, for it is because of their works that they are hewn down; therefore remember the things that I have told you.

13. Behold I have given unto you my gospel, and this is the gospel which I have given unto you—that I came into the world to do the will of my Father, because my Father sent me.

14. And my Father sent me that I might be lifted up upon the cross; and after that I had been lifted up upon the cross, that I might draw all men unto me, that as I have been lifted up by men even so should men be lifted up by the Father, to stand before me, to be judged of their works, whether they be good or whether they be evil—

15. And for this cause have I been lifted up; therefore, according to the power of the Father I will draw all men unto me, that they may be judged according to their works.

16. And it shall come to pass, that whoso repenteth and is baptized in my name shall be filled; and if he endureth to the end, behold, him will I hold guiltless

"Their blossoms shall go up as dust; because they have cast away the Law of the Lord of Hosts, and despised the word of the Holy One of Israel." (II Nephi 15:24; Compare Isaiah 5:24)

Man and his works, and the works of Satan, go hand in hand, and are fit only "to be hewn down and cast into the fire." (v. 11) It is, moreover, that the works of men and the works of devils condemn the doers thereof, and because their works are evil, their works and they themselves will be hewn down and be consumed by fire.

VERSES 13-15. *This is the Gospel which I have given unto you.* The Gospel includes all truth. *The Plan of Salvation* is what we may call, the Blueprint of the Gospel. It is a simple drawing. All may read and understand it who have a desire to know the Mind and Will of God.

Christ, Himself, gives the key to its great meaning: "That I came into the world to do the will of My Father . . ." (v. 13) And, you will remember that among His last words when His mission unto the Jews was about ended: "Father, if Thou be willing, remove this cup from Me: nevertheless, not My will, but Thine be done." (Luke 22:42)

Obedient, Jesus Christ, the Eternal Son of God, came to Earth to fulfill a mission His Father sent Him to perform. We may not comprehend the metaphysics of *Why?*, but we do understand that such a mission as was Christ's became necessary to further the Designs of Providence. A price was demanded to Redeem mankind from the effects of Adam's Fall. What was that price? *God alone could pay the price.* Jesus Christ, the Lord God, paid it; *The Great Redeemer died.* The reason for it being, the Savior explains: "And for this cause have I been lifted up; therefore, according to the power of the Father I will draw all men unto Me, that they may be judged according to their works." (v. 15)

VERSES 16-22. *The works ye have seen Me do that shall ye also do.* We have heard from His Own lips, words telling us what Jesus Christ did, and for what purpose. Now let us hear, from those same lips, the things we should do. ". . . This is the commandment: Repent, all ye ends of the Earth, and come unto Me and be baptized in My Name, that ye may be sanctified by the reception of the Holy Ghost, before my Father at that day when I shall stand to judge the world.

17. And he that endureth not unto the end, the same is he that is also hewn down and cast into the fire, from whence they can no more return, because of the justice of the Father.

18. And this is the word which he hath given unto the children of men. And for this cause he fulfilleth the words which he hath given, and he lieth not, but fulfilleth all his words.

19. And no unclean thing can enter into his kingdom; therefore nothing entereth into his rest save it be those who have washed their garments in my blood, because of their faith, and the repentance of all their sins,

---

that ye may stand spotless before Me at the Last Day. Verily, verily, I say unto you, this is My Gospel; and ye know the things that ye must do in My Church; for the works which ye have seen Me do that shall ye also do; for that which ye have seen Me do even that shall ye do. . . ." (vv. 20-21)

Now we being imperfect, nevertheless are commanded to do the things we have seen our Lord and Savior do, Who to us is perfect. However, it is not a hard thing that is required of us. Remember the words of one of God's holy prophets: "He hath shewed thee, O man, what is good; and what doth the Lord require of thee, but to do justly, and to love mercy, and to walk humbly with thy God?" (Micah 6:8) To walk with God is to go where He goes and to do the things you see Him do. No more, no less is our allotted portion. The reason for so doing is made clear in verse 19, where we are told: ". . . no unclean thing can enter into His Kingdom; therefore nothing entereth into His rest save it be those who have washed their garments in My blood, because of their faith, and the repentance of all their sins, and their faithfulness unto the end."

Sin is something unclean, it is filthy; evil also is unclean. The Savior said: "No unclean thing can enter into God's Kingdom."

Through faith on Christ's Name, and repentance from sin, man is washed clean of evil by being immersed in the Waters of Baptism by one who has been commissioned to perform that sacred Ordinance. Not only is he cleansed from sin, but if his repentance is sincere he will receive the Holy Ghost which will guide him along that Path which is straight and narrow. And what is more, as blood is the life-giver in this mortal existence he may look to the shedding of Christ's blood and to His resurrection from the dead as salvation from the effects of Adam's Sin, and therein, with hope, look forward to Immortality, and by the grace of God,[1] to that Life in the Kingdom of God which is eternal. Man may see his uncleanness swallowed up *in everlasting and glorious victory through our Lord Jesus Christ.*

The Ordinance of Baptism, when upheld by our faith and repentance, cleanses us from all sin and blameworthiness; our garments, or in other words, our lives, are made white as snow. Our transgressions are forgiven, and, therefore, if we continue in well-doing unto the end, the Savior also said that such a one may enter the rest that abides in God's Kingdom.

In words the most beautiful and simple, Nephi, the son of the Prophet Lehi, in a discourse delivered before his elder brothers, deals emphatically with this very subject. He tells them how the voices of both the *Father and the Son* came to him, the voice of the Father testifying of the Son, and the voice of the Son, saying: "Wherefore, follow Me, and do the things which ye see Me do." But, said Nephi,

---

[1] By the phrase *Grace of God,* we mean something we could not do for ourselves.

and their faithfulness unto the end.

20. Now this is the commandment: Repent, all ye ends of the earth, and come unto me and be baptized in my name, that ye may be sanctified by the reception of the Holy Ghost, that ye may stand spotless before me at the last day.

"My beloved brethren, can we follow Jesus save we shall be willing to keep the commandments of the Father?"

The passage of Book of Mormon Scripture to which we refer is in detail Nephi's comments, and for us to comment on his comments is like a novice attempting to improve the work of a master. Therefore we reproduce Chapter 31, II Nephi, with the prayer in our hearts that the Holy Spirit will render its message, most for our good and greatest for the glory of our Father which is in Heaven.

"And now I, Nephi, make an end of my prophesying unto you, my beloved brethren. And I cannot write but a few things, which I know must surely come to pass; neither can I write but a few of the words of my brother Jacob.

"Wherefore, the things which I have written sufficeth me, save it be a few words which I must speak concerning the doctrine of Christ; wherefore, I shall speak unto you plainly, according to the plainness of my prophesying.

"For my soul delighteth in plainness; for after this manner doth the Lord God work among the children of men. For the Lord God giveth light unto the understanding; for he speaketh unto men according to their language, unto their understanding.

"Wherefore, I would that ye should remember that I have spoken unto you concerning that prophet which the Lord showed unto me, that should baptize the Lamb of God, which should take away the sins of the world.

"And now, if the Lamb of God, he being holy, should have need to be baptized by water, to fulfil all righteousness, O then, how much more need have we, being unholy, to be baptized, yea, even by water!

"And now, I would ask of you, my beloved brethren, wherein the Lamb of God did fulfil all righteousness in being baptized by water?

"Know ye not that he was holy? But notwithstanding he being holy, he showeth unto the children of men that, according to the flesh he humbleth himself before the Father, and witnesseth unto the Father that he would be obedient unto him in keeping his commandments.

"Wherefore, after he was baptized with water the Holy Ghost descended upon him in the form of a dove.

"And again, it showeth unto the children of men the straightness of the path, and the narrowness of the gate, by which they should enter, he having set the example before them.

"And he said unto the children of men: Follow thou me. Wherefore, my beloved brethren, can we follow Jesus save we shall be willing to keep the commandments of the Father?

"And the Father said: Repent ye, repent ye, and be baptized in the name of my Beloved Son.

"And also, the voice of the Son came unto me, saying: He that is baptized in my name, to him will the Father give the Holy Ghost, like unto me; wherefore, follow me, and do the things which ye have seen me do.

"Wherefore, my beloved brethren, I know that if ye shall follow the Son, with full purpose of heart, acting no hypocrisy and no deception before God, but with real intent, repenting of your sins, witnessing unto the Father that ye are willing to take upon you the name of Christ, by baptism—yea, by following your Lord and your Savior down into the water, according to his word, behold, then shall ye receive the Holy Ghost; yea, then cometh the baptism of fire and of the Holy Ghost; and then can ye speak with the tongue of angels, and shout praises unto the Holy One of Israel.

21. Verily, verily, I say unto you, this is my gospel; and ye know the things that ye must do in my church; for the works which he have seen me do that shall ye also do; for that which ye have seen me do even that shall ye do;

22. Therefore, if ye do these things blessed are ye, for ye shall be lifted up at the last day.

2. *All things are written by the Father.*

3. *Men to be judged by what is written in the books.*

23. Write the things which ye have seen and heard, save it be those which are forbidden.

24. Write the works of this

"But, behold, my beloved brethren, thus came the voice of the Son unto me, saying: After ye have repented of your sins, and witnessed unto the Father that ye are willing to keep my commandments, by the baptism of water, and have received the baptism of fire and of the Holy Ghost, and can speak with a new tongue, yea, even with the tongue of angels, and after this should deny me, it would have been better for you that ye had not known me.

"And I heard a voice from the Father, saying: Yea, the words of my Beloved are true and faithful. He that endureth to the end, the same shall be saved.

"And now, my beloved brethren, I know by this that unless a man shall endure to the end, in following the example of the Son of the living God, he cannot be saved.

"Wherefore, do the things which I have told you I have seen that your Lord and your Redeemer should do; for, for this cause have they been shown unto me, that ye might know the gate by which ye should enter. For the gate by which ye should enter is repentance and baptism by water; and then cometh a remission of your sins by fire and by the Holy Ghost.

"And then are ye in this straight and narrow path which leads to eternal life; yea, ye have entered in by the gate; ye have done according to the commandments of the Father and the Son; and ye have received the Holy Ghost, which witnesses of the Father and the Son, unto the fulfilling of the promise which he hath made, that if ye entered in by the way ye should receive.

"And now, my beloved brethren, after ye have gotten into this straight and narrow path, I would ask if all is done? Behold, I say unto you, Nay; for ye have not come thus far save it were by the word of Christ with unshaken faith in him, relying wholly upon the merits of him who is mighty to save.

"Wherefore, ye must press forward with a steadfastness in Christ, having a perfect brightness of hope, and a love of God and of all men. Wherefore, if ye shall press forward, feasting upon the word of Christ, and endure to the end, behold, thus saith the Father: Ye shall have eternal life.

"And now, behold, my beloved brethren, this is the way; and there is none other way nor name given under heaven whereby man can be saved in the kingdom of God. And now, behold, this is the doctrine of Christ, and the only and true doctrine of the Father, and of the Son, and of the Holy Ghost, which is one God, without end. Amen.

We hesitate to comment further on these wondrous promises of the Lord which He gave to us through His Nephite Disciples, but in humility we repeat the Savior's words which in the end is the sum and substance of all our joy, our happiness and peace: "Therefore, if ye do these things blessed are ye, for ye shall be lifted up at the Last Day." (v. 22)

VERSES 23-27. *Write the things which ye have seen and heard.* The members of Christ's Church have always been a record-keeping people. Even in great detail

people, which shall be, even as hath been written, of that which hath been.

25. For behold, out of the books which have been written, and which shall be written, shall this people be judged, for by them shall their works be known unto men.

26. And behold, all things are written by the Father; therefore out of the books which shall be written shall the world be judged.

---

has the Church in modern days kept the record of all those who have taken upon themselves the Name of Christ.[2] Whether or not they have been diligent in their labors, attending their meetings, paying their tithing, keeping the Word of Wisdom; their Temple Marriages, sealings, and in doing work for the dead, all these and more a sacred record of them is made. At the Last Day when all men shall stand before Christ to be judged, many will attempt to sway the Judge, one way or the other. Some will even dispute what we may say are the findings of that Court. But the Records are there and there will be no hearsay; what we have said and done while on the Earth will be an open book, and from them we will be rewarded justly, whether our works have been good or whether they have been bad. The Judge at that Day will be impartial; all will stand before Him on equal ground, save those who have not served Him, and their reward will be according to merit.

Christ commanded His Nephite Disciples to "Write the things which ye have seen and heard, save it be those which are forbidden."[3] (v. 23)

VERSE 26. *All things are written by the Father.* We refer to the first five books of the Bible as the Writings of Moses although serious objection is made of that fact. Nevertheless, if they were not written by him personally, they were done so under his supervision, and therefore are truly called his writings.

God has commanded men everywhere to write their records,[4] and they are written under the supervision of His servants, therefore without any pretext whatsoever, God has written them, and man will be judged therefrom.

---

[2]"And after they had been received unto baptism, and were wrought upon and cleansed by the power of the Holy Ghost, they were numbered among the people of the Church of Christ; and their names were taken, that they might be remembered and nourished by the Word of God, to keep them in the right way, to keep them continually watchful unto prayer, relying alone on the merits of Christ, Who was the Author and the Finisher of their faith." (Moroni 6:4)

"And now there are many records kept of the proceedings of this people, by many of this people, which are particular and very large, concerning them . . . But behold, a hundredth part of the proceedings of this people cannot be contained in this work. But behold, there are many books and many records of every kind, and they have been kept chiefly by the Nephites." (Helaman 13-15)

[3]"Behold, it came to pass on the morrow that the multitude gathered themselves together, and they both saw and heard these children; yea, even babes did open their mouths and utter marvelous things; and the things which they did utter were forbidden that there should not any man write them . . . And many of them saw and heard unspeakable things, which are not lawful to be written." (III Nephi 26:16-18)

[4]"Thou fool, that shall say: A Bible, we have got a Bible, and we need no more Bible. Have ye obtained a Bible save it were by the Jews? Know ye not that there are more nations than one? Know ye not that I, the Lord your God, have created all men, and that I remember those who are upon the isles of the sea; and that I rule in the heavens above and in the earth beneath; and I bring forth my word unto the children of men, yea, even upon all the nations of the earth? Wherefore murmur ye, because that ye shall receive more of my word? Know ye not that the testimony of two nations is a witness unto you that I am God, that I remember one nation like unto another? Wherefore, I speak the same words unto one nation like unto another. And when the two nations shall run together the testimony of the two nations shall run together also. And I do this that I may prove unto many that I am the same yesterday, today, and forever; and that I speak forth my words according to

27. And know ye that ye shall be judges of this people, according to the judgment which I shall give unto you, which shall be just. Therefore, what manner of men ought ye to be? Verily I say unto you, even as I am.

28. And now I go unto the Father. And verily I say unto you, whatsoever things ye shall ask the Father in my name shall be given unto you.

29. Therefore, ask, and ye shall receive; knock, and it shall be opened unto you; for he that asketh, receiveth; and unto him that knocketh, it shall be opened.

VERSE 27. *Ye shall be judges of this people.* Not by strangers, not by others who had no first-hand knowledge of the trials and vicissitudes by which the Nephites had been confronted, but they will be judged by their own—the Disciples whom Jesus had chosen from among the people.[5] They should judge justly according to the manner of judgment Christ promised to give unto them. "Therefore," He said, "what manner of men ought ye to be?" "Even as I am," was Christ's answer to His Own query.

From footnote number five we learn that the Twelve Apostles who were chosen by the Savior from among the Jews at Jerusalem — because they were to judge the Twelve Tribes of the House of Israel — would judge the Twelve Disciples from among the people of Nephi because the Nephite Twelve were of Israel themselves.

VERSES 28-29. *And now I go unto the Father.* The Nephite Twelve were not left to be alone. Before leaving them and going to His Father, realizing that He had accomplished the work His Father had sent Him to do, the Risen Redeemer promised the Twelve Disciples "Whatsoever things ye shall ask the Father in My Name shall be given unto you. Therefore, ask, and ye shall receive; knock, and it shall be opened unto you; for he that asketh, receiveth; and unto him that knocketh, it shall be opened."

---

mine own pleasure. And because that I have spoken one word ye need not suppose that I cannot speak another; for my work is not yet finished; neither shall it be until the end of man, neither from that time henceforth and forever. Wherefore, because that ye have a Bible ye need not suppose that it contains all my words; neither need ye suppose that I have not caused more to be written. For I command all men, both in the east and in the west, and in the north and in the south, and in the islands of the sea, that they shall write the words which I speak unto them; for out of the books which shall be written I will judge the world, every man according to their works, according to that which is written. For behold, I shall speak unto the Jews and they shall write it; and I shall also speak unto the Nephites and they shall write it; and I shall also speak unto the other tribes of the house of Israel, which I have led away, and they shall write it; and I shall also speak unto all nations of the earth and they shall write it. And it shall come to pass that the Jews shall have the words of the Nephites, and the Nephites shall have the words of the Jews; and the Nephites and the Jews shall have the words of the lost tribes of Israel; and the lost tribes of Israel shall have the words of the Nephites and the Jews. And it shall come to pass that my people, which are of the house of Israel, shall be gathered home unto the lands of their possessions; and my word also shall be gathered in one. And I will show unto them that fight against my word and against my people, who are of the house of Israel, that I am God, and that I covenanted with Abraham that I would remember his seed forever." (II Nephi 29:6-14)

[5]"And the angel spake unto me, saying: Behold the Twelve Disciples of the Lamb, who are chosen to minister unto thy seed. And he said unto me: Thou rememberest the Twelve Apostles of the Lamb? Behold they are they who shall judge the Twelve Tribes of Israel; wherefore, the Twelve ministers of thy seed shall be judged of them; for ye are of the House of Israel. And these Twelve ministers whom thou beholdest shall judge thy seed. And, behold, they are righteous forever; for because of their faith in the Lamb of God their garments are made white in His blood." (I Nephi 12:8-10)

30. And now, behold, my joy is great, even unto fulness, because of you, and also this generation; yea, and even the Father rejoiceth, and also all the holy angels, because of you and this generation; for none of them are lost.

31. Behold, I would that ye should understand; for I mean them who are now alive of this generation; and none of them are lost; and in them I have fulness of joy.

32. But behold, it sorroweth me because of the fourth generation from this generation, for they are led away captive by him even as was the son of perdition; for they will sell me for silver and for gold, and for that which moth doth corrupt and which thieves can break through and steal. And in that day will I visit them, even in turning their works upon their own heads.

33. And it came to pass that when Jesus had ended these sayings he said unto his disciples: Enter ye in at the strait gate; for strait is the gate, and narrow is the way that leads to life, and few there be that find it; but wide is the gate, and broad the way which leads to death, and many there be that travel therein, until the night cometh, wherein no man can work.

VERSES 30-33. *Behold, My joy is great . . . because of you. . . .* The Nephite people, as a whole, received Jesus as the Redeemer of tthe world. They believed on Him, that He was the Christ, the Son of God, the promised Messiah of Whom the Prophets had foretold. There were none, not even Lamanites, who rejected Him. "My joy is great, even unto fulness, because of you, and also this generation; yea, and even the Father rejoiceth, and also all the holy angels, because of you and this generation; for none of them are lost . . . and in them I have fulness of joy."

The Savior took time to emphasize to His Disciples, that, in the statement just made, He meant those "who are now alive of this generation," because the fourth generation, counting as the first "those who are now alive," gave Him great sorrow. He perceived that they would be led away by Satan "even as was the son of perdition."[6] They, in their iniquity, would sell Him for silver, and for gold; they will put their hearts more on the world and the things of the world than they will upon righteousness.[7] "And in that day," Christ said of them to His Disciples, "will I visit them, even in turning their works upon their own heads." This prophecy of the Savior's was fulfilled when in the fourth generation they were destroyed.

[6]Some think this refers to Judas Iscariot. We do not know, and prefer not to make a statement as to whom is meant. We doubt that Judas ever received the Holy Ghost, and therefore could not be a son of perdition.

[7]Mormon notes that when two hundred years had passed away, "There began to be among them those who were lifted up in pride, such as the wearing of costly apparel, and all manner of fine pearls, and of the fine things of the world." (IV Nephi 24)

CHAPTER 28

1. Each of the Twelve is granted his heart's desire—2. Three elect to remain on Earth until the Lord comes in His glory—3. Marvelous manifestations to the three—4. They are made immune to death and disaster.

1. *Each of the Twelve is granted his heart's desire.*

1. And it came to pass when Jesus had said these words, he spake unto his disciples, one by one, saying unto them: What is it that ye desire of me, after that I am gone to the Father?

2. And they all spake, save it were three, saying: We desire that after we have lived unto the age of man, that our ministry, wherein thou hast called us, may have an end, that we may speedily come unto thee in thy kingdom.

3. And he said unto them: Blessed are ye because ye desired this thing of me; therefore, after that ye are seventy and two years old ye shall come unto me in my kingdom; and with me ye shall find rest.

4. And when he had spoken unto them, he turned himself unto the three, and said unto them: What will ye that I should do unto you, when I am gone unto the Father?

5. And they sorrowed in their hearts, for they durst not speak unto him the thing which they desired.

6. And he said unto them: Behold, I know your thoughts, and ye have desired the thing which John, my beloved, who was with me in my ministry, before that I was lifted up by the Jews, desired of me.

7. Therefore, more blessed are ye, for ye shall never taste of death; but ye shall live to behold

---

VERSES 1-40. *What is it that ye desire of Me, after that I am gone to the Father?* After Jesus had reminded His Disciples that all things should be done in His Name, and therefore the Church should be called the Church of Jesus Christ, calling their attention to the Scriptures "which say ye must take upon you the Name of Christ, which is My Name?" He asked each one of the Twelve "What is it that ye desire of Me, after that I am gone to the Father?"

Then nine of them, all but three, answered saying: "We desire that after we have lived unto the age of man, that our ministry, wherein Thou hast called us, may have an end, that we may speedily come unto Thee in Thy Kingdom."

Now, Jesus Who previously had expressed His fulness of joy in them, saying that "even the Father rejoiceth, and also all the holy angels, because of you and this generation," continued His benedictions. He answered their expressed desire with blessings upon them as He said: "Blessed are ye because ye desired this thing of Me; therefore, after that ye are seventy and two years old ye shall come unto Me in My Kingdom; and with Me ye shall find rest."

Here we wish to note the beautiful yet simple words used by the Savior in His instructions and blessings to the Twelve. The plainness in which the Savior spoke reminds us of the words of His Prophet, Nephi, in which Nephi expresses

all the doings of the Father unto the children of men, even until all things shall be fulfilled according to the will of the Father, when I shall come in my glory with the powers of heaven.

8. And ye shall never endure the pains of death; but when I shall come in my glory ye shall be changed in the twinkling of an eye from mortality to immortality; and then shall ye be blessed in the kingdom of my Father.

9. And again, ye shall not have pain while ye shall dwell in the flesh, neither sorrow save it be for the sins of the world; and all this will I do because of the thing which ye have desired of me, for ye have desired that ye might bring the souls of men unto me, while the world shall stand.

10. And for this cause ye shall have fulness of joy; and ye shall sit down in the kingdom of my Father; yea, your joy shall be full, even as the Father hath given me fulness of joy; and ye shall be even as I am, and I am even as the Father; and the Father and I are one;

11. And the Holy Ghost beareth record of the Father and me; and the Father giveth the Holy Ghost unto the children of men, because of me.

12. And it came to pass that when Jesus had spoken these words, he touched every one of them with his finger save it were the three who were to tarry, and then he departed.

13. And behold, the heavens were opened, and they were caught up into heaven, and saw and heard unspeakable things.

14. And it was forbidden them that they should utter; neither was it given unto them power that they could utter the things which they saw and heard;

15. And whether they were in the body or out of the body, they could not tell; for it did seem unto them like a transfiguration of them, that they were changed from this body of flesh into an immortal state, that they could behold the things of God.

2. Three elect to remain on Earth until the Lord comes in His glory.

his unrestrained gladness in the use of such words. He says: "Wherefore, hearken, O my people, which are of the House of Israel, and give ear unto my words; for because the words of Isaiah are not plain unto you, nevertheless they are plain unto all those that are filled with the spirit of prophecy. But I give unto you a prophecy, according to the spirit which is in me; wherefore I shall prophesy according to the plainness which hath been with me from the time that I came out of Jerusalem with my father; for behold, my soul delighteth in plainness unto my people, that they may learn." (II Nephi 25:4) Also, "For my soul delighteth in plainness; for after this manner doth the Lord God work among the children of men. For the Lord God giveth light unto the understanding; for He speaketh unto men according to their language, unto their understanding." (*Ibid.*, 31:3)

Then Jesus turned to the three who had not answered, and again asked them what they would have Him do for them. But they faltered in their answer; their

16. But it came to pass that they did again minister upon the face of the earth; nevertheless they did not minister of the things which they had heard and seen, because of the commandment which was given them in heaven.

17. And now, whether they were mortal or immortal, from the day of their transfiguration, I know not;

18. But this much I know, according to the record which hath been given—they did go forth upon the face of the land, and did minister unto all the people, uniting as many to the church as would believe in their preaching; baptizing them, and as many as were baptized did receive the Holy Ghost.

19. And they were cast into prison by them who did not belong to the church. And the prisons could not hold them, for they were rent in twain.

20. And they were cast down into the earth; but they did smite the earth with the word of God, insomuch that by his power they were delivered out of the depths of the earth; and therefore they could not dig pits sufficient to hold them.

21. And thrice they were cast into a furnace and received no harm.

22. And twice were they cast into a den of wild beasts; and behold they did play with the beasts as a child with a suckling lamb, and received no harm.

23. And it came to pass that thus they did go forth among all the people of Nephi, and did preach the gospel of Christ unto all people upon the face of the

---

wish seemed to them to be so peculiar that they were loathe to express it. Then He said unto those who still were backward in voicing their desire: "Behold, I know your thoughts, and ye have desired the thing which John, My beloved, who was with Me in My ministry, before that I was lifted up by the Jews, desired of Me."[1]

[1]Revelation given to Joseph Smith, the Prophet, and Oliver Cowdery, at Harmony, Pennsylvania, April 1829, when they inquired through the Urim and Thummim as to whether John, the beloved Disciple, tarried in the flesh or had died. The revelation is the translated version of the record made on parchment by John and hidden up by himself. (See, History of the Church, Volume I, pp. 35-36)

"And the Lord said unto me: John, My beloved, what desireth thou? For if ye shall ask what you will, it shall be granted unto you.

"And I said unto Him: Lord, give me power over death, that I may live and bring souls unto Thee.

"And the Lord said unto me: Verily, verily, I say unto thee, because thou desireth this thou shalt tarry until I come in My glory, and shall prophesy before nations, kindreds, tongues, and people.

"And for this cause the Lord said unto Peter: If I will that he tarry till I come, what is that to thee? For he desired of Me that he might bring souls unto Me, but thou desirest that thou mightest speedily come unto Me in My Kingdom.

"I say unto thee, Peter, this was a good desire; but My beloved has desired that he might do more, or a greater work yet among men than what he has before done.

"Yea, he has undertaken a greater work; therefore I will make him as flaming fire and a ministering angel; he shall minister for those who shall be heirs of Salvation who dwell on the Earth.

"And I will make thee to minister for him (we presume Peter) and for thy brother, James; and unto you three I will give this power and the keys of this ministry until I come.

"Verily I say unto you, ye shall both have according to your desires, for ye both joy in that which ye have desired.

land; and they were converted unto the Lord, and were united unto the church of Christ, and thus the people of that generation were blessed, according to the word of Jesus.

24. And now I, Mormon, make an end of speaking concerning these things for a time.

25. Behold, I was about to write the names of those who were never to taste of death, but the Lord forbade; therefore I write them not, for they are hid from the world.

26. But behold, I have seen them, and they have ministered unto me.

27. And behold they will be among the Gentiles, and the Gentiles shall know them not.

28. They will also be among the Jews, and the Jews shall know them not.

3. Marvelous manifestations to the Three.

29. And it shall come to pass, when the Lord seeth fit in his wisdom that they shall minister unto all the scattered tribes of Israel, and unto all nations, kindreds, tongues and people, and shall bring out of them unto Jesus many souls, that their desire may be fulfilled, and also because of the convincing power of God which is in them.

30. And they are as the angels

"Wherefore," the Savior said to the Three, "more blessed are ye, for ye shall never taste of death; but ye shall live to behold all the doings of the Father unto the children of men, even until all things shall be fulfilled according to the will of the Father, when I shall come in My glory with the powers of Heaven. And ye shall never endure the pains of death; but when I shall come in My glory ye shall be changed in the twinkling of an eye from mortality to immortality; and then shall ye be blessed in the Kingdom of My Father. And again, ye shall not have pain while ye shall dwell in the flesh, neither sorrow save it be for the sins of the world; and all this will I do because of the thing which ye have desired of Me, for ye have desired that ye might bring the souls of men unto Me, while the world shall stand. And for this cause ye shall have fulness of joy; and ye shall sit down in the Kingdom of My Father; yea, your joy shall be full, even as the Father hath given Me fulness of joy; and ye shall be even as I am, and I am even as the Father; and the Father and I are One; And the Holy Ghost beareth record of the Father and Me; and the Father giveth the Holy Ghost unto the children of men, because of Me."

Thus Christ spoke to the Three Nephites of whom we sometimes hear, and who either singly or together have appeared to believers in this generation.

Then Jesus with His finger touched the nine who were to die, but the Three who were to live He did not touch; He then departed. And behold, the heavens were opened, and the Three were caught up into Heaven, and saw and heard unspeakable things. And it was forbidden them that they should utter, neither was it given unto them power that they could utter, the things which they saw and heard.

Mormon here gives an interesting observation which he made from reading the Plates he was abridging. It is one of his many comments on the incidents passing before him as if in panorama. He says of the Three that were "caught up in Heaven," "Whether they were in the body or out of the body, they could not tell; for it did seem to them like a transfiguration of them, that they were changed

of God, and if they shall pray unto the Father in the name of Jesus they can show themselves unto whatsoever man it seemeth them good.

31. Therefore, great and marvelous works shall be wrought by them, before the great and coming day when all people must surely stand before the judgment-seat of Christ;

32. Yea even among the Gentiles shall there be a great and marvelous work wrought by them, before that judgment day.

33. And if ye had all the scriptures which give an account of all the marvelous works of Christ, ye would, according to the words of Christ, know that these things must surely come.

4. They are made immune to death and disaster.

from this body of flesh into an immortal state, that they could behold the things of God." (v. 15)

However, the change under which they passed that they might receive the blessings the Savior pronounced as theirs, (See, vv. 7-9) in no way hindered them from going about ministering, for they from that time forth went throughout the land preaching and baptizing all who believed on their words. In preaching the Savior's Gospel of Repentance and Baptism, many were added to the Church of Christ, and the Holy Ghost which was received by each one of them, affirmed in their hearts that Jesus, of Whom they both saw and heard, was indeed the Christ, the Messiah Whose coming they long had waited.

Great were the wonders that attended the labors of these servants of God who were to tarry on earth unto the end. Death had no power over them; they passed through the most terrible ordeals unhurt. Swords could not touch them; fire could not burn them; savage beasts could not harm them; prisons could not hold them; chains could not bind them; the grave could not entomb them; the earth would not conceal them. No matter how much they were abused or maltreated, they triumphed over all their persecutors.

The age in which the Three lived, marked especially by its people to whom they ministered, was a peculiar one. Under ordinary circumstances the superhuman powers shown by them would have brought the wicked to repentance. But the happy age of peace and innocence that had followed the Savior's ministry was fast passing away; the people were hardening their hearts; they were relapsing into iniquity with their eyes open; they were sinning knowingly and understandingly. Angels from Heaven would not have converted them; they had given themselves up to Satan, and every manifestation of the power of God in behalf of His servants only made them more angry and more determined upon the destruction of those who sounded in their ears the unwelcome message of divine wrath. The hurricane might demolish the dungeon; the earthquake overthrow the walls of the prison; the earth refuse to close when the Disciples were cast into it; these protests of nature simply caused their hardened hearts to conjure up fresh methods of torture and devise new means to destroy those whom they so intensely, and yet so unwarrantably hated.

But they ever failed; the Three Nephites still live!

Of what change passed upon John, the Apostle, or how it was brought about that he should not taste of death, we are not told. But insofar as the Three Nephites are concerned, we are told that they were "caught up into Heaven," and there experienced a *change* which is not explained; and that they there saw and heard

34. And wo be unto him that will not hearken unto the words of Jesus, and also to them whom he hath chosen and sent among them; for whoso receiveth not the words of Jesus and the words of those whom he hath sent receiveth not him; and therefore he will not receive them at the last day;

35. And it would be better for them if they had not been born. For do ye suppose that ye can get rid of the justice of an offended God, who hath been trampled under feet of men, that thereby salvation might come?

36. And now behold, as I spake concerning those whom the Lord hath chosen, yea, even three who were caught up into the heavens, that I knew not whether they were cleansed from mortality to immortality—

37. But behold, since I wrote, I have inquired of the Lord, and he hath made it manifest unto me that there must needs be a change wrought upon their bodies, or else it needs be that they must taste of death;

38. Therefore, that they might not taste of death there was a change wrought upon their bod-

---

unspeakable things. Mormon writing about them, says, "And now behold, as I spake concerning those whom the Lord had chosen, yea, even three who were caught up into the Heavens, that I knew not whether they were cleansed from mortality to immortality — But behold, since I write, I have inquired of the Lord, and He hath made it manifest unto me that must needs be a change wrought upon their bodies, or else it needs be that they must taste of death; Therefore, that they might not taste of death there was a change wrought upon their bodies, that they might not suffer pain or sorrow save it were for the sins of the world. Now this change was not equal to that which shall take place at the last day; but there was a change wrought upon them, insomuch that Satan could have no power over them, that he could not tempt them; and they were sanctified in the flesh, that they were holy, and that the powers of the earth could not hold them."

In the Hebrew Scriptures we read of two men who lived before the advent of the Savior — Moses and Elijah — who did not taste of death; we also read in the Book of Mormon of two — Alma and Nephi — who were translated.

The Sacred Record gives no information as to who the Three were who were not to taste of death. Mormon was about to write their names, but the Lord forbade him.

Some have supposed that Nephi, the senior of the Disciples, was one of these three undying ones, who remained to minister on the earth to the people of the latter-days; that is hid from our knowledge, no doubt for a wise purpose. If he was, he lived through that most happy era of Nephite history, when all was righteousness, and joy, and peace, throughout America's vast domain; he lived to suffer with his two brethren all the persecutions which the wicked, in latter days, so frequently imposed upon those three favored servants of the Lord, and in the end he retired from the midst of mankind when overwhelming corruption again paralyzed the life of the Nephite Nation. If he was one of the nine who passed away to the presence of the Savior and their God after they had dwelt three score and twelve years in mortality, he must have laid aside his earthly tabernacle under as happy circumstances as ever prophet or apostle died, surrounded by a loving, faithful people, among whom the practice of iniquity was a memory of the past. In the

ies, that they might not suffer pain nor sorrow save it were for the sins of the world.

39. Now this change was not equal to that which shall take place at the last day; but there was a change wrought upon them, insomuch that Satan could have no power over them, that he could not tempt them; and they were sanctified in the flesh, that they were holy, and that the powers of the earth could not hold them.

40. And in this state they were to remain until the judgment day of Christ; and at that day they were to receive a greater change, and were to be received into the kingdom of the Father to go no more out, but to dwell with God eternally in the heavens.

---

midst of the most holy peace he passed away to the glories of Eternal Life among the righteous.

In verse twenty-six, Mormon testifies that he had seen the Nephite Disciples of Christ who were to tarry upon the earth, and also that they had ministered to him. What a glorious experience that must have been. Men like unto himself; men who had ministered with the Lord, visited him, and like angels of God (v. 30), comforted him and to his strength added more strength. No doubt that to him they administered the Sacrament of the Lord's Supper, and some other holy ordinances of the Gospel which had been forgotten or neglected by the Nephites during the long period of strife which had destroyed their observance among them.

Thoughts of Christ's Disciples ministering to him inspired Mormon to great heights of his office and calling, that of God's Prophet. Like Nephi of old, his words are plain that all may understand. These holy men of God, he says, "Will be among the Gentiles, and the Gentiles shall know them not. They will also be among the Jews, and the Jews shall know them not. And it shall come to pass, when the Lord seeth fit in His wisdom that they shall minister unto all the scattered tribes of Israel, and unto all nations, kindreds, tongues, and people, and shall bring out of them unto Jesus many souls, that their desire may be fulfilled, and also because of the convincing power of God which is in them."

CHAPTER 29

1. *Mormon's Warning to Those Who Spurn the Words and Works of the Lord.*

1. *Mormon's warning to those who spurn the words and works of the Lord.*

1. And now behold, I say unto you that when the Lord shall see fit, in his wisdom, that these sayings shall come unto the Gentiles according to his word, then ye may know that the covenant which the Father hath made with the children of Israel, concerning their restoration to the lands of their inheritance, is already beginning to be fulfilled.

VERSE 1. *The Covenant is already beginning to be fulfilled.* When, in the wisdom of Him Who knoweth all things, the Lord shall cause that the knowledge of the ancient Nephites and Lamanites should be made known unto the Gentiles according to the promises He made to the fathers of the much-favored Nephite people, then will we know that the Covenant which He made with Israel has already begun to be fulfilled, wherein the Lord covenanted that all of Israel's Tribes would be restored to the Lands of their Inheritance.[1]

---

[1]*The Lands of their Inheritance — The Holy Land or Palestine — The Land of Jerusalem*
"This is the land which ye shall divide by lot unto the Tribes of Israel for inheritance, and these are their portions, saith the Lord God." (Ezekiel 48:29; also read *Ibid.*, 47:13ff)
    In connection with the Prophecy of Ezekiel it is well to read III Nephi 5:24-26: "And as surely as the Lord liveth, will He gather in from the four quarters of the earth all the Remnant of the seed of Jacob, who are scattered abroad upon all the face of the earth. And as He hath covenanted with all the House of Jacob, even so shall the Covenant wherewith He hath covenanted with the House of Jacob be fulfilled in His own due time, unto the restoring all the House of Jacob unto the knowledge of the Covenant that He hath covenanted with them. And then shall they know their Redeemer, Who is Jesus Christ, the Son of God; and then shall they be gathered in from whence they have been dispersed; yea, as the Lord liveth so shall it be."
    The Holy Land would, some have calculated, extend from about 30-34 degrees north latitude, and from 34-37 degrees east longitude. It would be about 280 miles in length and 150 in width. It would be divided into twelve provinces, each named for one of the sons of Jacob and containing a strip of land 20 by 150 miles. Between Judah and Benjamin there would be a holy oblation. This reservation, dedicated to the public service, would be about 50 by 150 miles and the City of Jerusalem with suburbs would occupy an area in it 10 miles square.
    The entire area of the Palestine of Ezekiel's vision is small, but it is only a beginning of a "Greater Palestine" which will, in all probability, extend from the River Euphrates on the north to the Red Sea, and from the Mediterranean to the mouth of the Euphrates on the east. For the deserts will be made to blossom as the rose, just as has come to pass, by the power of God, where Israel has gathered on the American Continent. The country which the Lord promised to give to Abraham and his seed after him is, according to the divine Covenant, bounded by the River of Egypt and the Euphrates (Genesis 15:18), and his descendants will some time come into possession of their inheritance.
    Palestine will once more become the gathering place of the scattered Children of Judah, through the power of the Mighty One of Jacob, but He always accomplishes His purposes through the instrumentality of His children. When Israel was to be redeemed from Egyptian bondage, Moses was raised up and made the instrument of deliverance. At the end of the Babylonian Captivity, Cyrus, the mighty Prince of Persia, was moved upon to set the captives free and his successors continued to extend to them their protection while they were restoring their Temple, and repairing the ruined walls of their City. In the same way,

2. And ye may know that the words of the Lord, which have been spoken by the holy prophets, shall all be fulfilled; and ye need not say that the Lord delays his coming unto the children of Israel.

3. And ye need not imagine in

---

it is to be expected that, when the time comes for the last gathering and final restoration, the promises will all be fulfilled by means of natural agencies.

Cyrus was entrusted with power for the very purpose of enabling him to make the return of Israel to Palestine possible. For, about two hundred years before his birth, the Prophet Isaiah foretold his mission in these words: "Thus saith the Lord . . . that saith of Cyrus, He is My shepherd, and shall perform all My pleasure: even saying to Jerusalem, Thou shalt be built; and to the Temple, Thy foundation shall be laid." (Isaiah 44:24-28) Possibly this remarkable prediction was placed on record by divine inspiration, for the effect it naturally would produce on the Persian Ruler when his attention should be called to it. He, himself, acknowledged his obligation to God and issued his famous decree as an expression of his gratitude for the success he had achieved. He says: "The Lord God of Heaven hath given me all the Kingdoms of the earth; and He hath charged me to build Him an house at Jerusalem, which is in Judah. Who is there among you of all His people? his God be with him, and let him go up to Jerusalem." (Ezra 1:2-3) That was a graceful act of acknowledgment of divine providence in the military and diplomatic achievements through whch Cyrus had risen to prominence and power.

Is there, we may ask, a prophetic word by which we who live today may know by what human instrumentality the restoration of Palestine will be effected?

There is!

For the same Prophet who indicated Cyrus was the deliverer of the Jews from Babylonian Captivity, directed us to look to the *real sovereign of Egypt* for the final restoration and deliverance of the Holy Land, when he placed on record the following word of the Lord: "For I am the Lord thy God, the Holy One of Israel, thy Savior: I gave Egypt for thy ransom." (Isaiah 43:3)

Will not God, perhaps in our own day, literally entrust Egypt into the care of the great democratic powers. Notwithstanding the turmoil that divides the earth into two great armed camps, the future of Egypt is assured. It may cause men to wonder at His purposes, but, in the end, His Will will be done, and His Covenant made with the House of Jacob be fulfilled unto their gathering together in the Lands of their Inheritance.

Let us acknowledge the hand of the Almighty in all things leading to the fulfillment of the words of His prophets, their development and their accomplishment. He will give Egypt to the great nations of the earth, as we have said, as *a ransom for Israel*. It will rest with these great powers to restore the property unto the Lord, they having accepted the price.

There are indications that the thoughts of men are now being directed, as never before, toward the political necessity of restoring Palestine and the establishment in the ancient City of David, of a kind of International Court that will solve the problems that now divide and array nation against nation. Such an action would be due recognition of the interest all enlightened nations naturally have in the place where the cradle of their civilization stood.

When that question shall be actually brought up, good statesmanship will prompt the great nations to proclaim the independence of all Palestine, and to issue an invitation to the Children of Israel to return to the land of their fathers.

The establishment of the independent state of *Israel* is an auspicious beginning that will yet grow until all the kingdoms of the earth shall become the Kingdom of our Lord.

"Israel, youngest true democracy in the world, enters its seventh year amidst austerity, sacrifice and violence. These elements are not new, historically, to young states nor to the indomitable people who carved their homeland out of the hostile desert.

"Achievements have been noteworthy since Israel was born in 1948. Not the least of these was the founding of a nation in an unproductive, ferment-ridden area. Thousands of persons, persecuted and discriminated against in other countries, hailed Israel as their own free country and flocked there in an historic migration. They set up truck farms and factories where jackals once roamed and nomads grazed their sheep. They made the desert blossom; they conquered disease where pestilence had made it unsafe for humans. They established compulsory education; they gave women the right to vote and other rights. They created a symbol of man's faith in himself and his great potentialities.

your hearts that the words which | his covenant which he hath made
have been spoken are vain, for | unto his people of the house of
behold, the Lord will remember | Israel.

VERSES 2-3. *The words of the Lord will all be fulfilled.* "The Words of the
Lord," spoken by His servants, "will all be fulfilled." For the Lord says: "I am
He Who speaketh,"[2] and we may be assured His speech is not idle talk. Let us not
be deceived into thinking that the Lord is unmindful of any of His promises. Let
us not fan ourselves into that silly delusion that the Almighty Father is whimsical
and liable to a change in fancy. He is not governed by the events of the day, nor
does He await their fruition before He acts. The Lord Himself makes the decisions;
the incidents of the day do not regulate or vary the Plan of Salvation. The coming
of the Lord will be according to His own pleasure. However, He is not a god of
caprice, acting on impulse without good reason therefor. The Lord knows all, even
the end from the beginning, "And ye need not say that the Lord delays His coming
unto the Children of Israel," because, in His wisdom we may be well assured that
the time has not arrived that His coming shall be fulfilled. Remember the words
of Moroni: "For the eternal purposes of the Lord shall roll on, until all His
promises shall be fulfilled." (Mormon 8:22)

*   *   *   *   *   *

"Six years ago the United States was the first nation to recognize the Israeli republic.
Without this action and other friendly acts the state would not have survived its fight for life
against superior armies of its six neighbors. Irrespective of what else we may consider necessary to compromise the thorny issues of the Middle East, the United States should make it
abundantly clear to the Arabs and the world that we are resolved that Israel has come to stay.
Recognition of Israel as an entity is the prerequisite to any formula for peace in this part
of the globe." (*Salt Lake Tribune,* May 10, 1954)

The gathering of the Children of Israel and the rehabilitation of Palestine must be considered from the widest possible panoramic view. It is, by no means, a matter of sentiment.
That measure would be the beginning of a regenerative movement affecting the entire world.
Paul, in his letter to the Romans, takes this view, when he says: "For if the casting away
of them [the Jews] be the reconciling of the world, what shall the receiving of them be, but
life from the dead?" If, in the dispersed condition, they were an influence for good in the world,
how much greater will that influence be when they are re-united and can take a place in the
family of nations? That will be, to the entire world, as "life from the dead."

There is no other salvation for the world than the establishment of that Kingdom of
which the prophets have spoken from the beginning. All merely human governments have
proved inadequate to the moral, spiritual, and physical needs of the children of men. No
matter how well the machinery has worked to begin with, after a while it has become
deranged and, in many instances, unfit for the service for which it was intended. Therefore,
God Himself will give to the children of men a form of government, perfect and adequate
to all their needs. And this form of government will come from Zion and Jerusalem.

The race that has given to the world such lawgivers and leaders as Moses and Ezra;
such philosophers as Solomon and poets as David; and, in later ages, such teachers as
Maimonides and Mendelssohn, will yet bring forth the genius, the religious force, and the
statesmanship necessary for the true solution of the moral, social, and political problems that
cause trouble in the world today, and with this, the establishment of the Universal Brotherhood of Man. For that is the next stage to which our civilization must advance.

[2]"And he that will contend against the word of the Lord, let him be accursed; and he
that shall deny these things, let him be accursed; for unto them will I show no greater things,
saith Jesus Christ; for I am He Who speaketh." (Ether 4:8)

"Verily, verily, I say unto you, that My people shall know My Name; yea, in that day
they shall know that I am He that doth speak." (III Nephi 20:39)

"And he that believeth not My words believeth not My Disciples; and if it so be that
I do not speak, judge ye; for ye shall know that it is I that speaketh, at the last day."
(Ether 4:10)

4. And when ye shall see these sayings coming forth among you, then ye need not any longer spurn at the doings of the Lord, for the sword of his justice is in his right hand; and behold, at that day, if ye shall spurn at his doings he will cause that it shall soon overtake you.

5. Wo unto him that spurneth at the doings of the Lord; yea, wo unto him that shall deny the Christ and his works!

6. Yea, wo unto him that shall

VERSES 4-5. *Wo unto him that spurneth at the doings of the Lord.* When the knowledge of their fathers shall come unto the Remnant of the Lamanites who shall be living at that day, and Christ is preached unto its benighted people by the Gentiles, who themselves believe in His Holy Name, "Then ye need not any longer spurn at the doings of the Lord." *Spurn,* means to reject with disdain, or to treat a thing with contempt. "Wo unto him," Moroni says that he, who by disdainful rejection of the Word of God, or by contemptuous treatment of His works, casts aside these signs as a thing unworthy of any notice, "For the Sword of His Justice is in His right hand," and such a one will reap a harvest of tares, and not a storehouse of plenty. In other words, the Lord will visit him with despair and disappointment. He has seen the signs of His coming, but has rejected the Lord's works, now the *Sword of His Justice* cuts along that line which he himself has marked out.

VERSE 6. *Wo unto him that shall deny the revelations of the Lord.* "Surely the Lord God will do nothing," said Amos, "but He revealeth His secrets unto His servants the prophets." (Amos 3:7) It was ever thus. The great Ruler of the Universe has so decreed, and from the beginning He has, for the benefit and betterment of His children, taught them His Ways that they, in a higher and greater degree, might understand His Salvation. Through His servants, the prophets, the Lord has revealed to them His holy Mind and Will that they may not stumble in darkness over every unseen obstacle placed in their way, but walk uprightly before Him.

By His power, God revealed unto Adam, the venerable ancestor of the human family, the things he should do, and what he should not do; in doing, or not doing them, Adam would be pleasing in the sight of the Lord. The same is true of us.

Moses, Israel's great leader in its Exodus from Egypt, was caught up into a high mountain, and in vision saw, "God face-to-face, and he talked with Him . . . And God spake unto Moses, saying: Behold, I am the Lord God Almighty, and Endless is My Name; for I am without beginning of days or end of years; and is not this endless? And, behold, thou art My son; wherefore look, and I will show thee the workmanship of Mine hands; but not all, for My works are without end, and also My words, for they never cease. . . . And now, behold, this one thing I show unto thee, Moses, My son; for thou art in the world, and now I show it unto thee. And it came to pass that Moses looked, and beheld the world upon which he was created; and Moses beheld the world and the ends thereof, and all the children of men which are, and which were created; of the same he greatly marvelled and wondered." (*Pearl of Great Price,* Moses 1:2-8)

Moses, continuing in that vision, saw father Adam, and that in his day, "Adam blessed God and was filled, and began to prophesy concerning all the families of the Earth. . . . And Adam and Eve blessed the Name of God, and they made known all things unto their sons and daughters." (*Ibid.,* 5:10-12)

Enoch, the seventh from Adam, by that same power, was shown the world and its inhabitants that were to come for many generations. Moses, *in his writings as they were revealed to the Prophet Joseph Smith* in December 1830, said, quoting Enoch: "And it came to pass that I turned and went up on the mount; and as I

deny the revelations of the Lord, | by prophecy, or by gifts, or by
and that shall say the Lord no | tongues, or by healings, or by the
longer worketh by revelation, or | power of the Holy Ghost!

stood upon the mount, I beheld the Heavens open, and I was clothed upon with glory. And I saw the Lord; and He stood before my face, and He talked with me, even as a man talketh one with another, face-to-face; and He said unto me: "Look, and I will show unto thee the world for the space of many generations." (*Ibid.*, 7:3-4)

"And the Lord showed Enoch all things, even unto the end of the world; and he saw the day of righteousness, the hour of their redemption; and received a fulness of joy." (*Ibid.*, 7:67)

The Brother of Jared, one of the leaders of that wonderful people, the Jaredites, whom the Lord said should become the greatest nation of the Earth, was shown all the inhabitants of this planet, both those who had been and those who were to be. The great Giver of that vision, Who was the Lord, told Mahonri Moriancumr, for that was the name of the Brother of Jared, to write down the things he had both seen and heard and seal them up; and said the Lord: "I will show them in Mine Own due time unto the children of men." (Ether 3:25-27) The Gospel, in its purity, has been revealed to God's children in every age.

Let us now turn to the history of the Nephites who were a people blessed beyond measure in Heavenly Gifts. Their story is one marked everywhere with the proofs of Providential care. Revelations from Heaven were their constant guide; angels from the Courts of Glory ministered to them; the Savior Himself, personally and with His Own mouth, taught them the principles of Life and Salvation. Mormon, the abridger of their record, says of them that during the period of their national life when they all listened to what God revealed to them through His servants, "Surely there could not be a happier people among all the people who had been created by the hand of God," because, he noted in the preceding verse, "of the love of God which did dwell in the hearts of the people." (IV Nephi 15-16)

Nephi, the son of the Prophet Lehi, because of his righteousness, had revealed to him of the Lord, His wonderful ways, and the beauties of Christ's Gospel. These marvelous things Nephi recorded in the Record he was making upon metal plates the Lord had commanded him to make. This record became the first of the Nephite Scriptures, and the revelations of God which were therein guided and admonished them even as long as righteousness prevailed among them. Not only that, but to us, the Saints of these latter days, they are as a light unto our feet which cannot be darkened, and a voice as of one from the dead, not saying, but shouting *praises to the Holy One of Israel.* (*See,* Mormon 9:30; *also. see,* II Nephi 31:13)

"Behold," said Jacob, Nephi's brother, "great and marvelous are the works of the Lord. How unsearchable are the depths of the mysteries of Him; and it is impossible that man should find out all His ways. And no man knoweth of His ways save it be revealed unto him; wherefore. brethren, *despise not the revelations of God.* For behold, by the power of His word man came upon the face of the Earth, which Earth was created by the power of His word. . . . Wherefore, brethren, seek not to counsel the Lord, but to take counsel from His hand. For behold, ye yourselves know that He counseleth in wisdom, and in justice, and in great mercy, over all His works." (Jacob 4:8-10)

The words of revelation among the Nephites were many, and the exhortations of their leaders were fearless and mighty. "Behold, will ye reject these words?" asked Jacob, of whom we have just referred. "Will ye reject the words of the prophets; and will ye reject all the words which have been spoken concerning Christ, after so many have spoken concerning Him; and deny the good word of Christ, and the

7. Yea, and wo unto him that | that there can be no miracle
shall say at that day, to get gain, | wrought by Jesus Christ; for he

---

power of God, and the gift of the Holy Ghost, and quench the Holy Spirit, and
make a mock of the great Plan of Redemption, which hath been laid for you? Know
ye not that if ye will do these things, that the power of the Redemption and the
Resurrection, which is in Christ, will bring you to stand with shame and awful
guilt before the Bar of God?" (*Ibid.*, 6:8-9)

In speaking of the revelations of God, Nephi declared in a few words the thing
of which we have been writing: "And He surely did show unto the prophets of old
all things concerning them. . . ." (I Nephi 19:21) "O then despise not, and wonder
not, but hearken unto the words of the Lord. . . . Doubt not, but be believing, and
begin as in times of old, and come unto the Lord with all your heart, and work
out your own Salvation with fear and trembling before Him." (Mormon 9:27)

The words, *deny* and *despise*, as used in the Book of Mormon are not synony-
mous, but to us they connote the same thing, reject. To reject the commandments
of the Lord, would be adding the burdens of blameworthiness upon our shoulders.
Blame because of guilt, therefore we are made recipients of blame because of our
enlightenment, or in spite of it; and in it we choose not to acknowledge the truth
of God's Holy Words.

"But, behold, ye not only deny my words, but ye also deny all the words
which have been spoken by our fathers, and also the words which were spoken by
this man, Moses, who had such great power given unto him, yea, the words which
he hath spoken concerning the coming of the Messiah." (Nephi, the son of Helaman,
Helaman 8:13)

"I speak unto you who deny the revelations of God, and say that they are
done away, that there are no revelations, nor prophecies, nor gifts, nor healing, nor
speaking with tongues, and the interpretation of tongues. Behold, I say unto you,
he that denieth these things knoweth not the Gospel of Christ. . . ." (Mormon 9:7-8)

We are told in many places of Scripture that the Lord knows the end from
the beginning, therefore, we say, "He can command and it is done!" The Earth
is not a great laboratory in which the Creator experiments. Life is not empirical,
neither is it fortuitous. Things are not by chance. The Bible or the Book of Mormon
does not even recognize the word. By chance or by accident, things do not so
occur to the writers thereof. What we sometimes call accidents are really not so.
As we have said: "The accidents of man are the inspirations of God, and the
incidents of this life, are the leadings and the guidings of Him Who made it."

"And again, I exhort you, my brethren, that ye deny not the gifts of God, for
they are many; and they come from the same God. And there are different ways
that these gifts are administered; but it is the same God Who worketh all in all;
and they are given by the manifestations of the Spirit of God unto men, to profit
them." (Moroni 10:8)

"For behold, I am the Father, I am the Light, and the Life, and the Truth
of the world." Therefore Jesus Christ says: "Come unto Me, O ye Gentiles, and
I will show unto you the greater things, the knowledge which is hid up because
of unbelief." (Ether 4:12-13)

Yea, wo unto him that shall deny the revelations of the Lord, and that shall say the
Lord no longer worketh by revelation, or by prophecy, or by gifts, or by tongues, or
by healings, or by the power of the Holy Ghost!" (v. 6)

VERSE 7. *Yea, and wo unto him . . . that shall say, to get gain, that there can
be no miracle wrought by Jesus Christ.* Mormon was constrained, by the spirit of
prophecy which was in him, to warn them that a miserable and sorrowful state
awaits all those who, at that last day, shall preach the Gospel only for money.

that doeth this shall become like unto the son of perdition, for | whom there was no mercy, according to the word of Christ!

He saw that at that time wicked and crafty men would turn preaching the message of Life and Salvation from a duty of love towards Christ to a money-making proposition. To do so is to turn religion into an industrial craft, and that is "priestcraft."

Priestcraft means, not only crafty and wicked ruses to lead the unwary astray, but also the making of religion a profession in which the aim is to obtain worldly honor, gold and silver, and the plaudits of men.

The rejection of the Messiah by the Jews, and their consequent dispersion, are traced to the existence of priestcrafts and the attendant iniquities thereof. By the words, *priestcrafts* and *iniquities* we do not merely mean such subtlety as is ascribed to the serpent in the Garden of Eden (Genesis 3:1), or such wickedness as originates in the realm of Lucifer. It has a special meaning which should be carefully noted. To us, it means, the practice of religion for worldly gain and the praise of men.

Not only that, but in doing so, the great and glorious saving truths of the Gospel of Jesus Christ are bought and sold as common merchandise, and God's sanctuary, a place where we bring our prayers and our praise, and our offerings of homage, is turned into a market-place where all manner of hucksters with raucous voices peddle their wares in the Name of Him Who to us is most holy.

The Lord, knowing the mercenary desires of many men, commanded them that there should be no priestcrafts among them. "For," He said to the early fathers of the Nephites, "behold priestcrafts are that men preach and set themselves up for a light unto the world, that they may get gain and praise of the world; but they seek not the welfare of Zion. Behold, the Lord hath forbidden this thing; wherefore, the Lord God hath given a commandment that all men should have charity, which charity is love. And except they should have charity they were nothing. Wherefore, if they should have charity they would not suffer the laborer in Zion to perish. *But the laborer in Zion shall labor for Zion; for if they labor for money they shall perish.*" (II Nephi 26:29-31)

To those who want to see the contrast complete between the work of the Lord, and the work of priestcrafts, which are the works of the devil, we offer the following Nephite Scriptures. Their substance is this: Our Lord God never does a thing but that which will benefit His children. (II Nephi 26:24) He loveth the world. He invites all to come unto Him and get "milk and honey" freely. (*Ibid.,* v. 25) In other words, Salvation is offered freely to all. (*Ibid.,* vv. 27-28) There shall be no "priestcrafts"— no preaching for money and fame, but only for the welfare of Zion. (*Ibid.,* v. 29; compare II Nephi 10:5; III Nephi 16:10-20)

Isaiah, speaking of this same thing, says: "Ho, every one that thirsteth, come ye to the waters, and he that hath no money; come ye, buy, and eat; yea, come, buy wine and milk without money and without price. Wherefore do ye spend money for that which is not bread? and your labor for that which satisfieth not? hearken diligently unto me, and eat ye that which is good, and let your soul delight itself in fatness." (Isaiah 55:1-2)

There can be no miracle wrought by Jesus Christ. There are only two churches— the Church of God and the church of the devil. This may seem a hard statement to make, but Jesus Christ is the Founder and Creator of but one. All the opposing ones, with their contending and dissenting factions, form the other. It has become infiltrated with different modes of "priestcraft." Any excuse and every pretext is offered by its founders to apologize for its shortcomings. Even fraud and deception

8. Yea, and ye need not any longer hiss, nor spurn, nor make | game of the Jews, nor any of the remnant of the house of Israel;

---

are called in by them to reinforce the claims they make to divine authority. The Church of Christ, otherwise the Church of God, must be founded upon His authority, or under His jurisdiction. All others are vain.

Christ's promise to His followers among the Jews in Jerusalem, and to the Nephites in the new Land of Promise, that these signs shall follow them that believe, "In My Name shall they cast out devils; they shall speak with new tongues; they shall take up serpents; and if they drink any deadly thing it shall not hurt them; they shall lay hands on the sick and they shall recover; and whosoever shall believe in My Name, doubting nothing, unto him will I confirm all My words, even unto the ends of the Earth," (Mormon 9:24-25) is now declared to be foolishness, and the followers of the meek and lowly Lamb, victims of their own folly.

In their ignorance and infatuation, priests ordained by men, and preachers of religion, "to get gain" "Deny the power of God, the Holy One of Israel; and they say unto the people: Hearken unto us, and hear ye our precept; for behold there is no God today, for the Lord and the Redeemer hath done His work, and He hath left His power unto men; Behold, hearken unto my precept; if they shall say there is a miracle wrought by the hand of the Lord, believe it not; for this day He is not a God of miracles; He hath done His work." (II Nephi 28:5-6)

There can be no miracle wrought by Jesus Christ, means this: Do not believe in miracles, for now there are no more miracles; God has done His work. In the 19th century, during what is called "the age of enlightenment," certain men who, according to their own notions, were known as *rationalists,* advocated exactly the same thing. They made human, scientific, knowledge the highest standard of truth. Being unable to explain scientifically what we know as miraculous, they treated *the signs Christ promised* with disdain, or as myths; either that, or denied them. Rationalism became the wet-nurse of infidelity.

"Yea, and there shall be many which shall teach after this manner, false and vain and foolish doctrines, and shall be puffed up in their hearts and shall seek to hide their counsels from the Lord; and their works shall be in the dark. . . . O the wise, and the learned, and the rich, that are puffed up in the pride of their hearts, and all those who preach false doctrines, and all those who commit whoredoms, and pervert the right way of the Lord, wo, wo, wo, be unto them, saith the Lord God Almighty, for they shall be thrust down to hell." (*Ibid.,* 28:9, 15)

That is exactly what Mormon tells us in the 7th verse of our text. Those who deny that through the power of the Lord God Who is Jesus Christ these *gifts,* sometimes called *signs,* shall follow them that believe "shall become like unto the Son of Perdition, for whom there is no mercy." "For they shall be thrust down to hell," as Nephi expresses the thought, has the same meaning as when Mormon says: "shall become like the Son of Perdition."

VERSE 8. *Yea, and ye need not any longer hiss, nor spurn, nor make game of the Jews.* To make game of the Jews, or as Mormon says, "Any of the remnant of the House of Israel," is to subject them to sport or to ridicule them. In ridiculing the Jews, God's purposes are also ridiculed. The Lord has given them a great part in furthering the Plan of Salvation, and the Jews with gladness will perform everything their prophets have said they would.

In days now past, (thank Almighty God they are), Jews were thought to be the natural prey of Christian people. And even today, they are the target of raucous gibes, or prejudice and intolerance. The world is guilty of downright ignorance in its anti-Semitic aggressions, of having insufficient knowledge concerning them, and

for behold, the Lord remember- | he will do unto them according
eth his covenant unto them, and | to that which he hath sworn.

---

an unreasonable prediliction of what is right and what is wrong in dealing with them. What is still more offensive to the humble follower of Jesus is that in persecuting the Jews, open rebellion is carried on in defiance of God and His laws. They are made to appear as something to be spurned and despised; a hiss and a by-word among the nations of the earth. For ages persecution has been their lot. Great nations have openly sought their martyrdom. But in spite of great and powerful enemies, the Jews, today, after two thousand years of censure and unjust treatment, remain with us a magnificent source of unbounded energy, and also a reminder to all "That the Lord He is God in Heaven above, and upon the Earth beneath: there is none else." (Deuteronomy 4:39) Through the Jews, mankind has inherited knowledge of *the True and Living God,* and that alone should make us love and not hate them.

In all our contemplation of the Jews, let us remember that the Jews have given to the world much that is most noble and fine; much to advance the science of medicine, mathematics, and all forms of discovery. Music and the arts have benefited greatly by their contributions, and we will not forget the great moral and intellectual ethics to which they as a people have attained.

A full and complete answer to all appeals that are made to passion and prejudice in our rendering of judgment on the Jews, let us consider that they are truly the Chosen People of the Lord, and too, the Savior and the Redeemer of the world is a Jew.

"And now comes an event in the history of the Church that causes the most intensive faith in the work of the Lord in this day. The Prophet Joseph Smith sent Apostle Orson Hyde to the Holy Land in 1841, where he dedicated that Land for the return of the Children of Judah. The prayer was prophetic in every way. Beautiful are the words of Orson Hyde as he prayed to God that the Holy Land of the Jews should be saved. I give only a few words of the prayer:

Now, O Lord! Thy servant has been obedient to the heavenly vision which Thou gavest him in his native land; and under the shadow of Thine outstretched arm, he has safely arrived in this place to dedicate and consecrate this land unto Thee, for the gathering together of Judah's scattered remnants, according to the predictions of the holy Prophets—for the building up of Jerusalem again after it has been trodden down by the Gentiles so long, and for rearing a Temple in honor of Thy name. . . .

Grant therefore, O Lord, in the name of Thy well-beloved Son, Jesus Christ, to remove the barrenness and sterility of this land, and let springs of living water break forth to water its thirsty soil. Let the vine and olive produce in their strength, and the fig-tree bloom and flourish. Let the land become abundantly fruitful when possessed by its rightful heirs; let it again flow with plenty to feed the returning prodigals who come home with a spirit of grace and supplication; upon it let the clouds distil virtue and richness, and let the fields smile with plenty. Let the flocks and the herds greatly increase and multiply upon the mountains and the hills; and let Thy great kindness conquer and subdue the unbelief of Thy people. Do Thou take from them their stony heart, and give them a heart of flesh; and may the Sun of Thy favor dispel the cold mists of darkness which have beclouded their atmosphere. *Incline them to gather in upon this land according to Thy word.* Let them come like clouds and like doves to their windows. Let the large ships of the nations bring them from the distant isles; and let kings become their nursing fathers, and queens with motherly fondness wipe the tear of sorrow from their eye. (*Documentary History of the Church* IV, pp. 456-457, italics added. Quoted by President Levi Edgar Young in a sermon delivered in the Salt Lake Tabernacle April 5, 1957)

9. Therefore ye need not suppose that ye can turn the right hand of the Lord unto the left, that he may not execute judgment unto the fulfilling of the covenant which he hath made unto the house of Israel.

VERSE 9. *Therefore ye need not suppose that ye can turn the right hand of the Lord unto the left.* Mormon here warns those who spurn, and treat the words and works of the Lord as something of no worth, that His work will go on in spite of their ill will, and by it they can in nowise hope to have Him nullify that which "He hath sworn."

In the bloody pages of history that record the persecutions of the Jews in many parts of the world, we see not only the wrath of God displayed in their dispersion, but also love for His chosen people in preparing the way for their gathering together again; that they may again be a light unto the world, and that again the Word of the Lord shall go forth from Jerusalem. (*See,* Isaiah 2:3) Yes, the Lord has and will "execute judgment unto the fulfilling of the Covenant which He hath made unto the House of Israel."

GENERAL NOTES

The Lands of their inheritance. (v. 1) We understand the *Lands of their Inheritance* to mean all the countries in which their possessions, that is the Twelve Tribes of Israel, were once allotted to them; the entire region between the River of Egypt and the Euphrates, once inhabited by Kenites, Kenizzites, Kadmonites, Hittites, Perizzites, Rephaims, Canaanites, Girganites, and Jebusites. (Genesis 15: 18-21) According to the Mosaic Law, land possessions disposed of by the owner thereof returned automatically every fiftieth year to its original owner: "In the year of the jubilee the field shall return to him of whom it was bought, even to him to whom the possession did belong." (Numbers 27:24) The original Covenant was made with the descendants of Abraham, and this fact may have to be considered in the solution of what now appears to be a difficult problem, involving perfect justice between Hebrews and Arabs.

Tel Aviv. This is the name of a Jewish City on the Mediterranean Sea, near the City of Jaffa. It was founded in 1909. In 1913 it had a population of only 908. Now its inhabitants number many, many, times that. In Tel Aviv, the ancient language of the Hebrews, thought to be dead because it was used only by scholars and of no commercial value, has been revived. Newspapers there are printed in pure Hebrew. Theaters and even signboards use that tongue. The streets are thronged with well-dressed people, with new motor cars and motor buses. The traffic policemen are dressed much like the American policemen in summer uniform. The shops are bright and modern. The homes are of the California type of bungalow, or flat buildings. Jews from South Africa, from Argentina, from Brazil, from the United States, from Yemen in central Arabia, in large numbers from Russia and from Poland, Austria, England, and many other countries. There, they are adapting themselves to the new civilization being built up in a purely Jewish atmosphere.

Tel Aviv is only one of the manifestations of the establishment of the Jewish home, and in it we can see that the Covenant God made with their fathers "is already beginning to be fulfilled." (v. 1)

CHAPTER 30

1. Mormon Calls the Gentiles to Repentance.

1. Hearken, O ye Gentiles, and hear the words of Jesus Christ, the Son of the living God, which he hath commanded me that I should speak concerning you, for, behold he commandeth me that I should write, saying:

2. Turn, all ye Gentiles, from your wicked ways; and repent of your evil doings, of your lyings and deceivings, and of your whoredoms, and of your secret abominations, and your idolatries, and of your murders, and your priestcrafts, and your envyings, and your strifes, and from all your wickedness and abominations, and come unto me, and be baptized in my name, that ye may receive a remission of your sins, and be filled with the Holy Ghost, that ye may be numbered with my people who are of the house of Israel.

VERSE 1. *Hearken, O ye Gentiles, and hear the Words of Jesus Christ.* After urgently imploring those of the Remnant of Israel to be prepared for the coming of that Day when the Lord in His wisdom shall fulfill the promise He made to their forefathers, Mormon directs an appeal to the Gentiles, or to those not favored as the seed of Abraham.

Jews, although they are only part thereof, are spoken of as the Children of Israel, or the House of Israel. Jews and Gentiles are on an equal level before God, save those who do not keep His commandments. Gentiles who repent, thereby join the Covenant People of the Lord, and share its privileges and prerogatives, as well as its duties and responsibilities. Likewise, Jews, who will not repent, will be cast off.

Nephi, the son of Lehi, in speaking to his brethren, some of whom were in reality his brothers, said: "I, Nephi, would not suffer that ye should suppose that ye are more righteous than the Gentiles shall be. For behold, except ye shall keep the commandments of God ye shall all likewise perish; and because of the words which have been spoken ye need not suppose that the Gentiles are utterly destroyed. For behold, I say unto you that as many of the Gentiles as will repent are the Covenant People of the Lord; and as many of the Jews as will not repent shall be cast off; for the Lord covenanteth with none save it be with them that repent and believe in His Son, Who is the Holy One of Israel." (II Nephi 30:1-2)

Paul teaches the same doctrine. He says: "For the promise was not to Abraham, or his seed, through the law, but through the righteousness of faith." (Romans 4:13) Faith as used here means the Gospel of Christ. Again Paul says: "For there is no difference between the Jew and the Greek (Gentiles): for the same Lord over all is rich unto all that call upon Him." (*Ibid.*, 10-12) And again: "As many as are led by the Spirit of God, they are the sons of God." (*Ibid.*, 8:14)

Mormon is emphatic in that he had been commanded by the Lord to call all the Gentiles to repent of ". . . all your wickedness and abominations," and return unto your Father that "ye may receive a remission of your sins, and be filled with the Holy Ghost, that ye may be numbered with My people who are of the House of Israel."

THE GOSPEL OF JESUS CHRIST AMONG THE NEPHITES

The Religion of the Nephites was the Gospel of our Lord and Savior, Jesus Christ. It embraced, before His advent, those offerings and sacrifices typical of His life and death, the observance of which was enjoined upon the House of Israel by the Law of Moses. As soon as He was offered upon the cross at Calvary these sacrifices stopped, as the Law was fulfilled, and its intent and purpose was accomplished.

Nephi epitomizes the religious faith of his people in the following graphic and comprehensive language:

"For we labor diligently to write, to persuade our children, and also our brethren, to believe in Christ, and to be reconciled to God; for we know that it is by grace that we are saved, after all we can do. And, notwithstanding we believe in Christ, we keep the Law of Moses, and look forward with steadfastness unto Christ, until the Law shall be fulfilled; For, for this end was the Law given; wherefore the Law hath become dead unto us, and we are made alive in Christ because of our faith; yet we keep the Law because of the commandments: And we write according to our prophecies, that our children may know to what source they may look for a remission of their sins. Wherefore, we speak concerning the Law that our children may know the deadness of the Law; and they, by knowing the deadness of the Law, may look forward unto that life which is in Christ, and know for what end the Law was given. And after the Law is fulfilled in Christ, that they need not harden their hearts against Him when the Law ought to be done away." (II Nephi 25:23-27)

Here are a hundred sermons in a few sentences, and every sentence is pregnant with the force and glory of God's Eternal Truth. Again, how concisely the Plan of Salvation is explained in the following passages:

"O how great is the holiness of our God! For He knoweth all things, and there is not anything, save He knows it. And He cometh into the world that He may save all men, if they will hearken unto His voice; for behold, He suffereth the pains of all men; yea, the pains of every living creature, both men, women and children, who belong to the family of Adam. And He suffereth this, that the resurrection might pass upon all men, that all might stand before Him at the great and judgment day. And He commandeth all men that they must repent, and be baptized in His Name, having perfect faith in the Holy One of Israel, or they cannot be saved in the Kingdom of God. And if they will not repent and believe in His Name, and be baptized in His Name, and endure to the end, they must be damned; for the Lord God, the Holy One of Israel, has spoken it." (II Nephi 9:20-24)

The Priesthood held by the Nephites was the same as ours. We read of High-Priests, Elders, Priests, and Teachers, in their Church, but Evangelists, Bishops, and Deacons, are not mentioned. They also had numerous prophets minister to them the pleasing or the awful word of God, as their condition warranted or their lives deserved. But the spirit of prophecy, then as now, was not confined to any particular grade of the Priesthood; those holding none of the several offices therein being frequently endowed with this precious gift.

The Twelve special witnesses whom Jesus chose on this continent, of whom Nephi was the first, are never called Apostles in the Book of Mormon, but always Disciples; the word *apostles* is used in that Book only when applied to the Twelve who ministered with the Savior in the Land of Jerusalem.

The Nephite Church when fully organized in the ages before the visit of the Redeemer was always presided over by a High Priest. He held the keys of the Holy Priesthood. Whether these keys remained with the Nephites at all times is doubtful. But many of the Church heads were undoubtedly thus empowered. The Lord made covenant with Nephi, the son of Helaman, with His own voice as follows:

"Blessed art thou, Nephi, for those things which thou hast done; for I have beheld how thou hast with unwearyingness declared the word which I have given unto thee, unto this people. And thou hast not feared them, and hast not sought thine own life, but have sought My will, and to keep My commandments. And now because thou hast done this with such unwearyingness, behold, I will bless thee forever; and I will make thee mighty in word and in deed, in faith and in works; yea, even that all things shall be done unto thee according to thy word, for thou shalt not ask that which is contrary to My will. Behold, thou art Nephi, and I am God. Behold, I declare it unto thee in the presence of mine angels, that ye shall have power over this people, and shall smite the earth with famine, and with pestilence, and destruction, according to the wickedness of this people. Behold, I give unto you power, that whatsoever ye shall seal on earth shall be sealed in Heaven; and whatsoever ye shall loose on earth shall be loosed in Heaven; and thus shall ye have power among this people. And thus, if ye shall say unto this temple it shall be rent in twain, it shall be done. And if ye shall say unto this mountain, Be thou cast down and become smooth, it shall be done. And behold, if ye shall say that God shall smite this people, it shall come to pass, And now behold, I command you that ye shall go and declare unto this people, that thus saith the Lord God, who is the Almighty: Except ye repent ye shall be smitten, even unto destruction." (Helaman 10:4-11)

What greater powers than these has God ever given to man?

The Churches in the various lands or districts appear to have each been presided over locally by a High Priest, as the different stakes of Zion are in these days. In this and other respects a close resemblance can be perceived between the organization of the ancient Nephite Church and the Church of Jesus Christ of Latter-day Saints. As an example of these local High Priests, we refer to the case of Ammon, the son of King Mosiah, who held this office among the Christian Lamanites in the Land of Jershon at the same time that Alma was the Presiding High Priest over the whole Church.

The duties, responsibilities, and powers, of the various orders of the Priesthood were evidently identical with those possessed by the same officers in the Church of God here in these last days. Were we arguing from a doctrinal standpoint we should claim that this must necessarily be so because of the unity of the Church of the Lamb in all ages; but we are now simply affirming that which appears from the statements, historical and otherwise, that are to be found in the Book of Mormon. The fact of these identities of duties and powers is apparent in the instructions which are recorded as being given regarding the ordinance of Baptism, the Bestowal of the Holy Ghost, the administration of the Sacrament of the Lord's Supper, the ordination of Priests and Teachers, etc.

Not only was the Priesthood identical, but the ordinances of both Churches were the same. The same words were spoken in the baptism of converts as are used now. The same mode of Baptism was then observed as now used. The same persons—the penitent believers—were baptized. The baptism of little children was forbidden in the most energetic language.[1] When Jesus instructed His Disciples on the subject of baptism, He said:

"On this wise shall ye baptize; and there shall be no disputations among you. Verily I say unto you, that whoso repenteth of his sins through your words and desireth to be baptized in My Name, on this wise shall ye baptize them—Behold, ye shall go down and stand in the water, and in My Name shall ye baptize them. And now behold, these are the word which ye shall say, calling them by name, saying: Having authority given me of Jesus Christ, I baptize you in the Name of the Father, and of the Son, and of the Holy Ghost. Amen. And then shall ye immerse them in the water, and come forth again out of the water. (III Nephi 11:22-26)

The words spoken by the Elder or Priest who blessed the Bread and Wine in the administration of the Sacrament were in the Nephite Church identical with those that we use. In fact, the words of the prayer uttered by them in this sacred ordinance were recorded by Moroni, and are found in the Book under his name, Moroni, Chapters 4 and 5. The officers who officiated in the blessing of the Emblems, Elders and Priests, were the same.

In ordinations to the Priesthood, a similar form was employed by them as that used in this dispensation, and men were ordained to the same calling. It is written: "The manner which the Disciples, who were called the Elders of the Church, ordained Priests and Teachers—After they had prayed unto the Father in the Name of

[1]"And their little children need no repentance, neither baptism. Behold, baptism is unto repentance to the fulfilling the commandments unto the remission of sins. But little children are alive in Christ, even from the foundation of the world; if not so, God is a partial God, and also a changeable God, and a respecter of persons; for how many little children have died without baptism! Wherefore if little children could not be saved without baptism, these must have gone to an endless hell. . . . Little children cannot repent; wherefore, it is awful wickedness to deny the pure mercies of God unto them, for they are all alive in Him because of His mercy. And he that saith that little children need baptism denieth the mercies of Christ, and setteth at naught the Atonement of Him and the power of His Redemption." (Mormon, Moroni 8:11-20)

Christ, they laid their hands upon them and said: In the Name of Jesus Christ I ordain you to be a Priest (or, if he be a teacher) I ordain you to be a Teacher, to preach repentance and remission of sins through Jesus Christ, by the endurance of faith on His Name to the end. Amen." (Moroni 3)

With regard to the manner of conducting their meetings, we are told: "And their meetings were conducted by the Church after the manner of the workings of the Spirit, and by the power of the Holy Ghost; for as the power of the Holy Ghost led them whether to preach, or to exhort, or to sing, even so it was done." (Moroni 6:9)

The same parallel between the two Churches can also be found when we consider the subject of Spiritual Gifts. The Savior, when delivering His charge to the Twelve Nephite Disciples, said:

"Go ye into all the world, and preach the Gospel to every creature; And He that believeth and is baptized shall be saved, but he that believeth not shall be damned; And these signs shall follow them that believe—in My Name shall they cast out devils; they shall speak with new tongues; they shall take up serpents; and if they drink any deadly thing it shall not hurt them; they shall lay hands on the sick and they shall recover; And whosoever shall believe in My Name, doubting nothing, unto him will I confirm all My words, even unto the ends of the Earth." (Moroni 9:22-25)

Moroni treating on this same subject, states:

"For behold, to one is given by the Spirit of God, that he may teach the word of wisdom; And to another, that he may teach the word of knowledge by the same Spirit; And to another, exceeding great faith; and to another the gifts of healing by the same Spirit; And again, to another, that he may work mighty miracles; And again, to another, that he may prophesy concerning all things; And again, to another, the beholding of angels and ministering spirits; And again, to another, all kinds of tongues; And again, to another, the interpretation of languages and divers kinds of tongues. And all these gifts come by the power of Christ; and they come to every man severally, according as he will. And I would exhort you, my beloved brethren, that ye remember that every good gift cometh of Christ." (Moroni 10:9-18)

From these quotations all can perceive that the Gifts of the Spirit were the same in the Nephite Church as among the Saints in Old Jerusalem and the people of God in these days.

FOURTH NEPHI

THE BOOK OF NEPHI

Who is the son of Nephi — One of the Disciples of Jesus Christ

An Account of the People of Nephi, According to His Record

1. *The Church of Christ flourishes* — 2. *Nephites and Lamanites converted* — 3. *They have all things in common*—4. *Two centuries of righteousness followed by division and degeneracy*—5. *Amos and Ammaron in turn keep the records.*

1. *The Church of Christ flourishes.*

2. *Nephites and Lamanites converted.*

3. *They have all things in common.*

1. And it came to pass that the thirty and fourth year passed away, and also the thirty and fifth, and behold the disciples of Jesus had formed a church of Christ in all the lands round about. And as many as did come unto them, and did truly repent of their sins, were baptized in the name of Jesus; and they did also receive the Holy Ghost.

2. And it came to pass in the thirty and sixth year, the people were all converted unto the Lord, upon all the face of the land, both Nephites and Lamanites, and there were no contentions and disputations among them, and every man did deal justly one with another.

3. And they had all things common among them; therefore there were not rich and poor, bond and free, but they were all made free, and partakers of the heavenly gift.

4. And it came to pass that the thirty and seventh year passed away also, and there still continued to be peace in the land.

5. And there were great and marvelous works wrought by the disciples of Jesus, insomuch that they did heal the sick, and raise the dead, and cause the lame to walk, and the blind to receive

---

These are strange times. If we look out over the world today, the people of the Earth are confronted by problems and vicissitudes quite unprecedented in the past. Never before have our pathways been strewn with such failure and disaster. "Rarely has this Earth known such peril as to-day." (President Dwight D. Eisenhower, *Inaugural Address,* January 21, 1957) The awful tumult of things to come, things yet unseen, fill our hearts with fear and trembling. Only the bravest look towards the future; no one knows what the morrow may bring forth.

These are strange times! Strife and angry passions mark the roads we travel. Fraud and deception are re-enforced by every pretext and excuse the ingenuity of man can suggest. Waters from the stinking springs of iniquity have flooded the Earth, deep as an ocean, with their impurities. The upright man is upbraided because

their sight, and the deaf to hear; and all manner of miracles did they work among the children of men; and in nothing did they work miracles save it were in the name of Jesus.

6. And thus did the thirty and eighth year pass away, and also the thirty and ninth, and forty and first, and the forty and second, yea, even until forty and nine years had passed away, and also the fifty and first, and the fifty and second; yea, and even until fifty and nine years had passed away.

7. And the Lord did prosper them exceedingly in the land; yea, insomuch that they did build cities again where there had been cities burned.

8. Yea, even that great city Zarahemla did they cause to be built again.

9. But there were many cities which had been sunk, and waters came up in the stead thereof;

therefore these cities could not be renewed.

10. And now, behold, it came to pass that the people of Nephi did wax strong, and did multiply exceedingly fast, and became an exceedingly fair and delightsome people.

11. And they were married, and given in marriage, and were blessed according to the multitude of the promises which the Lord had made unto them.

12. And they did not walk any more after the performances and ordinances of the law of Moses; but they did walk after the commandments which they had received from their Lord and their God, continuing in fasting and prayer, and in meeting together oft both to pray and to hear the word of the Lord.

13. And it came to pass that there was no contention among all the people, in all the land; but there were mighty miracles

---

of his righteousness, and the sinful one held in repute. Where joy and thanksgiving once resounded throughout the Earth, there is remorse; there is sorrow where there should be gladness.

Nor, is that all! *Hymns of Hate* are heard in every land. Madness steers the *Ships of State.* Reason has lost its footing. Sanity has upset its throne. Men, in vast numbers, are leaving the beliefs and traditions of their fathers; others seek in religion that which will deaden the terrible forebodings of coming woe. Great nations openly proclaim a disavowal of belief in God. The teachings of the Savior, for ages the vanguard of our civilization, are now declared to be foolishness.

Indeed, these are strange times.

They are, however, not particularly new.

Every generation has had its problems, and wise men, and good men, for the benefit and betterment of mankind, have sought to solve them. From the very first many attempts have been made to do just that. If we search the past, we find the many laws that have been made to lift mankind to higher levels of goodness and purity. We see the philosophies and the religions that today are merely academic. We hear again the appeals that were once made to passion and prejudice, to ignorance and infatuation, to arrogance and to pride.

wrought among the disciples of Jesus.

14. And it came to pass that the seventy and first year passed away, and also the seventy and second year, yea, and in fine, till the seventy and ninth year had passed away; yea, even an hundred years had passed away, and the disciples of Jesus, whom he had chosen, had all gone to the paradise of God, save it were the three who should tarry; and there were other disciples ordained in their stead; and also many of that generation had passed away.

15. And it came to pass that there was no contention in the land, because of the love of God which did dwell in the hearts of the people.

16. And there were no envyings, nor strifes, nor tumults, nor whoredoms, nor lyings, nor murders, nor any manner of lasciviousness; and surely there could not be a happier people among all the people who had been created by the hand of God.

17. There were no robbers, nor murderers, neither were there Lamanites, nor any manner of -ites; but they were in one, the children of Christ, and heirs to the kingdom of God.

18. And how blessed were they! For the Lord did bless them in all their doings; yea, even they were blessed and prospered until an hundred and ten years had passed away; and the first generation from Christ had passed away, and there was no contention in all the land.

19. And it came to pass that Nephi, he that kept this last record, (and he kept it upon the plates of Nephi) died, and his son Amos kept it in his stead; and he kept it upon the plates of Nephi also.

20. And he kept it eighty and four years, and there was still peace in the land, save it were a small part of the people who had revolted from the church and taken upon them the name of Lamanites; therefore there began to be Lamanites again in the land.

All have failed!

We know of only one that was lasting and real. *The Book of Mormon tells of one that did not fail.*

We refer the student to the visit of the Risen Redeemer to the Nephites here in this land. You will remember that the Savior taught His Gospel to the Nephites the same as He, aforetime, had taught it to the Jews at Jerusalem.

From their annals as recorded in the Sacred Record you will learn that when the Nephites kept the commandments of the Lord, they were prospered and otherwise blessed far beyond our poor powers of description. We, in the record which was kept by Nephi, son of Nephi the Disciple of Christ, and called by us, THE BOOK OF IV NEPHI may learn this truth which is today as forceful to us as it was then to them.

Here, in brief, is their own account written in our words: When Jesus left the Nephites to the care of His Disciples, He had so thoroughly filled the people with the influences and powers of the Eternal Worlds that evil utterly ceased in their

21. And it came to pass that Amos died also, (and it was an hundred and ninety and four years from the coming of Christ) and his son Amos kept the record in his stead; and he also kept it upon the plates of Nephi; and it was also written in the book of Nephi, which is this book.

22. And it came to pass that two hundred years had passed away; and the second generation had all passed away save it were a few.

23. And now I, Mormon, would that ye should know that the people had multiplied, insomuch that they were spread upon all the face of the land, and that they had become exceeding rich, because of their prosperity in Christ.

24. And now, in this two hundred and first year there began to be among them those who were lifted up in pride, such as the wearing of costly apparel, and all manner of fine pearls, and of the fine things of the world.

25. And from that time forth they did have their goods and their substance no more common among them.

26. And they began to be divided into classes; and they began to build up churches unto themselves to get gain, and began to deny the true church of Christ.

27. And it came to pass that when two hundred and ten years had passed away there were many churches in the land; yea, there were many churches which professed to know the Christ, and yet they did deny the more parts of his gospel, insomuch that they did receive all manner of wickedness, and did administer that which was sacred unto him to whom it had been forbidden because of unworthiness.

28. And this church did multiply exceedingly because of iniquity and because of the power of Satan who did get hold upon their hearts.

29. And again, there was an-

midst. They were united in all things, temporal and spiritual. Universal peace prevailed. Love, joy, harmony, everything desirable to make the life of man a perfect condition of unalloyed, holy happiness, reigned supreme. Indeed, it may be said that a type, a foreshadowing of the Millennium, for once found place and foothold among the erring sons of humanity.

At this blessed period, Nephi, the son of Nephi and the grandson of Helaman, received the sacred Plates. His duty, as the recorder of the doing of his people was a happy one. He had nothing but good to relate of their lives and actions, and to record that perfect peace prevailed upon all these vast Western Continents. The Nephites increased in numbers—there were no Lamanites—they prospered in circumstances; they grew in material wealth, all of which was held *in common* according to *God's Order.* They colonized and spread far abroad; they rebuilt their ancient capital and many other cities; they also founded new ones. Above all, they were rich in heavenly treasures; the Holy Spirit reigned in every heart and illumined every soul.

When Nephi died (110 A.D.) this happy, heavenly, inexpressibly peaceful state still continued in undiminished warmth of divine and brotherly love. All the gen-

other church which denied the Christ; and they did persecute the true church of Christ, because of their humility and their belief in Christ; and they did despise them because of the many miracles which were wrought among them.

30. Therefore they did exercise power and authority over the disciples of Jesus who did tarry with them, and they did cast them into prison; but by the power of the word of God, which was in them, the prisons were rent in twain, and they went forth doing mighty miracles among them.

31. Nevertheless, and notwithstanding all these miracles, the people did harden their hearts, and did seek to kill them, even as the Jews at Jerusalem sought to kill Jesus, according to his word.

32. And they did cast them into furnaces of fire, and they came forth receiving no harm.

33. And they also cast them into dens of wild beasts, and they did play with the wild beasts even as a child with a lamb; and they did come forth from among them, receiving no harm.

34. Nevertheless, the people did harden their hearts, for they were led by many priests and false prophets to build up many churches, and to do all manner of iniquity. And they did smite upon the people of Jesus; but the people of Jesus did not smite again. And thus they did dwindle in unbelief and wickedness, from year to year, even until two hundred and thirty years had passed away.

35. And now it came to pass in this year, yea, in the two hundred and thirty and first year, there was a great division among the people.

4. *Two centuries of righteousness followed by division and degeneracy.*

5. *Amos and Ammaron in turn keep the records.*

36. And it came to pass that in this year there arose a people who were called the Nephites, and they were true believers in Christ; and among them there were those who were called by the Lamanites — Jacobites, and Josephites, and Zoramites;

eration to which Nephi belonged entered in God's Kingdom at the Strait Gate and walked the Narrow Way to the Eternal City of God; not one of them was lost.

At Nephi's death, his son, Amos, became the custodian of the *Holy Things,* and he held them for 84 years, or from 110 to 194 A.D. He lived in the days of the Nephites' greatest prosperity and happiness. The perfect law of righteousness was still their only guide. But before he passed away to his heavenly home, a small cloud, a fatal harbinger of an approaching devastating storm had gathered. A few that were weary of the uninterrupted bliss, the perfect harmony, the universal love, that everywhere prevailed, seceded from the Church and took upon themselves the title of Lamanite, which ill-boding name had only been known to the Nephites in tradition for more than 100 years.

37. Therefore the true believers in Christ, and the true worshipers of Christ, (among whom were the three disciples of Jesus who should tarry) were called Nephites, and Jacobites, and Josephites, and Zoramites.

38. And it came to pass that they who rejected the gospel were called Lamanites, and Lemuelites, and Ishmaelites; and they did not dwindle in unbelief, but they did wilfully rebel against the gospel of Christ; and they did teach their children that they should not believe, even as their fathers, from the beginning, did dwindle.

39. And it was because of the wickedness and abomination of their fathers, even as it was in the beginning. And they were taught to hate the children of God, even as the Lamanites were taught to hate the children of Nephi from the beginning.

40. And it came to pass that two hundred and forty and four years had passed away, and thus were the affairs of the people. And the more wicked part of the people did wax strong, and became exceedingly more numerous than were the people of God.

41. And they did still continue to build up churches unto themselves, and adorn them with all manner of precious things. And thus did two hundred and fifty years pass away, and also two hundred and sixty years.

42. And it came to pass that the wicked part of the people

It may be asked, "How was it possible that men and women should withdraw from such a holy order or society where all was perfect peace; where every man dealt justly with his neighbors; where none afflicted wrongs and none suffered from injustice done them; where angels ministered to the children of mortality, and heavenly revelations were their constant guides?"

If the inquirer will answer why Lucifer, the Son of the Morning, in Heaven itself, rebelled against the Almighty Father and led astray one-third of the angelic hosts, we will reply by saying that he, Satan, tempted the dissenting Nephites with the same spirit of rebellion to the Divine Power and that he succeeded in ensnaring them and leading them away captive to his will.

A second Amos followed his father as keeper of the Records. His duties were not the happy ones of his immediate predecessors. Instead of good, he had much to chronicle of evil.

Amos, himself, was a righteous man, but he lived to witness an ever-increasing flood of iniquity inundate the land, a phase of evil-doing that rose not from false tradition or from ignorance, but from direct and wilful rebellion against God, and apostasy from His laws. The wholesome checks to vice and misery found in the Plan of Salvation were knowingly or intentionally removed and done away with. The voice of reason was disregarded. The promptings of the Holy Spirit were defiantly repelled. Man's unbridled passions again bore sway; disunion, dissension, violence, hatred, distress, dismay, bloodshed, and havoc, spread the wide continents over; and from their high pinnacle of righteousness, peace, happiness, refinement, social advantage, etc., the Nephites were once more hurled into an abyss of misery and barbarism, now more profound, more torturing, and more degrading than ever.

We may conclude of the Nephites as did Isaiah many hundreds of years before concerning the Jews, and whose words were written upon the Brass Plates of Laban. The Prophet, after pronouncing woe upon the wicked and the wise who were wise

began again to build up the secret oaths and combinations of Gadianton.

43. And also the people who were called the people of Nephi began to be proud in their hearts, because of their exceeding riches, and become vain like unto their brethren, the Lamanites.

44. And from this time the disciples began to sorrow for the sins of the world.

45. And it came to pass that when three hundred years had passed away, both the people of Nephi and the Lamanites had become exceeding wicked one like unto another.

46. And it came to pass that the robbers of Gadianton did spread over all the face of the land; and there were none that were righteous save it were the disciples of Jesus. And gold and silver did they lay up in store in abundance, and did traffic in all manner of traffic.

47. And it came to pass that after three hundred and five years had passed away, (and the people did still remain in wickedness) Amos died; and his brother, Ammaron, did keep the record in his stead.

48. And it came to pass that when three hundred and twenty years had passed away, Ammaron, being constrained by the Holy Ghost, did hide up the records which were sacred—yea, even all the sacred records which had been handed down from gen-

---

in their own eyes, also the mighty who justify the wicked for reward and who take away the the righteousness of the righteous, exclaimed: "Therefore, as the fire devoureth the stubble, and the flame consumeth the chaff, their root shall be as rottenness, and their blossoms shall go up as dust; because they have cast away the law of the Lord of Hosts, and despised the word of the Holy One of Israel. Therefore, is the anger of the Lord kindled against His people, and He hath stretched forth His hand against them, and He hath smitten them. . . ." (II Nephi 15:24-25)

The commencement of the apostasy. Let us consider a little more fully the events leading up to the catastrophic destruction of the Nephite Race about 400 A.D. By the year 201 A.D., all the second generation had passed away save a few; the people had greatly multiplied and spread over the face of the land, north and south, and had become exceedingly rich; they wore costly apparel which they adorned with ornaments of gold and silver, with pearls and precious stones. From this date they had no more their property in common, but like the rest of the world, every man sought gain, wealth, power and influence for himself and his. All the old evils arising from selfishness were revived. Soon they began to build churches after their own fashion, and hire preachers who pandered to their lusts; some even began to deny the Savior.

From 210 A.D. to 230 A.D., the people waxed greatly in iniquity and impurity of life. Different dissenting sects multiplied, infidels abounded. The three remaining Disciples were sorely persecuted notwithstanding that they performed many mighty miracles. They were shut up in prison, but the prisons were rent in twain by the power of God; they were cast into fiery furnaces, but the flames harmed them not; they were thrown into dens of wild beasts, but they played with the savage inmates as a child does with a lamb, and they received no harm; they were not subject to

eration to generation, which were
sacred—even until the three hundred and twentieth year from the
coming of Christ.

49. And he did hide them up
unto the Lord, that they might

come again unto the remnant of
the house of Jacob, according to
the prophecies and the promises
of the Lord. And thus is the end
of the record of Ammaron.

---

many of the laws that govern our mortal bodies; they had passed through a
glorious change by which they were freed from earthly pain, suffering, and death.
Not only did the wicked persecute these three blessed ones, but others also of God's
people suffered from their unhallowed anger and bitter hatred; but the faithful
neither reviled at the reviler nor smote the smiter; they bore these things with
patience and fortitude, remembering the pains of their Redeemer.

In the year 231 A.D., there was a great division among the people. The old
party lines were again definitely marked. Again the old animosity assumed shape,
and Nephite and Lamanite once more became implacable foes. Those who rejected
and renounced the Gospel assumed the latter name, and with their eyes open, and
a full knowledge of their inexcusable infamy, they taught their children the same
base falsehoods that in ages past had caused the unceasing hatred that reigned in
the hearts of the children of Laman and Lemuel toward the seed of their younger
brothers.

By 244 A.D., the more wicked portion of the people had become exceedingly
strong, as well as far more numerous than the righteous. They deluded themselves
by building all sorts of churches, with creeds to suit the increasing depravity of
the masses.

When 260 years had passed away, the Gadianton Bands, with all their secret
signs and abominations, through the cunning of Satan, again appeared and increased until, in the year 300 A.D., they had spread all over the land. By this time
also, the Nephites, having gradually forsaken their first love, had so far sunk in
the abyss of iniquity that they had grown as wicked, as proud, as corrupt, and as
vile as the Lamanites. All were submerged in an overwhelming flood of infamy,
and there were none that were righteous, save it were the followers of Christ.

Amos entrusted the Records to his son, Ammaron, in the year 306 A.D. Owing
to the increasing depravity and vileness of the Nephites, Ammaron was constrained
by the Holy Spirit to hide up all the sacred things which had been handed down
from generation to generation. (320 A.D.) The place where he hid them, Moroni,
in his comments, said was a Hill called Shim, in the Land Antum. After he hid
them he informed Mormon, then a child of ten years, and placed the buried
treasures in his charge.

THE BOOK OF MORMON

CHAPTER 1

1. Ammaron's Charge to Mormon Respecting the Sacred Engravings—2. War and Wickedness—3. The Three Nephite Disciples Depart—4. Mormon Restrained from Preaching—5. Predictions of Abinadi and Samuel the Lamanite Fulfilled.

1. *Ammaron's charge to Mormon respecting the Sacred Engravings.*

1. And now I, Mormon, make a record of the things which I have both seen and heard, and call it the Book of Mormon.

2. And about the time that Ammaron hid up the records unto the Lord, he came unto me, (I being about ten years of age, and I began to be learned somewhat after the manner of the learning of my people) and Ammaron said unto me: I perceive that thou art a sober child, and art quick to observe;

3. Therefore, when ye are about twenty and four years old I would that ye should remember the things that ye have observed concerning this people; and when ye are of that age go to the land Antum, unto a hill which shall be called Shim; and there have I deposited unto the Lord all the sacred engravings concerning this people.

4. And behold, ye shall take the plates of Nephi unto yourself, and the remainder shall ye leave in the place where they are; and ye shall engrave on the plates

---

VERSES 1-6. *And now I, Mormon, make a record . . . and call it the Book of Mormon.* Mormon was the last great Prophet-General of the Nephite Race, but better known to us as the custodian and compiler of the records of his people, and the writer of the greater portion of the work named after him, and known to us as the *Book of Mormon.* The father of Mormon who was a descendant of Nephi bore the same name as his illustrious son. The younger Mormon was born on the Northern Continent (311 A.D.), but when he was eleven years of age his father and he traveled to the land southward, "even to the Land of Zarahemla."

Before his departure south, Mormon formed the acquaintance of Ammaron whose name is the last word in the Book of Fourth Nephi. Ammaron was the brother of the younger Amos, and when Amos died, Ammaron took possession of the Sacred Things which because of the wickedness of the people he had hidden in a hill in the Land Antum. Ammaron perceived that Mormon was a lad of unusual perspicacity and that he was somewhat learned, Mormon himself notes "after the manner of the learning of my people." Impressed by Mormon's soberness and his ability to observe things quickly and accurately, he informed Mormon — then a child ten years old — of what he had done and placed the buried treasures in his charge. He instructed Mormon to go, when he was about twenty-four years old, to the hill where they were hidden and take the Plates of Nephi and record thereon what he had observed concerning the people. The remainder of the Plates, or the Records, etc., he was to leave where they were.

of Nephi all the things that ye have observed concerning this people.

5. And I, Mormon, being a descendant of Nephi, (and my father's name was Mormon) I remembered the things which

2. War and wickedness.

7. The whole face of the land had become covered with buildings, and the people were as numerous almost, as it were the sand of the sea.

8. And it came to pass in this year there began to be a war between the Nephites, who consisted of the Nephites and the Jacobites and the Josephites and the Zoramites; and this war was between the Nephites, and the Lamanites and the Lemuelites and the Ishmaelites.

9. Now the Lamanites and the Lemuelites and the Ishmaelites were called Lamanites, and the two parties were Nephites and Lamanites.

10. And it came to pass that

Ammaron commanded me.

6. And it came to pass that I, being eleven years old, was carried by my father into the land southward, even to the land of Zarahemla.

the war began to be among them in the borders of Zarahemla, by the waters of Sidon.

11. And it came to pass that the Nephites had gathered together a great number of men, even to exceed the number of thirty thousand. And it came to pass that they did have in this same year a number of battles, in which the Nephites did beat the Lamanites and did slay many of them.

12. And it came to pass that the Lamanites withdrew their design, and there was peace settled in the land; and peace did remain for the space of about four years, that there was no bloodshed.

3. The Three Nephite Disciples depart.

VERSES 7-12. *The whole face of the land had become covered with buildings.* In the journey with his father to the Land of Zarahemla, or to the Land Southward, Mormon observed that the whole face of the land through which they traveled was covered with buildings, and the people who dwelt thereon were as numerous as the "sand of the sea." This observation made by such a sober young man should verify the fact that the Nephite people had grown great in numbers, and *fat* in material things.

It was in the year 322 A.D., that actual war broke out between the Nephites and the Lamanites for the first time since the Redeemer's appearing. It commenced in the Land of Zarahemla near the Waters of Sidon. A number of battles were fought in which the armies of the Nephites were victorious, the Nephites having gathered together more than thirty thousand men to do battle. The Lamanites, unprepared to meet such a formidable array withdrew their design of conquest, and retreated to an uneasy peace which lasted for four years.

13. But wickedness did prevail upon the face of the whole land, insomuch that the Lord did take away his beloved disciples, and the work of miracles and of healing did cease because of the iniquity of the people.

14. And there were no gifts from the Lord, and the Holy Ghost did not come upon any, because of their wickedness and unbelief.

4. Mormon restrained from preaching.

15. And I, being fifteen years of age and being somewhat of a sober mind, therefore I was visited of the Lord, and tasted and knew of the goodness of Jesus.

16. And I did endeavor to preach unto this people, but my mouth was shut, and I was forbidden that I should preach unto them; for behold they had wilfully

---

VERSES 13-14. *The Lord did take away His Three beloved Nephite Disciples.* Wickedness became widespread throughout all the land. Pride and the love for the things of the world, crowded all thoughts of obedience to God's laws from the peoples' hearts, and all manner of iniquity took the place of goodness and purity. Many did whatever pleased their fancy, or gratified their whims; they forgot the peace that filled the hearts of their ancestors for over two hundred years immediately after the visit of the Risen Redeemer. Now all was changed. They no longer joyfully kept God's commandments; what once they loved, they now hated, and where once the teachings of the Savior was a light unto their feet, they now walked in darkness. Surely, sin lay at their door, their cup of iniquity was almost full, and was filling rapidly. Tumult, strife, and angry passions, murders and whoredoms, deceit and lying, marked these times as worthy only the designs of hell.

In such an unholy atmosphere the influence of which pervaded not only the religious and moral, but also the political lives of the people, the Spirit of the Lord could not dwell. In spite of the many marvelous miracles performed by God's servants, and His watchful care over them, His children quickly forgot their Father. Insomuch did the iniquity of the people increase day by day that "the work of miracles and of healing did cease," Mormon notes, among them. The gifts that are the rewards of righteous living also ceased, and the Holy Ghost "did not come upon any," to confirm them in their most holy faith, and to lead and guide them along the Paths of Holiness in which Paths their fathers had trod. The Three Disciples whom the Lord loved so well, and to whom He gave marvelous powers, failed longer to minister to the people, and all except the followers of Christ were left with no succor coming from Above to guide them. Mormon says that the Lord took away His beloved Disciples who for almost two hundred years had tarried among the Nephites and had ministered to their spiritual wants and needs.

VERSES 15-17. *I was visited of the Lord.* In these verses Mormon relates that when he was but fifteen years of age (about 326 A.D.), the Lord visited him, and he tasted of the "goodness of Jesus" in, we may imagine, a spiritual feast served as it were upon the *Table of our Lord* wherein he ate and drank of God's Holy Word. We can conceive the sweetness thereof. (*See,* I Nephi 8:11) For as a result of this marvelous outpouring of the Spirit, Mormon was anxious in the Work of the Lord. With a clarion voice he wanted to cry unto the people, "Repent ye, repent ye," but the Spirit restrained him; "My mouth," he says, "was shut, and I was forbidden that I should preach unto them. . . ."

It is recorded of this generation (the third after Christ), "They did not dwindle

rebelled against their God; and the beloved disciples were taken away out of the land, because of their iniquity.

17. But I did remain among them, but I was forbidden to preach unto them, because of the hardness of their hearts; and because of the hardness of their hearts the land was cursed for their sake.

5. Predictions of Abinadi and Samuel the Lamanite fulfilled.

18. And these Gadianton robbers, who were among the Lamanites, did infest the land, insomuch that the inhabitants thereof began to hide up their treasures in the earth; and they became slippery, because the Lord had cursed the land, that they could not hold them, nor retain them again.

19. And it came to pass that there were sorceries, and witchcrafts, and magics; and the power of the evil one was wrought upon all the face of the land, even unto the fulfilling of all the words of Abinadi, and also Samuel the Lamanite.

---

in unbelief, but they did wilfully rebel against the Gospel of Christ; and they did teach their children that they should not believe, even as their fathers." (IV Nephi 38) Mormon says of them, "They had wilfully rebelled against their God." We repeat a comment we made on this subject beforehand: "Amos, the son of Amos, and the grandson of Nephi, the Disciple, was the keeper of the Sacred Record during this period of Nephite history. He himself was a righteous man, but he witnessed an ever-increasing flood of iniquity break over the land. A phase of evil-doing that arose not from ignorance and false tradition, but from direct and wilfull rebellion against God, and apostasy from His laws. The wholesome checks to vice and misery found in the *Plan of Salvation* were knowingly done away with, or intentionally removed; the voice of reason was disregarded; the promptings of the Holy Spirit were defiantly repelled; man's unbridled passions again bore sway; disunion, dissension, violence, hatred, distress, dismay, bloodshed and havoc, spread the wide continents over; and from their high pinnacle of righteousness, peace, happiness, refinement, social advantage, etc., the people were hurled once more into an abyss of misery and barbarism, now more profound, more torturing, and more degrading than ever."

VERSES 18-19. *The Lord had cursed the land.* In verse seventeen we read: "And because of the hardness of their hearts the land was cursed for their sake." For many years the people had no more *all things in common,* but like the rest of the world, every man sought gain, wealth, power, and influence for himself and his. All the old evils arising from selfishness were revived. The Gadianton Bands, with all their secret signs and abominations, through the cunning of Satan, again appeared and increased until, in 300 A.D., they had spread over all the land. They were feared by the Nephites, not only because the Robbers were numbered among the Lamanites, but also because their name implied just what they were, robbers, indeed. The inhabitants of the land, Mormon notes, "began to hide up their treasures in the earth; and they became slippery, because the Lord had cursed the land, that they could not hold them, nor retain them again." (v. 18; *See also,* Helaman 13:30-32; Mosiah 17:14-20) Just as in the Dark Ages of Europe when Satan seemed to control men's hearts and minds, there was an overwhelming flood of "sorceries, and witchcrafts, and magics," let loose upon the people; anything that would blind the minds or harden the hearts of an already stiff-necked generation was made to appear to them as desirable. Yes, all that human ingenuity could suggest, or evil power achieve, was woven into their lives, until at this time the Nephites, having forsaken their first love, had so far sunk in the abyss of iniquity that they had grown as wicked, as proud, as corrupt and as vile as the Lamanites. All were submerged in an overpowering deluge of infamy, and there were none who were righteous save it were the followers of Jesus.

Thus we see that the prophecies of the Lord's servants, Abinadi and Samuel, the Lamanite, were fulfilled even to every word which they uttered.

CHAPTER 2

1. Mormon Leads the Nephite Armies—2. More of the Gadianton Robbers— 3. By Treaty the Land Northward is Given to the Nephites, and the Land Southward to the Lamanites.

1. *Mormon leads the Nephite Armies.*

1. And it came to pass in that same year there began to be a war again between the Nephites and the Lamanites. And notwithstanding I being young, was large in stature; therefore the people of Nephi appointed me that I should be their leader, or the leader of their armies.

2. Therefore it came to pass that in my sixteenth year I did go forth at the head of an army of the Nephites, against the Lamanites; therefore three hundred and twenty and six years had passed away.

3. And it came to pass that in the three hundred and twenty and seventh year the Lamanites did come upon us with exceeding great power, insomuch that they did frighten my armies; therefore they would not fight, and they began to retreat towards the north countries.

4. And it came to pass that we did come to the city of Angola, ·and we did take possession of the city, and make preparations to defend ourselves against the Lamanites. And it came to pass that we did fortify the city with our might; but notwithstanding all our fortifications the Lamanites did come upon us and did drive us out of the city.

5. And they did also drive us

VERSES 1-2. *The people of Nephi appointed me to be the leader of their armies.* Near the end of the four years of peace spoken of in verse 12, of the preceding Chapter, war was again commenced between the Nephites and the Lamanites. Notwithstanding his youth, Mormon, being large of stature, was appointed to lead the armies of the Nephites.

Mormon must have had many qualities of leadership besides being physically large, such as unusual power, or strength, ability to see and observe, quick to make decisions, honest, true and comprehensive, but above all else, he was faithful to God and His laws. He was, like the Brother of Jared, "a large and mighty man" (Ether 1:34) in personal appearance, and undoubtedly as strong in his integrity to God and in his moral courage as he was in physical characteristics. In the short autobiography he gives us, Mormon states that "three hundred and twenty-six years had passed away," since the birth of Christ, and that "in my sixteenth year I did go forth at the head of an army of the Nephites, against the Lamanites."

The next year saw disaster follow the Nephite cause. Mormon's troops retreated before the Lamanites who came against them showing great strength and resourcefulness, insomuch so that the Nephite armies were terrified when they beheld their battle array. Mormon's soldiers fled northward, and did not stop until they "did come to the City of Angola." Here the Nephites made a stubborn stand, yet in spite of the fortifications they had built, Mormon says: "The Lamanites did

forth out of the land of David.

6. And we marched forth and came to the land of Joshua, which was in the borders west by the seashore.

7. And it came to pass that we did gather in our people as fast as it were possible, that we might get them together in one body.

2. More of the Gadianton Robbers.

8. But behold, the land was filled with robbers and with Lamanites; and notwithstanding the great destruction which hung over my people, they did not repent of their evil doings; therefore there was blood and carnage spread throughout all the face of the land, both on the part of the Nephites and also on the part of the Lamanites; and it was one complete revolution throughout all the face of the land.

9. And now, the Lamanites had a king, and his name was Aaron; and he came against us with an army of forty and four thousand. And behold, I withstood him with forty and two thousand. And it came to pass that I beat him with my army that he fled before me. And behold, all this was done, and three hundred and thirty years had passed away.

---

come upon us and did drive us out of the City." Nor did the Nephite retreat stop in the land round about Angola, but the Land of David whereunto they fled offered them no assylum. Escape from the results of their iniquity did not come to them because of repentance which they did not, for the old habits and practices of wickedness pursued them as well as the Lamanite hordes. An attempt was made by Mormon and others of their leaders to assemble all the Nephites into one place that the full strength of their numbers could be felt. With this end in view, the armies of the Nephites marched into the Land of Joshua which was on the borders of the Western Sea.

VERSE 8. *The land was filled with Robbers and with Lamanites.* In addition to the fact that the Lamanite warriors stood ready to destroy them, and the terrifying thoughts of coming woe which overshadowed their every move, even their search for safety, the Nephites were constantly harrassed by the Gadianton Robbers who filled the land. Bloody forays and murderous assaults on them by the Robbers, were the wages Satan paid the staggering Nephites who now had become as wicked and as vile as the Lamanites. Of Satan, one thing is sure: He always pays his servants their wages. Nevertheless, and notwithstanding the threatened destruction that awaited them, the Nephites "did not repent of their evil doings." Surrounded by forces that were to them superior in numbers; left to their own devices by the God Whom they had forsaken; floundering about as if searching for something which they could not find—something they once had, but which they no longer possessed; the Spirit of the Lord to guide them—the Nephites, the people of God, joined hand-in-hand with the Lamanites in an orgy of blood and carnage that spread throughout the whole land. Here Mormon notes that "It was one complete revolution throughout all the face of the land."

VERSE 9. *A king named Aaron.* In 300 A.D., the King of the Lamanites, whose name was Aaron, was defeated by an inferior army under the command of Mormon. Aaron commanded 44,000 men, and Mormon 42,000.

10. And it came to pass that the Nephites began to repent of their iniquity, and began to cry even as had been prophesied by Samuel the prophet; for behold no man could keep that which was his own, for the thieves, and the robbers, and the murderers, and the magic art, and the witchcraft which was in the land.

11. Thus there began to be a mourning and a lamentation in all the land because of these things, and m o r e especially among the people of Nephi.

12. And it came to pass that when I, Mormon, saw their lamentation and their mourning and their sorrow before the Lord, my heart did begin to rejoice within me, knowing the mercies and the long-suffering of the Lord, therefore supposing that he would be merciful unto them that they would again become a righteous people.

13. But behold this my joy was vain, for their sorrowing was not unto repentance, because of the goodness of God; but it was rather the sorrowing of the damned, because the Lord would not always suffer them to take happiness in sin.

14. And they did not come unto Jesus with broken hearts and contrite spirits, but they did curse God, and wish to die. Nevertheless they would struggle with the sword for their lives.

15. And it came to pass that my sorrow did return unto me

VERSE 10. *The Nephites began to repent of their iniquity.* Realizing the perilous straits into which their evil ways had beguiled them, and with a dread inspired by the *Sword of Vengeance* that hung over them, the Nephites, in fear and trembling because of their wickedness, began to sorrow and lament their fallen condition. The words of the Prophet Samuel were in them literally fulfilled: "And the day shall come that they shall hide up their treasures, because they have set their hearts upon riches; and because they have set their hearts upon riches, I will hide up their treasures when they shall flee before their enemies; because they will not hide them up unto Me, cursed be they and also their treasures; and in that day shall they be smitten, saith the Lord." (*Samuel,* Helaman 13:20) Mormon comments: "No man could keep that which was his own, for the thieves, and the robbers, and the murderers, and the magic art, and the witchcraft which was in the land." (v. 10)

VERSES 11-15. *When I, Mormon, saw their lamentation . . . before the Lord, my heart did begin to rejoice.* Mormon notes that not only were the Lamanites cursed in these things, but more especially were the Nephites. Both divisions of the people had reached that point in their evil ways, or doings, where human wickedness cannot pass. Yet Mormon perceived that among the Nephites the spirit of repentance was beginning to work. Their lamentation and their mourning, and he says: "Their sorrow before the Lord," which were expressed, no doubt, in supplication to Him Who reigns Above, so softened Mormon's heart that he, too, bowed before the *Majesty on High,* because "My heart did begin to rejoice within me, knowing the mercies and the long-suffering of the Lord." I supposed "that He would be merciful unto them that they would again become a righteous people." (v. 12)

But Mormon's joy in his people's changed attitude was only of short duration. By it, for awhile, he was inspirited. He sought greater ends for them to accomplish, but he tells us that his joy was vain. He hoped for that which he saw not, for

again, and I saw that the day of grace was passed with them, both temporally and spiritually; for I saw thousands of them hewn down in open rebellion against their God, and heaped up as dung upon the face of the land. And thus three hundred and forty and four years had passed away.

16. And it came to pass that in the three hundred and forty and fifth year the Nephites did begin to flee before the Lamanites; and they were pursued until they came even to the land of Jashon, before it was possible to stop them in their retreat.

17. And now, the city of Jashon was near the land where Ammaron had deposited the records unto the Lord, that they might not be destroyed. And behold I had gone according to the word of Ammaron, and taken the plates of Nephi, and did make a record according to the words of Ammaron.

18. And upon the plates of Nephi I did make a full account of all the wickedness and abominations; but upon these plates I did forbear to make a full account

of their wickedness and abomination, for behold, a continual scene of wickedness and abominations has been before mine eyes ever since I have been sufficient to behold the ways of man.

19. And wo is me because of their wickedness; for my heart has been filled with sorrow because of their wickedness, all my days; nevertheless, I know that I shall be lifted up at the last day.

20. And it came to pass that in this year the people of Nephi again were hunted and driven. And it came to pass that we were driven forth until we had come northward to the land which was called Shem.

21. And it came to pass that we did fortify the city of Shem, and we did gather in our people as much as it were possible, that perhaps we might save them from destruction.

22. And it came to pass in the three hundred and forty and sixth year they began to come upon us again.

23. And it came to pass that I did speak unto my people, and did urge them with great energy,

---

while their cries to the Lord were heart-rending, their actions belied their intentions. They still indulged their wicked appetites and practices. Their sorrow was not unto repentance, but was "because the Lord would not always suffer them to take happiness in sin." Their lamentations were not words of praise and thanksgiving to God for His goodness, but in them they expressed resentment because He allowed them to be visited with His wrath.

VERSES 16-27. *They did not come unto Jesus with broken hearts and contrite spirits.* Amid much that was painful to their hearts, and perplexing to their minds, conditions which could have been alleviated by righteous appeal, the Nephites, nevertheless, refused to bow their heads in grateful acknowledgment of the many blessings God had bestowed upon them. Like their ancestors, the Jews, they were stiff-necked. They refused to listen to the words of God's servants, and sought the satisfaction of their lusts and appetites by indulging in carnal gratification. Their

that they would stand boldly before the Lamanites and fight for their wives, and their children, and their houses, and their homes.

24. And my words did arouse them somewhat to vigor, insomuch that they did not flee from before the Lamanites, but did stand with boldness against them.

25. And it came to pass that we did contend with an army of thirty thousand against an army of fifty thousand. And it came to pass that we did stand before them with such firmness that they did flee from before us.

26. And it came to pass that

when they had fled we did pursue them with our armies, and did meet them again, and did beat them; nevertheless the strength of the Lord was not with us; yea, we were left to ourselves, that the Spirit of the Lord did not abide in us; therefore we had become weak like unto our brethren.

27. And my heart did sorrow because of this the great calamity of my people, because of their wickedness and their abominations. But behold, we did go forth against the Lamanites and the robbers of Gadianton, until we had again taken possession of the lands of our inheritance.

3. By Treaty the land is divided.

28. And the three hundred and forty and ninth year had passed away. And in the three hundred and fiftieth year we made a treaty with the Lamanites and the robbers of Gadianton, in which we did get the lands of our inherit-

ance divided.

29. And the Lamanites did give unto us the land northward, yea, even to the narrow passage which led into the land southward. And we did give unto the Lamanites all the land southward.

---

lives were a strange admixture of sin, and a desire therein for happiness. All sin is wickedness, and "Wickedness never was happiness"; (Alma 41:10) also, "If there be no righteousness, there be no happiness." (II Nephi 2:13) The people now seemed to be the same as those to whom the Prophet Samuel spoke about 350 years previously in Zarahemla: "Ye have sought all the days of your lives for that which ye could not obtain; and ye have sought for happiness in doing iniquity, which thing is contrary to the nature of that righteousness which is in our great and Eternal Head." (Helaman 13:38)

In their folly and foolishness the Nephites thought to deceive the Almighty with outward appearances of grief and penitence. But they did not come unto Him with broken hearts and contrite spirits, meaning hearts that were broken down with sorrow for sin; being humbly and thoroughly penitent; contrite spirits; spirits evincing sincere repentance. But instead of praising Him for His goodness and mercy, they cursed God, and expressed a wish to die. However, Mormon notes that "they would struggle with the sword for their lives."

VERSES 28-29. The land southward, we understand, is the land of South America, and the land northward refers to the land north of the Isthmus of Panama.

CHAPTER 3

1. Nephites continue in wickedness.

1. And it came to pass that the Lamanites did not come to battle again until ten years more had passed away. And behold, I had employed my people, the Nephites, in preparing their lands and their arms against the time of battle.

2. And it came to pass that the Lord did say unto me: Cry unto this people—Repent ye, and come unto me, and be ye baptized, and build up again my church, and ye shall be spared.

3. And I did cry unto this people, but it was in vain; and they did not realize that it was the Lord that had spared them, and granted unto them a chance for repentance. And behold they did harden their hearts against the Lord their God.

VERSE 1. *The Lamanites did not come up to battle again until ten years had passed away.* The treaty that was made between the Nephites on one hand, and the Lamanites with their many dissident Nephites on the other, lasted for ten years, in which interim of warfare, the peaceful pursuits of the Nephites were largely devoted to the preparation for war that seemed to Mormon as inevitable. During that time, he says, "I had employed my people, the Nephites, in preparing their lands and their arms against the time of battle."

VERSE 2. The long-suffering of the Lord was again made manifest in offering mercy to the wayward Nephites, if only they would repent, "and come unto Me. . . ." "Build up again My Church," came the voice of the Lord to Mormon, and at the same time he was commanded to cry this message to his people. The Lord promised them in doing so, that "ye shall be spared," from the ravages of their foes which for years, barring short intervals of an uncertain peace, had been the plague and scourge of their lives. In His offer of forbearance the Lord again makes known that He does not desire the death of the transgressor, but that the sinner live and return unto Him.

VERSE 3. *I did cry unto this people, but it was in vain.* Mormon's people were so steeped in sin, and had become so hardened to sensibility that they were no longer able to choose between good and evil, let alone see the right when opposed by that which was wrong. They had the idea that whatsoever pleased the fancy or gratified the demands of their carnal selves would bring happiness. In this they were mistaken! Mormon says that they did not realize, nor did they bring into actual existence the fact that it was God alone Who spared them in times past. The loving-kindness of the Lord for His wayward children during their period of offense was made evident in His patience and endurance for them which countered every move of their enemies to destroy them. Notwithstanding the offer the Lord made to spare them, if they would repent, and save them from the adversary who sought to destroy them, "They did harden their hearts against the Lord their God."

4. And it came to pass that after this tenth year had passed away, making, in the whole, three hundred and sixty years from the coming of Christ, the king of the Lamanites sent an epistle unto me, which gave unto me to know that they were preparing to come again to battle against us.

5. And it came to pass that I did cause my people that they should gather themselves together at the land Desolation, to a city which was in the borders, by the narrow pass which led into the land southward.

6. And there we did place our armies, that we might stop the armies of the Lamanites, that they might not get possession of any of our lands; therefore we did fortify against them with all our force.

7. And it came to pass that in the three hundred and sixty and first year the Lamanites did come down to the city of Desolation to battle against us; and it came to pass that in that year we did beat them, insomuch that they did return to their own lands again.

8. And in the three hundred and sixty and second year they did come down again to battle. And we did beat them again, and did slay a great number of them, and their dead were cast into the sea.

2. Mormon refuses to be their military leader.

9. And now, because of this great thing which my people, the Nephites, had done, they began to boast in their own strength, and began to swear before the heavens that they would avenge themselves of the blood of their brethren who had been slain by their enemies.

10. And they did swear by the heavens, and also by the throne of God, that they would go up to battle against their enemies, and would cut them off from the face of the land.

11. And it came to pass that I, Mormon, did utterly refuse from this time forth to be a commander

---

VERSES 4-8. *The King of the Lamanites in the year 360 after the coming of Christ again declared war.* In the year 360 after the coming of Christ, the King of the Lamanites again declared war by sending an epistle to Mormon telling him that they (the Lamanites) were preparing to come to battle against the Nephites. To repel the threatened invasion, the people of Nephi were gathered at the Land of Desolation. There the Lamanites attacked them, were defeated, and returned home. Not content with this repulse, the following year the Lamanites made another inroad into the Northern Country, and were again repulsed with many who were slain. The dead bodies of the slain were cast into the sea.

VERSES 9-16. *The Nephites began to boast in their own strength.* The hard hearts of the Nephites, which had become like stone, rejected Mormon's appeals, and unmindful of His help, refused to admit they conquered in the strength of the Lord, but boasted in their own might. Day by day they went their way forgetting His wisdom and guidance. They forgot that their utmost strength when compared

and a leader of this people, because of their wickedness and abomination.

12. Behold, I had led them, notwithstanding their wickedness I had led them many times to battle, and had loved them, according to the love of God which was in me, with all my heart; and my soul had been poured out in prayer unto my God all the day long for them; nevertheless, it was without faith, because of the hardness of their hearts.

13. And thrice have I delivered them out of the hands of their enemies, and they have repented not of their sins.

14. And when they had sworn by all that had been forbidden them by our Lord and Savior Jesus Christ, that they would go up unto their enemies to battle, and avenge themselves of the blood of their brethren, behold the voice of the Lord came unto me saying:

15. Vengeance is mine, and I will repay; and because this people repented not after I had delivered them, behold, they shall be cut off from the face of the earth.

16. And it came to pass that I

to God's was absolute weakness, and their wisdom but foolishness. They had no alliance with a power greater than theirs. In their folly this they would not recognize, but swore "before the Heavens that they would avenge themselves of the blood of their brethren." Not only that, but they called upon God to witness their determination to cut their enemies "off from the face of the land."

For them to rely upon their own impregnability and ignore His might was repugnant to the Lord's purposes as proclaimed by Mormon. The wickedness and abandonment of the Nephite people were fast reaching their maximum. They sought not the Lord, but repelled His Spirit and knowingly rebelled against His mandates. For this reason, and this reason alone, Mormon refused to longer be their Commander.

Here Mormon recalls that in spite of their waywardness, he had led the Nephites many times into battle, and had done so because they were his people, and therefore he had loved them with a fervor almost divine. And in this love he had unceasingly poured out his heart in prayer unto God that He in His might would save them from their own folly. But, Mormon sadly notes that because "of the hardness of their hearts" his petitions did not prevail before Him Who reigns On High.

Notwithstanding the fact of which they were aware, that in recent years Mormon had led the Nephite Armies to victory when the Nephites were attacked by the Lamanites, the people nevertheless did not repent of their wickedness. They continued on in their iniquity, and in their unhallowed wrath swore by the Heavens and by the Throne of God in what they thought was their newly found strength that they would persist in battle until the blood of their brethren who had been slain in previous encounters was avenged.

This was not pleasing unto the Lord Who had commanded that man should not swear by anything. And inasmuch as all thoughts of God had been crowded from their hearts, and no praise or thanksgiving offered Him by the Nephites for their deliverance, His voice came to Mormon: "Vengeance is Mine, and I will repay." It was not for the Nephites to mete out punishment, or to inflict it for past injuries or offenses committed by the Lamanites as the Nephites had sworn to do, but to leave it to God in Heaven Who knoweth the end from the beginning. Evidently,

utterly refused to go up against mine enemies; and I did even as the Lord had commanded me; and I did stand as an idle witness to manifest unto the world the things which I saw and heard, according to the manifestations of the Spirit which had testified of things to come.

3. Moroni's address to future generations.

4. The Twelve Apostles whom Jesus had chosen in Jerusalem to judge the House of Israel.

17. Therefore I write unto you, Gentiles, and also unto you, house of Israel, when the work shall commence, that ye shall be about to prepare to return to the land of your inheritance;

18. Yea, behold, I write unto all the ends of the earth; yea, unto you, twelve tribes of Israel, who shall be judged according to your works by the twelve whom Jesus chose to be his disciples in the land of Jerusalem.

19. And I write also unto the remnant of this people, who shall also be judged by the twelve whom Jesus chose in this land; and they shall be judged by the other twelve whom Jesus chose in the land of Jerusalem.

20. And these things doth the Spirit manifest unto me; therefore I write unto you all. And for this cause I write unto you, that ye may know that ye must all stand before the judgment-seat of Christ, yea, every soul who belongs to the whole human family of Adam; and ye must stand to be judged of your works, whether they be good or evil;

21. And also that ye may believe the gospel of Jesus Christ, which ye shall have among you;

---

the Lord had become weary of the Nephites' sinful ways,[1] and now His long-suffering was at an end, He said: "They shall be cut off from the face of the earth."

VERSES 17-22. *I write unto you, Gentiles . . . and unto you, House of Israel . . . and also unto the Remnant of this people.* Anxious in the work of the Lord, and eager to advance its cause, Mormon never ceased to proclaim its great message. Under every circumstance whatsoever as the opportunity presented, he published the Name of Christ whom he declared to be the very Eternal God. For this cause that the Jews who slew Jesus "Whom they saw and heard," (v. 21) might have another witness of His Godhood, Mormon testified to all the world—knowing that his words shall come to them at some future time—both Gentiles and Jews, and the Tribes of Israel, wherever they may be, that this same Jesus was the Christ Whose coming they awaited, and therefore he admonished all to believe the teachings of Jesus which, he promised "ye shall have among you." (v. 21)

---

[1]Of the Jews in Jerusalem: "Thou hast forsaken Me, saith the Lord, thou art gone backward: therefore will I stretch out My hand against thee, and destroy thee; I am weary with repenting." (Jeremiah 15:6) *I am weary with repenting,* many times the Lord had thought to destroy the wicked Jews, and just as many times had relented because of the prayers of the righteous, but now their cup of iniquity was full and He refused to alter His decision to destroy them. He would not again change the verdict He had given. Also read Mormon 5:1 where the word *repent* is used in exactly the same sense.

and also that the Jews, the covenant people of the Lord, shall have other witness besides him whom they saw and heard, that Jesus, whom they slew, was the very Christ and the very God.

22. And I would that I could persuade all ye ends of the earth to repent and prepare to stand before the judgment-seat of Christ.

The great purpose for which Mormon addressed his exhortation was that all men must "stand before the Judgment-Seat of Christ . . . to be judged of your works, whether they be good or evil." (v. 20) To the end that no one shall have an excuse for his actions and thereby be prepared when that time comes, Mormon, with sincere purpose of heart, closes his warning with a prayer: "I would that I could persuade all ye ends of the earth to repent and prepare to stand before the Judgment-Seat of Christ."

CHAPTER 4

1. *Nephites begin a war of revenge upon Lamanites.*

1. And now it came to pass that in the three hundred and sixty and third year the Nephites did go up with their armies to battle against the Lamanites, out of the land Desolation.

2. And it came to pass that the armies of the Nephites were driven back again to the land of Desolation. And while they were yet weary, a fresh army of the Lamanites did come upon them; and they had a sore battle, insomuch that the Lamanites did take possession of the city Desolation, and did slay many of the Nephites, and did take many prisoners.

3. And the remainder did flee and join the inhabitants of the city Teancum. Now the city Teancum lay in the borders by the seashore; and it was also near the city Desolation.

4. And it was because the armies of the Nephites went up unto the Lamanites that they began to be smitten; for were it not for that, the Lamanites could have had no power over them.

5. But, behold, the judgments of God will overtake the wicked;

VERSE 1. *The Nephites went up to battle with the Lamanites.* The Nephites, emanating confidence in themselves because of the victories gained by them in the last two struggles with the Lamanites—and therein overestimating their own strength —were convinced that they could, by a might all their own, overcome and vanquish their unyielding foe.

The Nephites congregated all their forces in the Land Desolation, and from there as a base for operations invaded the Land Southward.

VERSE 2. *The Armies of the Nephites were driven back.* Quickly, with overpowering numbers the Lamanites drove the attacking Nephites back to the place from which they had started. Not only did the warriors from the south follow them into the Land Desolation, but while the Nephites were yet resting from the terrible ordeal just enacted, a fresh army of Lamanites came upon them. The battle that ensued was a sore one; the Nephites fought in vain, and were eventually driven from the City Desolation which they had formed into a bastion. (*See*, Mormon 3:5-6) "The Lamanite warriors did slay many of the Nephites and did take many prisoners."

VERSES 3-16. *The remainder did flee to the City Teancum.* Those of the Nephites who were not slain in the recent battle, nor were taken prisoners by the Lamanites, fled to the nearby City Teancum which was close to the seashore. Here the refugees joined the defenders of that city, and by their joint efforts they did prevail. The next year, it being the 364th, the Lamanites came against it, but by the united efforts of its protectors the Lamanites' attack was repelled and they were driven back. (v. 8)

Again the hue and cry of victory resounded throughout the Nephites' possessions,

and it is by the wicked that the wicked are punished; for it is the wicked that stir up the hearts of the children of men unto bloodshed.

6. And it came to pass that the Lamanites did make preparations to come against the city Teancum.

7. And it came to pass in the three hundred and sixty and fourth year the Lamanites did come against the city Teancum, that they might take possession of the city Teancum also.

8. And it came to pass that they were repulsed and driven back by the Nephites. And when the Nephites saw that they had driven the Lamanites they did again boast of their strength; and they went forth in their own might, and took possession again of the city Desolation.

9. And now all these things had been done, and there had been thousands slain on both sides, both the Nephites and the Lamanites.

10. And it came to pass that the three hundred and sixty and sixth year had passed away, and the Lamanites came again upon the Nephites to battle; and yet the Nephites repented not of the evil they had done, but persisted in their wickedness continually.

11. And it is impossible for the tongue to describe, or for man to write a perfect description of the horrible scene of the blood and carnage which was among the people, both of the Nephites and of the Lamanites; and every heart was hardened, so that they delighted in the shedding of blood continually.

12. And there never had been

---

and drowned out all appeals for a spirit of thanksgiving. They would not acknowledge that God overruled all, but again they felt strong in their own might. They were, in their opinion, sufficient to the end they had in view. In a way they were successful, but only temporarily. They marched forth in their self-supposed might, and exhibiting all the strength they possessed, recaptured from the Lamanites the City Desolation.

This state of things continued yet for about ten years. War, contention, rapine, pillage, and all the horrors incident to the letting loose of men's most depraved and brutal passions, filled the land. Sometimes one army conquered, sometimes the other. Now it was the Nephites who were pouring their forces into the south; then the Lamanites were overflowing the north. Whichever side triumphed, that triumph was of short duration; but it all meant sacrifice, cruelty, blood-guiltiness, and woe.

Mormon here observes what we, too, may take as a warning. We may compare our lives with the actions of the Nephites at this time. They sought trouble by going out for it. They attacked the Lamanites. Mormon notes that "it was because the armies of the Nephites went up unto the Lamanites that they began to be smitten; for if it were not for that, the Lamanites could have had no power over them." How often do we approach evil, thinking we are strong enough to overcome its blandishments. It is then we begin "to be smitten." Little by little we fall a prey to the things we once hated, and love the things to which we were once indifferent. Only God Himself can save such a man, and that by man's sincere repentance, for, "Behold," Mormon says, "the judgments of God will overtake the wicked." (v. 5) The Nephites sought things which would satisfy their depraved appetites; if we seek righteousness, Satan can have no power over us, just the

so great wickedness among all the children of Lehi, nor even among all the house of Israel, according to the words of the Lord, as was among this people.

13. And it came to pass that the Lamanites did take possession of the city Desolation, and this because their number did exceed the number of the Nephites.

14. And they did also march forward against the city Teancum, and did drive the inhabitants forth out of her, and did take many prisoners both women and children, and did offer them up as sacrifices unto their idol gods.

15. And it came to pass that in the three hundred and sixty

---

opposite of Lamanitish might that had power over the Nephites when they sought the things God had forbidden—bloodshed and murder even if it was called "warfare."

A story we heard in our youth, although its allegory is imperfect, will tend to illustrate our point. In the old days before good roads, an owner of a stage line advertised for a competent and careful driver. Three men in particular answered, and them he took to a high mountain pass overlooking a steep cliff. The road, which we may call it, narrowed down as it negotiated a turn. To the first, he said, "How near can you get to the edge of that cliff and not go over?" The owner of the stage line was assured that the job's prospect could go almost to the edge of the cliff, and not any farther. "Good," said the inquirer, and asked the second applicant the same question. "I can get my back wheels over the cliff, and still regain the roadway." That was still better. But the third man in answer to the same question, replied: "I don't know how near the edge I can go, but I will stay as far away from it as I can." He got the job. The moral is: Stay away from even the appearance of evil. "Seek not after riches nor the vain things of this world; for behold, you cannot carry them with you." (Alma 39:14) But before ye seek for riches, seek ye for the Kingdom of God.

It is by the wicked that the wicked are punished. How often has this been the case in the history of the Jews as well as in the history of the Nephites. The wicked Jews in crucifying our Lord, brought disaster to their descendants, who are still unbelievers in Christ's Divinity. The idolatrous nations, Egypt, Babylonia, Assyria, and others, sought to bring apostate Jerusalem into bondage. This they did many times. But we do not hear of Jewish bondage in their Golden Age when they served the Lord. When they did not, but left the worship of the Only True and Living God, it so happened that the wicked nations of the earth came upon them and at one time carried many of their great ones into captivity at Babylon.

This was also the case with the Lamanites and those Nephites who forsook the Way of Righteousness, and entered by and forbidden paths. After the final battle at Cumorah when only the Lamanites survived the carnage, they battled one with the other. Moroni, in finishing his father's (Mormon) record, says: "The Lamanites are at war one with another; and the whole face of the land is one continual round of murder and bloodshed." (Mormon 8:8) The wicked survivors killed other wicked survivors of that battle.

In the case at point, Mormon informs us that the Lamanites, who were notoriously wicked, punished the wicked Nephites. Both had become so embroiled in sin that they actually delighted in the shedding of blood. They "sought for happiness in doing iniquity." (Helaman 13:38) At no time in the history of Lehi's descendants, or even among the Jews, had the people sunk so far in debasement, in profligacy, and in crime, as did both the Nephites and Lamanites of this period. Mormon

and seventh year, the Nephites being angry because the Lamanites had sacrificed their women and their children, that they did go against the Lamanites with exceeding great anger, insomuch that they did beat again the La-

manites, and drive them out of their lands.

16. And the Lamanites did not come again against the Nephites until the three hundred and seventy and fifth year.

2. The Nephites no longer prevail.

17. And in this year they did come down against the Nephites with all their powers; and they were not numbered because of the greatness of their number.

18. And from this time forth did the Nephites gain no power over the Lamanites, but began to be swept off by them even as a dew before the sun.

19. And it came to pass that the Lamanites did come down against the city Desolation; and there was an exceedingly sore battle fought in the land Desolation, in the which they did beat the Nephites.

20. And they fled again from before them, and they came to the city Boaz; and there they did

---

says: "And it is impossible for the tongue to describe, or for man to write a perfect description of the horrible scene of the blood and carnage which was among the people, both of the Nephites and the Lamanites; and every heart was hardened, so that they delighted in the shedding of blood continually." (v. 11)

After again capturing the City Desolation, because of their superior numbers, the Lamanites also came in their might against the City Teancum. They overcame all resistance, and took many women and children prisoners. The Lamanites had become so debased and so corrupt that they offered their captives — both women and children — up "as sacrifices unto their idol gods." This so enraged the husbands and fathers of the Nephites that they "did go against the Lamanites with exceeding great anger." So fiercely did the Nephites fight, and so violently did they combat the Lamanites that they drove them entirely out of all Nephite lands. These things all happened in the 367th year, and the Lamanites were so beaten that they did not again come to battle with the Nephites for eight years, or until the year 375.

VERSE 18. *From this time forth did the Nephites gain no power over the Lamanites.* In the year 375, as we have noted, the Lamanites "with all their power," came to battle again with the decadent Nephites. The number of the Lamanite invaders was so great that they were not counted. They were numberless. First, the Lamanites attacked the wicked City Desolation, and again it fell to the assault of the Lamanites; the whole Land of Desolation was turned into a battlefield where men fought in hand-to-hand combat, neither giving nor taking quarter; neither did they think of God Who in times past often planted victory upon the banners of those who called upon His holy Name. Again the Nephites were sorely beaten.

VERSE 20. *The Nephites again fled before the onslaught of the Lamanites.* Unable to withstand the overwhelming tide of the soldiers of the Lamanites, the Nephites again fled before the oncoming foe, this time until they came to the City Boaz. At last when all else seemed vain, the Nephites turned upon the invading

stand against the Lamanites with exceeding boldness, insomuch that the Lamanites did not beat them until they had come again the second time.

21. And when they had come the second time, the Nephites were driven and slaughtered with an exceedingly great slaughter; their women and their children were again sacrificed unto idols.

22. And it came to pass that the Nephites did again flee from before them, taking all the inhabitants with them, both in towns and villages.

3. Sacred Records taken from the Hill Shim.

23. And now I, Mormon, seeing that the Lamanites were about to overthrow the land, therefore I did go to the hill Shim, and did take up all the records which Ammaron had hid up unto the Lord.

---

force of Lamanites, and gave battle to them with such fierceness that it was not until the Lamanites came upon them the second time that the Nephites gave way. The previous scene was reenacted. The Nephites lost many men in those who were slain, and again the women and children captives were "sacrificed unto idols."

The Nephites continued to flee. They seemed utterly routed.

VERSE 23. *The Lamanites were about to overthrow the land.* Mormon, realizing the ascendancy of the Lamanites, and that no longer could he rely on any form of order, went to the Hill Shim where Ammaron had hid them from the Lamanites, and took all the records to a safer place of concealment. Mormon does not say whereunto he took them, but they eventually found their way to the Hill Cumorah.

CHAPTER 5

1. *Mormon Relents and Again Leads the Nephite Armies—2. Lamanites Outnumber the Nephites—3. Crime and Carnage—4. Mormon's Abridgment of the Records.*

1. *Mormon relents and again leads the Nephite Armies.*

1. And it came to pass that I did go forth among the Nephites, and did repent of the oath which I had made that I would no more assist them; and they gave me command again of their armies, for they looked upon me as though I could deliver them from their afflictions.

2. But behold, I was without hope, for I knew the judgments of the Lord which should come upon them; for they repented not of their iniquities, but did struggle for their lives without calling upon that Being who created them.

3. And it came to pass that the Lamanites did come against us as we had fled to the city of Jordan; but behold, they were driven back that they did not take the city at that time.

4. And it came to pass that they came against us again, and we did maintain the city. And there were also other cities which were maintained by the Nephites,

---

VERSE 1. *I did repent of the oath which I had made that I would no more assist them.* In going forth among his people, no doubt to comfort and give them courage, Mormon observed their pitiable condition. The awful straits they were in appalled him; he perceived that Satan had deceived them. Thoughts of the world and the things of the world had crowded all thoughts of God from their hearts. Their hopes in life had become a fight for survival. Although their condition existed as an occasion of their wickedness, Mormon's heart was full of compassion for them. He relented of the decision he had made to lead them no more to battle, and once more took upon himself command of the Nephite Armies. This change in Mormon's plans pleased them, for they thought there was only one among them who could lead them from their many afflictions which according to Mormon came upon them because of their wickedness.

VERSE 2. *They repented not of their iniquity.* However, Mormon was depressed: "I was without hope, for I knew the judgments of the Lord which should come upon them." No matter if disasters, one after another, almost overwhelmed them, they refused to repent, and call upon Him Who had created them, that He might give them succor according to the hour and the power of their need. They would fight for their lives, Mormon says, evidently thinking that life, however bitter, was the only thing worth the fight.

VERSES 3-7. *More battles and more cities destroyed.* Again the Nephites were forced to retreat; this time they fled to the City of Jordan, the Lamanites in hot pursuit. But, notwithstanding their many troops, they were driven back and the Lamanites failed in the attempt to capture the City. The Lamanites made yet another attack upon Jordan, but the Nephite forces with almost superhuman efforts

which strongholds did cut them off that they could not get into the country which lay before us, to destroy the inhabitants of our land.

5. But it came to pass that whatsoever lands we had passed by, and the inhabitants thereof were not gathered in, were destroyed by the Lamanites, and their towns, and villages, and cities were burned with fire; and thus three hundred and seventy and nine years passed away.

6. And it came to pass that in the three hundred and eightieth year the Lamanites did come again against us to battle, and we did stand against them boldly; but it was all in vain, for so great were their numbers that they did tread the people of the Nephites under their feet.

7. And it came to pass that we did again take to flight, and those whose flight was swifter than the Lamanites' did escape, and those whose flight did not exceed the Lamanites' were swept down and destroyed.

2. *Lamanites outnumber Nephites.*

3. *Crime and carnage.*

4. *Mormon's abridgment of the records.*

8. And now behold, I, Mormon, do not desire to harrow up the souls of men in casting before them such an awful scene of blood and carnage as was laid before mine eyes; but I, knowing that these things must surely be made known, and that all things which

---

"did maintain the City." Mormon notes that there were other cities which did not fall to Lamanitish aggression. These cities stood in the way of their further advancement so at that time the inroads of the Lamanite hordes were stopped, and the inhabitants of the regions round about were spared from destruction.

As the Nephites retreated farther northward, they gathered up all the inhabitants of the lands through which they passed. Those who would not join them in their flight from the Lamanites were slain by the pursuing Lamanites, and the villages and towns were destroyed by fire. Thus ended the 379th year after the birth of Christ.

In the 380th year, the Lamanites again came against the Nephites to battle. Inspired by the fear of what would happen if the Lamanites won, the Nephites stood before them "boldly." But Mormon notes that it was useless and to no avail, because the number of Lamanites was so great that they literally overran the field of battle, and "did tread the people of the Nephites under their feet." (v. 6)

The flight of the Nephites now became a rout; a state of confused running for safety, or from danger. Those Nephites who were swifter in their movements than were the Lamanites, escaped the horrors of Lamanitish brutality; however, those whose flight did not carry them faster than the Lamanites, were slaughtered under circumstances of atrocity and cruelty.

VERSES 8-24. *I, Mormon do not desire to harrow up the souls of men in casting before them such an awful scene of bloodshed and carnage as was laid before mine eyes.* By any words of his own that would depict the awful scenes presented here, Mormon, with great care and anxiety, hesitated to picture to any future readers of

are hid must be revealed upon the house-tops—

9. And also that a knowledge of these things must come unto the remnant of these people, and also unto the Gentiles, who the Lord hath said should scatter this people, and this people should be counted as naught among them— therefore I write a small abridgment, daring not to give a full account of the things which I have seen, because of the commandment which I have received, and also that ye might not have too great sorrow because of the wickedness of this people.

10. And now behold, this I speak unto their seed, and also to the Gentiles who have care for the house of Israel, that realize and know from whence their blessings come.

11. For I know that such will sorrow for the calamity of the house of Israel; yea, they will sorrow for the destruction of this people; they will sorrow that this people had not repented that they might have been clasped in the arms of Jesus.

12. Now these things are written unto the remnant of the house of Jacob; and they are written after this manner, because it is known of God that wickedness will not bring them forth unto them; and they are to be hid up unto the Lord that they may come forth in his own due time.

13. And this is the command-

his account what lay about him lest it "harrow up" their souls, and at the same time, be too painful to their hearts and perplexing to their minds. But, nevertheless, for a wise purpose, the knowledge of them must be made known to future generations that they might learn to be more wise than his people, the Nephites, were. Therefore, Mormon makes but brief mention of the brutality exhibited on each side of the war. In the preceding chapter, he refers to the conditions then existing in these words: "And it is impossible for the tongue to describe, or for man to write a perfect description of the horrible scene of the blood and carnage which was among the people, both of the Nephites and of the Lamanites; and every heart was hardened, so that they delighted in the shedding of blood continually." (Mormon 4:11)

Although his words were restrained, his purpose was not. In this chapter (5) Mormon brings forth and emphasizes a great lesson that permeates the history of Lehi's seed as found in the Book of Mormon. It is this: When the fathers of the Nephite and Lamanite Races were about to embark upon the unchartered journey which the Lord had commanded, Nephi was promised of the Lord: "And inasmuch as ye shall keep My commandments, ye shall prosper, and shall be led to a Land of Promise; yea, even a land which I have prepared for you; yea, a land which is choice above all other lands. And inasmuch as thy brethren shall rebel against thee, they shall be cut off from the presence of the Lord. And inasmuch as thou shalt keep My commandments, thou shalt be made a ruler and a teacher over thy brethren. For behold, in that day that they shall rebel against Me, I will curse them even with a sore curse, and they shall have no power over thy seed except they shall rebel against Me also. And if it so be that they (thy seed) rebel against Me, they (the Lamanites) shall be a scourge unto thy seed, to stir them up in the ways of remembrance." (I Nephi 2:20-24; Italics and parentheses are the Editor's)

Throughout the whole of the Sacred Record this promise of the Lord to Nephi

ment which I have received; and behold, they shall come forth according to the commandment of the Lord, when he shall see fit, in his wisdom.

14. And behold, they shall go unto the unbelieving of the Jews; and for this intent shall they go — that they may be persuaded that Jesus is the Christ, the Son of the living God; that the Father may bring about, through his most Beloved, his great and eternal purpose, in restoring the Jews, or all the house of Israel, to the land of their inheritance, which the Lord their God hath given them, unto the fulfilling of his covenant;

15. And also that the seed of this people may more fully believe his gospel, which shall go forth unto them from the Gentiles; for this people shall be scattered, and shall become a dark, a filthy, and a loathsome people, beyond the description of that which ever hath been amongst us, yea, even that which hath been among the Lamanites, and this because of their unbelief and idolatry.

---

is referred to, and in turn was repeated by God's Nephite servants to each succeeding generation of His children. As in this case of which Mormon writes, it was because the people refused to obey the Lord and rebelled against keeping His commandments that the Lamanites had power over them. The Word of the Lord was repeatedly fulfilled both in the blessings promised and in the curses. It was so in the days of Mormon almost a thousand years after the promise was given to Nephi.

That promise also was made to the Brother of Jared, and is, as we have stated before, unto us who now dwell in this much favored land, and it is unto those who ever shall.[1]

Amid all the destruction that was about Mormon, the bloodshed and carnage, he delivered a message to all the inhabitants of the earth, to Jew and to Gentile; to the House of Israel wherever they may be scattered, and also to "a remnant of this people," who "were once a delightsome people, and they had Christ for their Shepherd; yea, they were led even by God the Father." (v. 17)

To the Jew, he says: "Jesus is the Son of God,"[2] and he prayed "that the Father may bring about, through His most Beloved, His great and eternal purpose, in restoring the Jews, or all the House of Israel, to the Land of their Inheritance, which the Lord their God hath given them, unto the fulfilling of His covenant."

---

[1]"And the Lord would not suffer that they should stop beyond the sea in the wilderness, but He would that they should come forth even unto the Land of Promise, which was choice above all other lands, which the Lord God had preserved for a righteous people. And He had sworn in His wrath unto the Brother of Jared, that whoso should possess this Land of Promise, from that time henceforth and forever, should serve Him, the true and only God, or they should be swept off when the fulness of His wrath should come upon them. And now we can behold the decrees of God concerning this land, that it is a Land of Promise; and whatsoever nation shall possess it shall serve God, or they shall be swept off when the fulness of His wrath cometh upon them when they are ripened in iniquity.

"For behold, this is a land which is choice above all other lands; wherefore he that doth possess it shall serve God or shall be swept off; for it is the everlasting decree of God. And it is not until the fulness of iniquity among the children of the land, that they are swept off. . . . Behold, this is a choice land, and whatsoever nation shall possess it shall be free from bondage, and from captivity, and from all other nations under heaven, if they will but serve the God of the land, who is Jesus Christ. . . ." (Ether 2:7-12)

[2]Mormon's son, Moroni, also addresses this message to "Jew and Gentile that Jesus is the Christ, the Eternal God, manifesting Himself unto all nations. . . ." Read the inspired Preface to the Book of Mormon.

16. For behold, the Spirit of the Lord hath already ceased to strive with their fathers; and they are without Christ and God in the world; and they are driven about as chaff before the wind.

17. They were once a delightsome people, and they had Christ for their shepherd; yea, they were led even by God the Father.

18. But now, behold, they are led about by Satan, even as chaff is driven before the wind, or as a vessel is tossed about upon the waves, without sail or anchor, or without anything wherewith to steer her; and even as she is, so are they.

19. And behold, the Lord hath reserved their blessings, which they might have received in the land, for the Gentiles who shall possess the land.

20. But behold, it shall come to pass that they shall be driven and scattered by the Gentiles; and after they have been driven and scattered by the Gentiles, behold, then will the Lord remember the covenant which he made unto Abraham and unto all the house of Israel.

21. And also the Lord will remember the prayers of the righteous, which have been put up unto him for them.

22. And then, O ye Gentiles, how can ye stand before the power of God, except ye shall repent and turn from your evil ways?

23. Know ye not that ye are in the hands of God? Know ye not that he hath all power, and at his great command the earth shall be rolled together as a scroll?

24. Therefore, repent ye, and humble yourselves before him, lest he shall come out in justice against you—lest a remnant of the seed of Jacob shall go forth among you as a lion, and tear you in pieces, and there is none to deliver.

To the Gentiles, he says: "Repent ye, and humble yourselves before Him, lest He come out in justice against you—lest a Remnant of the seed of Jacob shall go forth among you as a lion, and tear you in pieces, and there is none to deliver." (v. 24)

To a Remnant of this people, he says: "that," they "may more fully believe His Gospel, which shall go forth unto them from the Gentiles"; and to all the House of Israel, he says: That when that part of the House of Israel that had been transplanted to the Promised Land shall have been driven and scattered by the Gentiles—who esteemed them as naught—"Then will the Lord remember the Covenant which He made unto Abraham and unto all the House of Israel." (v. 20)

Of the Remnant of Lehi's seed which was left after the war of extermination that was then going on, Mormon tells us that they "shall be scattered, and shall become a dark, a filthy, and a loathsome people, beyond the description of that which ever hath been amongst us, yea, even that which hath been among the Lamanites, and this because of their unbelief and idolatry." Mormon further says: "And behold, the Lord hath reserved their blessings, which they might have received in the land, for the Gentiles who shall possess the land." (v. 19)

CHAPTER 6

1. *The Hill Cumorah and its records.*

1. And now I finish my record concerning the destruction of my people, the Nephites. And it came to pass that we did march forth before the Lamanites.

2. And I, Mormon, wrote an epistle unto the king of the Lamanites, and desired of him that he would grant unto us that we might gather together our people unto the land of Cumorah, by a hill which was called Cumorah, and there we could give them battle.

3. And it came to pass that the king of the Lamanites did grant unto me the thing which I desired.

4. And it came to pass that we did march forth to the land of Cumorah, and we did pitch our tents round about the hill Cumorah; and it was in a land of many waters, rivers, and fountains; and here we had hope to gain advantage over the Lamanites.

5. And when three hundred and eighty and four years had passed away, we had gathered in all the remainder of our people unto the land of Cumorah.

Verse 6. *I made this record out of the Plates of Nephi, and hid up in the Hill Cumorah all the records which had been entrusted to me by the hand of the Lord.* Mormon, almost overwhelmed with grief; his hopes vanished, and his fears fully realized, took the Plates of Nephi which Ammaron, the last of the Nephite historians, had placed in his care, and, finding space thereon, finished the record of his peoples' destruction.

Only a few details of their mass extermination is given by him, but enough is told us that we can see the power and the purpose of the Lord in the Nephites being swept off the face of the earth.

To begin the story of this phase of the struggle which Mormon knew was the last battle in the long period of warfare that had engulfed both the wicked Lamanites and the still more wicked Nephites, he tells of writing an epistle to the King of the Lamanites, requesting him to grant unto the Nephites time that therein might be gathered together his people in the Land called by them, Cumorah; near a Hill by the same name, and there give him battle. The King granted Mormon's request.

Mormon at its head, the Nephite Armies began the march which eventually took them to the Land of Cumorah. Only he, it seems, sensed that the proposed battle there would be the final struggle between the Nephites and the Lamanites. Only he, but it may be a few others, realized that God was not with them, nor with the Lamanites. Arrived at Cumorah, the Nephites pitched their tents around a Hill which was called by the same name. Cumorah was a land where there were many rivers and lakes, and here Mormon hoped "to gain advantage over the Lamanites."

6. And it came to pass that when we had gathered in all our people in one to the land of Cumorah, behold I, Mormon, began to be old; and knowing it to be the last struggle of my people, and having been commanded of the Lord that I should not suffer the records which had been handed down by our fathers, which were sacred, to fall into the hands of the Lamanites, (for the Lamanites would destroy them) therefore I made this record out of the plates of Nephi, and hid up in the hill Cumorah all the records which had been entrusted to me by the hand of the Lord, save it were these few plates which I gave unto my son Moroni.

2. *The final struggle between the two nations.*

3. *The Lamanites victorious.*

4. *Only twenty-four Nephites survive.*

7. And it came to pass that my people, with their wives and their children, did now behold the armies of the Lamanites marching towards them; and with that awful fear of death which fills the breasts of all the wicked, did they await to receive them.

8. And it came to pass that they came to battle against us, and every soul was filled with terror because of the greatness of their numbers.

9. And it came to pass that they did fall upon my people with the sword, and with the bow, and with the arrow, and with the ax, and with all manner of weapons of war.

10. And it came to pass that my men were hewn down, yea, even my ten thousand who were with me, and I fell wounded in the midst; and they passed by me that they did not put an end to my life.

Now, in the 385th year, the Nephites had gathered into one group all those who claimed an affiliation with their cause. But by this time Mormon was getting old, and perhaps a little feeble for such a strenuous undertaking as the one in which he was engaged. He, knowing as we have stated, that the impending battle would be the last violent effort of both sides to annihilate the other, took the records and other sacred things which were in his possession, for the Lord had commanded him to suffer them not to fall into the hands of the Lamanites, for he says, "The Lamanites would destroy them," and after making a record of these times on the Plates of Nephi, he hid them all in the Hill Cumorah save "these few plates which I gave to my son, Moroni."

VERSES 8-22. *The Lamanites did come to battle against us.* When the forces of the Nephites, plus their women and children, saw the Lamanites approaching, they were filled with terror, a sort of intense or violent dread, that filled their hearts. The wicked fear and tremble when brought face to face with death. The awful fear of which Mormon writes, is the opposite of the fear of God, which means that reverence for Him that leads to obedience because of one's realization of His power,

11. And when they had gone through and hewn down all my people save it were twenty and four of us, (among whom was my son Moroni) and we having survived the dead of our people, did behold on the morrow, when the Lamanites had returned unto their camps, from the top of the hill Cumorah, the ten thousand of my people who were hewn down, being led in the front by me.

12. And we also beheld the ten thousand of my people who were led by my son Moroni.

13. And behold, the ten thousand of Gidgiddonah had fallen, and he also in the midst.

14. And Lamah had fallen with his ten thousand; and Gilgal had fallen with his ten thousand; and Limhah had fallen with his ten thousand; and Joneam had fallen with his ten thousand; and Camenihah, and Moronihah, and Antionum, and Shiblom, and Shem, and Josh, had fallen with their ten thousand each.

15. And it came to pass that

as well as of His love toward man. The Psalmist wrote of evil men and their works; his words may apply not only to the Lamanites, but also to the Nephites: ". . . They are corrupt, they have done abominable works, there is none that doeth good. The Lord looked down from Heaven upon the children of men, to see if there were any that did understand, and seek God. They are all gone aside, they are all together become filthy: there is none that doeth good, no, not one. Have all the workers of iniquity no knowledge? who eat up My people as they eat bread, and call not upon the Lord. There were they in great fear; for God is in the generation of the righteous. . . ." (Psalm 14:1-5) A better description of both peoples cannot be had than this.

Despair and anguish took possession of the hearts of the Nephites because the numbers of the Lamanites were so great.

The Jews, when apostate nations and men defiled their Altars of God, it is said that one of their number, Judah Maccabaeus led the loyal and dutiful members of his faith to a grand and glorious victory. However, there were many righteous among them, but their numbers were small. When they saw the greatness of the numbers of their enemies, they said, "How can we be able, being a small company, to fight against so great and strong a multitude?" Judah answered: "With the God of Heaven it is all one to save by many or by few. And all the people shall know that there is One Who redeemeth and saveth Israel." Would to God there had been some righteous ones among the Nephites. Their history might have been different; their end less horrible.

With terrifying yells, we imagine, the Lamanites pounced upon the waiting Nephites with every weapon of which they knew. Soon the whole battlefield was covered with the dead and wounded, and it was not long until the ten thousand soldiers commanded by Mormon who led the Nephites into the fray were "hewn down." Presently other thousands followed in death. Thousands upon thousands of Nephites were hewn down, and at length the battle-weary Lamanites left the field, their gory work accomplished and their hatred gratified.

Of the many thousands of Nephites who only a short time before had prepared for the ensuing battle which they hoped to win, only twenty-four — who included Mormon and his son, Moroni — were spared from Lamanitish fury, and on the

there were ten more who did fall
by the sword, with their ten thousand each; yea, even all my people, save it were those twenty and
four who were with me, and also
a few who had escaped into the
south countries, and a few who
had dissented over unto the Lamanites, had fallen; and their
flesh, and bones, and blood lay
upon the face of the earth, being
left by the hands of those who
slew them to molder upon the
land, and to crumble and to return to their mother earth.

16. And my soul was rent with
anguish, because of the slain of
my people, and I cried:

17. O ye fair ones, how could
ye have departed from the ways
of the Lord! O ye fair ones, how
could ye have rejected that Jesus,
who stood with open arms to receive you!

18. Behold, if ye had not done
this, ye would not have fallen.
But behold, ye are fallen, and I
mourn your loss.

19. O ye fair sons and daughters, ye fathers and mothers, ye
husbands and wives, ye fair ones,
how is it that ye could have
fallen!

20. But behold, ye are gone,
and my sorrows cannot bring
your return.

21. And the day soon cometh
that your mortal must put on immortality, and these bodies which
are now moldering in corruption
must soon become incorruptible
bodies; and then ye must stand
before the judgment-seat of
Christ, to be judged according to

---

morrow, from the top of the Hill Cumorah, beheld the work of the Lamanites.
Although Mormon was wounded in the combat and left by the enemy as dead,
he survived, but was later killed by the marauding Lamanites who sought every
Nephite to slay, even those who had escaped into the country south.

We may conceive the anguish with which Mormon said his "soul was rent," as
he viewed the remains of "what might have been," and pondered in his heart
that his people who were now gone and their dead bodies left on the field to
molder, and crumble, and to return to their mother earth, might have still lived
if only they had been faithful and firm in keeping the commandments of God
as did their fathers in former generations.

In bitter distress, he cried: "O ye fair ones, how could ye have departed from
the ways of the Lord! O ye fair ones, how could ye have rejected that Jesus, Who
stood with open arms to receive you!" But now it was vain to ask them, *Why?*
They had procrastinated too long the day of their repentance, and the vengeance of
a just God had been visited upon them even to their utter destruction.

In the Nephites' destruction we are reminded of the words of the Prophet Isaiah
concerning the Jews of his day. They are akin in thought to the words of Mormon.
Isaiah said: "Therefore as the fire devoureth the stubble, and the flame consumeth
the chaff, so their root shall be as rottenness, and their blossom shall go up as
dust: because they have cast away the law of the Lord of hosts, and despised the
word of the Holy One of Israel. Therefore is the anger of the Lord kindled against
His people, and He hath stretched forth His hand against them, and hath smitten
them. (Isaiah 5:24-25)

Mormon continued his prayerful cries, not so much to his fallen brethren, for
they were dead, but more to us, the living, unto us to whom his words have come.
"Your mortal," he says, "must put on immortality, and your bodies which are now

your works; and if it so be that ye are righteous, then are ye blessed with your fathers who have gone before you.

22. O that ye had repented before this great destruction had come upon you. But behold, ye are gone, and the Father, yea, the Eternal Father of heaven, knoweth your state; and he doeth with you according to his justice and mercy.

---

moldering in corruption must soon become incorruptible bodies." And then when your bodies have rid themselves of all earthly impurities, and are no longer subject to decay, "You must stand before the Judgment-Seat of Christ to be judged according to your works; and if it so be that ye are righteous, then are ye blessed with your fathers who have gone before you." (v. 21)

But again his sorrowful heart returns to thoughts of his brethren. Again their pitiable state calls forth another prayer from him, and again despair and anguish rend his soul. Again Mormon cries: "O that ye had repented before this great destruction had come upon you. But, ye are gone, and the Father of Heaven, knoweth your state; and He doeth with you according to His justice and mercy." (v. 22)

CHAPTER 7

1. Mormon affirms to Lamanites that they are of the House of Israel.

1. And now, behold, I would speak somewhat unto the remnant of this people who are spared, if it so be that God may give unto them my words, that they may know of the things of their fathers; yea, I speak unto you, ye remnant of the house of Israel; and these are the words which I speak:

2. Know ye that ye are of the house of Israel.

2. Admonishes them for their Salvation.

3. Know ye that ye must come unto repentance, or ye cannot be saved.

4. Know ye that ye must lay down your weapons of war, and delight no more in the shedding

---

VERSES 1-2. *Know ye not that ye are of the House of Israel.* Mormon's great concern now was about the survivors of the battle that had ended so ingloriously for the Nephites. They had lost many thousands of men, not counting women and children, but the Lamanites also had suffered severe losses. Both nations were near equal in strength, man for man. However, the Lamanites were more numerous than were the Nephites, but in spite of their numerical superiority we may assume that their losses were equal in manpower to that of the Nephites. Wickedness had a great accounting that day.

Many of the Lamanites were Nephite apostates, but nevertheless they were of the House of Israel, and entitled to the blessings of the Covenant God made with Abraham which was repeated to his grandson, Jacob. All true Lamanites, that is, we mean, actual descendants of Laman and Lemuel, were also Israelites, which brings Mormon to express the point: "Know ye that ye are of the House of Israel."

VERSE 3. *Know ye that ye must come unto repentance, or ye cannot be saved.* Mormon knew of the many faults and iniquities of the Lamanites, for had he not battled against their wicked ways, lo, for many years? Had he not been a preacher of righteousness, as well as military leader? Many times, especially in his younger days, he had called on them to repent, and now, as by inspiration, he wrote to the remnant of those who survived the slaughter of the recent battle that they, too, must repent of the wicked ways into which their fathers had led them, or, he warned, "Ye cannot be saved."

VERSE 4. *Know ye that ye must lay down your weapons of war.* Murder and bloodshed, even if it is called war, unless God commands it, is not consistent with the Gospel of Christ. In no way does it find place in the Plan of Salvation. Taking a human life, except by law, is murder, and is the greatest of sins when committed against the light and knowledge of God. (Alma 39:6)

Mormon's teachings wherein he says that "ye must lay down your weapons of war, and delight no more in the shedding of blood, and take them not again, save it be that God shall command you," are an important part of the Gospel's fulness.

of blood, and take them not again, save it be that God shall command you.

5. Know ye that ye must come to the knowledge of your fathers, and repent of all your sins and iniquities, and believe in Jesus Christ, that he is the Son of God, and that he was slain by the Jews, and by the power of the Father he hath risen again, whereby he hath gained the victory over the grave; and also in him is the sting of death swallowed up.

6. And he bringeth to pass the resurrection of the dead, whereby man must be raised to stand before his judgment-seat.

7. And he hath brought to pass the redemption of the world, whereby he that is found guiltless before him at the judgment day hath it given unto him to dwell in the presence of God in his kingdom, to sing ceaseless praises with the choirs above, unto the Father, and unto the Son, and unto the Holy Ghost, which are one God, in a state of happiness which hath no end.

When the converted Lamanites who took upon themselves the name of their King, Anti-Nephi-Lehi, who also was a convert to the teachings of Christ as announced by the sons of Mosiah, they buried deep in the earth their weapons of war, and covenanted not to again take them up even in defense of their own lives. We recommend the reader to peruse most carefully Chapters 24 and 25 of the Book of Alma wherein this doctrine is fully elucidated.

VERSE 5. . . . *Ye must believe in Jesus Christ.* . . . Know that ye must come to the knowledge your fathers once had, "that Jesus is the Christ, that He is the Son of God, and that He was slain by the Jews, and by the power of the Father He hath risen again, whereby He hath gained the victory over the grave; and also in Him is the sting of death swallowed up."[1] (v. 5)

The foregoing is a brief, but consistent statement of Gospel truths. In a concise form, these are the requirements of the Gospel Plan and every believer in the divinity of Christ must have faith that they are true. Believing so, in him is made manifest the power of God unto Salvation. To Mormon's mind he recalled the history of those times of the Nephites (there were no Lamanites) when the knowledge of God and His marvelous ways was had by even the humblest among the people. He remembered reading the words of Jesus as recorded by Nephi, the Disciple who kept the records: "And now, behold, My joy is great, even unto fulness, because of you, and also this generation; yea, and even the Father rejoiceth, and also all the holy angels, because of you and this generation; for none of them are lost." (III Nephi 27:30) Now, to Mormon, all seemed lost. But he also remembered the promises of the Lord to his fathers that the remnant of this people would some

---

[1]These Doctrines as preached by Mormon are briefly stated, and were so proclaimed by Paul when he preached unto the Corinthians. You will remember that Paul was a very little man; he was lame and personally unimpressive as he himself says in one of his Epistles. The Apostle Paul, dwelling in that poor, miserable, decrepit tent, the body of Paul, the tentmaker; feeling his infirmities, but realizing his victory through Jesus Christ, solemnly laid his hand upon his breast, and we imagine he said something like this: You may wonder at it, ye sophists of Greece, and you incredulous of Rome, but this poor mortal that you see, with all these certain traces of death, shall be swallowed up in everlasting and glorious victory; as it is written; O death, where is thy sting? O grave, where is thy victory? And then he says: The sting of death is sin . . . and concludes in a most triumphal shout: *Thanks be to God, which giveth us the victory through our Lord Jesus Christ.* (See, last ten verses of I Corinthians)

8. Therefore repent, and be baptized in the name of Jesus, and lay hold upon the gospel of Christ, which shall be set before you, not only in this record but also in the record which shall come unto the Gentiles from the Jews, which record shall come from the Gentiles unto you.

---

day have the Gospel preached unto them, and they should become a white and a delightsome people. Mormon rejoiced in the promises of the Lord, and the thought that at some future time when righteousness again prevailed, he with them would dwell in the presence of God in His Kingdom, and there sing ceaseless praises with the choirs above,[2] unto the Father, and unto the Son, and unto the Holy Ghost, which are one God, in a state of happiness which hath no end." (v. 7)

VERSE 8. *Repent, and be baptized in the Name of Jesus.* Mormon, now admonishes all who may at some future time read the words he writes, "to repent, and be baptized in the Name of Jesus, and lay hold upon the Gospel of Christ." Which Gospel shall be made known unto them, he affirms, not only in the records of their fathers that have been kept from generation to generation, but also a record of the Jews that contain these things which shall come unto them through the Gentiles.[3]

---

[2]*With the choirs above.* Mormon, here expresses the thought that those who are found guiltless before the Judgment-Seat of Christ, shall be given a place to dwell in the Kingdom of God, and there sing ceaseless praises with the choirs above, unto the Father, and unto the Son, and unto the Holy Ghost. Compare Mosiah 28, King Benjamin also expresses a desire to be fully prepared to "join the choirs above."

Does it seem improbable that there are choirs in the realm inhabited by the Redeemed? The ability to sing and compose music is a divine gift. The very purpose of it is to enable man to praise the Lord and to glorify His name.

We know that John the Beloved, on several occasions in his Apocalyptic visions, became aware of singing and music of heavenly origin. (Revelation 5:9; 14:3; 15:3) We also know that at the time of the birth of our Lord, a heavenly host sang praises to God, audible to mortal ear. (Luke 2:13-14)

And here, let me, Janne M. Sjodahl (co-author of this commentary), in all humility, place on record that to my own personal knowledge, singing and music were heard in the Manti Temple at the time of its dedication. On two separate occasions I had the privilege of hearing the super-earthly harmonies. The first was just before the beginning of the services on the day I attended. It sounded as a very distant organ music, for a brief moment, as if a door had been suddenly opened, and then almost immediately closed. The second occasion was a few days later, when I was preparing to do some ordinance work for some of my friends on the other side. It sounded as the singing of male voices, also for a brief moment, and came as from far distance. There were other manifestations during those days, never to be forgotten. During the service I noticed that some of the Twelve, notably Elder Heber J. Grant, and also John W. Taylor, were surrounded by rays of light, resembling the colors of a rainbow, only softer.

Yes, there are choirs on the other side, and bands, and John describes their performances as "the voice of many waters, and as the voice of a great thunder . . . and the voice of harpers harping with their harps." (Revelation 14:2)

[3]"And it came to pass that I, Nephi, beheld that they did prosper in the land; and I beheld a book, and it was carried forth among them. And the angel said unto them: Knowest thou the meaning of the book? And I said unto him: I know not. And he said: Behold it proceedeth out of the mouth of a Jew. And I, Nephi, beheld it; and he said unto me: The book that thou beholdest is a record of the Jews, which contains the covenants of the Lord, which he hath made unto the house of Israel; and it also containeth many of the prophecies of the holy prophets; and it is a record like unto the engravings which are upon the plates of brass, save there are not so many; nevertheless, they contain the covenants of the Lord, which he hath made unto the house of Israel; wherefore, they are of great worth unto the Gentiles. And the angel of the Lord said unto me: Thou hast beheld that the book proceeded forth from the mouth of a Jew; and when it proceeded forth from the mouth of a Jew it contained the plainness of the gospel of the Lord, of whom the twelve apostles bear record

9. For behold, this is written for the intent that ye may believe that; and if ye believe that ye will believe this also; and if ye believe this ye will know con- | cerning your fathers, and also the marvelous works which were wrought by the power of God among them.

VERSE 9. *This is written that ye may believe these things.* This verse contains Mormon's appeal to those who should live, when, in the Lord's own due time, He will cause the Records of their forefathers, and the Records of the Jews to come unto them whose father's bodies are now moldering in dust upon the field of battle, and whose time of repentance was procrastinated too long. His desire was to add his own to the testimony of these two records. For, Mormon infers, that if you believe the Gospel as it is made known to you by the Jewish Records which will come to you through the Gentiles, you will believe my words; and further he says that if you believe what is written in the Records of the Jews, you will believe what is written about your forefathers, and will also see wherein the words of Lehi, your venerable ancestor, were indeed true when in past ages they were literally fulfilled in God's wonderful ways among his descendants: "Great and marvelous are Thy works, O Lord God Almighty." (I Nephi 1:14) Mormon here uses other words, but in them expresses the same idea; he says: "Ye will know concerning your fathers, and also the marvelous works which were wrought by the power of God among them." (v. 9)

according to the truth which is in the Lamb of God. Wherefore, these things go forth from the Jews in purity unto the Gentiles, according to the truth which is in God.

"And after they go forth by the hand of the twelve apostles of the Lamb, from the Jews unto the Gentiles, thou seest the foundation of a great and abominable church, which is most abominable above all other churches; for behold, they have taken away from the gospel of the Lamb many parts which are plain and most precious; and also many covenants of the Lord have they taken away. And all this have they done that they might pervert the right ways of the Lord, that they might blind the eyes and harden the hearts of the children of men. Wherefore, thou seest that after the book hath gone forth through the hands of the great and abominable church, that there are many plain and precious things taken away from the book, which is the book of the Lamb of God. And after these plain and precious things were taken away it goeth forth unto all the nations of the Gentiles; and after it goeth forth unto all the nations of the Gentiles, yea, even across the many waters which thou hast seen with the Gentiles which have gone forth out of captivity, thou seest—because of the many plain and precious things which have been taken out of the book, which were plain unto the understanding of the children of men, according to the plainness which is in the Lamb of God—because of these things which are taken away out of the gospel of the Lamb, an exceeding great many do stumble, yea insomuch that Satan hath great power over them." (I Nephi 13:20-29)

"And it came to pass that I beheld the remnant of the seed of my brethren, and also the book of the Lamb of God, which had proceeded forth from the mouth of the Jew, that it came forth from the Gentiles unto the remnant of the seed of my brethren. And after it had come forth unto them I beheld other books, which came forth by the power of the Lamb, from the Gentiles unto them, unto the convincing of the Gentiles and the remnant of the seed of my brethren, and also the Jews who were scattered upon all the face of the earth, that the records of the prophets and of the twelve apostles of the Lamb are true. And the angel spake unto me, saying: These last records, which thou hast seen among the Gentiles, shall establish the truth of the first, which are of the twelve apostles of the Lamb, and shall make known the plain and precious things which have been taken away from them; and shall make known to all kindreds, tongues, and people, that the Lamb of God is the Son of the Eternal Father, and the Savior of the world; and that all men must come unto him, or they cannot be saved. And they must come according to the words which shall be established by the mouth of the Lamb; and the words of the Lamb shall be made known in the records of thy seed, as well as in the records of the twelve apostles of the Lamb; wherefore they both shall be established in one; for there is one God and one Shepherd over all the earth." (*Ibid.,* 38-41)

10. And ye will also know that ye are a remnant of the seed of Jacob; therefore ye are numbered among the people of the first covenant; and if it so be that ye believe in Christ, and are baptized, first with water, then with fire and with the Holy Ghost, following the example of our Savior, according to that which he hath commanded us, it shall be well with you in the day of judgment. Amen.

VERSE 10. *You will also know that ye are a remnant of the Seed of Jacob.* With a pride only exceeded by his knowledge of their mutual heritage, Mormon avers that they are of the Seed of Jacob, and as such are numbered among those of the House of Israel. They are by the fact of being such, heirs of the Priesthood, and children—even if they were wayward—of the Most High God. They were estitled to every blessing of righteousness which the Lord, the Mighty Judge, promised, if only they would repent and do no more the things they should not do, and do that which they should do.

"And if it so be that ye believe in Christ," Mormon tells them in his admonishing them, "and are baptized, first with water, then with fire and with the Holy Ghost, following the example of our Savior, according to that which He hath commanded us, it shall be well with you in the Day of Judgment."

CHAPTER 8

1. *Moroni finishes his father's record.*

2. *After the carnage of Cumorah.*

1. Behold I, Moroni, do finish the record of my father, Mormon. Behold, I have but few things to write, which things I have been commanded by my father.

2. And now it came to pass that after the great and tremendous battle at Cumorah, behold, the Nephites who had escaped into the country southward were hunted by the Lamanites, until they were all destroyed.

3. *Mormon among the slain.*

3. And my father also was killed by them, and I even remain alone to write the sad tale of the destruction of my people. But behold, they are gone, and I fulfil the commandment of my father. And whether they will slay me, I know not.

VERSES 1-2. *Behold, I, Moroni, do finish the record of my father, Mormon.* Feeling that the Lamanites, who already were in ascendancy of the Nephites, would destroy the records if they fell into their hands, Mormon hid all of the plates which contained said records in the Hill Cumorah. He hid all of them except a few which he gave to his son, Moroni, with instructions to engrave thereon certain things the nature of which is evident in the things Moroni thereafter wrote.

The spite which they had in their hearts for all Nephites, and their intense hatred towards them, were so keen and inexhaustible that the Lamanites, even after their victory at Cumorah, hunted and destroyed those of the Nephites who had escaped into "the country southward."

VERSE 3. *My father also was killed by them.* The lonesomeness that filled Moroni's heart was made the more acute by the realization also that the Lamanites had killed his father, Mormon. Through all the vicissitudes of battle and preaching the Gospel, in their anxiety for the safety of each other, Mormon and Moroni had been more than father and son; they had been companions. Now that relationship was broken by Mormon's death, and Moroni was left alone to write "the sad tale of the destruction of my people." To this end and because his father had so commanded, Moroni wrote the bitter story of the extinction of this once divinely favored people.

Moroni, all his kinsfolk slain by the Lamanites, expected that he himself would, at any moment, be a victim of Lamanitish hatred; not knowing, he says, "whether they will slay me," he takes a collected retrospect of all his past life, and expresses no regrets and offers no apologies, pretexts or excuses, but enters calmly and even joyously upon the prospect of his coming doom and neither flinches nor fears it. He says, "How long the Lord will suffer that I may live I know not."

4. Therefore I will write and hide up the records in the earth; and whither I go it mattereth not.

5. Behold, my father hath made this record, and he hath written the intent thereof. And behold, I would write it also if I had room upon the plates, but I have not; and ore I have none, for I am alone. My father hath been slain in battle, and all my kinsfolk, and I have not friends nor whither to go; and how long the Lord will suffer that I may live I know not.

4. Lamanites and robbers possess the land.

6. Behold, four hundred years have passed away since the coming of our Lord and Savior.

7. And behold, the Lamanites have hunted my people, the Nephites, down from city to city and from place to place, even until they are no more; and great has been their fall; yea, great and marvelous is the destruction of my people, the Nephites.

8. And behold, it is the hand of the Lord which hath done it. And behold also, the Lamanites are at war one with another; and the whole face of this land is one continual round of murder and bloodshed; and no one knoweth the end of the war.

9. And now, behold, I say no more concerning them, for there are none save it be the Lamanites and robbers that do exist upon the face of the land.

VERSE 4. *I will write and hide the Records in the earth.* Complying with the instructions Moroni had received from his father, he commenced the work of finishing the Record Mormon had made. At length, not only did he consummate the work he had been assigned, but for its safety he decided to hide the Record in the earth.

In the fifth verse, Moroni notes that his father had included in the Record he was making the intent for which he wrote. (*See,* Mormon 7:9) If there had been more space upon the Plates to write, Moroni informs us that he, too, would write his own purpose. However, that he was forced to forego. The intent, or purpose of both father and son was that in any future development, their testimony concerning God's wonderful ways in dealing with the former inhabitants of this Promised Land might be made known to some future generations of their descendants. But, he says that he has no "ore" to make additional plates, therefore the intent expressed by Mormon would also give vent to the satisfaction of his own desires.

VERSE 9. *There are none save it be the Lamanites and robbers that do exist upon the face of the land.* It was now four hundred years since the birth of the Savior, or the year 401 A.D., that the Lamanites became the complete and sole masters of the Western Hemisphere. They would not let what was left of the people of Nephi rest in the ignominy of defeat, but hunted them down wherever they might be, until all had been found and slain. The wonder of it was that their utter destruction had been brought about by their own iniquity, the Lord using the Lamanites to punish the Nephites for their wickedness.

The Lamanites, not content with the defeat of the Nephites, began a war among themselves. Their bloodthirstiness, and the love they had for killing, were not gratified in the slaying of their enemies, but that measure of their want was

10. And there are none that do know the true God save it be the disciples of Jesus, who did tarry in the land until the wickedness of the Lord would not suffer them to remain with the people; and whether they be upon the face of the land no man knoweth.

11. But behold, my father and I have seen them, and they have ministered unto us.

in a way gratified only with them taking the lives of their neighbors. Moroni tells us that "the Lamanites are at war one with another; and the whole face of this land is one continual round of murder and bloodshed; and no one knoweth the end of the war." (v. 8)

Moroni closes his description of Lamanitish atrocities, because he could find no good to relate of them; noting in doing so that there are none but "the Lamanites and robbers that do exist upon the face of the land."

When the days of that last fearful struggle were ended, all but twenty-four of the Nephite Race had been, by the hand of violence, swept into untimely graves, save a few, a very few, who had fled into the South Country. The powers, the glories, the beauties of this favored branch of Israel's chosen Tribe had sunk beneath a sea of blood; the Word of God, which they had so long disregarded, was vindicated; the warnings of His servants were fulfilled.

The Lamanites were now rulers of the Western World, their traditional enemies being utterly destroyed. But they did not cultivate peace; no sooner were the Nephites obliterated, than they commenced fighting among themselves. The lonely Moroni, the last of the Nephites, tells us, 400 A.D., that the Lamanites are at war one with another; and the face of the land is one continual round of murder and bloodshed; and no man knoweth the end of the war. And again, he writes yet later: "Their wars are exceeding fierce among themselves."

Such was the sad condition of the Lamanite race in the early part of the fifth century after Christ. There the inspired Record closes; henceforth we have nothing but uncertain tradition. The various contending tribes, in their thirst for blood so long slaked, sank deeper and deeper into savage degradation; the arts of civilization were almost entirely lost to the great mass of the people. Decades and centuries passed away, and after a time, in some parts of this chosen land, a better state of things slowly arose. In Central America and Mexico, in Peru and other places, the foundations of new empires were laid, in which were built up gradually civilizations peculiarly their own, but in many ways bearing record to the idiosyncrasies of their ancient predecessors. Of this we have here little to do; many of their traditions (though disregarded by nearly all) bear testimony to the truth of the Book of Mormon, and we have the unequivocal assurance that the words of their ancient prophets recorded therein have been fulfilled to the very letter in their humiliation; and as they have drunk to the dregs from the cup of bitterness of the wrath of God, so is the glorious day now dawning, when the light of the eternal Gospel shall illumine the hearts of their children; fill them with the love of God; renew their ancient faith and steadfastness, and make them the fitting instruments in His hands of accomplishing all His holy purposes with regard to them, in which also shall be fulfilled all the gracious, glorious promises made by Jehovah to this transplanted Branch of the Olive Tree of Israel.

VERSE 10. *There are none that do know the true God save it be the Disciples of Jesus.* (See, III Nephi, Chapter 28) The three Disciples of Christ, who, Moroni says, "did tarry in the land until the wickedness of the people was so great that the Lord would not suffer them to remain with the people," alone of all the inhabitants of

5. Mormon's record to come out of the earth.

12. And whoso receiveth this record, and shall not condemn it because of the imperfections which are in it, the same shall know of greater things than these. Behold, I am Moroni; and were it possible, I would make all things known unto you.

13. Behold, I make an end of speaking concerning this people. I am the son of Mormon, and my father was a descendant of Nephi.

14. And I am the same who hideth up this record unto the Lord; the plates thereof are of no worth, because of the commandment of the Lord. For he truly saith that no one shall have them to get gain; but the record thereof is of great worth; and whoso shall bring it to light, him will the Lord bless.

15. For none can have power to bring it to light save it be given him of God; for God wills that it shall be done with an eye single to his glory, or the welfare of the ancient and long dispersed covenant people of the Lord.

16. And blessed be he that shall bring this thing to light; for

---

the land, knew the true God, and he further says: "Whether they be upon the face of the land no man knoweth. But behold, my father and I have seen them, and they have ministered unto us."

VERSE 12. *And whoso receiveth this record, and shall not condemn it because of the imperfections which are in it, the same shall know of greater things than these.* (See, Foreword COMMENTARY ON THE BOOK OF MORMON, Volume VII, The Bible and the Book of Mormon)

VERSES 13-14. *I am the son of Mormon, and my father was a descendant of Nephi.* After giving a brief notation of his ancestry, Moroni avers that he it is who "hideth up this Record unto the Lord," meaning that it is hidden up awaiting the purposes of the Almighty which in due time will be made known. The Record, or the Plates upon which the Record is engraven, is of no material value to the holder thereof because the Word of the Lord is to that effect. The gold of which they are made, shall be, in the case of false ownership, counted as dross, as skum from molten ore or metal; waste matter or refuse. But, however, the Record itself is of great worth, and him will the Lord bless whosoever bringeth forth unto man, the knowledge therein impounded.

VERSES 15-16. *None can have power to bring it to light save it be given unto him of God.* The great purpose to which the Record of these ancient people is consecrated, is that it might be, by His holy Spirit, rendered greatest to the glory of God, and most for the welfare of "the ancient and long-dispersed covenant people of the Lord," the House of Israel.

By the power of God, and none other, this Record shall come unto the knowledge of the people who dwell upon all the earth. That which is hidden shall be made known; it shall be found, and that which is dark shall be made light; as a lamp that was hid in a dark place, it shall shine forth.

The coming forth of this Record was prophesied of by Lehi when that great leader gave a blessing to his son, Joseph. In words most easily understood, he told Joseph, his son, in speaking of Joseph, who was sold into Egypt:

it shall be brought out of darkness unto light, according to the word of God; yea, it shall be brought out of the earth, and it shall shine forth out of darkness, and come unto the knowledge of the people; and it shall be done by the power of God.

"For Joseph truly testified, saying: A seer shall the Lord my God raise up, who shall be a choice seer unto the fruit of my loins.

"Yea, Joseph truly said: Thus saith the Lord unto me: A choice seer will I raise up out of the fruit of thy loins; and he shall be esteemed highly among the fruit of thy loins. And unto him will I give commandment that he shall do a work for the fruit of thy loins, his brethren, which shall be of great worth unto them, even to the bringing of them to the knowledge of the covenants which I have made with thy fathers.

"And I will give unto him a commandment that he shall do none other work, save the work which I shall command him. And I will make him great in mine eyes; for he shall do my work.

"And he shall be great like unto Moses, whom I have said I would raise up unto you, to deliver my people, O house of Israel.

"And Moses will I raise up, to deliver thy people out of the land of Egypt.

"But a seer will I raise up out of the fruit of thy loins; and unto him will I give power to bring forth my word unto the seed of thy loins—and not to the bringing forth my word only, saith the Lord, but to the convincing them of my word, which shall have already gone forth among them.

"Wherefore, the fruit of thy loins shall write; and the fruit of the loins of Judah shall write; and that which shall be written by the fruit of thy loins, and also that which shall be written by the fruit of the loins of Judah, shall grow together, unto the confounding of false doctrines and laying down of contentions, and establishing peace among the fruit of thy loins, and bringing them to the knowledge of their fathers in the latter days, and also to the knowledge of my covenants saith the Lord.

"And out of weakness he shall be made strong, in that day when my work shall commence among all my people, unto the restoring thee, O house of Israel, saith the Lord.

"And thus prophesied Joseph, saying: Behold, that seer will the Lord bless; and they that seek to destoy him shall be confounded; for this promise, which I have obtained of the Lord, of the fruit of my loins, shall be fulfilled. Behold, I am sure of the fulfilling of this promise;

"And his name shall be called after me; and it shall be after the name of his father. And he shall be like unto me; for the thing which the Lord shall bring forth by his hand, by the power of the Lord shall bring my people unto salvation.

"Yea, thus prophesied Joseph: I am sure of this thing, even as I am sure of the promise of Moses; for the Lord hath said unto me, I will preserve thy seed forever." (II Nephi 3:6-16)

And the means whereby these Records will be made known to the children of men has been provided by the Lord. The *means* to this end were told by one Ammon from Zarahemla to King Limhi, in the Land of Nephi, as follows:

"Now Ammon said unto him: I can assuredly tell thee, O king, of a man that can translate the records; for he has wherewith that he can look, and translate all records that are of ancient date; and it is a gift from God. And the things are called interpreters, and no man can look in them except he be commanded, lest he should look for that he ought not and he should perish. And whosoever is commanded to look in them, the same is called seer.

"And behold, the king of the people who are in the land of Zarahemla is the man that is commanded to do these things, and who has this high gift from God.

"And the king said that a seer is greater than a prophet.

"And Ammon said that a seer is a revelator and a prophet also; and a gift which is greater can no man have, except he should possess the power of God, which no man can; yet a man may have great power given him from God.

"But a seer can know of things which are past, and also of things which are to come, and by them shall all things be revealed, or, rather, shall secret things be made manifest, and hidden things shall come to light, and things which are not known shall be made known by them, and also things shall be made known by them which otherwise could not be known.

"Thus God has provided a means that man, through faith, might work mighty miracles; therefore he becometh a great benefit to his fellow beings." (Mosiah 8:13-17)

The *means* whereby the knowledge contained in these Records shall be given unto the covenant people of the House of Israel is made mention in that which follows:

"And it came to pass that the Lord said unto the brother of Jared: Behold, thou shalt not suffer these things which ye have seen and heard to go forth unto the world, until the time cometh that I shall glorify my name in the flesh; wherefore, ye shall treasure up the things which ye have seen and heard, and show it to no man.

"And behold, when ye shall come unto me, ye shall write them and shall seal them up, that no one can interpret them; for ye shall write them in a language that they cannot be read.

"And behold, these two stones will I give unto thee, and ye shall seal them up also with the things which ye shall write.

"For behold, the language which ye shall write I have confounded; wherefore I will cause in my own due time that these stones shall magnify to the eyes of men these things which ye shall write.

"And when the Lord had said these words, he showed unto the brother of Jared all the inhabitants of the earth which had been, and also all that would be; and he withheld them not from his sight, even unto the ends of the earth.

"For he had said unto him in times before, that if he would believe in him that he could show unto him all things—it should be shown unto him; therefore the Lord could not withhold anything from him, for he knew that the Lord could show him all things.

"And the Lord said unto him: Write these things and seal them up; and I will show them in mine own due time unto the children of men.

"And it to pass that the Lord commanded him that he should seal up the two stones which he had received, and show them not, until the Lord should show them unto the children of men. (Ether 3:21-28)

The words of Jesus Christ, the Savior of mankind, spoken to the Nephites in the Land Bountiful when He ministered among them thereby confirm the words of his servants:

"And verily I say unto you, I give unto you a sign, that ye may know the time when these things shall be about to take place—that I shall gather in, from their long dispersion, my people, O house of Israel, and shall establish again among them my Zion;

"And behold, this is the thing which I will give unto you for a sign—for verily I say unto you that when these things which I declare unto you, and which I shall declare unto you hereafter of myself, and by the power of the Holy Ghost which shall be given unto you of the Father, shall be made known unto the Gentiles that they may know concerning this people who are a remnant of the house of Jacob, and concerning this my people who shall be scattered by them;

"Verily, verily, I say unto you, when these things shall be made known unto them of the Father, and shall come forth of the Father, from them unto you;

"For it is wisdom in the Father that they should be established in this land, and be set up as a free people by the power of the Father, that these things might come forth from them unto a remnant of your seed, that the covenant of the Father may

17. And if there be faults they be the faults of a man. But behold, we know no fault; nevertheless God knoweth all things; therefore, he that condemneth, let him be aware lest he shall be in danger of hell fire.

18. And he that saith: Show unto me, or ye shall be smitten— let him beware lest he command-

---

be fulfilled which he hath covenanted with his people, O house of Israel;

"Therefore, when these works and the works which shall be wrought among you hereafter shall come forth from the Gentiles, until your seed which shall dwindle in unbelief because of iniquity;

"For thus it behooveth the Father that it should come forth from the Gentiles, that he may show forth his power unto the Gentiles, for this cause that the Gentiles, if they will not harden their hearts, that they may repent and come unto me and be baptized in my name and know of the true points of my doctrine, that they may be numbered among my people, O house of Israel;

"And when these things come to pass that thy seed shall begin to know these things—it shall be a sign unto them, that they may know that the work of the Father hath already commenced unto the fulfilling of the covenant which he hath made unto the people who are of the house of Israel.

"And when that day shall come, it shall come to pass that kings shall shut their mouths; for that which had not been told them shall they see; and that which they had not heard shall they consider.

"For in that day, for my sake shall the Father work a work, which shall be a great and a marvelous work among them; and there shall be among them those who will not believe it, although a man shall declare it unto them.

"But behold, the life of my servant shall be in my hand; therefore they shall not hurt him, although he shall be marred because of them. Yet I will heal him, for I will show unto them that my wisdom is greater than the cunning of the devil.

"Therefore it shall come to pass that whosoever will not believe in my words, who am Jesus Christ, which the Father shall cause him to bring forth unto the Gentiles, and shall give unto him power that he shall bring them forth unto the Gentiles, (it shall be done even as Moses said) they shall be cut off from among my people who are of the covenant." (III Nephi 21:8-11)

VERSE 17. *If there be faults they be the faults of men.* (*See* Inspired Preface of the Book of Mormon; also *Foreword,* COMMENTARY ON THE BOOK OF MORMON, Volume VII, The Finger of God)

VERSE 18. *Show unto me, or ye shall be smitten.* Many there were who said to the Prophet Joseph Smith, 'Show unto me, or ye shall be smitten," demanding thereby to see the Gold Plates themselves from which God's Prophet, the promised Seer, translated the ancient Record. They threatened the Prophet, abused and sought to intimidate him that by any chance they might force him to show unto them the Plates. By them he was "smitten." He was arrested, tried, beaten, scourged, imprisoned; he was brought before their courts and accused of false crimes by witnesses suborned for that purpose. They imagined in their hearts that to destroy the Prophet, would be to get rid of the very idea of Mormonism. To this end they lost no time, nor left a thing undone. In consequence, the Prophet died as a Martyr. He sealed his testimony with his own blood. "Now," they said, "Mormonism must surely die." They thought that the heart-beats in the Prophet's breast, were the great heart-throbs of Mormonism. But in this they were mistaken! Mormonism is immortal. The Sacred Record is immortal. It will live on forever, because it has God for its author, Omnipotence for its Shield, and Eternity for its glorious life. Thanks, be to God, it like the Bible, will go on and on, to help the helpless and those who have no other helper but the Lord.

eth that which is forbidden of the Lord.

19. For behold, the same that judgeth rashly shall be judged rashly again; for according to his works shall his wages be; therefore, he that smiteth shall be smitten again, of the Lord.

20. Behold what the scripture says—man shall not smite, nei-

their shall he judge; for judgment is mine, saith the Lord, and vengeance is mine also, and I will repay.

21. And he that shall breathe out wrath and strifes against the work of the Lord, and against the covenant people of the Lord who are the house of Israel, and shall say: We will destroy the work of

---

The Prophet's enemies, as we have said, threatened him that if he did not show the Plates unto them, they would "smite" him; nevertheless, and in spite of their openly expressed intentions to inflict evil upon him, he remained firm in not doing that which the Lord had forbidden. (v. 18)

VERSES 19-20. *Man shall not smite, neither shall he judge.* It takes one higher than you or me to be a judge. We, being mortals, sometimes allow passion and prejudice to pronounce the opinions and judgments of our consciences. Therefore is the commandment given, "Thou shalt not judge." When it matters most, there will be but one Judge Who will preside in that court of righteous and holy decisions at the Last Day. The verdict of that tribunal will be final. Its findings of fact cannot be appealed. It will, nevertheless, judge justly, and its decisions will be according to mercy and truth.

Moroni cautions us not to judge imprudently, or as he says, "rashly," meaning thereby, not to be over-hasty, or false to ourselves in making our decisions. Therefore, if our decisions are not according to justice, we can expect that measure to be given us in return. "For according to his works shall his wages be." (v. 19) Moroni, in great regard for that eternal truth, reminds us, "He that smiteth shall be smitten again, of the Lord." Those who rashly judged the Prophet Joseph Smith to be a pious fraud and one worthy of death, were themselves smitten of the Lord.

We are reminded of a comment we made when studying IV Nephi, 34th verse; it concerns the Nephites in the days of Amos. The wicked, it appears, reviled at the righteous because of their righteousness, and the wrong-doer, they held in repute. The Sacred Record says, "And they did smite upon the people of Jesus." But, however, the righteous did not revile at the reviler, nor did they smite the smiter. They bore all these things with courage and fortitude, remembering the pains of their Redeemer.

VERSES 21-22. *He that shall breathe out wrath and strifes against the Work of the Lord . . . is in danger to be hewn down and cast into the fire.* In the annals of the Germanic peoples, especially the Scandinavians of Northern Europe, and the Anglo-Saxon tribes that invaded England in the 5th and 6th Centuries, together with native and Danish elements, all of which intermingled and formed one great race, we can see the Finger of God in the incidents of their lives that thereafter developed.

In no place in history is it more clearly to be seen than here, that the work of the Lord is progressing in all parts of the earth. And in it we may behold that what we sometimes call accidents, are really not so. But, we conclude, that in all righteous nations the incidents of their history are the inspirations of God, and the so-called accidents therein are the leadings and guidings of Him Who caused their foundations to be laid.

It is certain that many of the people above mentioned are of Israel, the Covenant People of the Lord.

the Lord, and the Lord will not remember his covenant which he hath made unto the house of Isra- | el—the same is in danger to be hewn down and cast into the fire; 22. For the eternal purposes of

---

There is another race of God's children which some delight to imprecate, and to say of them all manner of evil. These are the descendants of Judah, the son of Jacob and the great grandson of Abraham.

The Jews, although they have gone astray, and no longer remember the Covenant their fathers made with God at Sinai, are still His chosen people, and as such have been given a mighty work to perform to the honor and glory of God. They have already paid heavily for their errors, and are still paying, but notwithstanding the trials and the humiliation that have been for over two thousand years, heaped upon them by their neighbors, they will fulfil every word spoken by their holy prophets. Instead of their homeland being a dry and unyielding place where only jackals roam; a land of poverty and suffering, the Land of their Inheritance shall again "be as a watered garden, and they will sorrow no more." Prophesying of this time when Judah, which is now scattered abroad throughout the whole earth, shall return to its native home, the Land of Jerusalem, Jeremiah, one of its great prophets, says: "Hear the word of the Lord, O ye nations, and declare it in the isles afar off, and say, 'He that scattered Israel will gather him, and keep him, as a shepherd does his flock. For the Lord hath redeemed Jacob, and ransomed him from the hand of him that was stronger than he. Therefore they shall come in the height of Zion, and shall flow together to the goodness of the Lord, for wheat, and for wine, and for oil, and for the flock and the herd: and their soul shall be as a watered garden; and they shall not sorrow any more at all . . . for I will turn their mourning into joy, and will comfort them, and make them rejoice from their sorrow . . . !' (Jeremiah 31:10-13)

The abridger of the Larger Plates of Nephi, Mormon, also prophesied of these times. He says: "And as surely as the Lord liveth, will He gather in from the four quarters of the earth all the Remnant of the seed of Jacob, who are scattered abroad upon all the face of the earth. And as He hath covenanted with all the House of Jacob, even so shall the covenant wherewith He hath covenanted with the House of Jacob be fulfilled in His Own due time, unto the restoring all the House of Jacob unto the knowledge of the Covenant that He hath covenanted with them. And then shall they know their Redeemer, Who is Jesus Christ, the Son of God; and then shall they be gathered in from the four quarters of the earth unto their own lands, from whence they had been dispersed; yea, as the Lord liveth so shall it be." (III Nephi 5:24-26)

The angel who accompanied Nephi in his vision of events that would thereafter transpire, and explained to him the meaning thereof, spake to Nephi concerning certain records which Nephi saw, and of them, the angel said: 'These last records, which thou hast seen among the Gentiles,' meaning the Book of Mormon, 'shall establish the truth of the first,' which is the Bible . . . 'and shall make known to all kindreds, tongues, and people, that the Lamb of God is the Son of the Eternal Father, and the Savior of the world; and that all men must come unto Him, or they cannot be saved.' " (I Nephi 13:40)

To cry this truth to Jew and Gentile is our work which is also the Lord's work, and let us beware that in any thought or action, we do not attempt to sabotage His work by decrying and denying the Jews. No power on earth, or in hell, can destroy His work, or cause Him to forget the Covenant which He made with the House of Israel. "For the eternal purposes of the Lord shall roll on, until all His promises shall be fulfilled."

the Lord shall roll on, until all his promises shall be fulfilled.

23. Search the prophecies of Isaiah. Behold, I cannot write them. Yea, behold I say unto you, that those saints who have gone before me, who have possessed this land, shall cry, yea, even from the dust will they cry unto the Lord; and as the Lord liveth he will remember the covenant which he hath made with them.

24. And he knoweth their prayers, that they were in behalf of their brethren. And he knoweth their faith, for in his name could they remove mountains; and in his name could they cause the earth to shake; and by the power of his word did they cause prisons to tumble to the earth; yea, even the fiery furnace could not harm them, neither wild beasts nor poisonous serpents, because of the power of his word.

VERSES 23-24. *Those Saints who have possessed this land, shall cry, yea, even from the dust will they cry unto the Lord.* The prophecies of Isaiah tell of this thing; Moroni would have written them, but he had no space upon the Plates wherein to write. But Moroni points out that the cries of the Saints "who have possessed this land" in the ages that are gone, have been "unto the Lord," that He will not forget their brethren who may stray, and in His mercy "remember the Covenant which He hath made with them."

In the last verse of the last chapter of the Book of Mormon (9:37) in which Moroni fulfilled a solemn compact he had made with his father that he would finish writing the history of their people, Moroni notes that the cries of his people unto the Lord "are according to the prayers of all the Saints who have dwelt in the land." That their brethren who had "dwindled in unbelief" would some day have the Gospel of Christ preached unto them, and again have restored to them the knowledge of Christ that their fathers had, was the earnest supplication of their sires who had gone on before.[1]

---

[1]Now, it came to pass that when I had heard these words I began to feel a desire for the welfare of my brethren, the Nephites; wherefore, I did pour out my whole soul unto God for them. And while I was thus struggling in the spirit, behold, the voice of the Lord came into my mind again, saying: I will visit thy brethren according to their diligence in keeping my commandments. I have given unto them this land, and it is a holy land; and I curse it not save it be for the cause of iniquity; wherefore, I will visit thy brethren according as I have said; and their transgressions will I bring down with sorrow upon their own heads. And after I, Enos, had heard these words, my faith began to be unshaken in the Lord; and I prayed unto him with many long strugglings for my brethren, the Lamanites. And it came to pass that after I had prayed and labored with all diligence, the Lord said unto me: I will grant unto thee according to thy desires, because of thy faith. And now behold, this was the desire which I desired of him—that if it should so be, that my people, the Nephites, should fall into transgression, and by any means be destroyed, and the Lamanites should not be destroyed, that the Lord God would preserve my people, the Nephites; even if it so be by the power of his holy arm, that it might be brought forth at some future day unto the Lamanites, that, perhaps, they might be brought unto salvation—For at the present our strugglings were vain in restoring them to the true faith. And they swore in their wrath that, if it were possible, they would destroy our records and us, and also all the traditions of our fathers. Wherefore, I knowing that the Lord God was able to preserve our records, I cried unto him continually, for he had said unto me: Whatsoever things ye shall ask in faith, believing that ye shall receive in the name of Christ, ye shall receive it. And I had faith, and I did cry unto God that he would preserve the records; and he covenanted with me that he would bring them forth unto the Lamanites in his own due time. And I, Enos, knew it would be according to the covenant which he had made; wherefore my soul did rest." (Enos 9-16)

25. And behold, their prayers were also in behalf of him that the Lord should suffer to bring these things forth.

26. And no one need say they shall not come, for they surely shall, for the Lord hath spoken it; for out of the earth shall they come, by the hand of the Lord, and none can stay it; and it shall come in a day when it shall be said that miracles are done away; and it shall come even as if one should speak from the dead.

6. Conditions and calamities of latter days depicted.

27. And it shall come in a day when the blood of saints shall cry unto the Lord, because of secret combinations and the works of darkness.

28. Yea, it shall come in a day when the power of God shall be denied, and churches become defiled and be lifted up in the pride of their hearts; yea, even in a day

---

VERSES 25-26. *Their prayers were also in behalf of him that the Lord should suffer to bring forth these things.* The Lord having promised their fathers that the record of the Nephites should come forth to those who did survive among their Remnant, it was an almost constant prayer with them that God's servant who was to be the instrument in His hands to bring these Records forth, should be made strong and firm, and in every way be blessed that he may accomplish God's purpose in bringing them out of darkness into the light.

To one who doubted these things, Moroni became emphatic. "The Lord hath spoken it," and for that reason, no one need say, "They shall not." "Out of the earth shall they come, by the hand of the Lord, and none can stay it,[2] was his further elaboration.

VERSES 27-32. *It shall come in a day when it shall be said that miracles are done away.* In that day when miracles no longer "shall follow them that believe," and sham and deceit shall take their place, these things shall be heard as one from the dead. The world conditions that shall mark that time are occasions that bring fear and trembling. They fathom the depths into which men plunge in following after the pseudo-joys and follies of the world. Even in the church that men build up, pride and vanity will usurp the place of humility and meekness. Secret combinations shall shed the blood of the innocent, and the guilty shall devour the guiltless. Crime, degradation, and filth, shall pollute the earth, and waters from the stinking springs of iniquity shall cover the earth, deep as an ocean, with their impurities. Not only that, but many shall seek to excuse their iniquity by lying and

---

[2]"But behold, I prophesy unto you concerning the last days; concerning the days when the Lord God bring these things forth unto the children of men. After my seed and the seed of my brethren shall have dwindled in unbelief, and shall have been smitten by the Gentiles; yea, after the Lord God shall have camped against them round about, and shall have laid siege against them with a mount, and raised forts against them; and after they shall have been brought down low in the dust, even that they are not, yet the words of the righteous shall be written, and the prayers of the faithful shall be heard, and all those who have dwindled in unbelief shall not be forgotten. For those who shall be destroyed shall speak unto them out of the ground, and their speech shall be low out of the dust, and their voice shall be as one that hath a familiar spirit; for the Lord God will give unto him power, that he may whisper concerning them, even as it were out of the ground; and their speech shall whisper out of the dust. For thus saith the Lord God: They shall write the things which shall be done among them, and they shall be written and sealed up in a book, and those who have dwindled in unbelief shall not have them, for they seek to destroy the things of God." (II Nephi 26:14-17)

when leaders of churches and teachers shall rise in the pride of their hearts, even to the envying of them who belong to their churches.

29. Yea, it shall come in a day when there shall be heard of fires, and tempests, and vapors of smoke in foreign lands;

30. And there shall also be heard of wars, rumors of wars, and earthquakes in divers places.

31. Yea, it shall come in a day when there shall be great pollutions upon the face of the earth; there shall be murders, and robbing, and lying, and deceivings,

and whoredoms, and all manner of abominations; when there shall be many who will say, Do this, or do that, and it mattereth not, for the Lord will uphold such at the last day. But wo unto such for they are in the gall of bitterness and in the bonds of iniquity.

32. Yea, it shall come in a day when there shall be churches built up that shall say: Come unto me, and for your money you shall be forgiven of your sins.

33. O ye wicked and perverse and stiffnecked people, why have ye built up churches unto yourselves to get gain? Why have ye

---

deceiving, and all manner of abominations. In their wickedness they shall say, "Do this, or do that, it mattereth not, for when overtaken by the Lord's own, He will excuse a little folly and uphold us at the last day." O, how mistaken they will be. Their pretexts and their excuses therefore will find them in the gall of bitterness and in the bonds of iniquity. At the last day they will be the slaves of passion, the victims of corruption.[3]

VERSE 33. *O ye wicked . . . and stiffnecked people.* Moroni, who was greatly imbued with the spirit of righteousness could not understand the ways of wickedness. He could not comprehend why man should choose to do evil when the good is placed before him. Man, he knew, was endowed with reason to distinguish between right and wrong, with freedom to choose between good and evil. He, no doubt, thought of the wonders of creation. How that the eyes of man had, by the grace of Him Who created all things, been opened to the beauties round about him. But nevertheless and notwithstanding the glory of God therein seen, he pondered, Why does man seek the things of the world that pass swiftly by, and not the Lord Who is always near to the hearts of the lowly? We remember here the prayer of King David which we find in the 119 Psalm, verses 33-40. We hereby give the Jewish translation. (Union Prayer Book) In spite of his vision of things to come in the Last Days, it expresses the hope that Moroni had concerning these times. "Teach me, O Lord, the way of Thy statutes and I will keep it at every step. Give me understanding that I keep Thy law and observe it with my whole heart. Make me tread in the path of Thy commandments; for therein do I delight. Incline my heart unto Thine testimonies,

---

[3]Continuing his prophecy, Nephi said: "And the Gentiles are lifted up in the pride of their eyes, and have stumbled, because of the greatness of their stumbling block, that they have built up many churches; nevertheless, they put down the power and miracles of God, and preach up unto themselves their own wisdom and their own learning, that they may get gain and grind upon the face of the poor. And there are many churches built up which cause envyings, and strifes, and malice. And there are also secret combinations, even as in times of old, according to the combinations of the devil, for he is the foundation of all these things; yea, the foundation of murder, and works of darkness; yea, and he leadeth them by the neck with a flaxen cord, until he bindeth them with his strong cords forever." (*Ibid.*, 20-22)

tranfigured the holy word of God, that ye might bring damnation upon your souls? Behold, look ye unto the revelations of God; for behold, the time cometh at that day when all these things must be fulfilled.

34. Behold, the Lord hath shown unto me great and marvelous things concerning that which must shortly come, at that day when these things shall come forth among you.

35. Behold, I speak unto you as if ye were present, and yet ye are not. But behold, Jesus Christ hath shown you unto me, and I know your doing.

36. And I know that ye do walk in the pride of your hearts; and there are none save a few only who do not lift themselves up in the pride of their hearts, unto the wearing of very fine apparel, unto envying, and strifes, and malice, and persecutions, and all manner

and not to covetousness. Turn away mine eyes from beholding vanity, and quicken me in Thy ways. Confirm unto Thy servant Thy Word, which pertaineth unto the fear of Thee. Turn away my reproach which I dread, for Thine ordinances are good. Behold, I have longed after Thy precepts; quicken me in Thy righteousness."

"O ye wicked and perverse and stiffnecked people, why have ye built up churches unto yourselves to get gain?" Moroni queried. Why have ye perverted God's holy word, and twisted and turned it to make it appear that therein your souls are damned? "Behold," he said, "look ye into the revelations of God;[4] for behold, the time cometh at that day when all these things must be fulfilled." (v. 23)

VERSES 34-40. *The Lord hath shown unto me great and marvelous things concerning that which must shortly come, at that day when these things shall come forth among you.* The Lord showed unto Moroni, as He had shown others of His servants, a panoramic picture of His children down to the Last Days. *Great and marvelous* were the things Moroni saw. All of which, Moroni indirectly intimated, "shall come forth among you" before that great and last day. Although many generations separate our times, he noted, "I," nevertheless, "speak unto you as if ye were present," for I know your faults, and your failings, and your subversions. That in His mercy, the Lord, he said, for a wise purpose, has shown you unto me that I may warn you of these things which are to come, and that seeing the errors of your ways, you may repent before it is everlastingly too late. We conceive these and other thoughts crowded each other through his mind as Moroni contemplated the scenes of his vision that passed before his astonished eyes.

4"And it came to pass that the angel spake unto me, saying: Look! And I looked and beheld a man, and he was dressed in a white robe. And the angel said unto me: Behold one of the twelve apostles of the Lamb. Behold, he shall see and write the remainder of these things; yea, and also many things which have been. And he shall also write concerning the end of the world. Wherefore, the things which he shall write are just and true; and behold they are written in the book which thou beheld proceeding out of the mouth of the Jew; and at the time they proceeded out of the mouth of the Jew, or, at the time the book proceeded out of the mouth of the Jew, the things which were written were plain and pure, and most precious and easy to the understanding of all men. And behold, the things which this apostle of the Lamb shall write are many things which thou hast seen; and behold, the remainder shalt thou see. But the things which thou shalt see hereafter thou shalt not write; for the Lord God hath ordained the apostle of the Lamb of God that he should write them. And also others who have been, to them hath he shown all things, and they are sealed up to come forth in their purity, according to the truth which is in the Lamb, in the own due time of the Lord, unto the house of Israel. And I, Nephi, heard and bear record, that the name of the apostle of the Lamb was John, according to the word of the angel." (I Nephi 14:18-27)

of iniquities; and your churches, yea, even every one, have become polluted because of the pride of your hearts.

37. For behold, ye do love money, and your substance, and your fine apparel, and the adorning of your churches, more than ye love the poor and the needy, the sick and the afflicted.

38. O ye pollutions, ye hypocrites, ye teachers, who sell yourselves for that which will canker, why have ye polluted the holy church of God? Why are ye ashamed to take upon you the name of Christ? Why do ye not think that greater is the value of

---

May we here add what we consider the best comment on the next few verses. It is part of what Nephi, the son of Lehi who was the learned ancestor of the Nephites and the Lamanites, predicted would come to pass in the latter days:

"And now, behold, my brethren, I have spoken unto you, according as the Spirit hath constrained me; wherefore, I know that they must surely come to pass.

"The things which shall be written out of the book shall be of great worth unto the children of men, especially unto our seed, which is a remnant of the house of Israel.

"For it shall come to pass in that day that the churches which are built up, and not unto the Lord, when the one shall say unto the other: Behold, I, I am the Lord's; and the other shall say: I, I am the Lord's; and thus shall every one say that hath built up churches, and not unto the Lord—

"And they shall contend one with another; and their priests shall contend one with another, and they shall teach with their learning, and deny the Holy Ghost, which giveth utterance.

"And they deny the power of God, the Holy One of Israel; and they say unto the people: Hearken unto us, and hear ye our precept; for behold there is no God today, for the Lord and the Redeemer hath done his work, and he hath given his power unto men;

"Behold, hearken ye unto my precept; if they shall say there is a miracle wrought by the hand of the Lord, believe it not; for this day he is not a God of miracles; he hath done his work.

"Yea, and there shall be many which shall say: Eat, drink, and be merry, for tomorrow we die; and it shall be well with us.

"And there shall also be many which shall say: Eat, drink, and be merry; nevertheless, fear God—he will justify in committing a little sin; yea, lie a little, take the advantage of one because of his words, dig a pit for thy neighbor; there is no harm in this; and do all these things, for tomorrow we die; and if it so be that we are guilty, God will beat us with a few stripes, and at last we shall be saved in the kingdom of God.

"Yea, and there shall be many which shall teach after this manner, false and vain and foolish doctrines, and shall be puffed up in their hearts, and shall seek deep to hide their counsels from the Lord; and their works shall be in the dark.

"And the blood of the saints shall cry from the ground against them.

"Yea, they have all gone out of the way; they have become corrupted.

"Because of pride, and because of false teachers, and false doctrine, their churches have become corrupted, and their churches are lifted up; because of pride they are puffed up.

"They rob the poor because of their fine sanctuaries; they rob the poor because of their fine clothing; and they persecute the meek and the poor in heart, because in their pride they are puffed up.

"They wear stiff necks and high heads; yea, and because of pride, and wickedness, and abominations, and whoredoms, they have all gone astray save it be a few, who are the humble followers of Christ; nevertheless, they are led, that in many instances they do err because they are taught by the precepts of men.

an endless happiness than that misery which never dies—because of the praise of the world?

39. Why do ye adorn yourselves with that which hath no life, and yet suffer the hungry, and the needy, and the naked, and the sick and the afflicted to pass by you, and notice them not?

40. Yea, why do ye build up your secret abominations to get gain, and cause that widows

---

"O the wise, and the learned, and the rich, that are puffed up in the pride of their hearts, and all those who preach false doctrine, and all those who commit whoredoms, and pervert the right way of the Lord, wo, wo, wo be unto them, saith the Lord God Almighty, for they shall be thrust down to hell!

"Wo unto them that turn aside the just for a thing of naught and revile against that which is good, and say that is of no worth! For the day shall come that the Lord God will speedily visit the inhabitants of the earth; and in that day that they are fully ripe in iniquity they shall perish.

"But behold, if the inhabitants of the earth shall repent of their wickedness and abominations they shall not be destroyed, saith the Lord of Hosts.

"But behold, that great and abominable church, the whore of all the earth, must tumble to the earth, and great must be the fall thereof.

"For the kingdom of the devil must shake, and they which belong to it must needs be stirred up unto repentance, or the devil will grasp them with his everlasting chains, and they be stirred up to anger, and perish;

"For behold, at that day shall he rage in the hearts of the children of men, and stir them up to anger against that which is good.

"And others will he pacify, and lull them away into carnal security, that they will say: All is well in Zion; yea, Zion prospereth, all is well—and thus the devil cheateth their souls, and leadeth them away carefully down to hell.

"And behold, others he flattereth away, and telleth them there is no hell; and he saith unto them: I am no devil, for there is none—and thus he whispereth in their ears, until he grasps them with his awful chains, from whence there is no deliverance.

"Yea, they are grasped with death, and hell; and death, and hell, and the devil, and all that have been seized therewith must stand before the throne of God, and be judged according to their works, from whence they must go unto the place prepared for them, even a lake of fire and brimstone, which is endless torment.

"Therefore, wo be unto him that is at ease in Zion!

"Wo be unto him that crieth: All is well!

"Yea, wo be unto him that hearkeneth unto the precepts of men, and denieth the power of God, and the gift of the Holy Ghost!

"Yea, wo be unto him that saith: We have received, and we need no more!

"And in fine, wo unto all those who tremble, and are angry because of the truth of God! For behold, he that is built upon the rock receiveth it with gladness; and he that is built upon a sandy foundation trembleth lest he shall fall.

"We be unto him that shall say: We have received the word of God, and we need no more of the word of God, for we have enough!

"For behold, thus saith the Lord God: I will give unto the children of men line upon line, precept upon precept, here a little and there a little; and blessed are those who hearken unto my precepts, and lend an ear unto my counsel, for they shall learn wisdom; for unto him that receiveth I will give more; and from them that shall say, We have enough, from them shall be taken even that which they have.

"Cursed is he that putteth his trust in man, or maketh flesh his arm, or shall hearken unto the precepts of men, save their precepts shall be given by the power of the Holy Ghost.

"Wo be unto the Gentiles, saith the Lord God of Hosts! For notwithstanding I shall length out mine arm unto them from day to day, they will deny me; nevertheless,

should mourn before the Lord, and also orphans to mourn before the Lord, and also the blood of their fathers and their husbands to cry unto the Lord from the ground, for vengeance upon your heads?

41. Behold, the sword of vengeance hangeth over you; and the time soon cometh that he avengeth the blood of the saints upon you, for he will not suffer their cries any longer.

I will be merciful unto them, saith the Lord God, if they will repent and come unto me; for mine arm is lengthened out all the day long, saith the Lord God of Hosts." (II Nephi, Chapter 28)

VERSE 41. *Behold, the sword of vengeance hangeth over you.* The Sword of Vengeance spoken of here is a mighty weapon. In the hands of the Lord, it is terrible. It *hangeth heavily* over the doers of iniquity. It was forged in the fires of righteousness because of wickedness. Its keen blade and sharp point pierce to the inmost parts. *The Wielder of that Sword is the King of all the Earth.* He uses it against the devil to protect His Majesty, and to prepare a path before His people, unto whom He says: Seek not vengeance to recompense evil by doing evil; seek not to destroy that which ye cannot build; seek not to take that which ye cannot give. "Vengeance is mine, and I will repay."[5]

"O ye pollutions, ye hypocrites, ye teachers, who sell yourselves for that which will canker . . . why are you ashamed to take upon you the Name of Christ? . . . Yea, why do ye build up your secret abominations to get gain, and cause that widows should mourn before the Lord, and also orphans to mourn before the Lord, and also the blood of their fathers and their husbands to cry unto the Lord from the ground, for vengeance upon your heads? Behold, the Sword of Vengeance hangeth over you; and the time soon cometh that He avengeth the blood of the Saints upon you, for He will not suffer their cries any longer."

---

[5]"Behold what the Scripture says—man shall not smite, neither shall he judge; for judgment is mine, saith the Lord, and vengeance is mine also, and I will repay." (Mormon 8:20)

CHAPTER 9

1. Moroni's Address to Unbelievers—2. His Testimony Concerning the Christ—3. The Nephite Language Known as Reformed Egyptian.

1. Moroni's address to unbelievers.

1. And now, I speak also concerning those who do not believe in Christ.

2. Behold, will ye believe in the day of your visitation—behold, when the Lord shall come, yea, even that great day when the earth shall be rolled together as a scroll, and the elements shall melt with fervent heat, yea, in that great day when ye shall be brought to stand before the Lamb of God—then will ye say that there is no God?

3. Then will ye longer deny the Christ, or can ye behold the Lamb of God? Do ye suppose that ye shall dwell with him under a consciousness of your guilt? Do ye suppose that ye could be happy to dwell with that holy Being, when your souls are racked with a consciousness of guilt that ye have ever abused his laws?

VERSE 1. *I speak also concerning those who do not believe.* Moroni left off admonishing the perverse and stiffnecked people whom he had seen in his vision, those people whose wickedness was a will to do iniquity, and plead with those of whom it has been said that *there are none so deaf as those who will not hear, and none so blind as those who will not see.* At this point, we imagine Moroni saying, "Hear, ye deaf; and look, ye blind, that ye may see." (Isaiah 42:18)

VERSE 2. *Then will ye say that there is no God.* Will you who do not believe in Christ remain in your unbelief until the earth shall mourn and fade away "and the haughty people of the earth do languish?" (*See, Ibid.*, 24:4) Will you persist in your unbelief until the things of which I have spoken shall be visited upon you? "Yea," said Moroni, "in that great Day when ye shall be brought to stand before the Lamb of God—then will ye say that there is no God?

VERSE 3. *Do you suppose that ye could be happy to dwell with that Holy Being?* At that Day when you are brought before Him to be judged for your works on earth, whether they have been good or evil; and with your own eyes behold the Lamb of God, will ye still insist that He is not? Can you gainsay the fact that He presides over that august body there assembled? And therein reject Him. In that great Day, when the glorious splendor of His presence and of His Majesty shall illumine both the Heavens and the Earth, when they shall be rolled up as a scroll, what will it profit you when the Heavens and the Earth shall pass away if you do not know that bright and morning Star which is the Sun of Righteousness? Do you imagine that in the consciousness of your guilt you would be happy "to dwell with that Holy Being?" Moroni, no doubt, remembered reading from the Brass Plates of Laban, "Light is sown for the righteous, and gladness for the upright in heart." (Psalm 97:11) Neither light nor gladness will be your portion "when your souls are racked" with an awareness of a life of sin while on Earth. Do not longer delay your belief in Christ, but put on His armor and be prepared for that Day. In the anxiety of his heart, Moroni made such an appeal to those who give little time or thought to the welfare of their souls.

4. Behold, I say unto you that ye would be more miserable to dwell with a holy and just God, under a consciousness of your filthiness before him, than ye would to dwell with the damned souls in hell.

5. For behold, when ye shall be brought to see your nakedness before God, and also the glory of God, and the holiness of Jesus Christ, it will kindle a flame of unquenchable fire upon you.

6. O then ye unbelieving, turn ye unto the Lord; cry mightily unto the Father in the name of Jesus, that perhaps ye may be found spotless, pure, fair, and white, having been cleansed by the blood of the Lamb, at that great and last day.

7. And again I speak unto you who deny the revelations of God, and say that they are done away, that there are no revelations, nor prophecies, nor gifts, nor healing, nor speaking with tongues, and the interpretation of tongues;

VERSE 4. *Ye would be more miserable.* . . . Knowing that sin has defiled your body, and corruption your mind; conscious that pride and deceit has made you filthy in His sight, "Ye," Moroni said, "Would be more miserable to dwell with a holy and just God . . . than ye would to dwell with damned souls in hell."

VERSE 5. *It will kindle a flame of unquenchable fire upon you.* At that Day when you stand before the Judgment-Seat of Christ, and you can find nothing to hide under; stripped of all pretense and hypocrisy; left alone to ponder; when you see God's glory, and the holiness of Jesus Christ, and be cognizant that you could have been a partaker therein if only you had followed Him, the loss you see you have sustained, will "kindle a flame of unquenchable fire upon you."

VERSE 6. *O then ye unbelieving, turn ye unto the Lord.* O then that you may thwart the designs of the devil, "turn ye unto the Lord"; forsake the ways of Satan. Pray earnestly to the Father in the Name of His Son, Jesus, for light that you may see the right way and for strength that you may continue therein, that in the end at that great Day "ye may be found spotless, pure, fair, and white, having been cleansed by the blood of the Lamb." Moroni invited all to prepare for that Day.

VERSES 7-10. *I speak, also, unto you who deny the revelations of God, and say that they are done away.* In this day when any excuse is sufficient, and any pretext is enough to deceive those that would believe in the Lamb, it is not surprising to find many who say that the Gifts of the Spirit no longer follow, as was promised, them that believe. Parallels in belief between the Nephite Church of God, the worship of the ancient Saints in Jerusalem, and the Church of Jesus Christ of Latter-day Saints can be found in the history of each. The Savior, when giving His charge to the Twelve Nephite Disciples, said, "Go ye into all the world, and preach the Gospel to every creature. And he that believeth and is baptized shall be saved, but he that believeth not shall be damned; And these signs shall follow them that believe—in My Name shall they cast out devils; they shall speak with new tongues; they shall take up serpents; and if they drink any deadly thing it shall not hurt them; they shall lay hands on the sick and they shall recover; And whosoever shall believe in My Name, doubting nothing, unto him will I confirm all My words, even unto the ends of the Earth." (Mormon 9:22-25)

Moroni, treating on the same subject, states:

8. Behold I say unto you, he that denieth these things knoweth not the gospel of Christ; yea, he has not read the scriptures; if so, he does not understand them.

9. For do we not read that God is the same yesterday, today, and forever, and in him there is no variableness neither shadow of changing?

10. And now if ye have imagined up unto yourselves a god who doth vary, and in whom there is shadow of changing, then have ye imagined up unto yourselves a god who is not a God of miracles.

"Ye may know that He is, by the power of the Holy Ghost; wherefore I would exhort you that ye deny not the power of God; for He worketh by power, according to the faith of the children of men, the same today and tomorrow, and forever.

"And again, I exhort you, my brethren, that ye deny not the gifts of God, for they are many; and they come from the same God. And there are different ways that these gifts are administered; but it is the same God who worketh all in all; and they are given by the manifestations of the Spirit of God unto men, to profit them.

"For behold, to one is given by the Spirit of God, that he may teach the word of wisdom;

"And to another, that he may teach the word of knowledge by the same Spirit;

"And to another, exceeding great faith; and to another, the gifts of healing by the same Spirit;

"And again, to another, that he may work mighty miracles;

"And again, to another, that he may prophesy concerning all things;

"And again, to another, the beholding of angels and ministering spirits;

"And again, to another, all kinds of tongues;

"And again, to another, the interpretation of languages and of divers kinds of tongues.

"And all these gifts come by the Spirit of Christ; and they come unto every man severally, according as He will.

"And I would exhort you, my beloved brethren, that ye remember that every good gift cometh of Christ.

"And I would exhort you, my beloved brethren, that ye remember that He is the same yesterday, today, and forever, and that all these gifts of which I have spoken, which are spiritual, never will be done away, even as long as the world shall stand, only according to the unbelief of the children of men (Moroni 10:7-19)

This is a full and complete answer to those who contend that there are no more revelations given of God, "nor prophecies, nor gifts, nor healing, nor speaking with tongues, and the interpretation of tongues."

VERSE 8. *He that denieth these things knoweth not the Gospel of Christ.* To deny that these Gifts of the Spirit do exist in the Church of Christ, is to admit that we are destitute of understanding, and that even if we have read the Scriptures we do not apprehend their meaning. That statement, Moroni wrote for us as well as to the Remnant of his brethren. He saw a further decline in belief in Christ, and God Who doeth all things according to men's faith, offers these Gifts only to those whose faith is evidenced by their keeping His commandments. It is well to remember that by our actions, we prove our belief in the truth of the things we proclaim.

VERSE 9. *Do we not read that God is the same yesterday, today, and forever?* (See, Moroni 10:19)

VERSE 10. *Have ye imagined up unto yourselves a god who is not a God of miracles.* The Gifts of the Spirit are themselves indeed miracles. The Book of Mormon teaches in very strong language that God is a God of miracles. Were it not

2. Moroni's Testimony Concerning the Christ.

11. But behold, I will show unto you a God of miracles, even the God of Abraham, and the God of Isaac, and the God of Jacob; and it is that same God who created the heavens and the earth, and all things that in them are.

12. Behold he created Adam, and by Adam came the fall of man. And because of the fall of man came Jesus Christ, even the Father and the Son; and because of Jesus Christ came the redemption of man.

13. And because of the redemption of man, which came by Jesus Christ, they are brought back into the presence of the Lord; yea, this is wherein all men are redeemed, because the death of Christ bringeth to pass the resurrection, which bringeth to pass a redemption from an endless sleep, from which sleep all men shall be awakened by the power of God when the trump shall sound; and they shall come forth, both small and great, and all shall stand before his bar,

---

so, He would cease to be an unchangeable Being. He would be a partial God, blessing one people more than another; but in Him, Moroni lays considerable stress "there is no variableness neither shadow of changing." Moroni warns against letting our imaginations conjure up a god who is not a God of miracles.

VERSE 11. *I will show unto you a God of miracles.* To witness that He who Moroni proclaims is a God of miracles, Moroni calls upon all Creation to attest that truth. He himself bears testimony that he speaks of "the God of Abraham, and the God of Isaac, and the God of Jacob; that same God," he noted, "who created the Heavens and the Earth, and all things that in them are." Moroni thought of other words of King David than those above already noted: "O Lord, our God, how glorious is Thy Name in all the Earth, whose majesty is rehearsed above the Heavens. When I behold Thy Heavens, the work of Thy fingers, the Moon and the stars which Thou hast established; what is man, that Thou art mindful of him, and the son of man, that Thou thinkest of him? . . . O Lord, our God, how glorious is Thy Name in all the Earth. (Psalm 8; Jewish Rendition)

VERSES 12-14. *Behold, He created Adam.* The entire Plan of Salvation was offered by Moroni as further proof that the God of Whom he spoke was One of miracles. (A miracle, we may understand to be an event or its effect in the physical world deviating from the known laws of nature, or transcending our knowledge of these laws; an extraordinary event brought about by superhuman agency; *Mary Baker Eddy*, of Christian Science fame, calls a miracle, *something that is divinely natural, but must be learned humanly.*)

Moroni then introduces Adam, the first man who God created in His own image. Adam sinned and brought death and sorrow onto the Earth which had been created by God for the benefit and blessing of mankind. Adam bequeathed to his offspring his legacy of sin. As a result, God the loving Father of all men, Who Himself is sinless, was separated from His children who as we have noted, were carnal, and who had become sinful and sensual in their fallen state. A redemption from the effects of Adam's Fall must be made that again man and his Father may be united. That Redemption, Moroni points out, came about by the Sacrifice Christ made that man might live, and therein brought back into the presence of God, his Father.

Through the Redemption of all mankind came man's deliverance from an endless sleep which is the grave. When Moroni's father, who was the Prophet

being redeemed and loosed from this eternal band of death, which death is a temporal death.

14. And then cometh the judgment of the Holy One upon them; and then cometh the time that he that is filthy shall be filthy still; and he that is righteous shall be righteous still; he that is happy shall be happy still; and he that is unhappy shall be unhappy still.

15. And now, O all ye that have imagined up unto yourselves a god who can do no miracles, I would ask of you, have all these things passed, of which I have spoken? Has the end come yet? Behold I say unto you, Nay; and God has not ceased to be a God of miracles.

16. Behold, are not the things that God hath wrought marvelous

---

Mormon, engraved an address to the Lamanites who survived the Battle of Cumorah, he said — and his words are particularly important here — "Know ye that ye must come to the knowledge of your fathers, and repent of all your sins and iniquities, and believe in Jesus Christ, that He is the Son of God, and that He was slain by the Jews, and by the power of the Father He hath risen again, whereby He hath gained the victory over the grave; and also in Him is the sting of death swallowed up." (Mormon 7:5)

Now that man has been Redeemed from death and the grave by the Sacrifice made by Christ, man is held responsible for his actions here upon the Earth, whether they have been good or whether they have been bad. If he has not repented of sin and still remains in his guilt, he will still be *filthy*, or unclean, but the righteous shall be happy because of their righteousness, and will go on forever being happy and righteous in that they delight in keeping the commandments of God. That is wisdom. "Behold, the fear of the Lord, that is wisdom, and to depart from evil is understanding." (Job 28:28) The wise old Jewish King, Solomon, gave his experience in these beautiful and never-to-be-forgotten words: "Happy is the man that findeth wisdom, and the man that getteth understanding." (Proverbs 3:13) We can easily see the truth of Moroni's assertion "he that is happy shall be happy still . . ." (v. 14) Therefore, "Trust in the Lord with all thy heart, and lean not upon thine own understanding." (Proverbs 3:5) Let the words of Peter forever be in our minds: "If ye suffer for righteousness' sake, happy are you." (I Peter 3:14)

VERSES 15-19. *Are not the things God hath wrought marvelous in your eyes?* Again, we are reminded of the words of Lehi, when that holy man, in vision, saw many wonderful things concerning the purposes of the Lord and therein rejoiced, he exclaimed: "Great and marvelous are Thy works, O Lord God Almighty!" (I Nephi 1:14) To the minds of mortals, the marvelous works of the Lord are incomprehensible; to us they are inscrutable. Except through revelation (See, v. 7) they cannot be found out. The revealed word of God is a lamp unto our feet, and a light unto our path, (See, Psalm 119:105) and here we remember the words of Isaiah: "Who is among you that feareth the Lord, that obeyeth the voice of His servant, that walketh in darkness, and hath no light? let him trust in the Name of the Lord, and stay upon his God." (Isaiah 50:10)

Moroni now sums up the proofs which he has thus far brought to bear upon his contention that God is a God of miracles. To those who contend the opposite that God can do no miracles, he asks: "Have all these things passed, of which I have spoken? Has the end come yet? Moroni answers his own question: "Nay; and God has not ceased to be a God of miracles." (v. 15)

The Creation of the Heavens and the Earth was in Moroni's mind, a great

in our eyes? Yea, and who can comprehend the marvelous works of God?

17. Who shall say that it was not a miracle that by his word the heaven and the earth should be; and by the power of his word man was created of the dust of the earth; and by the power of his word have miracles been wrought?

18. And who shall say that Jesus Christ did not many mighty miracles? And there were many mighty miracles wrought by the hands of the apostles.

19. And if there were miracles wrought then, why has God ceased to be a God of miracles and yet be an unchangeable Being? And behold, I say unto you he changeth not; if so he would cease to be God; and he ceaseth not to be God, and is a God of miracles.

---

miracle, as also that by God's holy Word, man was created of the dust of the Earth. Not only that, but by the power of His Word have His servants, in the Name of Christ, wrought many mighty miracles.

All the works of the Lord are miracles. Listen to the wisdom of the ancient Hebrews; therein is the word of Moroni verified:

"How manifold are Thy works, O Lord! In wisdom hast Thou made them all; the Earth is full of the riches of Thy bounty." (Psalm 104:24)

"From the rising of the Sun to the going down thereof, we will praise Thy holy Name." (See, Psalm 50:1)

"The Heavens are the Lord's, the Earth also and all that is therein." Expressed somewhat differently:

"The Heavens are Thine, the Earth also is Thine: as for the world and the fulness thereof, Thou hast founded them." (Psalm 89:11)

"He made great lights, the Sun to rule the day, the Moon and stars to rule by night." (See, Psalm 136:7)

"He commanded and they were created, He gave a law they cannot transgress.

"He covereth the heaven with clouds, and prepareth rain for the earth. He causeth the grass to spring up for the cattle, and herb for the service of man.

"God ruleth the proud swelling of the sea; when the waves thereof arise, He stilleth them.

"The everlasting God hath laid the foundations of the earth; He hath placed the corner-stone thereof.

"The Creator of the Earth fainteth not, neither is He weary; His discernment is past finding out.

"The way of the Lord is perfect, His word is tried, and His counsels stand forever.

"The Lord liveth. Exalted be the God of my Salvation." (*Jewish Union Prayer Book*)

The wisdom of the Jews lies in knowing the Only True and Living God, the God of their fathers; while by the wisdom of the Gentiles, Paul says, "The world . . . knew not God." (I Corinthians 21)

May we, in all humility, quote the 111th Psalm as it is by the Jews: "I will give thanks unto the Lord with my whole heart, in the council of the upright, and in the congregation. The works of the Lord are great, sought out of all them that have delight therein. His work is glory and majesty, and His righteousness endureth forever. He hath made a memorial for His wonderful works; the Lord is gracious and full of compassion. He hath given food unto them that fear Him; He will be mindful of His Covenant. He hath declared to His people the great power of His works, in giving to them the heritage of the nations. The works of

20. And the reason why he ceaseth to do miracles among the children of men is because that they dwindle in unbelief, and depart from the right way, and know not the God in whom they should trust.

21. Behold, I say unto you that whoso believeth in Christ, doubting nothing, whatsoever he shall ask the Father in the name of Christ it shall be granted him; and this promise is unto all, even unto the ends of the earth.

22. For behold, thus said Jesus Christ, the Son of God, unto his disciples who should tarry, yea, and also to all his disciples, in the hearing of the multitude: Go ye into all the world, and preach the gospel to every creature;

23. And he that believeth and is baptized shall be saved, but he that believeth not shall be damned;

24. And these signs shall follow them that believe in my name shall they cast out devils; they shall speak with new tongues; they shall take up serpents; and if they drink any deadly thing it shall not hurt them; they shall lay hands on the sick and they shall recover;

25. And whosoever shall believe in my name, doubting nothing, unto him will I confirm all my words, even unto the ends of the earth.

26. And now, behold, who can stand against the works of the Lord? Who can deny his sayings? Who will rise up against the almighty power of the Lord? Who will despise the works of the Lord? Who will despise the children of Christ? Behold, all ye who are despisers of the works of the Lord, for ye shall wonder and perish.

27. O then despise not, and wonder not, but hearken unto the words of the Lord, and ask the Father in the name of Jesus for what things soever ye shall stand in need. Doubt not, but be believing, and begin as in times of old, and come unto the Lord with all your heart, and work out your own salvation with fear and trembling before him.

28. Be wise in the days of your probation; strip yourselves of all uncleanness; ask not, that ye may consume it on your lusts, but ask with a firmness unshaken, that ye will yield to no temptation, but that ye will serve the true and living God.

29. See that ye are not baptized unworthily; see that ye

His hands are truth and justice; all His precepts are sure. They are established forever and ever, they are done in truth and righteousness. He hath sent Redemption unto His people; He hath commanded His Covenant forever; holy and awful is His Name. The fear of the Lord is the beginning of wisdom; a good understanding have all they that do thereafter; His praise endureth forever."

VERSE 20. *The reason why God has ceased to do miracles.* Because unbelievers have no faith, and even many of those who believe have little, "God can do no miracle among them." (*Moroni*, Ether 12:12) "Yea, and even all they who wrought miracles wrought them by faith, even those who were before Christ and also those who were after." (*Ibid.*, 16)

partake not of the sacrament of Christ unworthily; but see that ye do all things in worthiness, and do it in the name of Jesus Christ, the Son of the living God; and if ye do this, and endure to the end, ye will in nowise be cast out.

30. Behold, I speak unto you as though I spake from the dead; for I know that ye shall hear my words.

31. Condemn me not because of mine imperfection, neither my father, because of his imperfection, neither them who have written before him; but rather give thanks unto God that he hath made manifest unto you our imperfections, that ye may learn to be more wise than we have been.

3. The Nephite Language known as Reformed Egyptian.

32. And now, behold, we have written this record according to our knowledge, in the characters which are called among us the reformed Egyptian, being handed down and altered by us, according to our manner of speech.

33. And if our plates had been

It is the case with many of us, we go our way, day-by-day, forgetting His wisdom and guidance. The task and trials of life absorbs us, and crowd all thoughts of God from our hearts. In that condition of mind, we reject even His great Name; we "know not the God in whom" we "should trust." To eyes that are blind and hearts that are hardened to the word of the Lord, that He can do no miracle among them, again may we offer one of King David's Psalms, also a Jewish rendition; it awakens in nearly every one a sense of remorse when they think of these last words of Moroni, "They know not the God in Whom they should trust. Answer me when I call, O God of my righteousness, Thou Who didst set me free when I was in distress; be gracious unto me, and hear my prayer. O ye sons of men, how long shall My glory be put to shame, in that ye love vanity and seek after falsehood? But know that the Lord hath set apart the godly man as His own; the Lord will hear when I call unto Him. Tremble, and sin not; commune with your own heart upon your bed, and be still. Offer the sacrifices of righteousness, and put your trust in the Lord. Many are they who say: O that we could see some good! Lord, lift Thou up the light of Thy countenance upon us. Thou hast put gladness in my heart, more than their corn and their wine increase. In peace will I both lay me down and sleep; for Thou, Lord, makest me dwell alone in safety." (Psalm 4)

VERSES 32-33. *We have written this Record in the Characters called among us the Reformed Egyptian.* Near what he thought was to be the close of the Record of his people, an abridgment of which his father had made from the Larger Plates of Nephi, and which Moroni himself had completed, together with the personal writings of his father, Mormon, and himself, Moroni informs us that they had written them according to their own knowledge and the knowledge they had gleaned from the study of their ancestors as it was written upon the Larger Plates.

Also, he tells us that the writings of both him and his father were made in certain characters known to them as the "reformed Egyptian." Moroni notes that in the thousand years which had elapsed between his own and the time of their fathers when they left Jerusalem for the Promised Land, many changes had been made in their manner of speech, therefore, they had altered the characters so that in them they better could express their thoughts.

sufficiently large we should have
written in Hebrew; but the Hebrew hath been altered by us also;
and if we could have written in

Hebrew, behold, ye would have
had no imperfection in our record.

Again, Moroni tells us that if they could have written in Hebrew they would have done so. But this they could not do because the plates upon which they engraved the Record were insufficiently large to contain the necessary Hebrew Characters. However, he says that the Hebrew also was modified, or made different without changing its meaning into something else. Moroni here expresses, we imagine, a regret that they had not written in Hebrew, because the imperfections in the Record for which he apologizes (*See,* v. 31) would then not have existed.

Questions concerning the writing upon the Plates, their number, and also the weight thereof, are repeatedly projected both by believers in the divine origin of the Sacred Record, and by unfriendly critics. There are, as far as we know, no data from which to calculate, with accuracy, any answers thereto.

That we may not be considered negligent in not discussing these questions in point, we hereby reproduce a portion of what we, after careful study, caused to be printed in the Second Volume of this work. (COMMENTARY ON THE BOOK OF MORMON, Volume II, p. 308ff)

CONCERNING THE PLATES OF THE BOOK OF MORMON

The Reverend Mr. M. T. Lamb's Objections. The Reverend Mr. M. T. Lamb who, in 1886 or 1887, favored the Saints in Utah, with a series of lectures against the sacred volume, and was courteously tendered the use of ward houses for that purpose, told us that the 563 pages of the Liverpool text, would have required at least an equal number of plates. Consequently, he said there were on the most liberal estimate possible, enough plates only for from one-third to one-eighth of the text as printed in the edition then in common use. He arrived at this conclusion by accepting the dimensions of the plates as 7 x 8 inches, and the thickness of the volume as four inches. But the Prophet, he said, did not translate more than one-third of the two hundred which he allowed for the plates at fifty per inch; that is to say, sixty-six or sixty-seven plates, and Joseph Smith could not have obtained the entire book as we have it from such a small number of plates.[1]

Others have asserted that if the Prophet Joseph Smith had a sufficient number of gold plates to contain the entire text of the Book of Mormon, they would have been too heavy to handle as a book. They would have weighed 500 pounds or more.

By such statements the critics have hoped to break the "Mormon" pitcher at the threshold, as the Greek saying is. If they could make it appear that the Prophet could not have had a sufficient number of plates; or, if he had, that he could not have lifted them, they felt thereby they could remove the entire foundation of the Church, and have nothing more to discuss. It is therefore, interesting to consider just what data is available, and what conclusions may be drawn from them.[2]

---

[1]M. T. Lamb, *The Golden Bible,* pp. 245-250.

[2]*The Prophet Joseph Smith's Own Account.* The Prophet writes: "These records were engraven on plates which had the appearance of gold; each plate was six inches wide and eight inches long and not quite as thick as common tin. They were filled with engravings, in Egyptian characters, and bound together in a volume as the leaves of a book with three rings running through the whole. The volume was something near six inches in thickness, part of which was sealed. The characters on the unsealed part were small, and beautifully engraved. The whole book exhibited many marks of antiquity in its construction, and much skill in the art of engraving. With the records was found a curious instrument, which the ancients called 'urim and thummim,' which consisted of two transparent stones set in the rim of

No Definite Data now on Hand. It should be noted, however, that the Prophet Joseph does not enlighten us on the number or weight of the plates, any more than Moses does on the size and avoirdupois of the tables on which the Lord engraved the Law. It should also be remembered that the particulars furnished by eyewitnesses were given many years after they had seen the plates, in answer to questions pressed upon them in the course of what amounted almost to cross examination. They gave, therefore, their individual estimates and nothing more.

Suppose, for the sake of illustration, that two or more men should be examined on the dimensions of a book — say *Webster's Dictionary* — twenty years after they had seen it. What would their answers be, provided there was no collusion between them? They would call up from the depths of their minds the images produced there many years ago and then each would give his own estimate, as best he could.

We remember an occasion on which some students were together, and the question of estimating dimensions came up. A "stovepipe hat" was placed in the middle of the floor, where there was no object close to it to compare it with, and the question was asked, "What is the height of the hat?" The estimates, quickly made, varied and ranged all the way from four to ten inches. The actual height, we believe, was five-and-a-half inches. We dare say a carpenter, or any other mechanic, would have come closer to the right figure, when the object was before him, but what would be his estimate many years afterward? Probably it would have been more or less than the actual figure, but that would not affect his credibility as a witness to the fact that he had actually seen and handled the object in question.

Size of the Plates. The Prophet Joseph Smith gave the size as six-by-eight inches.

David Whitmer, in an interview in the *Kansas City Journal*, said of the plates, shortly before his death: "They appeared to be of gold, about six by nine inches in size, about as thick as parchment, a great many in number and bound together like the leaves of a book by massive rings passing through the edges."

Martin Harris, according to *Myth of the Manuscript Found*,[3] estimated the plates at eight-by-seven inches and the thickness of a volume of four inches, each plate being as thick as thick tin.

Orson Pratt had not seen the plates, himself, but his intimacy with the Prophet and the eyewitnesses lend some weight to his words. He tells us that the plates were eight-by-seven inches, while each plate was about as thick as common tin, and also that the entire volume was about six inches thick. Orson Pratt also said that two-thirds of the volume was sealed.

Such are the statements made on the dimensions of the plates and all show really slight variations. David Whitmer's estimate of the size amounts to fifty-four square inches, but he says nothing of the thickness of the volume. Martin Harris gives us fifty-six square inches as the size of the plates and four inches as the thickness of the volume. Orson Pratt accepts the first figure of Martin Harris but gives six inches as the thickness, as does the Prophet Joseph Smith. According to the latter, each plate had a surface of forty-eight square inches.

The real question is: "Could one-third (two-thirds being sealed) of a volume of metal plates (leaves) 6 x 8 x 6 (the Prophet Joseph), or 8 x 7 x 4 (Martin Harris), or 8 x 7 x 6 (Orson Pratt), contain a sufficient number of plates, each as thick as parchment or tin, to yield the necessary space for the entire text of the Book of Mormon? If so, what about their immense weight?

---

a bow fastened to a breastplate. Through the medium of the Urim and Thummim I translated the record by the gift and power of God." Joseph Smith, in a letter to John Wentworth, editor of the *Chicago Democrat*, March 1, 1842. *History of the Church*, Vol. 4, p. 535.

[3]A little book by George Reynolds.

Two remarkable Illustrations. The accompanying illustrations answer these questions.

The first is a facsimile of a sheet of paper, eight by seven inches, upon which a Hebrew translation of fourteen pages of the American text of the Book of Mormon have been written in the modern, square Hebrew letters in common use. The translation was made by our friend, Mr. Henry Miller, a Hebrew by birth, thoroughly versed in the Hebrew language, and a member of the Church. On this sheet it is demonstrated that the entire text of the Book of Mormon could have been written in Hebrew on 40-3/7 pages — twenty-one plates in all.

If it is thought that these characters are too small to be read with alacrity, it may be said that the illustrations, as Mr. Miller wrote them, were quite legible. But turn to the second illustration. This is a reproduction of a translation into Hebrew, also by Mr. Miller, and written in the old Phœnician or Israelitic characters which were known to Lehi and his contemporaries. It contains seven pages of the American text of the Book of Mormon. It proves that even if these larger characters are used, the entire book should be written or engraved on 80-6/7 pages — forty-one plates in all. Illustration No. 2 is also on seven by eight inch paper.

Hebrew translation of II Nephi, Chapters 5:20 to 11:3 inclusive,

(about 14¾ pages of the English version)

In the Old World the ancient Semitic Alphabet was, in due time, superceded by the Aramean. This system of writing was adopted by the Hebrew after the Babylonian captivity, chiefly, as Jewish tradition avers, through the influence of Ezra. The square Hebrew letters now in use are the modern offspring of the Aramean ancestors.

In Egypt the Hieroglyphic letters gradually receded into oblivion, and the Demotic or Enchorian script became popular. At the time of Herodotus, about B.C. 450, only the Hieratic and the Demotic characters were known outside the small circle of scholars.[4] It appears, therefore, that Nephi, in this part of the world, took the same course as regards the reformation of the alphabet as that followed by the scholars of the Old World, as their literary taste and requirements developed.

Seven English Pages

(Seven pages of text in Phoenician or Old Israelitic characters)

II Nephi 11:4-16:9; Hebrew Text; Phoenician Letters.

Hebrew translation of II Nephi, Chapter 11:4 to 16:9 inclusive
(Phœnician or Old Israelitic characters. Seven English pages)

Some time in the dim past, perhaps two thousand years before our era, Semitic scholars, probably Phœnicians, feeling the need of simpler and more practical signs

---

[4]E. A. Wallis Budge, *A History of Egypt*, Vol. 6, p. 198. *Scribner's Bible Dictionary*, "Alphabet."

than those in use in Egypt, picked out twenty-one of the old Hieratic characters, modified them, and renamed them. This according to the famed French Egyptologist Emmanuel de Rouge, was the origin of the oldest Semitic alphabet. It has been called the *Phoenician* or *Old Israelitic* alphabet. As a matter of fact, it was the *Egyptian Reformed,* and was adapted to Semitic speech. The *Law,* and most of the *Prophets,* were at one time written in these characters.

Lehi, the scholarly ancestor of the Nephites and the Lamanites, undoubtedly was familiar with it. It was the alphabet, we have no doubt, on the Brass Plates of Laban, referred to as "the language of the Egyptians,"[5] (Mosiah 1:4) meaning, as explained, "the characters which are called among us the reformed Egyptian." (Mormon 9:32) Nephi knew this system of writing, for he had been "taught somewhat in all the learning of my father." (I Nephi 1:1) It would, therefore, be natural for him to make use of this Old Semitic alphabet as a foundation for the signs he needed for his record, modified so as to require but little space for the ponderous material on which they were engraved.

Here it should be recalled, perhaps, that we are not in possession of all that the Prophet translated from the record. Martin Harris lost, as is well known, one hundred-sixteen written pages of completed manuscript, which were not retranslated. Just how much printed space they would have occupied, we know not; but fifty pages we consider a very generous allowance for that space. Fifty printed pages would be equal to a little more than seven pages—four plates— if the Phœnician characters were used. Four plates, then, should be added to the forty-one already mentioned, making a total number of plates needed for the entire book that was translated, forty-five.

Hebrew Writing Requires Small Space. This may sound incredible, but it is easily explained. The Hebrews of old did not write vowels. They wrote only consonants, and they did not leave much space between words and lines as we do. Nor did they need so many small words as we do to complete a sentence. Frequently their auxiliary words consisted of a single letter attached to the main word, either as a prefix or suffix. And, finally, they used many abbreviations. All this meant a great saving of space.[6]

The entire volume was four inches thick (Martin Harris), or about six inches (Orson Pratt). Let us take the smaller number as the most probable. Mr. Lamb has allowed fifty plates to an inch, or two hundred plates to the four inches. One-third only was translated; that is, sixty-six and a fraction plates. But we have demonstrated that the entire book including the lost pages, could have been written on forty-five plates. If we allow sixty-six, or even fifty, we have ample space for a text engraved in large, legible characters.[7]

Regarding the Weight. Thirty-five twenty-dollar gold pieces would cover a surface of about seven by eight inches. To make a column four inches high, forty-eight such pieces would be needed. Consequently, thirty-five times forty-eight twenty dollar gold pieces, or 1,680 in all, would make up the dimensions of the plates,

---

[5]This little colony brought with them from Jerusalem their ancient scriptures engraved in Egyptian characters, on brass plates." Orson Pratt, in an article on the Book of Mormon, written in 1874 for the *Universal Cyclopedia. Millennial Star,* Vol. 38, p. 692.

[6]It is well known that the subdivision of the Hebrew text of the Bible was not begun before the Thirteenth Century of our era. The Masoretic punctuation, including most of the vowels now in use to aid the student in pronouncing the words, was not introduced until some time between the Sixth and Ninth Centuries. The separation of the text into words is not found in the oldest manuscripts. The square letters of the consonants were not employed before the Third Century of our era.

[7]The first edition of the Book of Mormon, printed in Palmyra, New York, 1830, has 590 pages, 12:mo. The first European edition, Liverpool, 1841, reprinted from the second American edition, has 634 pages. The third American edition, Nauvoo, has 571 pages. The second edition, Liverpool, 1849, has 563 pages. The American edition, 1920, has 522 pages.

seven by eight by four inches. A twenty-dollar gold piece weighs twenty-one and one-half penny-weights. That would make a total of 123 pounds.[8]

From this estimate liberal deductions must be made. The Plates were not pure gold. The Plates of Nephi were made of *ore,* and Moroni also mentions *ore* as the material of which his plates were made. (Mormon 8:5) The *ore,* possibly a copper alloy, must have been considerably lighter in weight than the twenty-three karat gold of which a twenty-dollar piece is made. We cannot suppose that the plates fitted as closely together as gold coins do when stacked in a column. There must have been some space between each pair, especially if, as is probable, they were hammered[9] and not cast. Then again, allowance must be made for the metal cut away by the engraver, from each plate. Everything considered, the volume must have weighed considerably less than a hundred pounds, even on the supposition that the dimensions given are strictly accurate and not mere approximations.

Another Calculation. The subject of weight may also be approached from another premise. Let us suppose that the entire text was engraved on forty-five plates, as has been shown to be possible. Forty-five would then be the number of the unsealed one-third and there would be ninety in the sealed two-thirds; that is a total of 135 plates. But if two hundred weigh 123 pounds, 135 would weigh a small fraction over eighty-three pounds. When the necessary deductions, pointed out in the previous paragraph, are made, the entire volume could not have weighed fifty pounds. The plates that the Prophet had in his possession were not heavier than that he, who was an unusually strong man, could lift them and handle them.[10] That is the testimony of eyewitnesses, and that testimony stands.

Similar Objections to Bible Statements. Curiously enough, at one time certain critics of the Bible used to raise objections to the Old Testament description of the Tabernacle furniture on the ground that gold was too heavy to handle. We are told that Bezaleel made an ark or box of wood, in which the Law was deposited. It was overlaid with pure gold "within and without." The cover of this box was a lid made of pure gold (Exodus 25:17); two and one-half cubits long and one and one-half cubits wide. That is, it was an immense gold plaque four feet three inches by two feet seven inches, or about eleven square feet in size. On this lid two cherubs were placed, one at each end. These figures were hammered of pure gold. Their wings covered the lid, and they must have been of considerable size. This box, we are told, was carried by the priests before the Camp of Israel during the wanderings of the Children of Israel, but the critics referred to, used to tell us that was impossible. The box, with its solid gold lid, and immense solid gold statues, its stone tablets, its gold rings and staves, was too heavy to handle, except with machinery. But that kind of "criticism" is old and obsolete, whether applied to the Bible or Book of Mormon.

Metal Plates not Unknown. We have also been told the ancient scribes never used metal plates for their records, and that, therefore, Laban could not have had any brass plates.

Ivory tablets were used by the ancient Romans. They also used wooden tablets, beech and fir. Sometimes these were coated with wax, and the record was made with a *stylus.* Two or more of such tablets might be joined together by means of wire rings, similar to the Book of Mormon Plates. Parchment made of animal skins was a favorite material for important records, and vellum, or calf skin, was commonly used in early days for this purpose. But we also read that the High Priest wore a

[8]A solid brick of twenty-four karat gold, 7 x 8 x 4 inches in measurement, would weigh approximately 156 pounds, avoirdupois.
[9]*See,* Exodus 39:3. "And they did beat the gold into thin plates."
[10]*History of the Prophet Joseph by His Mother, Lucy Smith,* pp. 85 and 105. The incident told must have been related by the Prophet, himself.

34. But the Lord knoweth the things which we have written, and also that none other people knoweth our language; therefore he hath prepared means for the interpretation thereof.

35. And these things are written that we may rid our garments of the blood of our brethren, who have dwindled in unbelief.

36. And behold, these things which ye have desired concerning our brethren, yea, even their restoration to the knowledge of Christ, are according to the prayers of all the saints who have dwelt in the land.

37. And may the Lord Jesus Christ grant that their prayers may be answered according to

gold plate on his crown, on which words were engraved (Exodus 39:30), and Jeremiah exclaims: "The sin of Judah is written with a pen of iron, and with the point of a diamond: it is graven upon the table of their heart. . . ." (Jeremiah 17:1) This proves beyond question that the Israelites were familiar with engraved tables, for otherwise the words of the prophets would have been unintelligible to them. (See, statement by Padre Gay, page XI, Volume I, Commentary on the Book of Mormon.

VERSE 34. *The Lord hath prepared means for the interpretation thereof. See,* footnote No. 2.

VERSE 35. *Why these things are written.* That the blood of our brethren who have dwindled in unbelief may not soil our garments that at the Last Day we may stand spotless before the Judgment-Seat of Christ; and that through no fault of ours they may seek to excuse and palliate what they did, or did not do, while here upon the earth, this record is made.

VERSES 36-37. *These things which we have desired.* From the very first when contention among them divided into two groups, the sons of Lehi, the prayers of those who followed after Nephi, continually were for the welfare of their brethren who had followed Laman and Lemuel.

For the consideration of Book of Mormon students, we submit as proper evidence the words of Enos, who was a grandson of the Prophet Lehi. His words are to be found in the records of the Smaller Plates:

"And after I, Enos, had heard these words, my faith began to be unshaken in the Lord; and I prayed unto him with many long strugglings for my brethren, the Lamanites.

"And it came to pass that after I had prayed and labored with all diligence, the Lord said unto me: I will grant unto thee according to thy desires, because of thy faith.

"And now behold, this was the desire which I desired of him—that if it should so be, that my people, the Nephites, should fall into transgression, and by any means be destroyed, and the Lamanites should not be destroyed, that the Lord God would preserve a record of my people, the Nephites; even if it so be by the power of his holy arm, that it might be brought forth at some future day unto the Lamanites, that, perhaps, they might be brought unto salvation—

"For at the present our strugglings were vain in restoring them to the true faith. And they swore in their wrath that, if it were possible, they would destroy our records and us, and also all the traditions of our fathers.

"Wherefore, I knowing that the Lord God was able to preserve our records, I cried unto him continually, for he had said unto me: Whatsoever thing ye shall ask in faith, believing that ye shall receive in the name of Christ, ye shall receive it.

their faith; and may God the house of Israel; and may he bless Father remember the covenant them forever, through faith on which he hath made with the the name of Jesus Christ. Amen.

"And I had faith, and I did cry unto God that he would preserve the records; and he covenanted with me that he would bring them forth unto the Lamanites in his own due time.

"And I, Enos, knew it would be according to the covenant which he had made; wherefore my soul did rest.

"And the Lord said unto me: Thy fathers have also required of me this thing; and it shall be done unto them according to their faith; for their faith was like unto thine. (Enos 11-18)

VERSE 37. *May the Lord Jesus Christ grant that their prayers may be answered.* . . . Moroni finished the Record commenced by his father with a prayer unto God, the loving Father of all men, that the prayers offered by all the Saints who ever dwelt in the Land of Promise made for the benefit and blessing of his brethren, the Lamanites, would be answered, and also that He Who reigns On High would remember His Covenant made with the House of Israel, of which both the Nephites and the Lamanites were members; "and may He bless them forever, through faith on the Name of Jesus Christ. Amen."

THE BOOK OF MORONI

CHAPTER 1

1. *Moroni's Desolate State*—2. *He Writes, Hoping for the Welfare of the Lamanites.*

1. *Moroni's desolate state.*
2. *He writes, hoping for the welfare of the Lamanites.*

1. Now I, Moroni, after having made an end of abridging the account of the people of Jared, I had supposed not to have written more, but I have not as yet perished; and I make not myself known to the Lamanites lest they should destroy me.

2. For behold, their wars are exceedingly fierce among themselves; and because of their hatred they put to death every Nephite that will not deny the Christ.

3. And I, Moroni, will not deny the Christ; wherefore, I wander whithersoever I can for the safety of mine own life.

4. Wherefore, I write a few more things, contrary to that which I had supposed; for I had supposed not to have written any more; but I write a few more things, that perhaps they may be of worth unto my brethren, the Lamanites, in some future day, according to the will of the Lord.

VERSE 1. *I, Moroni.* Moroni's task having been completed, wherein he undertook to abridge the account of the Jaredites which Mosiah I, that great Prophet, Seer, and King of the Nephites, had translated from the twenty and four Gold Plates of Ether, he (Moroni) intended to write no more.

VERSE 2. *Their wars were exceedingly fierce among themselves.* After the final battle between the Nephites and the Lamanites in which the Lamanites were victorious, the Lamanites split into many contending factions, each contesting the dominance of the other, and all warring among themselves and pillaging and despoiling the countryside. Moroni notes that "Their wars are exceedingly fierce among themselves." His father, Mormon, had been slain by them, but he, himself, had not perished. By some marvelous power which was the power of God, Moroni's life was preserved for a wise purpose in which we can easily see the hand of God.[1] The power and the purpose of God is made manifest to us in Moroni's then uncontemplated writings which are preserved in the following chapters of his Book.

The bitter hatred of the Lamanites for all that was good, and their ferocious enmity toward God's servants, caused them to put to death "every Nephite who would not deny the Christ." (v. 2) All the bitter hatreds and angry passions that hell inspires, all that human wickedness could suggest, or evil power achieve, was let loose by Satan in the bloodthirsty carnival of crime that then bore sway.

But in spite of threatened death, one of the most horrible kind, Moroni was

---

[1]The expression, Hand of God, or Hand of the Lord, is used throughout the Scriptures, both Jewish and Nephite, and means the *purpose,* or the *presence,* or the *power* of God.

firm in his oft-repeated declaration of Christ's divinity; he knew that *Jesus was the Christ,* and he knew that God knew that he knew it, and I, Moroni, he says, "Will not deny the Christ, wherefore, I wander whithersoever I can for the safety of mine own life." (v. 3)

Inspired by his prophetic calling, and, no doubt, sensing the mind and will of the Lord, Moroni wrote down a few things which have proved to be of great worth to us in these last days. His prayer was that what he wrote may be of benefit to his brethren, the Lamanites, in some future day. His prayer is now being answered, for not only are we blessed and benefited by the things he wrote, but through us, the Lamanites, many of whom are fast becoming a white and delightsome people will by Heaven's gracious command also be blessed. This is, as Moroni prayed, according to the will of the Lord. (v. 4)

GENERAL NOTES

Moroni's literary work in the Book of Mormon, so far, consists of the last two chapters, 8 and 9, of the Book that bears his father's name, Mormon, and the fifteen chapters of the Book of Ether. He had finished the record concerning the final tragedy of Cumorah, and he had hidden it in the earth, presumably in the Hill on that battlefield. (Mormon 6:6; 8:4; 14:16) His first intention was not to make further additions to the completed volume. But, although his life had been spared in the general massacre, he had no opportunity, on account of the bitter enmity of the survivors against the followers of Christ, to testify to and exhort the people. In vain he held the office of a prophet of God bearing the holy Priesthood. He lived in hiding, or went about in disguise (v. 1), changing his places of refuge frequently. During this virtual exile, he committed the contents of this Book to writing. It was his only opportunity to bear his testimony.

I wander whithersoever I can. Moroni wandered in all probability not very far from Cumorah. He expected to seal up the records after he had spoken a few words "by way of exhortation." (Moroni 10:2) His hiding place could, consequently, not have been far from the underground repository that contained the other sacred records.

For the benefit of the Lamanites. Lamanites, means here, the *American Aborigines who have not accepted the Gospel as it was taught by the Nephites.* For genealogical purposes, Lamanites would be the lineal descendants of the sons of Lehi, Laman and Lemuel. But this natural division according to lineage was disregarded, except, we suppose, for special purposes, early in the history of the people. The Prophet Jacob, 50 or 60 years after the exodus from Jerusalem says that they were called, Nephites, Jacobites, Josephites, Lamanites, Lemuelites, and Ishmaelites, "But I, Jacob, shall not hereafter distinguish them by those names, but I shall call them Lamanites that seek to destroy the people of Nephi, and those who are friendly to Nephi I shall call Nephites, or the people of Nephi, according to the reigns of the kings." (Jacob 1:14)

In the Land of Zarahemla, during the Millennial conditions prevailing for two hundred years after the visit of the Risen Redeemer, the distinction between Nephites and Lamanites was completely obliterated (IV Nephi 17), until a war began between the two religio-political parties known as Nephites and Lamanites, respectively. (Mormon 1:9)

The future of the Lamanites. According to the prophetic word of the Book of Mormon, the Indians, also known as the Lamanites, may look forward to a glorious future. *See,* III Nephi 20 on the "remnant of the House of Israel," and the New Jerusalem. Moroni must have had this in mind when he wrote the concluding part of the Book of Mormon, in the hope that it might be "of worth unto my brethren, the Lamanites at some future day."

That the Indians of America had a bright future in store for them, was far from the popular belief at the time when the Prophet Joseph published the contents of the Sacred Record. The general view was that the American Natives were doomed to extinction. Their ultimate fate seemed to be approaching. It was argued that they had dwindled from an estimated total of about 800,000, at the time of the arrival of the first Europeans, to 294,000 in 1865, when the first government census was taken. As a matter of fact, the generation preceding the present one, expected the native Americans to perish, and some individuals even did what they could to bring about the expected tragedy.

It has been shown in a recent official report of the government that the Indians lost by various ways sixty per cent of the lands granted to them by Congress at the first enactment of any laws affecting their welfare. Few seemed to care whether the Indians were starving, or decimated by sickness and death; or sinking in ignorance through the indifference, or incompetence of the Indian Service. But the race did not perish, and a wonderful change has taken place in their condition and future prospects. In an official report published, it is shown that there were 523,591 native Americans (1960 census) under the care of the Indian Service. They are taught to be self-supporting as farmers, cattle-raisers, and makers of jewelry and blankets. Many Indians, the service reports, have gone into the professions of engineering, law, medicine, teaching, and forestry, after having been educated in reservation schools. Many of these so trained, according to the service, are returning to help their people. "They are imbued with an idea of bettering their race, and rebuilding the Indian Empire along present-day lines."

The Lamanite evidence for the Book of Mormon. This stage of Indian development should be of special interest to the readers of the Book of Mormon, since it furnishes another bit of evidence, the Lamanite evidence, probably new to many of them, for the divine inspiration of that venerable Volume. It makes the Indians, with their fabulous adventures and experiences, witnesses for their ancient record, for the same reason that the Hebrews, in their preservation throughout the ages, prove the truth of the Bible.

Here is a striking story which contains a volume in one brief sentence. When the Court Chaplain of Frederick the Great, of Prussia, was asked by the King for a proof in one word of the inspiration of the Bible, he answered, "The Jews, your Majesty." And the King was satisfied. If a friend should make a similar request of a student of the Book of Mormon, the latter might answer, confidently and emphatically, "The American Indians."

Moroni, we may suppose, through inspiration, wrote his Book which is an addition to that which he originally intended, and doing so had the Lamanites "in some future day," in prophetic prospect.

CHAPTER 2

1. Concerning the Bestowal of the Holy Ghost by the Nephite Twelve.

1. The words of Christ, which he spake unto his disciples, the twelve whom he had chosen, as he laid his hands upon them— 2. And he called them by name, saying: Ye shall call on the Father in my name, in mighty prayer; and after ye have done this ye shall have power that to him upon whom ye shall lay your hands, ye shall give the Holy Ghost; and in my name shall ye give it, for thus do mine apostles. 3. Now Christ spake these words unto them at the time of his first appearing; and the multitude heard it not, but the disciples heard it; and on as many as they laid their hands, fell the Holy Ghost.

---

1. *The words of Christ as He bestowed the Holy Ghost upon the Nephite Twelve Disciples.* Our Lord, in conferring on the Twelve Nephite Disciples the authority to give the Holy Ghost to baptized believers, instructed them to call upon the Father in His (Christ's) Name in mighty prayer. The Apostle Paul gives the same admonition thus: "And whatsoever ye do in word or in deed, do all in the Name of the Lord Jesus, giving thanks to God the Father through Him." (Colossians 3:17)

To ask in the Name of the Lord is not merely to repeat His Name at the beginning and the end of a petition, but is to come before the Almighty because we are granted that privilege, or authority, to do so by the Beloved Son Himself. That brings the desired results.

But a prayer in the Name of the Lord must, furthermore, be a "mighty" prayer. If it is mighty, it is sincere. It comes from the heart. It is a function as necessary to our spiritual life, as is breathing, or the circulation of the blood, to our physical being.

A "mighty" prayer is dictated by the Spirit of the Lord, and is, therefore, in harmony with His will. That is the secret of its power. The Father will not refuse to grant the prayers of a humble petitioner who asks for that which the Lord wants him to have, no more than He will turn a deaf ear to the pleadings of the Beloved Son Himself. Hence the essence of a "mighty prayer" is, "Not my will, but Thine be done."

This is an important Scriptural doctrine. Hear the Apostle Paul: "The Spirit also helpeth our infirmity: for we know not how to pray as we ought; but the Spirit Himself maketh intercession for us with groanings which cannot be uttered." (Romans 8:26) John says: "And this is the confidence which we have toward Him, that, if we ask anything according to His will, He heareth us. (I John 5:14) And also James: "Ye ask, and receive not, because ye ask amiss, that ye may spend it in your pleasures. (James 4:5)

The Importance of Prayer. Our Lord first authorized the Twelve Disciples to baptize. (III Nephi 11:27; 12:1) Then, as we learn from this text, He conferred upon them the power to impart the Holy Ghost by the Laying of the Hands. But this great gift would be bestowed on them only if they would call upon the Father in mighty prayer to be offered in Jesus' Name. The lesson is that the power of the Priesthood has its source in prayer, fervent, heartfelt, and that the Elder who expects to retain his spiritual vigor must attend to his prayers faithfully. Neglect of communion with God makes him weak spiritually, and his administrations may become ineffective.

Thus do Mine Apostles. The Apostles in the Church in Jerusalem were living when Jesus called the Twelve in the Land Bountiful.

The Multitude Heard it not. Our Lord gave the same instructions to all the Twelve, calling each by name and repeating, one by one it so appears, the same words. In so doing He naturally lowered His voice to a pitch of a private conversation. The Disciples and those who were close by heard Him, but the multitude in the distance heard Him not. "But the Disciples heard it; and on as many as they laid their hands, fell the Holy Ghost." (v. 3)

CHAPTER 3

1. Concerning the Ordination of Priests and Teachers.

1. The manner which the disciples, who were called the elders of the church, ordained priests and teachers—

2. After they had prayed unto the Father in the name of Christ, they laid their hands upon them, and said:

3. In the name of Jesus Christ I ordain you to be a priest, (or if he be a teacher) I ordain you to be a teacher, to preach repentance and remission of sins through Jesus Christ, by the endurance of faith on his name to the end. Amen.

4. And after this manner did they ordain priests and teachers, according to the gifts and callings of God unto men; and they ordained them by the power of the Holy Ghost, which was in them.

VERSE 1. *The manner which the Elders ordained Priests and Teachers.* The calling and duties of the Nephite Disciples were similar in some respects to those of the Apostles in Palestine (Moroni 2:2), and in the Church of Jesus Christ of Latter-day Saints. Their Priesthood was that of Elders (v. 1), and their commission was to declare the Gospel "unto this people," and unto "the ends of the earth." (III Nephi 11:41) We gather from the record of Moroni that they received this Priesthood and mission at the time when they were chosen and authorized to baptize (III Nephi 11:22; Moroni 2:2). In Moroni 3:3, the exact words which the Disciples used in ordaining Priests and Teachers are recorded.

In common, everyday parlance, a "priest" is an ordained preacher, one who teaches religion from the pulpit; he may be the spiritual guide of an ecclesiastical denomination or congregation. The word is an abbreviated form of "presbyter," which has been translated "elder" in the New Testament, (Titus 1:5; I Peter 5:11), in all passages except I Timothy 4:14, where the original "presbyter" has been retained. In the Book of Alma "priest" has another meaning. That Prophet, speaking of our first parents, says, "God gave commandments unto His children, and I would that ye remember that the Lord God ordained priests after His Holy Order, which was after the Order of His Son, to teach these things unto the people." (Alma 26-31; 13:1-2) The calling of these priests was to teach the people the commandments of God. They were teachers or prophets, and not only priests. They held the Melchizedek Priesthood, or Priesthood, as Alma said, after the *Order of His Son.*

"Priests and Teachers" in our text (Moroni 3) must, in our opinion, be understood to be of callings different from either of the two just explained. This conclusion may be drawn from the fact that they are mentioned separately as two distinct classes. Some of the novices were ordained Priests, others Teachers. We are, therefore, inclined to the view that those so ordained, were two divisions of what the Latter-day Saints, according to modern revelations, know as the Aaronic Priesthood.

Some would tell us that the Priesthood of Aaron ended with the advent of Christ in the Meridian of Time, and that, consequently, the Nephites could not have received that Priesthood through the Disciples of our Lord; and that the Latter-day Saints could not have gotten it in our day through the instrumentality of John the Baptist. But the idea that the Priesthood of Aaron was abolished by Christ is not correct. Some of the outward ordinances which were the essential features of worship during the Old Covenant ended with the coming of the New Dispensation. They were but morning twilight preceding the glorious dawn. They were types fulfilled in the life and death of Christ. Thus, many of the functions of the Aaronic Priests ceased with the Messiah's advent, but the Priesthood itself remained.

Our Lord Himself held the Aaronic Priesthood as well as the Melchizedek Priesthood, if we understand correctly what the Apostle Paul says on that subject. His argument is that every High Priest — he is speaking of Aaron, the Chief Priest of the Mosaic Covenant — is "taken from among men," and appointed for men in *things pertaining to God,* but that he must be called by God even "as was Aaron." "So," he says, "Christ also glorified not Himself to be made an High Priest," — He is still speaking of the office of Aaron — but He that said unto Him, THOU ART MY SON, TO DAY HAVE I BEGOTTEN THEE." (Hebrews 5:1-5)

That is, Christ's calling to the Aaronic as well as the Melchizedek Priesthood came from God. As an Aaronic High Priest He presided, and does still preside, over the Aaronic Priesthood, as did Aaron in the Mosaic religious services, and Aaron's successors after him. Our Lord, in mortality, offered His prayers and supplications (Hebrews 5:7) as did Aaron his gifts and sacrifices, and then, having been made perfect, He was named of God a High Priest after the order of Melchizedek.[1]

Aaron and his consecration. Aaron was the brother of Moses and Miriam and the son of Amron, of the Tribe of Levi. According to some calculations he was born about 1725 B.C., the year before the Egyptian tyrant ordered the destruction of all Hebrew male infants in the country, and three years before the birth of Moses. (Exodus 7:7) The name of his wife was Elisheba. She was of the Tribe of Judah. They had four sons, Nadab, Abihu, Eleazar, and Ithamar. Unlike Moses, Aaron was an eloquent speaker, wherefore the Lord, when Moses was about to refuse to accept the mission of liberator and law-giver of Israel, appointed him to assist and speak for the younger brother. On his way to Egypt, Moses met Aaron at Mt. Horeb. (Exodus 4:27) They proceeded together to their destination. On their arrival there, they began their mission by summoning the Elders of Israel, and announcing to them that they had come by divine command to lead the people out of bondage. Then they appeared before Pharaoh and proved their commission by a series of terrifying miracles. The consent of the rulers to the demand of the two Hebrews was obtained only when it appeared as if the entire Egyptian population was about to perish.

Aaron receives the Priesthood. In due time after the Exodus from Egypt, the Children of Israel arrived at Mt. Sinai. Here, on the Mount, the Lord graciously revealed Himself to Moses, after the Covenant between Him and Israel had been ratified by the people. Moses ascended the lofty heights. Aaron, his sons, and seventy of the Elders who represented the Twelve Tribes, accompanied Moses at a distance, but near enough to be witnesses to the divine manifestation. (Exodus 24:1-11) At this time the Lord commanded Moses to confer upon Aaron and his sons the Priesthood that their descendants were to inherit and hold forever. (Leviticus 8:12) The entire Tribe of Levi was at the same time called to devote themselves exclusively to the Divine Service.

---

[1]The title, High Priest, as applied to Aaron, is not free from ambiguity. In the Old Testament he is called *the great priest* (hakohen hagadol), or *head priest* (kohen harosh), or the *anointed priest* (kohen hamashiach). However, these titles are not ambiguous. In the New Testament he is the *first* or *chief* priest (archierevs). St. Paul, as already noted, says that he was appointed for men (to have charge) of things pertaining to God, the literal meaning of which is that Aaron, as Chief Priest presided, on behalf of the people, over temporal matters dedicated to the divine service. Aaron and his sons were the Presiding Bishopric of the Old Covenant. As a Bishop his office was, and still is, hereditary. (Exodus 29:9; Doctrine and Covenants 68:20; 21; 107:69; 70)

CHAPTERS 4 AND 5

Mode of Administering the Sacramental Bread.

Mode of Administering the Sacramental Wine.

1. The manner of their elders and priests administering the flesh and blood of Christ unto the church; and they administered it according to the commandments of Christ; wherefore we know the manner to be true; and the elder of priest did minister it—
2. And they did kneel down with the church, and pray to the Father in the name of Christ, saying:
3. O God, the Eternal Father, we ask thee in the name of thy Son, Jesus Christ, to bless and sanctify this bread to the souls of all those who partake of it; that they may eat in remembrance of the body of thy Son, and witness unto thee, O God, the Eternal Father, that they are willing to take upon them the name of thy Son, and always remember him, and keep his commandments which he hath given them, that they may always have his Spirit to be with them. Amen.

In the verses of these chapters, Moroni tells us what the words are that were used by the Elders and Priests in administering the holy Emblems of the flesh and blood of the Redeemer to the members of Christ's Nephite Church. He assures us that everything was done in accordance with certain commandments that were given them (the Nephite Saints of God) by Jesus Christ Himself. Therefore, Moroni notes that we know the manner of their administration to be true.

Eating of the Broken Bread and drinking of the Cup of Wine which is also called the Sacrament, is an ordinance observed by all devout Latter-day Saints in remembrance of the flesh and blood of our Lord and Savior, Jesus Christ, Who laid down His Own Life as a Ransom for sin that all might live forever, which is Life Eternal.

During His appearance in the Land Bountiful, observance of the Sacrament was instituted by our Lord for the spiritual benefit of those who believed in Him, and who had been baptized in His Name by the Nephite servants of God.

The Broken Bread, one of the emblems of this ordinance, is to be eaten in remembrance of the body of Jesus as a testimony to the Father that the partaker thereof is willing to take upon himself the Name of Christ, and also that His Son, Jesus Christ, the Holy One of Israel, will be by them always remembered.

The Cup of Wine, similarly, is partaken of in remembrance of the blood of our Savior which was shed for all mankind, and in doing so, we witness to the Father that we will always remember His Son. Also, in complying with the requirements of this ordinance we testify to God, the Eternal Father, that we are willing to keep the commandments which He commissioned His Son to give unto us. The great purpose of that commitment is that in keeping His commandments we may always have His Spirit to be with us, that we will be holy unto the Lord, our God.

Hearkening back to the time in their history when the Nephites were as one in serving the Lord, they, in solemn assembly, to evidence their reverence for the Sacramental Ordinance which was to be performed, knelt down in humble prayer

1. The manner of administering the wine—Behold, they took the cup, and said:

2. O God, the Eternal Father, we ask thee, in the name of thy Son, Jesus Christ, to bless and sanctify this wine to the souls of all those who drink of it, that they may do it in remembrance of the blood of thy Son, which was shed for them; that they may witness unto thee, O God, the Eternal Father, that they do always remember him, that they may have his Spirit to be with them. Amen.

---

to extol God's holy Name, and to invoke His blessings upon the Bread and Wine. Whereupon both Elders or Priests and the assembled congregation of Saints unitedly called upon the Father in the name of Jesus, Crucified, using the words Moroni notes:

"O God, the Eternal Father, we ask thee, in the name of thy Son, Jesus Christ, to bless and sanctify this bread to the souls of all those who partake of it; that they may eat in remembrance of the body of thy Son, and witness unto thee, O God, the Eternal Father, that they are willing to take upon them the name of thy Son, and always remember him, and keep his commandments which he hath given them, that they may always have his Spirit to be with them. Amen."

In blessing the Sacramental Wine that was in the Cup, which afterwards was passed around to Church members, the one who officiated in the ordinance uttered these words:

"O God, the Eternal Father, we ask thee, in the name of thy Son, Jesus Christ, to bless and sanctify this wine to the souls of all those who drink of it, that they may do it in remembrance of the blood of thy Son, which was shed for them; that they may witness unto thee, O God, the Eternal Father, that they do always remember him, that they may have his Spirit to be with them. Amen."

CHAPTER 6

1. Conditions of Baptism—2. Church Discipline.

1. Conditions of baptism.

1. And now I speak concerning baptism. Behold, elders, priests, and teachers were baptized; and they were not baptized save they brought forth fruit meet that they were worthy of it.

2. Neither did they receive any unto baptism save they came forth with a broken heart and a contrite spirit, and witnessed unto the church that they truly repented of all their sins.

3. And none were received unto baptism save they took upon them the name of Christ, having a determination to serve him to the end.

4. And after they had been received unto baptism, and were wrought upon and cleansed by the power of the Holy Ghost, they were numbered among the people of the church of Christ; and their names were taken, that they

---

VERSE 1. *I speak concerning baptism.* The Nephites, or the portion of them that observed God's holy laws, were strict in requiring certain mental and moral qualifications of those who presented themselves for baptism. Even those who afterwards held the holy Priesthood were, before baptism, enjoined to bring "forth fruit meet that they were worthy of it." Those who at a later time became Elders, Priests, or Teachers, merited baptism because of their good works.

VERSE 2. *Candidates for baptism witnessed . . . that they truly repented of all their sins.* However, good works alone do not entitle the applicant to receive entrance into God's Kingdom. Baptism, nevertheless, is the gate through which all must pass to gain admittance into that glorious place. Besides good works, be it said, those works must be accompanied by a heart broken down with sorrow for sin. Moreover, the seeker, seeking that gate, must approach it confessing his shortcomings, and must be thoroughly penitent therefore, witnessing, as did the Nephite hopefuls, before the other members of Christ's Church "that they truly repented of all their sins."

VERSE 3. *The Name of Christ.* Good works, plus a determination to continue therein, gives the doer thereof the key that unlocks the door to the mansions above. *That key is the Name of Christ.* It is the Name all who are baptized take upon themselves at the Waters of Baptism, and who at the same time make a holy resolve that they will do nothing to betray that Name, nor be found wanting in bringing forth fruit worthy to bear that Name.

VERSE 4. *After baptism they were numbered among the people of the Church of Christ.* Not content with only numbers, but more so in the welfare of those who had lately come into Christ's Church, those holding God's holy Priesthood — we may presume it was the active Elders, Priest, and Teachers — called upon the newcomers, nourishing them by the good word of God, teaching them to pray, and at length if any of them strayed, lead them back to the right path. None who were baptized, were forgotten, but their names were added to the records of the Church, and communion with their brethren was the just reward of righteous living.

might be remembered and nourished by the good word of God, to keep them in the right way, to keep them continually watchful

unto prayer, relying alone upon the merits of Christ, who was the author and the finisher of their faith.

2. Church discipline.

5. And the church did meet together oft, to fast and to pray, and to speak one with another concerning the welfare of their souls.

6. And they did meet together oft to partake of bread and wine, in remembrance of the Lord Jesus.

Relying not upon their own strength, but on God's Holy Word; not upon merits of their own, but on the worth and excellence of Christ, "Who," Moroni says, "was the author and the finisher of their faith," their thoughts undoubtedly are expressed in the beautiful but simple prayer of the Jews: "Lord of all worlds, not in reliance upon righteousness or merit in ourselves do we lay our supplications before Thee, but trusting in Thine infinite mercy alone. For what are we, what is our life, what our goodness, what our power? What can we say in Thy presence? Are not all the mighty men as naught before Thee, and those of great renown as though they had never been; the wisest as if without knowledge, and men of understanding as if without discernment? Many of our works are vain, and our days pass away like a shadow. Our life would be altogether vanity, were it not for our soul, which fashioned in Thine own image, gives us assurance of our higher destiny and imparts to our fleeting days an abiding value.

"Therefore we beseech Thee, O our God, to help us banish from our hearts all pride and vainglory, all confidence in worldly possessions, all self-sufficient leaning upon our own reason. Fill us with the spirit of meekness and the grace of modesty, that we may become wise in the fear of Thee. May we never forget that all we have and prize is but lent to us, a trust for which we must render account to Thee. O Heavenly Father, put into our hearts the love and fear of Thee, that we may consecrate our lives to Thy service and glorify thy Name in the eyes of all men." (Union Prayer Book)

VERSES 5-6. *The Church did meet together oft.* Near the end of the first paragraph of our comments on verse four, we made the statement *and communion with their brethren was the just reward of righteous living.* It is not strange, but enlightening to us, that Moroni says the same thing only in different words: *"The Church did meet together oft . . . to speak one with another concerning the welfare of their souls."* They often refrained from eating material food; fasting, that humility might leaven the bread of righteousness and of spirituality. They prayed for strength, not only for themselves, but for their brethren who knew weakness, not meekness. They prayed for courage that the light within them should not be darkened, but that as a lamp unto the feet of their brethren, it would lead them along that Path which is Strait and Narrow.

The Saints did not gather together for personal purposes, nor were they in pursuit of their own selfish happiness; they covenanted with God, by partaking of the Sacrament, that they did remember the Lord, Jesus Christ, and would thereafter keep His commandments. They were a happy, peaceful, association of God's children, because in all things they had love for their Father and all men in their hearts.

7. And they were strict to observe that there should be no iniquity among them; and whoso was found to commit iniquity, and three witnesses of the church did condemn them before the elders, and if they repented not, and confessed not, their names were blotted out, and they were not numbered among the people of Christ.

8. But as oft as they repented and sought forgiveness, with real intent, they were forgiven.

9. And their meetings were conducted by the church after the manner of the workings of the Spirit, and by the power of the Holy Ghost; for as the power of the Holy Ghost led them whether to preach, or to exhort, or to pray, or to supplicate, or to sing, even so it was done.

VERSES 7-9. *And they were strict to observe that there should be no iniquity among them.* The Nephites were not an inferior people. They were not born into poverty, nor nurtured in darkness. When they kept God's commandments, they were prospered. They became rich in worldly goods, and the light of God's Holy Word illumined the way before them. As we have said: "They had revelations from Heaven to guide them; angels from the Courts of Glory ministered unto them; they prospered in material things; and those who were zealous in keeping the Lord's commandments were benefited and blessed."

But, at length they were destroyed.

Their destruction came upon them because of wickedness; however, in the thousand years in which they dwelt upon the Promised Land of America, they were mostly a good and a just people, holy unto the Lord. Like the Jews who were a contemporary people in the East, the last generation of Nephites lived in the twilight of a brilliant past. In times of peace and prosperity, pride and class distinction because of the worldly things they possessed, became a menace to their welfare. Not only did the Nephites indulge themselves in all carnal pleasures, but pride in their fine clothes and their jewelry crowded all thoughts of God from their hearts.

We do not know the period in their history of which Moroni wrote, however our opinion is that the same things may be said of each. He notes, "They were strict to observe that there should be no iniquity among them." This became a rule, because time and time again the Nephites had seen in their own history where wickedness was the offspring of pride, and stiffneckedness the sire of both. Pride was the Nephites' undoing. If required, we could state the story of the Nephites in a very few words: Prosperity and Pride — Pride and Wickedness — Wickedness and Destruction.

Nevertheless, and notwithstanding the demands of clean and moral living which righteousness made, the Nephites were slow to condemn their fellow man. They gave him that was accused before the Elders of the Church, every opportunity to right a wrong if he was found guilty by that court of righteous and holy decisions. In that court for the Judges to accept any evidence whatsoever it was required that the testimony of at least three witnesses corroborate one another's word. If then the guilty one repented of the wrong he had done, and therein asked to be forgiven, he was forgiven. If he did not repent, his name was "blotted out and he was not numbered among the people of Christ."

The meetings of the Nephite Saints, wherever and whenever they might have been, were presided over by one in authority who by the power of the Holy Ghost and the united support of the congregation, "led them whether to preach, or to exhort, or to pray, or to supplicate, or to sing, even so it was done."

CHAPTER 7

1. *Moroni presents Mormon's teachings on faith, hope, and charity.*

1. And now I, Moroni, write a few of the words of my father Mormon, which he spake concerning faith, hope, and charity; for after this manner did he speak unto the people, as he taught them in the synagogue which they had built for the place of worship.

2. And now I, Mormon, speak unto you, my beloved brethren; and it is by the grace of God the Father, and our Lord Jesus Christ, and his holy will, because of the gift of his calling unto me, that I am permitted to speak unto you at this time.

3. Wherefore, I would speak unto you that are of the church, that are the peaceable followers of Christ, and that have obtained a sufficient hope by which ye can enter into the rest of the Lord, from this time henceforth until ye shall rest with him in heaven.

VERSE 1. *I, Moroni, write a few words of my father, Mormon, which he spake concerning faith, hope, and charity.* In this chapter an address concerning *Faith, Hope and Charity,* which was delivered by the Prophet Mormon to the Nephite Saints is preserved by his son, Moroni. For our edification, and our better understanding, we may be assured by Alma's admonishment to the Saints in Gideon: "See that ye have *faith, hope, and charity,* and then ye will always abound in good works." (Alma 7:24)

Where this address was given is not of the greatest importance, but it will suffice any inquiry thereof to quote Moroni's own words concerning it: "For after this manner did he speak unto the people, as he taught them in the synagogue which they had built for the place of worship."

VERSE 2. *I, Mormon, speak unto you by the grace of God.* To begin with, Mormon established his ability to speak unto the assembled congregation, and his authority for so doing. Being favored of God and our Lord Jesus Christ; in and through their kindness and mercy; it being Their will that I so do; having received from Them the blessings necessary unto this calling "I am permitted to speak unto you at this time."

VERSE 3. *I would speak unto you that are of the Church.* Mormon addresses his remarks to the members of the Church, those, he says, "Who are the peaceable followers of Christ." One of the first fruits of an association with Christ, or an acquaintance with His teachings, is peace, sometimes called "God's most precious gift." And in this connection, we will not forget the words of Isaiah; quoted by the Savior to the Nephites when He visited them in the Land Bountiful shortly after His resurrection: "And all thy children shall be taught of the Lord; and great shall be the peace of thy children." (III Nephi 22:13) Also the words of King David: "Mark the perfect man, and behold the upright: for the end of that man is peace," (Psalm 37:37) and "Great peace have they which love Thy law." (*Ibid.,* 119:165) Again, ". . . And His Name shall be called . . . *The Prince of Peace.*" (Isaiah 9:6)

From these and many other passages of both Nephite and Hebrew Scripture, we can easily see why Mormon addressed his words to the "peaceable followers of Christ."

Mormon coupled that quality of the Saints of God with another of outstanding importance, and thus we may read his salutation: "I speak unto the peaceable followers of Christ who have obtained a sufficient *hope* by which ye can enter into the rest of the Lord." Mormon adds further to his thought of hope, that the happy expectation of *rest in the Lord* will be followed by "rest with Him in Heaven." This doctrine is consistent with the magnific and sublime understanding which the Nephites had of the great Hereafter. Alma, in instructing his son upon some points of doctrine which his son, Corianton, wished to become enlightened, gave him this rather detailed description of what the "rest of the Lord" expression really did mean:

"Therefore, there is a time appointed that they shall rise from the dead; and there is a space between the time of death and the resurrection. And now, concerning this space of time, what becometh of the souls of men is the thing which I have inquired diligently of the Lord to know; and this is the thing of which I do know.

"And when the time cometh when all shall rise, then shall they know that God knoweth all the times which are appointed unto man.

"Now, concerning the state of the soul between death and the resurrection — Behold, it has been made known unto me by an angel, that the spirits of all men, as soon as they are departed from this mortal body, yea, the spirits of all men, whether they be good or evil, are taken home to that God who gave them life.

"And then shall it come to pass, *that the spirits of those who are righteous are received into a state of happiness, which is called paradise, a state of rest, a state of peace, where they shall rest from all their troubles and from all care, and sorrow.*

"And then shall it come to pass, that the spirits of the wicked, yea, who are evil—for behold, they have no part nor portion of the Spirit of the Lord; for behold, they chose evil works rather than good; therefore the spirit of the devil did enter into them, and take possession of their house—and these shall be cast out into outer darkness; there shall be weeping, and wailing, and gnashing of teeth, and this because of their own iniquity, being led captive by the will of the devil.

"Now this is the state of the souls of the wicked, yea, in darkness, and a state of awful, fearful looking for the fiery indignation of the wrath of God upon them; thus they remain in this state, as well as the righteous in paradise, until the time of their resurrection.

"Now, there are some that have understood that this state of happiness and this state of misery of the soul, before the resurrection, was a first resurrection. Yea, I admit it may be termed a resurrection, the raising of the spirit or the soul and their consignation to happiness or misery, according to the words which have been spoken.

"And behold, again it hath been spoken, that there is a first resurrection, a resurrection of all those who have been, or who are, or who shall be, down to the resurrection of Christ from the dead.

"Now, we do not suppose that this first resurrection, which is spoken of in this manner, can be the resurrection of the souls and their consignation to happiness or misery. Ye cannot suppose that this is what it meaneth.

"Behold, I say unto you, Nay; but it meaneth the reuniting of the soul with the body, of those from the days of Adam down to the resurrection of Christ.

"Now, whether the souls and the bodies of those of whom has been spoken shall be reunited at once, the wicked as well as the righteous, I do not say; let it suffice, that I say that they all come forth; or in other words, their resurrection cometh to pass before the resurrection of those who die after the resurrection of Christ.

"Now, my son, I do not say that their resurrection cometh at the resurrection of Christ; but behold, I give it as my opinion, that the souls and the bodies are reunited, of the righteous, at the resurrection of Christ, and his ascension into heaven.

"But whether it be at his resurrection or after, I do not say; but this much I say that *there is a space between death and the resurrection of the body, and a state of the soul in happiness or in misery until the time which is appointed of God that*

4. And now my brethren, I judge these things of you because of your peaceable walk with the children of men.

5. For I remember the word of God, which saith by their works ye shall know them; for if their works be good, then they are good also.

---

the dead shall come forth, and be reunited, both soul and body, and be brought to stand before God, and be judged according to their works.

"Yea, this bringeth about the restoration of those things of which has been spoken by the mouths of the prophets.

"The soul shall be restored to the body, and the body to the soul; yea, and every limb and joint shall be restored to its body; yea, even a hair of the head shall not be lost; but all things shall be restored to their proper and perfect frame.

"And now, my son, this is the restoration of which has been spoken by the mouths of the prophets—

"And then shall the righteous shine forth in the kingdom of God.

"But behold, an awful death cometh upon the wicked; for they die as to things pertaining to things of righteousness; for they are unclean, and no unclean thing can inherit the kingdom of God; but they are cast out, and consigned to partake of the fruits of their labors or their works, which have been evil; and they drink the dregs of a bitter cup." (Alma 40:9-26; Italics are the Editor's)

VERSES 4-11. *A man being evil cannot do that which is good.* Mormon was not deceived by outward appearances, but he saw and judged his brethren to whom he spoke, rightly and with great compassion. He saw how they walked peaceably, not only before God, but also before one another. To walk peaceably before God, is to walk in the Path of Righteousness. "There is no peace, saith my God, to the wicked." (Isaiah 57:21) The children of men, to part of whom Mormon spoke (v. 4), want peace, but not every or any peace. They do not want a worldly peace, worldly; but peace founded upon truth, upheld and sustained by righteousness. Any peace in opposition to righteousness, is all, Peace! Peace! when there is no peace. (Jeremiah 6:14)

Not only the peace that filled their hearts, but the lives of Mormon's brethren proved their belief in the great truths the Church of Christ proclaimed; their bearing toward their brethren, their faithfulness to God and His laws, their integrity in every line of duty, their determination to walk in the path of duty and loyalty, marked them as *peaceable followers of Christ* (v. 3), and in Him they had a *joyous hope* of eternal rest in the Kingdom of God, which is Life Everlasting.

We may conclude our introduction of Mormon by repeating the words of the Lord concerning Phinehas, the grandson of Aaron the brother of Moses: "The law of truth was in his mouth, and iniquity was not found in his lips: he walked with Me in peace and equity, and did turn many away from iniquity." (Malachi 2:6)

VERSE 5. *By their works ye shall know them.* The moral soundness, the integrity and uprightness, of the Nephite Saints of God unto whom Mormon declared His holy word, delighted Mormon's soul. Seeing their good works, he rejoiced in the words of the Lord, Who when speaking of false prophets "who come to you in sheep's clothing, but inwardly they are ravening wolves," said of them: "Ye shall know them by their fruits. Do men gather grapes of thorns, or figs of thistles? Even so every good tree bringeth forth good fruit; but a corrupt tree bringeth forth evil fruit. A good tree cannot bring forth evil fruit, neither a corrupt tree bring forth good fruit. Every tree that bringeth not forth good fruit is hewn down, and cast into the fire. Wherefore, by their fruits ye shall know them." (III Nephi 14:16-20)

6. For behold, God hath said a man being evil cannot do that which is good; for if he offereth a gift, or prayeth unto God, except he shall do it with real intent it profiteth him nothing.

7. For behold, it is not counted unto him for righteousness.

8. For behold, if a man being evil giveth a gift, he doeth it grudgingly; wherefore it is counted unto him the same as if he had retained the gift; wherefore he is counted evil before God.

9. And likewise also is it counted evil unto a man, if he shall pray and not with real intent of heart; yea, and it profiteth him nothing, for God receiveth none such.

10. Wherefore, a man being evil cannot do that which is good; neither will he give a good gift.

11. For behold, a bitter fountain cannot bring forth good water; neither can a good fountain bring forth bitter water; wherefore, a man being a servant

---

The works men do are like the fruit a tree brings forth. Mormon took great comfort and an unceasing joy in that his brethren were like unto good trees; their works were good,˙ so as the Savior said, "they were also good."

VERSES 6-10. *For if an evil man offereth a gift* . . . No matter what the gift, he that is evil attaches thereto a condition, or an unclean motive. At least he expects a gift in return. Someone has said that a gift without the giver is bare. That means just this, that the giver of a gift who gives not himself therewith, gives nothing, and the receiver thereof receives nothing that is of worth. Both gift and giver are vain. As a gift is empty which is given with no real intent of the heart, so prayer to God, without real intent, is void of meaning. Such a prayer profiteth the giver thereof nothing. It is only that a few words are recited, and like a shadow, it is but the outline of something real, and shall pass away. As to gifts, neither the giver nor the receiver profits unless that gift abounds to our credit in the world to come. In other words, a gift attached to evil, whether it is of the giver or of the receiver, is not a gift of righteousness, and it, too, as a shadow shall pass away, and as a treasure in Heaven it will not be counted.

VERSE 11. *If a man follow Christ he cannot be a servant of the devil.* Mormon further admonished the Nephite Saints who stood or sat before him—that was their custom—to continue walking together in the path of peace, and thereby he emphasized his great appeal to them for good works and good gifts. "Behold," he said, "a bitter fountain cannot bring forth good water; neither can a good fountain bring forth bitter water."[1] He then declared the solemn truth which was the high point of his sermon: "A man being a servant of the devil cannot follow Christ; and if he follow Christ he cannot be a servant of the devil."

The Bible, that good and precious Book says, however, in different words: "No servant can serve two masters: for either he will hate the one, and love the other; or else he will hold to the one, and despise the other. Ye cannot serve God and mammon." (Luke 16:13)

James, the brother of our Lord, in a letter to the Twelve Tribes "Who are scattered abroad," notes of those who are worldly wise and those of their own number who speak good and evil at the same time, "blessing and cursing out of the same

---

[1]The word *fountain* means the source or springhead of waters. It is often used meaning a *well*. Metaphorically, God is called the Fountain of Living Waters (Jeremiah 2:13) Springs or fountains are called *living*, when they never cease, but are always sending forth their waters.

of the devil cannot follow Christ; and if he follow Christ he cannot be a servant of the devil.

12. Wherefore, all things which are good cometh of God; and that which is evil cometh of the devil; for the devil is an enemy unto God, and fighteth against him continually, and inviteth and enticeth to sin, and to do that which is evil continually.

13. But behold, that which is of God inviteth and enticeth to do good continually; wherefore, every thing which inviteth and enticeth to do good, and to love God, and to serve him, is inspired of God.

---

mouth," says: "Doth a fountain send forth at the same place sweet water and bitter? Can a fig tree, my brethren, bear olive berries? either a vine, figs? so can no fountain both yield salt water and fresh." (James 3:10-11)

Here may we add that Waters of Life drawn from the Wells of Salvation are good waters; they are the Words of the Lord, and in drinking of the cup in which those waters are contained, we think of the Lord's servant and his exclamation of gladness: "Behold, God is my Salvation; I will trust, and not be afraid: for the Lord JEHOVAH is my strength and my song; He also is my Salvation. Therefore with joy shall ye draw water out of the Wells of Salvation." (Isaiah 12:2-3)

VERSES 12-13. *All things which are good cometh from God.* The works of God, like the fruits good trees bring forth, are good. *Only* good comes from the Maker and Creator of all. More properly we might say: *"All good comes from Him."*

As for the devil, the opposite is true, "that which is evil cometh from" him. From the very first, when after the great Council in Heaven, Lucifer, who became the devil, was cast out from His presence, he became an enemy of God, and thereafter without stoppage has fought truth and also the righteousness which is in God. He lures astray, the weak and unwary into paths of wickedness and in rebellion against the Counsels of Heaven. With promises of great reward to those who follow him, he puts into their mouths every pretext and excuse human nature can devise or evil power achieve to apologize for their actions. To thwart the plans of the Almighty, and destroy life, is the devil's aim.

"But behold," Mormon says, "that which is of God inviteth and enticeth to do good . . ." Nephi, after whom the Nephites took their name, and shortly after leaving Jerusalem with his father and a few others, enumerated some of the transgressions which are of the devil. He warned the doers thereof that because of "these things" they "shall perish." "None of these iniquities come of the Lord; for He doeth that which is good among the children of men; and He doeth nothing save it be plain unto the children of men; and He inviteth them all to come and partake of His goodness; and He denieth none that come unto Him. . . ." (II Nephi 26:33)

Too many to be numbered, are the works of God, how manifold are His blessings. The Earth is filled with His bounties. The Psalmist in meditating on His wonderful providences, praised God for His great and gracious works. With a "pen of iron, and the point of a diamond," he caused these words to be written, and they remain with us a tribute in words to Him Who is Most Holy:

"Bless the Lord, O my soul. O Lord my God, thou art very great; thou art clothed with honour and majesty.

"Who coverest thyself with light as with a garment: who stretchest out the heavens like a curtain:

"Who layeth the beams of his chambers in the waters: who maketh the clouds his chariot: who walketh upon the wings of the wind:

"Who maketh his angels spirits; his ministers a flaming fire:

"Who laid the foundations of the earth, that it should not be removed for ever.
"Thou coveredst it with the deep as with a garment: the waters stood above the mountains.
"At thy rebuke they fled; at the voice of thy thunder they hasted away.
"They go up by the mountains; they go down by the valleys unto the place which thou hast founded for them.
"Thou hast set a bound that they may not pass over; that they turn not again to cover the earth.
"He sendeth the springs into the valleys, which run among the hills.
"They give drink to every beast of the field: the wild asses quench their thirst.
"By them shall the fowls of the heaven have their habitation, which sing among the branches.
"He watereth the hills from his chambers: the earth is satisfied with the fruit of thy works.
"He causeth the grass to grow for the cattle, and herb for the service of man: that he may bring forth food out of the earth;
"And wine that maketh glad the heart of man, and oil to make his face to shine, and bread which strengtheneth man's heart.
"The trees of the Lord are full of sap; the cedars of Lebanon, which he hath planted;
"Where the birds make their nests: as for the stork, the fir trees are her house.
"The high hills are a refuge for the wild goats; and the rocks for the conies.
"He appointed the moon for seasons: the sun knoweth his going down.
"Thou makest darkness and it is night: wherein all the beasts of the forest do creep forth.
"The young lions roar after their prey, and seek their meat from God.
"The sun ariseth, they gather themselves together, and lay them down in their dens.
"Man goeth forth unto his work and to his labour until the evening.
"O Lord, how manifold are thy works! in wisdom hast thou made them all: the earth is full of thy riches.
"So is this great and wide sea, wherein are things creeping innumerable, both small and great beasts.
"There go the ships: there is that leviathan, whom thou hast made to play therein.
"These wait all upon thee; that thou mayest give them their meat in due season.
"That thou givest them they gather: thou openest thine hand, they are filled with good.
"Thou hidest thy face, they are troubled: thou takest away their breath, they die, and return to their dust.
"Thou sendest forth thy spirit, they are created: and thou renewest the face of the earth.
"The glory of the Lord shall endure for ever: the Lord shall rejoice in his works.
"He looketh on the earth, and it trembleth: he toucheth the hills, and they smoke.
"I will sing unto the Lord as long as I live: I will sing praise to my God while I have my being.
"My meditation of him shall be sweet: I will be glad in the Lord.
"Let the sinners be consumed out of the earth, and let the wicked be no more. Bless thou the Lord, O my soul. Praise ye the Lord." (Psalm 104)
"Praise ye the Lord. I will praise the Lord with my whole heart, in the assembly of the upright, and in the congregation.
"The works of the Lord are great, sought out of all them that have pleasure therein.
"His work is honourable and glorious: and his righteousness endureth for ever.
"He hath made his wonderful works to be remembered: the Lord is gracious and full of compassion.
"He hath given meat unto them that fear him: he will ever be mindful of his covenant.
"He hath shewed his people the power of his works, that he may give them the heritage of the heathen.

14. Wherefore, take heed, my beloved brethren, that ye do not judge that which is evil to be of God, or that which is good and of God to be of the devil.

15. For behold, my brethren, it is given unto you to judge, that ye may know good from evil; and the way to judge is as plain, that ye may know with a perfect

"The works of his hands are verity and judgment; all his commandments are sure.

"They stand fast for ever and ever, and are done in truth and uprightness.

"He sent redemption unto his people: he hath commanded his covenant for ever: holy and reverend is his name.

"The fear of the Lord is the beginning of wisdom: a good understanding have all they that do his commandments: his praise endureth for ever." (Psalm 111)

In the lives of the most humble, those who put their trust in Him, His marvelous works transcend the greatest of human achievements. Lehi, the scholarly ancestor of both the Nephites and the Lamanites, when shown in vision the wonderful purposes of God in bringing about the Salvation of His children, exclaimed in ecstasy: "Great and marvelous are Thy works, O Lord God ALMIGHTY! Thy throne is high in the Heavens, and Thy power and goodness, and mercy are over all the inhabitants of the Earth, and because Thou art merciful, Thou wilt not suffer those who come unto Thee that they shall perish!" (I Nephi 1:14) The power, goodness, and mercy, of God, are shown in His great and marvelous works.

May we in humility offer this Hebrew prayer; the words thereof express not only ours but the thoughts of the Elders of the Jews: "O Lord and God of our fathers, Thou art exalted above all human understanding; no tongue can tell Thy goodness and Thy mercy. Yet the countless tokens of Thy love, the innumerable signs of Thine unfailing providence and of Thy loving care for all Thy creatures, tell of Thee. Our eyes are opened to the wonders of this world, wherein Thy presence reveals itself in every star in heaven and in every flower of the field. The Heavens declare Thy glory, O God, and the firmament showeth Thy handiwork."

Lehi had learned to listen to that *still small voice* which is heard by the faithful, and which is of God; that comes to lead, and to direct, and to warn the hearer thereof, of things to come. To hear and recognize that voice is a gift of God, and in it is told the wonderful works of the Lord for the preservation of His Own. Not so with the adversary; his design is to preserve evil, and destroy that which is good. When the temptations of the devil that confront us are strongest—which connotes weakness on our part—he himself becomes stronger. Being an opportunist, he seizes this time as fit for our undoing, and leads us along his way until we are bound tightly by forces which we can neither see nor hear, and of which we have lost control. The result is: we do evil continually. "Wherefore," the Sacred Record says: "Every thing which inviteth and enticeth to do good . . . is inspired of God," and "that which is evil cometh of the devil."

VERSES 14-16. *For behold, my brethren, it is given you to judge, that ye may know good from evil.* He Who is the strength of all who put their trust in Him; the loving Father of all men, has endowed His children with reason to distinguish between right and wrong, and in wisdom has decreed that freedom to choose good or evil is their heritage. "With a great love hath He loved us." (See, Jeremiah 31:3) He has opened our eyes to behold the wonders of His Creation, and our minds to discern the glory of His works. But, notwithstanding His goodness and grace, we must realize that He has placed us here upon Earth, and enjoined to do His bidding. Sometimes we forget God's mighty works. Too often in pursuit of life's vanities we follow the evil inclinations with which Satan has filled our hearts, and therein transgress God's holy laws. The enticements of the devil, and his invitation to us

knowledge, as the daylight is from the dark night.

16. For behold, the Spirit of Christ is given to every man, that he may know good from evil; wherefore, I show unto you the way to judge; for every thing which inviteth to do good, and to persuade to believe in Christ, is sent forth by the power and gift of Christ; wherefore ye may know

with a perfect knowledge it is of God.

17. But whatsoever thing persuadeth men to do evil, and believe not in Christ, and deny him, and serve not God, then ye may know with a perfect knowledge it is of the devil; for after this manner doth the devil work, for he persuadeth no man to do good, no, not one; neither do his angels;

---

that we partake with his servants of the pseudo-joys and follies of the world — if we fall to his allurements — leaves us shackled by the bonds of sin, and fettered, both hands and feet, by the chains of hell.

Little by little, we are bound by Satan; little by little, we become his slaves — the victims of corruption. Our desires for the higher things of life become dulled, and our judgment of what is right, and what is wrong, warped. The *Spirit of Christ* is crowded from our hearts. The fears of Mormon expressed in verse 14, then become real. "Wherefore," he says, "take heed, my brethren, that ye do not judge that which is evil to be of God, or that which is good and of God to be of the devil."

The Spirit of Christ is given to every man. The Spirit of Christ is truth and light. "A light which is endless, that can never be darkened." (*Abinadi*, Mosiah 16:9) "I am the true light that lighteth every man that cometh into the world." (*Doctrine and Covenants* 93:2) "That which is of God is light; and he that receiveth light, and continueth in God, receiveth more light; and that light groweth brighter and brighter until the perfect day." (*Ibid.*, 50:24) Therefore, we repeat, as we have done before, the words of Isaiah concerning this great light which is the Light of Christ, Who is the Light and Life of the World: "O House of Jacob, come ye and let us walk in the light of the Lord . . ." (II Nephi 12:5) and coupled with it we will also repeat the words of the ancient Hebrew brethren who lived in the Golden Age of Jewish learning and wisdom: for *"In Thy light shall we see light."* (Psalm 36:9) Again, Mormon says: "Wherefore, I beseech of you, brethren, *that ye should search diligently in the light of Christ* that ye may know good from evil; and if ye will lay hold upon every good thing, and condemn it not, ye certainly will be a child of Christ." (v. 19) The *Spirit giveth light;* the admonishment of Mormon differs only in words from the reasoned judgment of the Jewish Elders. "That which is of God is light"; the prophets and teachers of Israel, in every age of the Gospel, have likened *light* to knowledge and truth; *darkness* to superstition and evil. All truth is of God.

The Lord Jesus, Himself, when instructing the Nephites upon His visit to them in the Land Bountiful, said: "Therefore it shall come to pass that whosoever will not believe My words, Who am Jesus Christ . . . shall be cut off from among My people who are of the Covenant" (III Nephi 21:11), and later, He said through Moroni — that same Moroni who recorded his father's sermon we are now considering — "But he that believeth these things which I have spoken, him will I visit with the manifestations of My Spirit, for he shall know and bear record. *For because of My Spirit he shall know that these things are true; for it persuadeth men to do good. And whatsoever thing persuadeth men to do good is of Me; for good cometh of none save it be of Me. I am the same that leadeth men to all good; he that will not believe My words will not believe Me—that I am; and he that will not believe*

neither do they who subject themselves unto him.

18. And now, my brethren, seeing that ye know the light by which ye may judge, which light is the light of Christ, see that ye do not judge wrongfully; for with that same judgment which ye judge ye shall also be judged.

19. Wherefore, I beseech of you, brethren, that ye should search diligently in the light of Christ that ye may know good from evil; and if ye will lay hold upon every good thing, and condemn it not, ye certainly will be a child of Christ.

20. And now, my brethren, how is it possible that ye can lay hold upon every good thing?

21. And now I come to that faith, of which I said I would speak; and I will tell you the way whereby ye may lay hold on every good thing.

22. For behold, God knowing all things, being from everlasting to everlasting, behold, he sent angels to minister unto the children of men, to make manifest concerning the coming of Christ; and in Christ there should come every good thing.

23. And God also declared unto prophets, by his own mouth, that Christ should come.

24. And behold, there were divers ways that he did manifest things unto the children of men, which were good; and all things

---

Me will not believe the Father Who sent Me. For behold, I am the Father, I am the light, and the life, and the truth of the world." (Ether 4:11-12)

"And I know that the Lord God will consecrate my prayers for the gain of my people. And the words which I have written in weakness will be made strong unto them; for it *persuadeth them to do good*; it maketh known unto them of their fathers; and it speaketh of Jesus, and *persuadeth* them to believe in Him, and to endure to the end, which is Eternal Life." (II Nephi 33:4)

In the development of the subject of his sermon, the theme of which he announced as "*Faith, Hope, and Charity,*" Mormon now gives the key by which all may know for a surety the things of God, and the things of the devil. He says: "But behold, that which is of God inviteth and enticeth to do good continually; wherefore, *everything which inviteth and enticeth to do good, and to love God, and to serve Him, is inspired of God.*" (v. 13) That is the truth upon which all things depend.

They knowing that all good things come from God, Mormon's brethren were urged by him to "lay hold upon every good thing." The weakness of the flesh in spite of the urging of a willing spirit, proposed to their minds a solemn inquiry: "How is it possible that ye can lay hold upon every good thing?" Mormon, perceiving their quandary, was quick to answer: "I will tell you the way whereby ye may lay hold on every good thing." *Faith*, that force or power by which all things are done, was Mormon's first assault on the dilemma they posed. It was the first part of his promised text, *Faith, Hope, and Charity.*

VERSES 22-26. *God sent angels to minister unto the children of men.* That the light of God's holy countenance should shine upon His children, and that they should not be left alone, in ignorance of the Plan of Salvation which in itself revealed Christ and His goodness, God sent messengers from His presence to minister

which are good cometh of Christ; otherwise men were fallen, and there could no good thing come unto them. 25. Wherefore, by the ministering of angels, and by every word which proceedeth forth out of the mouth of God, men began to exercise faith in Christ; and thus by faith, they did lay hold upon every good thing; and thus it was until the coming of Christ. 26. And after that he came men also were saved by faith in his name; and by faith, they become the sons of God. And as

to them, and acquaint them "concerning the coming of" their Redeemer in Whom should come every good thing.

In every age of the world, and all parts of the Earth, holy angels sent from God and commissioned by Him, have declared Salvation to all men through Jesus Christ, our Lord. Those who lived before His coming looked forward to that great event; we look back. Both visions are effectual to the working of grace in the hearts of men. These Heavenly messengers, sent from God's presence, were commissioned by Him to minister unto the children of men, as Mormon says, making known to them the power and authority of God, and His great love for them in that He gave His Only Begotten Son, through Whom, we repeat, "should come every good thing."

Heavenly manifestations became man's constant guide. Men were taught to pray to God, to rely on His justice and mercy, to do His will; and inasmuch as they did so, they were rewarded with greater knowledge of Christ and His Plan of Redemption.

Having transgressed God's holy laws by partaking of the Forbidden Fruit, men became as Gods, "knowing good from evil." In committing that same act, they were empowered to tell right and wrong, and were given the freedom to choose between them. Discretion, to this end, increased within them. Not only did they see and recognize the truth, but also they had power to act "according to their wills and pleasures, whether to do good or to do evil." (Alma 12:31)

When the Lord God saw that the children of men were capable in and of themselves to distinguish between truth and error, right and wrong, and also that they had the power or ability to choose good or evil, He gave unto them, by His holy prophets whom He sent among them, laws and certain commandments that by keeping them they would be benefited and blest. He also called priests and teachers and appointed them to instruct those among whom they labored all things concerning Himself and His Immortal Plans. In this way, by preachment and by example, the priests so set apart were able to guide and direct their brethren aright, and always hold before them the proper manner by which they were to look forward to the coming of Christ, Who was their Redeemer and Lord. Indeed, the Atonement of Christ, and the whole Plan of Salvation, God's grace and His loving-kindness, were proclaimed by holy prophets to whom God Himself "declared, by His Own mouth, that Christ should come." (v. 23)

"Wherefore, by the ministering of angels, and by every word which proceeded forth out of the mouth of God" — for God said through Moroni when speaking of the words of His holy prophets, 'I am He Who speaketh." — "Men began to exercise faith in Christ; and thus by faith, they did lay hold upon every good thing; and thus it was until the coming of Christ." (v. 25)

After Christ came among men, they, Mormon so enlightens us, were saved by faith just as had those who lived before His glorious advent. We have said earlier in this discussion that they who lived before, looked forward to His coming; we look back. We noted that both visions were effectual to the working of faith in our hearts.

342   COMMENTARY ON THE BOOK OF MORMON

sure as Christ liveth he spake these words unto our fathers, saying: Whatsoever thing ye shall ask the Father in my name, which is good, in faith believing that ye shall receive, behold, it shall be done unto you.

27. Wherefore, my beloved brethren, have miracles ceased because Christ hath ascended into heaven, and hath sat down on the right hand of God, to claim of the Father his rights of mercy which he hath upon the children of men?

28. For he hath answered the ends of the law, and he claimeth all those who have faith in him; and they who have faith in him will cleave unto every good thing;

wherefore he advocateth the cause of the children of men; and he dwelleth eternally in the heavens.

29. And because he hath done this, my beloved brethren, have miracles ceased? Behold I say unto you, Nay; neither have angels ceased to minister unto the children of men.

30. For behold, they are subject unto him, to minister according to the word of his command, showing themselves unto them of strong faith and a firm mind in every form of godliness.

31. And the office of their ministry is to call men unto repentance, and to fulfill and to do the work of the covenants of the

Here, we will not enter into a discussion of what faith is, except to say that it is the power or force which makes real the things we hope for, but cannot see. With an *eye of faith* we look forward continually, having in view those things which God's servants, the angels and His prophets, have placed verbally before us.

Christ said that if ye have faith in Me, that means if you believe earnestly, not doubting, that I Am, or that I live, that I am the Son of God, "Ye shall have power to do whatsoever thing is expedient in Me." (v. 33) *Whatsoever thing is expedient in Me,* means those things which will add to the glory of God by advancing the cause of righteousness; the cause of righteousness is His cause.

VERSES 27-34. *Have miracles ceased because Christ hath ascended into Heaven?* One of the favorite excuses with which the powers of evil seek to reinforce unbelief in Christ, is the assertion that there is no such thing as a miracle performed in His Name. Even to those who profess a belief in Him, the things they reject quickest as unworthy of belief, are those of which they know little. We may not be able to explain the metaphysics of what we call miracles, nor can we explain how God answer prayer—itself a miracle—but nevertheless, we know He does. It is no more difficult for the believer in a kind and wise Providence to accept as facts, the miracles recorded in Christ's ministry than the Miracle of Life, the evidences of which we see all about us.

To reject a truth because we do not understand it, is foreign to the principles of every science. It is unscientific. It is ignorance. As an example: will someone explain to us how it is that two plants placed side by side in a field, each produce, the one wheat and the other barley. Their roots intermingle in the same coarse sand; the same raindrops refresh the parched earth in which they grow; the same sunbeams warm the delicate leaves of both. Yet one produces wheat, the other barley. How is it? We do not know. But we would think him deranged, who would refuse to eat the beautiful white loaf, because, forsooth, he does not understand why

Father, which he hath made unto the children of men, to prepare the way among the children of men, by declaring the word of Christ unto the chosen vessels of the Lord, that they may bear testimony of him.

32. And by so doing, the Lord God prepareth the way that the residue of men may have faith in Christ, that the Holy Ghost may have place in their hearts, according to the power thereof; and after this manner bringeth to pass the Father, the covenants which he hath made unto the children of men.

33. And Christ hath said: If ye will have faith in me ye shall have power to do whatsoever thing is expedient in me.

34. And he hath said: Repent

---

that plant should in the end make a wheat loaf instead of a barley cake. However, that is just what the Anti-Christs would have us do. They would have us reject Christ and all good which comes in Him, because we cannot explain in detail the beauties and the glories of His works.

To complement the words of Mormon, give ear to Jacob, the brother of the Prophet Nephi and the son of Lehi: "Wherefore, we search the prophets, and we have many revelations and the spirit of prophecy; and having all these witnesses we obtain a *hope,* and our *faith* becometh unshaken, insomuch that we truly can command in the Name of Jesus and the very trees obey us, or the mountains, or the waves of the sea. Nevertheless, the Lord God showeth us our weakness that we may know that it is by His grace, and His great condescensions unto the children of men, that we have power to do these things. Behold, great and marvelous are the works of the Lord. How unsearchable are the depths of the mysteries of Him; and it is impossible that man should find out all His ways. And no man knoweth of His ways save it be revealed unto him; wherefore, brethren, despise not the revelations of God. For behold, by the power of His word man came upon the face of the Earth, which Earth was created by the power of His word. Wherefore, if God being able to speak and the world was, and to speak and man was created, O then, why not able to command the Earth, or the workmanship of His hands upon the face of it, according to His will and pleasure?" (Jacob 4:7-9) And still further Jacob says: "Wherefore, brethren, seek not to counsel the Lord, but to take counsel from His hand. For behold, ye yourselves know that He counseleth in wisdom, and in justice, and in great mercy, over all His works." (*Ibid.,* 4:10)

Someone has said: "There is a wisdom we cannot fathom, and an omnipotence upon which we can lean, but cannot grasp," and we can leave to that day, when the things we know not now, we shall know hereafter. What, here below, we call miracles and surround them with mysticism really do not deviate from natural law. They constitute part of the science of God's relationship to man. Angels from the Courts of Glory instruct men in its findings. It is the *heavenly science of Good Works.* The working of miracles is done by the faithful in the Name of Christ, the great Scientist of the Universe; all His works are good.

The Lord in speaking to Moroni as is shown in our comments on verse 16, further said: "And in that day that they (the Gentiles) shall exercise faith in Me . . . even as the Brother of Jared did, that they may become sanctified in Me, then will I manifest unto them the things which the Brother of Jared saw, even to the unfolding unto them all My revelations, saith Jesus Christ, the Son of God, the Father of the Heavens and of the Earth, and all things that in them are. And he that will contend against the word of the Lord, let him be accursed; and he that shall deny these things, let him be accursed; for unto them will I show no greater things,

all ye ends of the earth, and come unto me, and have faith in my name, and have faith in me, that ye may be saved.

35. And now, my beloved brethren, if this be the case that these things are true, which I have spoken unto you, and God will show unto you, with power and great glory at the last day, that they are true, and if they are true has the day of miracles ceased?

36. Or have angels ceased to appear unto the children of men? Or has he withheld the power of the Holy Ghost from them? Or will he, so long as time shall last, or the earth shall stand, or there shall be one man upon the face thereof to be saved?

37. Behold I say unto you, Nay; for it is by faith that mira-

cles are wrought; and it is by faith that angels appear and minister unto men; wherefore, if these things have ceased wo be unto the children of men, for it is because of unbelief, and all is vain.

38. For no man can be saved, according to the word of Christ, save they shall have faith in his name; wherefore, if these things have ceased, then has faith ceased also; and awful is the state of man, for they are as though there had been no redemption made.

39. But behold, my beloved brethren, I judge better things of you, for I judge that ye have faith in Christ because of your meekness; for if ye have not faith in him then ye are not fit to be numbered among the people of his church.

---

saith Jesus Christ; for I am He Who speaketh. And at My command the Heavens are opened and are shut; and at My word the Earth shall shake; and at My command the inhabitants thereof shall pass away, even as by fire." (Ether 4:7-9)

VERSES 35-38. *God will show unto you . . . at the Last Day, that these things are true.* Mormon witnessed to his brethren that the things whereof he spoke are true; that angels did communicate with man on Earth, that the Holy Ghost bore record in men's hearts that there was no other name than the Name of Christ whereby man can be saved. And that as long as the Earth shall stand, "or there shall be one man upon the face thereof to be saved," these visits by holy angels and the power of the Holy Ghost would not cease among men to the end that "the purposes of the Lord shall roll on, until all His promises shall be fulfilled." (Mormon 8:22) Mormon also called upon God to witness the truth of his words. A full and complete answer to Mormon's statement that "God will show unto you, with power and great glory at the Last Day, that they are true," is given by the Lord Himself when speaking of unbelievers in the latter days, "And he that believeth not My words believeth not My disciples; and if it so be that I do not speak, judge ye; for ye shall know that it is I that speaketh at the Last Day." (Ether 4:10)

VERSE 39. *I judge that ye have faith in Christ because of your meekness.* Mormon saw that his brethren to whom he spoke were meek and willing to show their faith in Christ by good works—works of righteousness. He also saw in their humility a complete dependence on God, and therein a meekness which the Lord Jesus Himself promised that such a one would inherit the Earth; not as conquering invaders, but as children and heirs of Him, Who is the Ruler of all. Mormon interpreted their integrity to Christ's teachings as a mark of their faith in Him, saying: "If ye have

40. And again, my beloved brethren, I would speak unto you concerning hope. How is it that ye can attain unto faith, save ye shall have hope?

41. And what is it that ye shall hope for? Behold I say unto you that ye shall have hope through the atonement of Christ and the power of his resurrection, to be raised unto life eternal, and this because of your faith in him according to the promise.

42. Wherefore, if a man have faith he must needs have hope; for without faith there cannot be any hope.

43. And again, behold I say unto you that he cannot have faith and hope, save he shall be meek, and lowly of heart.

44. If so, his faith and hope is vain, for none is acceptable before God, save the meek and lowly in heart; and if a man be meek and lowly in heart, and confesses by the power of the Holy Ghost that Jesus is the Christ, he must

---

not faith in Him then are ye not fit to be numbered among the people of His Church." (v. 39)

VERSES 40-43. *I would speak unto you concerning Hope.* Mormon now began to discourse on the second portion of his text, Hope, by first asking: "How is it that ye can attain unto faith, save ye shall have a hope?" and "And what is it that ye shall hope for?" Again, Mormon answered his own query: *"The Atonement of Christ and the power of His Resurrection, to be raised unto Life Eternal.* That, dear reader, is the sum and substance of all our joy, our happiness and peace. With an eye of faith we discern Life Eternal; with a clean mind, clean of all worldly things, we joyously hope for it. Our faith in Christ and our desire to obtain its promised reward, Life Everlasting, causes us to strive, for the glory of God, to lay hold upon every good thing (See, vv. 19-20), that in doing so we might attain (See, v. 40) that which we see through the eye of faith, and which in our minds we look forward to—hope for. "Wherefore, if a man have faith he must needs have hope"; for faith begets hope, "for without faith there cannot be any hope."

VERSE 43. *A man cannot have faith and hope, save he shall be meek, and lowly of heart.* The phrase, *lowly of heart,* does not mean a low, debased person, but one, the thoughts of whose heart are easily moulded by Christ-like appeals of virtue, purity, and goodness. We understand it is a mark of freedom from pride and arrogance; condescending in lowly (not low) service to others. It connotes humility, and humility engenders *faith,* begets *hope,* and makes *charity* man's first consideration in ameliorating man's woes. The word *charity* is used only in the New Testament, never in the Old. In the American Revised Version of the Bible, *charity* is always translated *love.*

VERSES 44-47. *A man must needs have charity.* Imbued with many Christ-like virtues, among them being meekness and lowliness of heart, a man whose faith in Christ brings forth good works, and whose hope for Eternal Life is shored up by his faith, offers a sacrifice to God which is acceptable to Him. If, on the other hand, a man is designing, ostentatious, and what he does is for display or show, to say the least, he is pharisaical; and will be like the early Christians who introduced pageantry and gaudy shows into the simple worshiping services of the Saints, he will gradually lose the vision he had through the eye of faith, and which once was bright and clear. Such a man we will find has become destitute of the greatest virtue God has infused into man—*Charity.*

needs have charity; for if he have not charity he is nothing; wherefore he must needs have charity.

45. And charity suffereth long, and is kind, and envieth not, and is not puffed up, seeketh not her own, is not easily provoked, thinketh no evil, and rejoiceth not in iniquity but rejoiceth in the truth, beareth all things, believeth all things, hopeth all things, endureth all things.

46. Wherefore, my beloved brethren, if ye have not charity, ye are nothing, for charity never faileth. Wherefore, cleave unto charity, which is the greatest of all, for all things must fail—

47. But charity is the pure love of Christ, and it endureth forever; and whoso is found possessed of it at the last day, it shall be well with him.

48. Wherefore, my beloved brethren, pray unto the Father with all the energy of heart, that ye may be filled with this love, which he hath bestowed upon all who are true followers of his Son, Jesus Christ; that ye may become

---

Charity is ennobling to the soul. Mormon lists many qualities that are evident in one when that one is sort of effervescent with the Spirit of Christ. Without charity, one is nothing, for Mormon says: "Charity is the pure love of Christ," (v. 47) and without it "all things must fail." (v. 46) Without charity, man is but an animal; survival of the fittest is the theme of his existence, and birth, but an accident. Charity, that is love, makes the weak, strong, and the strong, stronger.

The word, *Charity*, as used by Paul in his First Letter to the Corinthians, Chapter 23, and as it occurs elsewhere in the New Testament, has not been fully understood by Bible readers. It means *love*, and particularly *love of Christ*. This is made clear in the Book of Mormon. It does not mean *benevolence* or *alms-giving*, etc. The doctrine which St. Paul inculcates is that eloquence, learning, faith, alms-giving, and even martyrdom, are profitless to the soul, unless they are fruits of our love of Christ. Moroni must have felt that the time would come when this explanation would be necessary. It has come. We need to be told that love of Christ must be the spring by which the spiritual mechanism of a Christian life is set in motion and kept going. We need to be told that the purity of this powerful emotion (charity—the love of Christ) will have to stand the test of the Last Day. It must not be mixed with pretense.

St. Peter must have had that same thought in mind, when he wrote: "Adding . . .to your brotherly kindness *"philadelphia"* — love, not charity as the King James Version has it. The original is *agape*. Scholars tell us that paganism knew only *philantropia* and *philadelphia* as between relatives in blood, but the *agape*, the love of Christ, as applied to Peter's brethren, is original with revealed religion, which is the Gospel of Jesus Christ. (See, Second Epistle of Peter, 1:7-11)

VERSE 48. *Pray unto the Father . . . that ye may be filled with this love. . . .* Mormon closed his sermon on faith in Christ, the hope we have in Him of eternal rest in the Kingdom of God, and love of Christ and all men which will bring forth good works, meet for that just reward. He urged his *beloved brethren* to supplicate God in humble prayer that this love—the love of Christ—may fill their very beings, that truly they might be *sons of God*. And that when the Savior appears in all the

the sons of God; that when he shall appear we shall be like him, for we shall see him as he is; that we may have this hope; that we may be purified even as he is pure. Amen.

splendor of His might, this hope now fostered within our hearts will be realized by us unto the fulfilling of the vision we see through eyes of faith. "That we may be purified even as He is pure," was Mormon's prayer for all.

CHAPTER 8

1. *Mormon's Epistle to Moroni*—2. *Little Children have no Need of Repentance or Baptism.*

1. Mormon's epistle to Moroni.

1. An epistle of my father Mormon, written to me, Moroni; and it was written unto me soon after my calling to the ministry. And on this wise did he write unto me, saying:

2. My beloved son, Moroni, I rejoice exceedingly that your Lord Jesus Christ hath been mindful of you, and hath called you to his ministry, and to his holy work.

3. I am mindful of you always in my prayers, continually praying unto God the Father in the name of his Holy Child, Jesus, that he, through his infinite goodness and grace, will keep you through the endurance of faith on his name to the end.

2. Little children have no need of repentance or baptism.

4. And now, my son, I speak unto you concerning that which grieveth me exceedingly; for it grieveth me that there should disputations rise among you.

5. For, if I have learned the truth, there have been disputations among you concerning the baptism of your little children.

6. And now, my son, I desire

VERSES 1-3. *An epistle of my father, Mormon, written to me, Moroni . . . soon after my calling to the ministry.* No doubt that Moroni had kept the letter here recorded as a treasured reminder of his youth. He says that his father wrote it to him shortly after he, that is, Moroni, was called to the ministry of Christ.

The letter was of a personal nature, but as it deals with a subject of great importance, Moroni was constrained by the spirit of prophecy, to include it in his own writings. By that same spirit, he saw that the time would come when men, unenlightened by God's Holy Spirit, would consign innocent little children to an existence with the devil and his angels because, albeit through no fault of their own, they had not been baptized.

After rendering thanks to God that the Lord Jesus Christ had been mindful of his worthy son, and had called him to His holy work, Mormon invoked the continued blessings of the Holy One of Israel on Moroni, to the end that "through His infinite goodness and grace" Moroni would always be preserved "through the endurance of faith on His Name." It was a note that expressed a filial tenderness existing between father and son.

VERSES 4-6. *I speak unto you concerning that which grieveth me exceedingly.* Without burdening his father who was already high in the councils of the Church, with questions of doctrine, Moroni had evidently spared, or attempted to spare, him from the consideration of opinions that differed one from another concerning the necessity of baptizing little children. That there had been disputations among the Saints where Moroni lived regarding this departure from the "right way" had not previously reached Mormon's attention. However, Mormon had learned the truth that ye should labor diligently, that this gross error should be removed from among you; for, for this intent I have written this epistle.

7. For immediately after I had learned these things of you I inquired of the Lord concerning the matter. And the word of the Lord came to me by the power of the Holy Ghost, saying:

8. Listen to the words of Christ, your Redeemer, your Lord and your God. Behold, I came into the world not to call the righteous but sinners to repentance; the whole need no physician, but

they that are sick; wherefore, little children are whole, for they are not capable of committing sin; wherefore the curse of Adam is taken from them in me, that it hath no power over them; and the law of circumcision is done away in me.

9. And after this manner did the Holy Ghost manifest the word of God unto me; wherefore, my beloved son, I know that it is solemn mockery before God, that ye should baptize little children.

10. Behold I say unto you that this thing shall ye teach—repentance and baptism unto those who

---

(v. 5), and in this written message had urged his son to "labor diligently" that this malignant growth of error "should be removed from among you." To aid Moroni in its removal, was the end and objective to which Mormon had directed this letter stating in no uncertain language, the truth pertaining thereto.

VERSE 7. *I inquired of the Lord concerning this matter.* Without any delay on the part of Mormon, he, upon hearing of it, immediately put the matter of disputation before the Lord. Without delay, Mormon told Moroni: "The word of the Lord came to me by the power of the Holy Ghost," Mormon giving that source as authority for what he would thereafter say.

VERSE 8. *Listen to the words of Christ, your Redeemer . . .* "I came into the world not to call the righteous but sinners to repentance." The voice of Jesus then repeated words that need no interpreter. They were the words Christ spoke to the Scribes and the Pharisees who complained to His disciples when they saw Him (their Master—Matthew 9:12) eating with Publicans and Sinners: "They that are whole need not a physician; but they that are sick." (Luke 5:31)

The voice of our Lord then compared little children to one who needs no physician; "Little children are whole, for they are not capable of committing sin." Baptism is for the remission of sins, therefore, to baptize little children for the remission of sins which they did not commit, and could not, is to hold God to ridicule, and make a "solemn mockery" of His goodness and mercy.

VERSES 9-15. *This thing shall ye teach.* Many who profess religion, especially the teachers in the church of the devil, tell their followers what not to do, but, however, what to do, is not in their curriculum. Mormon tells Moroni what to do. "I say unto you that this thing shall ye teach—repentance and baptism unto those who are accountable and capable of committing sin; yea, teach parents that they must repent and be baptized, and humble themselves as their little children, and they shall all be saved with their little children." (v. 10)

Little children who die before they reach the age of accountability, are holy unto the Lord. They are pure, even as He is pure. They are not rebellious when the decrees of Heaven are made known to them. They are obedient to God's comare accountable and capable of committing sin; yea, teach parents that they must repent and be baptized, and humble themselves as their little children, and they shall all be saved with their little children.

11. And their little children need no repentance, neither baptism. Behold, baptism is unto repentance to the fulfilling the commandments unto the remission of sins.

12. But little children are alive in Christ, even from the foundation of the world; if not so, God is a partial God, and also a changeable God, and a respecter to persons; for how many little children have died without baptism!

13. Wherefore, if little children could not be saved without baptism, these must have gone to an endless hell.

14. Behold I say unto you, that he that supposeth that little children need baptism is in the gall of bitterness and in the bonds of iniquity, for he hath neither faith, hope, nor charity; wherefore, should he be cut off while in the thought, he must go down to hell.

15. For awful is the wickedness to suppose that God saveth one child because of baptism, and the

---

mands, and trust in His wisdom and His guidance as they do their earthly parents. From the very first, God has ordained their Salvation, and in His grace, has provided for their well-being. The command is given, "Be thou as a little child." Mormon draws the inevitable conclusion, that to remit a man's sins—wash his garments clean in the Blood of the Lamb—while a child whose garments never were soiled, but are white, goes to an everlasting punishment, is irreconcilable to the idea of a just and merciful God which those have who are righteous.

Little children are alive in Christ. Little children are spotless. They came from God's presence, pure, and so do they return if they die before their actions make them liable. God, in forgiving the sins of one who offends against knowledge, and, at the same time, retains in a child, who in itself is without sin, the sins of their First Parents—original sin as some call it—because of having not been baptized, is a "partial God," treating His children differently, and a "changeable God," deviating from His announced word. (v. 12) Little children are alive in Christ; they are not spiritually dead, but live in His protecting care. If a child dies, we are comforted by the promise of Eternal Life.

To suppose that little children must needs be baptized, lacks understanding of God's love, upon which all Creation was founded. It marks as unseeing, the eyes that should behold the beauties of the Heavens and the Earth. All things were made and fashioned by the love of God, and He will not depart therefrom. He is the loving Father of all men, and one of His children is as precious in His sight as another. He will not save one, and forsake the other. He has provided Salvation for all, and he who says that His ways are not straight is "in the gall of bitterness, and in the bonds of iniquity." Such a man has not the love of Christ in his heart, neither has he faith in divine promises, nor anything in which to look forward with joy. (v. 14) As Mormon wrote to Moroni, "He hath neither faith, hope, nor charity," which last is the "pure love of Christ." (Moroni 7:47)

VERSE 15. *Awful is the wickedness . . .* A man who is without love for God and all men, especially little children, is of all men, the most miserable, the most deeply to be pitied; he cannot see, nor can he feel, the rest which is in Christ. He

other must perish because he hath no baptism.

16. Wo be unto them that shall pervert the ways of the Lord after this manner, for they shall perish except they repent. Behold, I speak with boldness, having authority from God; and I fear not what man can do; for perfect love casteth out all fear.

17. And I am filled with charity, which is everlasting love; wherefore, all children are alike unto me; wherefore, I love little children with a perfect love; and they are all alike and partakers of salvation.

18. For I know that God is not a partial God, neither a changeable being; but he is unchangeable from all eternity to all eternity.

19. Little children cannot repent; wherefore, it is awful wickedness to deny the pure mercies of God unto them, for they are

---

goes about his task, day by day, unmindful of God's presence in every experience of his life. The follies and foolishness of the world, absorb him, and as we have noted before, "Crowd all thoughts of God from his heart." There is no peace to comfort him when faint, there is no joy in living. A state of *mental hell* awaits every move, and in its wake he curses both God and man. Awful is that hell into which he chooses to go. Awful is the wickedness of him who supposeth "that God saveth one child because of baptism, and the other must perish because he hath no baptism." Baptism of little children is a relic of the Dark Ages when men believed in witches and superstition guided the feet of those who sought Eternal Life.

VERSE 16. *Wo be unto them that pervert the ways of the Lord. Pervert,* means to twist, or to turn to error; to cause deviation from the right or true course; to lead astray, or to corrupt. In the manner of baptizing little children, Mormon pronounces wo upon those who insist that they should be. To perish will surely be the lot of them that do not repent; such a fate is possible to him in whom love does not abide. He who twists and turns (perverts) the right ways of the Lord, and corrupts the great saving principles of the Gospel of Christ, destroys himself. If one wants to make himself of no value in God's Kingdom, just break the laws by which it is governed. That is what Mormon meant when he said: "Wo be unto them that pervert the ways of the Lord." There is no surer way to pervert God's holy laws than not to keep them.

Mormon spoke boldly to his son, because he spoke by the authority of God, and with God at his side, Mormon feared no man. Let the dissidents declaim their beliefs, and the infirm of mind, their indifference, but Mormon, unlike them, had the truth with him and it made him strong. With the Word of God in his mouth, and the God of Truth nearby, Mormon knew no weakness. Fearing only the Lord Who is the Savior of all God's children, he without the restraint of the wicked, proclaimed Salvation through the mercy of Christ to "all little children . . . and also all they that are without the law." (v. 22)

VERSES 17-22. *I am filled with charity, which is everlasting love.* We imagine that for the sake of emphasis, Mormon repeated almost in detail, the things he wanted Moroni to declare as the Word of the Lord: That all little children are alike, and partakers of Salvation; God is not a partial God, neither a changeable Being; little children cannot repent, because they cannot sin; they are all alive in Christ because of His mercy; he that saith that little children need baptism setteth at naught the Atonement of Christ, and denieth the power of His Resurrection.

all alive in him because of his mercy.

20. And he that saith that little children need baptism denieth the mercies of Christ, and setteth at naught the atonement of him and the power of his redemption.

21. Wo unto such, for they are in danger of death, hell, and an endless torment. I speak it boldly; God hath commanded me. Listen unto them and give heed, or they stand against you at the judgment-seat of Christ.

22. For behold that all little children are alive in Christ, and also all they that are without the law. For the power of redemption cometh on all them that have no law; wherefore, he that is not condemned, or he that is under no condemnation, cannot repent; and unto such baptism availeth nothing—

23. But it is mockery before God, denying the mercies of Christ, and the power of his Holy Spirit, and putting trust in dead works.

24. Behold, my son, this thing

Wo, wo, wo, unto such, for they have neither faith, hope, nor charity, which is everlasting love. Of all the self-inflicted woes that occupy the human heart, the wo most bitter and malignant, is in him in whose heart there is no love. We mean by that, a heart like granite; a heart wherein love does not enter, neither does it abound and therefore cannot go out. In such a heart there is no hope of attaining that which the eye of faith reveals. And if a man has charity, which, we repeat is the pure love of Christ, his aim, like the purpose Christ had in offering His life for the good of mankind, will be to help the helpless and those who have no helper but the Lord. That is charity, which does not mean donations to the *Poor Box*, alms-giving.

The power of redemption cometh on all them that have no law. A great truth which is not understood by the people of the world, but the justice of it is made known in the love and mercy of God for all His children, is beautifully shown in the simple words of Nephi, who spoke as he was moved upon by the power of the Holy Ghost:

"And if they will not repent and believe in His name, and be baptized in His name, and endure to the end, they must be damned; for the Lord God, the Holy One of Israel, has spoken it.

"Wherefore, He has given a law; and where there is no law given there is no punishment; and where there is no punishment there is no condemnation; and where there is no condemnation the mercies of the Holy One of Israel have claim upon them, because of the Atonement; for they are delivered by the power of Him.

"For the atonement satisfieth the demands of His justice upon all those who have not the law given to them, that they are delivered from that awful monster, death and hell, and the devil, and the lake of fire and brimstone, which is endless torment; and they are restored to that God who gave them breath, which is the Holy One of Israel.

"But wo unto him that has the law given, yea, that has all the commandments of God, like unto us, and that transgresseth them, and that wasteth the days of his probation, for awful is his state! (II Nephi 9:24-27)

VERSES 23-26. *Putting trust in dead works.* Doing anything not needful is a *dead work.* Little children need no baptism, therefore to baptize them is a dead work, it availeth nothing. It makes a mockery of the sacred Ordinance, and in doing so, one denies the mercies of the Savior, and the power of His Holy Spirit ought not to be; for repentance is unto them that are under condemnation and under the curse of a broken law.

25. And the first fruits of repentance is baptism; and baptism cometh by faith unto the fulfilling the commandments; and the fulfilling the commandments bringeth remission of sins;

26. And the remission of sins

bringeth meekness, and lowliness of heart; and because of meekness and lowliness of heart cometh the visitation of the Holy Ghost, which Comforter filleth with hope and perfect love, which love endureth by diligence unto prayer, until the end shall come, when all the saints shall dwell with God.

unto Salvation. Christ came into the world to save all men, not just a few; and to condemn any or many unto eternal damnation is trusting in dead works, and not in Him Who is alive as are all those who put their trust in Him. "He is the light and the life of the world; yea, a light that is endless, that can never be darkened; yea, and also a life which is endless that there can be no more death." (*Abinadi,* Mosiah 16:8)

Mormon tells his son that this thing ought not to be, or in other words, there should be no contention among the Saints about baptizing little children. For baptism is unto repentance, and repentance is unto those who are under condemnation, because of *a broken law.* Little children cannot repent because they have broken no law, and are under no condemnation. But it is different with those who know the law and then break it. According to the requirements of the law they have need to repent, that the law may be fulfilled in them, and if their repentance is sincere, have their sins remitted by entering into the waters of baptism.

With the remission of sins come meekness and lowliness of heart. *Meekness* means complete dependence on God, and *lowliness of heart,* connotes, loving all men as brothers because we see in them sons of the same Father Who is God. Not pride, nor wealth, or station in life, distinguishes our place, but service to our fellow men. In serving our fellow men, we serve God. Christ, in serving us condescended to things of a lower estate (not low), so as His followers, is it impossible that we serve them with that same spirit of love, even as He served the children of men? *Lowliness of heart* does not even suggest a heart that is low, or one that is dead in trespass and sin, but one that is alive in Christ, and one that may be easily fashioned after that which is just and true. Not a heart of stone, like one of granite.

With hearts attuned to the harmonies of Heaven, and spirits aflame with the love of Christ, we remember that to serve Him is the soul's purest happiness, and to worship Him, life's greatest freedom. May we suggest in the spirit of prayer, that which follows: "And when we render Thee our homage, may we also remember that only by obedience to Thy commands, by faithfulness to our duties, by the goodness of our deeds, can we make our worship acceptable to Thee." This, dear reader, is the first expression of meekness and lowliness of heart, and for us to recognize Him in every experience of life, is to put a crown of glory upon the head of meekness, and to exalt the heart that is lowly to heights that are too great for mortals, and to realms of the glorified which to us are real, we having seen them through eyes of faith.

It is then, that the Holy Ghost, the Comforter, fills us "with hope and perfect love" which Mormon says: "Suffereth long, and is kind, and envieth not, and is not puffed up, seeketh not her own, is not easily provoked, thinketh no evil, and rejoiceth in the truth, beareth all things, believeth all things, hopeth all things, endureth all

27. Behold, my son, I will write unto you again if I go not out soon against the Lamanites. Behold, the pride of this nation, or the people of the Nephites, hath proven their destruction except they should repent.

28. Pray for them, my son, that repentance may come unto them. But behold, I fear lest the Spirit hath ceased striving with them; and in this part of the land they are also seeking to put down all power and authority which cometh from God; and they are denying the Holy Ghost.

29. And after rejecting so great a knowledge, my son, they must perish soon, unto the fulfilling of the prophecies which were spoken by the prophets, as well as the words of our Savior himself.

30. Farewell, my son, until I shall write unto you, or shall meet you again. Amen.

---

things." (7:45) Communion with God through prayer is then the natural desire of His children, and as they grow in years, so will they grow in grace, "and in the knowledge of the glory of Him that created them, or in the knowledge of that which is just and true," (See, Mosiah 4:12) "and this until the end shall come, when all the Saints shall dwell with God."

VERSES 27-30. *The pride ... of the Nephites hath proven their destruction except they repent.* Mormon was the Commander-in-Chief of the armies of the Nephites, and as such was at the scene of battle with the Lamanites. His grief was most bitter, not because of the greater number of the enemy for with the Lord's help it did not matter whether few or many, but by reason of the wickedness that abounded everywhere among his people.

Mormon promised that unless he went to battle soon with the Lamanites, he would write further instructions to his son, however, he asked Moroni to continue in prayer "that repentance may come unto them." Mormon was almost despondent for he realized that many times the Lord had rescued his people, but just as many times had they, after showing a sorrow for their iniquity, returned not only to their pride and false ways, but to wickedness, every time more degrading, more debasing, and more depraving, than ever. Mormon saw that his people were abounding in evil, and in that part of the Commonwealth wherein the war raged, they were openly rebelling against "all the power and authority which cometh from God." Not only were they in rebellion against the authority of the government, but also against the authority vested in the Church of God, insomuch so that those who had long relied upon its guidance, now "are denying the Holy Ghost." "I fear," wrote Mormon, "lest the Spirit hath ceased striving with them"; notwithstanding that they had been ministered to by angels from Heaven, and revelations from On High had been their almost constant guide, they, in spite of warnings by holy men, rejected further guidance and refused any longer to be led by One Who was mightier than they. In their own might they sought to vanquish the manpower of the Lamanites which was far greater than their own. Although Mormon was their military leader, besides being their spiritual mentor, saw only destruction awaiting them, for such were the words of the prophets, and even the Savior Himself if they did not repent. Unto the fulfilling of the prophecies, he knew that soon his people would perish.

A fond farewell, and with the added wish, which we may call a prayer, that they shall meet again, was Mormon's petition which we may judge was offered to God in humble supplication.

CHAPTER 9

THE SECOND EPISTLE OF MORMON TO HIS SON MORONI

1. *Atrocities Committed by Lamanites and Nephites*—2. *A Father's last and Affectionate Admonition.*

1. Atrocities committed by Lamanites and Nephites.

1. My beloved son, I write unto you again that ye may know that I am yet alive; but I write somewhat of that which is grievous.

2. For behold, I have had a sore battle with the Lamanites, in which we did not conquer; and Archeantus has fallen by the sword, and also Luram and Emron; yea, and we have lost a great number of our choice men.

3. And now behold, my son, I fear lest the Lamanites shall destroy this people; for they do not repent, and Satan stirreth them up continually to anger one with another.

4. Behold, I am laboring with them continually; and when I speak the word of God with sharpness they tremble and anger against me; and when I use no sharpness they harden their hearts against it; wherefore, I fear lest the Spirit of the Lord hath ceased striving with them.

5. For so exceedingly do they anger that it seemeth me that they have no fear of death; and they have lost their love, one

---

VERSES 1-6. *I fear lest the Lamanites shall destroy this people.* Some time after the great and last battle at Cumorah, Moroni recorded this letter which he had received from his father, Mormon, some time before, in which his father expressed anew his fears that the end of the Nephites as a distinct people was near at hand. He also told Moroni of a "sore battle" in which he had led the Nephites against the Lamanites, but as in many previous encounters the Lamanites were victorious. Archeantus, Luram, and Emron, together with a great number of the military captains and other "choice men" had been lost to the services of the Republic.

The spirit of the devil had infused into the lives of the Nephite people, hatred for everything that was good and pure. They rebelled against God by refusing to heed the voices of His servants. They knowingly elected to do evil, and chose those things that led them to do wickedly, until now, they loved what they had been taught to hate, and despised that which they should have loved. Instead of having one common enemy, strife and angry passions leavened their lives, and hostility towards each other added a dreadful agony to the death throes of their nation and divided them into contending factions, when there was great need of unity.

In spite of Mormon's oft-repeated attempts to unite the Nephites under one standard in meeting the demands made upon them by both the State and the Church of God, they recoiled when in criticism of them he uttered harsh or sharp words, and responded to every effort he made for their rehabilitation by heaping incense and abuse upon him, often inciting to anger those whom Satan held in his grasp as hostages in the momentous struggle then going on, and which ultimately ended in the extermination of what had, in the past, been a much-favored nation.

Mormon also notes that when in peaceful persuasion, he reprimands his people for their neglect of God, and reminds them of their duty in obeying His laws, they

towards another; and they thirst after blood and revenge continually.

6. And now, my beloved son, notwithstanding their hardness, let us labor diligently; for if we should cease to labor, we should be brought under condemnation; for we have a labor to perform whilst in this tabernacle of clay, that we may conquer the enemy of all righteousness, and rest our souls in the kingdom of God.

7. And now I write somewhat concerning the sufferings of this people. For according to the knowledge which I have received from Amoron, behold, the Lamanites have many prisoners, which they took from the tower of Sherrizah; and there were men, women, and children.

8. And the husbands and fathers of those women and children they have slain; and they feed the women upon the flesh of their husbands, and the children upon the flesh of their fathers; and no water, save a little, do they give unto them.

9. And notwithstanding this great abomination of the Lamanites, it doth not exceed that of our people in Moriantum. For behold, many of the daughters of the Lamanites have they taken prisoners; and after depriving them of that which was most dear and precious above all things, which is chastity and virtue—

10. And after they had done this thing, they did murder them in a most cruel manner, torturing their bodies even unto death; and after they have done this, they devour their flesh like unto wild beasts, because of the hardness of their hearts; and they do it for a token of bravery.

harden their hearts against being ruled by any unseen power, or be controlled by One, the vision of Whom they could not see, and about Whom they had only heard. "Therefore," Mormon says, "I fear lest the Spirit of the Lord hath ceased striving with them." (v. 4)

So intense became the anger of the Nephites towards the servants of the Lord, and so keen and inexhaustible their spite, that the voice of righteousness failed to reach the depths of depravity into which they had fallen. They appeared to Mormon to be insensate to death, he says: "They have lost their love, one towards another; and they thirst after blood and revenge continually." (v. 5)

The magnanimity of Mormon's great heart is seen in his exhortation to his son, not to let the transgressions of their people be a reason for them to relax their efforts. Mormon wanted the reverse. "We have a labor to perform," he told Moroni, therefore, let us labor diligently, "that we may conquer the enemy of all righteousness, and rest our souls in the Kingdom of God." (v. 6)

VERSES 7-10. *Now I write somewhat concerning the sufferings of this people.* A messenger from the battlefield, named Amoron, conveyed to Mormon the tidings of the horrible atrocities committed by the Lamanites upon the Nephite prisoners — men, women, and children — captured by them in the Tower of Sherrizah. These savagely cruel and outrageously brutal, really horrendous, acts, are too enormous to comment upon, suffice it to say that both Lamanites and Nephites had reached that point where the last effort of human wickedness cannot pass. Everything which evil power could suggest seemed to delight their fallen nature.

11. O my beloved son, how can a people like this, that are without civilization—

12. (And only a few years have passed away, and they were a civil and a delightsome people)

13. But O my son, how can a people like this, whose delight is in so much abomination—

14. How can we expect that God will stay his hand in judgment against us?

15. Behold, my heart cries: Wo unto this people. Come out in judgment, O God, and hide their sins, and wickedness, and abominations from before thy face!

16. And again, my son, there are many widows and their daughters who remain in Sherrizah; and that part of the provisions which the Lamanites did not carry away, behold, the army of Zenephi has carried away, and left them to wander whithersoever they can for food; and many old women do faint by the way and die.

17. And the army which is with me is weak; and the armies of the Lamanites are betwixt Sherrizah and me; and as many as have fled to the army of Aaron have fallen victims to their awful brutality.

18. O the depravity of my people! They are without order and without mercy. Behold, I am but a man, and I have but the strength of a man, and I cannot any longer enforce my commands.

19. And they have become strong in their perversion; and they are alike brutal, sparing none, neither old nor young; and they delight in everything save that which is good; and the suffering of our women and our children upon all the face of this land doth exceed everything; yea, tongue cannot tell, neither can it be written.

20. And now, my son, I dwell no longer upon this horrible scene. Behold, thou knowest the wickedness of this people; thou knowest that they are without principle, and past feeling; and their wickedness doth exceed that of the Lamanites.

21. Behold, my son, I cannot recommend them unto God lest he should smite me.

2. *A father's last and affectionate admonition.*

22. But behold, my son, I recommend thee unto God, and I trust in Christ that thou wilt be saved; and I pray unto God that

---

As did Mormon (v. 20), we close the annals of those times in disgust, and pray as he did, "Come out in judgment, O God, and hide their sins, and wickedness, and abominations from before Thy face."

Now, a last word from Mormon concerning the Nephites: "Their wickedness doth exceed that of the Lamanites. (v. 20) Behold, my son, I cannot recommend them unto God . . ." no doubt meaning that he could not even pray for them, he knowing their wickedness, "Lest," he says, "He should smite me." (v. 21)

he will spare thy life, to witness the return of his people unto him, or their utter destruction; for I know that they must perish except they repent and return unto him.

23. And if they perish it will be like unto the Jaredites, because of the wilfulness of their hearts, seeking for blood and revenge.

24. And if it so be that they perish, we know that many of our brethren have dissented over unto the Lamanites, and many more will also dissent over unto them; wherefore, write somewhat a few things, if thou art spared and I

VERSES 22-24. *I recommend thee unto God.* Knowing that his son, Moroni, continually walked in the path of duty and loyalty even though it might cost him all he held dear, Mormon humbly presented his son's name to God. Mormon's prayer for Moroni was simple, but it contained a request for that which of all things is most to be desired, all that is really worthwhile hoping for, *Salvation in Christ.* Also, Mormon's prayer was that Moroni's life be spared "to witness the return of His people" unto God, or to see "their utter destruction." For I know, Mormon sadly comments "that they must perish except they repent and return unto Him." (v. 22)

Mormon remembered King Mosiah's translation of the Twenty-four Gold Plates of Ether, wherein is told of the Jaredites, an earlier race of God's children who inhabited the Land in which the Nephites now dwelt. How they were destroyed because of just such wickedness as had befallen the Nephites, is set forth therein in no uncertain wording. Rejection of God's prophets, and wilfull disobedience of His holy laws, led the Jaredites to shed each other's blood, and seek revenge one against another, until, at last, because of iniquity, God ordered their destruction. Mormon saw in their fate, if so we may call it, a just warning to his own people that they, too, might suffer in like manner.

Hoping to escape His righteous judgment that comes upon those who transgress God's holy laws, many Nephites had dissented "over to the Lamanites," and many more, Mormon notes, "will also dissent over unto them." (v. 24)

Mormon's anxiety for the future spiritual welfare of his brethren — although they forswore allegiance to the Nephite Republic, and left his command, and many more would follow — grew greater every day as an increasing number of Nephites joined the ranks of the enemy all of whom were dissenters from the Church of Christ.

It must be remembered that only a few years had passed away since there were no Lamanites — all were Nephites and all belonged to His Church. A few not satisfied with the millennial conditions that had long held sway, quit the society of those among whom joy, harmony, and the love of Christ, prevailed, took upon themselves the name, Lamanites, and proceeded to destroy the tabernacle of peace that then spread the wide continents over. (*See,* IV Nephi v. 38ff)

By the names, Lamanite and Nephite, mostly, we think of the literal descendants of Laman and Nephi. Now it is different. At this period in their history the name, Lamanite, signified those who had apostatized from the Church of Christ, the members thereof took the name of Nephites by which they were afterwards known. They constituted two distinct religio-political groups. The Lamanites became greater in numbers because of the Nephite defections, and therefore, in war, stronger in manpower than the Nephites. But with the God in Heaven, it matters not whether there be few or many. However, increasing wickedness even among the Nephites robbed them of God's help, and they became, man-for-man, like the Lamanites.

Mormon sensed this mental and moral deficiency of his people, but he never-

shall perish and not see thee; but
I trust that I may see thee soon;
for I have sacred records that I
would deliver up unto thee.

25. My son, be faithful in
Christ; and may not the things
which I have written grieve thee,
to weigh thee down unto death;
but may Christ lift thee up, and
may his sufferings and death, and
the showing his body unto our
fathers, and his mercy and long-

suffering, and the hope of his
glory and of eternal life, rest in
your mind forever.

26. And may the grace of God
the Father, whose throne is high
in the heavens, and our Lord
Jesus Christ, who sitteth on the
right hand of his power, until all
things shall become subject unto
him, be, and abide with you forever. Amen.

---

theless realized that in Christ they could be forgiven, and in Him they could be
saved. To that end he never ceased to labor, and he told his son "if we should
cease to labor, we should be brought under condemnation; for we have a labor to
perform. . . ." (v. 6) Mormon knew that some day, in the wisdom of the Lord,
his own, or the words of Moroni, would be made known to their descendants,
(*Moroni*, Mormon 9:30) therefore he instructed Moroni to write somewhat of Christ
in the record Moroni was then making, that it would be a witness to them of His
being, and that in Him they might be saved.

This letter was written before the final battle between the Nephites and
Lamanites at Cumorah; in it Mormon expresses the hope that they may meet soon,
for, he says, "I have sacred records that I would deliver up unto thee." (v. 24; also
See, Mormon 6:6)

VERSES 25-26. *Be faithful in Christ.* These last two verses need no comment
from us. In great love, Mormon admonishes his son to be faithful in Christ, and
not let the wickedness portrayed by Mormon in his letter be an occasion for grief
unto Moroni's death. But let it be that in Moroni's faith, Christ may lift him up,
and the memory of Christ's "sufferings and death, His showing of His body unto
their fathers, and His mercy and long-suffering, and the hope of His glory and of
Eternal Life, rest in your mind forever. . . ."

CHAPTER 10

1. *Moroni's farewell to the Lamanites.*

2. *Conditions on which individual testimony of the truth of the Book of Mormon may be obtained.*

3. *Moroni seals up the record of his people.*

1. Now I, Moroni, write somewhat as seemeth me good; and I write unto my brethren, the Lamanites; and I would that they should know that more than four hundred and twenty years have passed away since the sign was given of the coming of Christ.

2. And I seal up these records, after I have spoken a few words by way of exhortation unto you.

3. Behold, I would exhort you that when ye shall read these things, if it be wisdom in God that ye should read them, that ye would remember how merciful the Lord hath been unto the children of men, from the creation of Adam even down unto the time that ye shall receive these things, and ponder it in your hearts.

VERSE 1. *I write unto my brethren, the Lamanites.* Conforming to the request made by his father, Mormon, which he made of his son in the epistle just recorded (v. 24, Chapter 9), Moroni wrote to the Lamanites concerning Christ, first noting that "more than four hundred and twenty years have passed away since the sign was given of the coming of Christ." Moroni was grieved because in what to him was a very few years, the Lamanites, whom he called "my brethren" had retrogressed from a pinnacle of peace and happiness in the Lord, to a condition of evil servitude. They, he remembered, were once a white and a delightsome people when, in humility, they served God, now they had given their hearts over to all manner of wickedness. The words he wrote were in witness that *Christ is; that all good comes of Him, and that through Him Eternal Life may be obtained by all who have "faith, hope, and charity."*

VERSES 2-3. *I seal up these records.* Moroni expresses his intention, that "after I have spoken a few words by way of exhortation unto you," "I will seal up these records." By "these records" he meant those "few plates" which his father "gave unto my son Moroni," (Mormon 6:6) and also the writings he himself had made, which included his abridgment of King Mosiah's translation of the Twenty-four Plates of Ether.

When, in the wisdom of the Lord, these Records shall come forth to the knowledge of the Remnant of the Lamanites who endure at that day, he exhorts them to remember "How merciful the Lord hath been unto the children of men, from the creation of Adam even down unto the time that ye shall receive these things, and ponder it in your hearts."